*The Language
of Puritan Feeling*

The Language
of Puritan Feeling

An Exploration in Literature, Psychology, and Social History

David Leverenz

Rutgers University Press
New Brunswick, New Jersey

I wish to thank Roy Huss, editor of *Psychocultural Review*, for permission to draw on my article, "Anxious fathers: Freud and the American Puritan Tradition," which originally appeared in *Psychocultural Review*, 1 (Fall 1977). My thanks also to Harry Slochower, editor of *American Imago*, and to Wayne State University Press for permission to reprint from my article, "Shared Fantasies in Puritan Sermons," which first appeared in *American Imago*, 32 (Fall 1975).

LIBRARY OF CONGRESS CATALOGING IN PUBLICATION DATA

Leverenz, David.
   The language of Puritan feeling.

   Includes bibliographical references and index.
   1. Puritans—Psychology.   2. American literature—
Colonial period, ca. 1600–1775—History and criticism.
3. New England—Intellectual life.   4. Patriarchy—
New England.   I. Title.
F7.L5   301.29′74   79-18579
ISBN 0-8135-0882-7

To my father and mother
for their love, strength, and good humor
and to Anne
"This is my beloved, and this is my friend."
(Canticles 5.16.)

Contents

Preface

Over a decade ago, Edmund Morgan wrote that we already know more about the Puritans than any sane man would want to know. Today we know much more, yet there is less agreement, more controversy, more emphasis on paradox and tensions, more sense of individual and demographic variety, more awareness of emotional sources. And here is yet another book that speaks to some of these concerns.

This book presents Puritanism as an ambivalent psychological response, expressed in theological language, to various tensions and conflicts in an age of dislocation. I especially emphasize dislocations in male roles and male authority. Most of the book is a speculative, sometimes idiosyncratic, reinterpretation of well-thumbed Puritan sermons and family tracts, from England to New England. As my subtitle indicates, the frame tries to link literary and psychological perspectives to social history, and I conclude with a glance at Franklin and nineteenth-century American literature.

Feeling—that invisible twentieth-century God—is the key. This book gives less weight than usual to Puritanism as an expression of middle-class political aggressiveness or intellectual tenacity. My concern is with underlying ambivalence, anxiety, and contradiction in the mainstream Puritan way, not with the more radical and separatist extremes. A central tenet is the idea of shared fantasy. But I am not arguing for a Puritan psyche to complement Perry Miller's Puritan mind. Rather, I try to show how the language of Puritanism transformed a great variety of conflicts and uncertainties about authority and social roles into a simplified vision of pure authority. Its genius lay in its ability to encompass contradictions in the name of order, to look backward and forward at once, and to resolve a wide spectrum of personal dilemmas into a collective assertion of worldly identity and heavenly dependence. In the current argument between Puritan intellectual historians, who see consensus, and social historians, who see discord, this study stands firmly on both sides, because rigid intellectual consensus and incessant social controversy are major aspects of Puritan discourse.

The reader should not expect another analysis of the antinomian controversy of the 1630s, or the witch trials of the 1650s and beyond. My focus is on male styles and fantasies, against a background of changing work and family roles, first in England and then in New England. Those who come to this book thinking of Puritanism primarily as oppressive to women will not find that chapter three lingers on the usual counterargument about increased equality in marriage. Instead, I hope readers will be surprised to find how vigorously Puritan men turned to female imagery to describe their inward state of mind. And I beg the reader's indulgence for sometimes repeating familiar material. What is obvious in one field may be new to another.

My thanks to Allison, Elizabeth, and lately Trevor, for helping to bring out my own language of feeling; to Frederick Crews and Norman S. Grabo, who faithfully shepherded a hardly recognizable version of these ideas too many years ago as part of a far more grandiose dissertation; to George Levine and Tom Edwards, for a decade of support and counsel; to Livingston College, faculty and students, for nourishing such a humane atmosphere of intellectual excitement and social concern; to Carey McWilliams and Murray Schwartz, good and helpful readers; to Rutgers University, for a year's leave in 1977–1978 that at last allowed me to get this book done right, and also to the British Library, as close as I expect to get to paradise; to Peggy Christ and Joe Esposito at Rutgers University Press, for thoughtful and attentive editorial work, and especially to Barbara Westergaard for her valiant copyediting and textual criticism; and above all to Anne Rutledge, not only for suggesting the subject in the first place but for repeatedly affirming that life is more real than books and at least as interesting. Anne has also helped me, and I hope this book, toward a feminist perspective by occasionally reminding me that "huswiferie" is neither spiritual nor wifery.

If I have an intellectual hero, it is Freud; my divergences from him will become clear, even as a debt is incurred on every page. My debt to many other writers is also enormous, especially to all the scholars whose work is absorbed in my text and fought with in my notes. If the notes seem copious, it is because the narrative is meant to stand alone, with scholarly documentation, placement, and infighting sent to the rear as a subtext. Readers may feel relieved to know that originally the references were twice as long. Several important works, notably those by Philip Greven and Lawrence Stone, came to hand as this study was in its last stages; I have tried nonetheless to signal both their findings and my disagreements.

Any study influenced by psychoanalysis brings some self-consciousness about one's own motives. I have tried to make my personal investment enliven the prose without obscuring the subject. I offer the book in the spirit of the Puritan minister who inscribed over his library door, "Lege, Lege, Aliquid Haerebit": "Read, read, something will stick!"

Introduction

> Fear not enemies without, but your
> selves at home.
>
> Thomas Shepard[1]

A surprising analogy often appears in Puritan sermons to describe
the minister's function. Without leering, and with no fear that their
manhood was threatened, preachers called themselves "breasts of
God." When I was poring through Puritan sermons for the first time,
over ten years ago, expecting images of a wrathful God, I was astonished to find such intimate and flexible imagery of the female body.
"It is said, (Cant. 8.8.) *We have a little Sister that has no Breast, what
shall we do for her*? So there are little places (and some considerable
ones too) in *New-England*, that have no Breasts, no Ministers from
whom they may receive the sincere milk of the Word," observed
Increase Mather in 1697. In a funeral sermon for his father (1723),
Cotton Mather also invoked what by then was a stale convention:
"Such *Ministers* are your *Mothers* too. Have they not *Travailed in
Birth* for you, that a CHRIST may be seen *formed in you*? Are not their
Lips the *Breasts* thro' which the *sincere Milk of the Word* has pass'd
unto you, for your Nourishment?"[2] The Song of Solomon ("Canticles")
legitimized their little allegory. The Bible was God's milk; the minister
was the breast at which the congregation suckled.

The analogy emphasizes one of the more unacknowledged aspects of
Puritanism: a readiness to use the body's natural functions to illustrate
things of the spirit. Thomas Shepard talked of sin as a menstruous cloth,
explicit birth imagery was applied to the soul's rebirth, bodily disease
and death became metaphors for the soul's sinful condition. But the
readiness of men to use *female* images to describe themselves, or
groups, or even their God, occasioned a psychological curiosity. What
assumptions did Puritans make, that fathers could portray themselves
as breasts of their still more fatherly God?

One simple answer is that the Bible told them so. "They were heavenly truths, but they were cloathed with earthly expressions," Samuel Willard said of biblical language; "hence the word is called *Logical milk*; 1 Pet. 2.2."[3] The sensuality of the Song of Solomon was "translated"—a favorite Puritan word—into a somewhat mechanical allegory of group nourishment, not individual pleasure. Still, the assumption of group identity seems strange. The congregation, not the self, collectively suckles. Moreover, the minister gains power in being the conduit for God's milk, not as he declares his patriarchal dominance. And the comparison is strictly verbal, asserting the power of metaphor as well as the Deity. To visualize the analogy at all is to make God and man ridiculous. The Word must remain in words.

Negative female images are more commonly associated with Puritan writings, especially the omnipresent "whore" of the Catholic Church. It is easy to find images of the wrathful patriarchal God rising to purify the contaminated Popish woman so that she can be worthy of the father again. Yet that God, like Puritan language, is curiously two-faced: a wrathful father to sinners, a nurturing mother to saints. And the readiness of Puritans to express their service to the Almighty in female self-images of group submission and fulfillment has no negative connotations. Ecstasy follows the self-transformation, and male conversion experiences are conventionally described with female analogies.

Another simple answer might be that ministers naturally reached for images of basic dependence and basic trust when trying to reach hard hearts. So John Cotton stated that ministers should "apply themselves to the estate of their people: If they bee babes in Christ, to be as breasts of Milke to suckle them: If they be grown to ripe yeares, to bee as clusters of grapes to refresh them with stronger liquor, be ready to poure out sweet and comfortable liquor." Milk for babes and wine for the "ripe" was sound biblical doctrine.[4] The comparison also shows practical knowledge of the varieties of faith in any congregation. Yet again, the unquestioning application of infantile feeding as an apt analogy for the newly converted surprises the modern secular reader, just as Cotton's "stronger liquor" for the more mature saints should also surprise.

Drinking the word became a metaphor so pervasive in Puritan culture that Cotton could entitle his standard catechism for New England children: "*Spiritual Milk for Boston Babes In either England. Drawn out of the Breasts of both Testaments for their souls nourishment.*" And Thomas Hooker could interpret Isaiah 66:11 to say, "The Church is compared to a childe, and the brests are the promises of the Gospell;

now the elect must suck out and be satisfied with it, and milke it out: . . . Ah beloved, this is our misery, we suffer abundance of milke to be in the promise, and we are like wainly children, that lye at the brest, and will neither sucke nor be quiet." The fantasy has more behind it than biblical exegesis or a search for arresting images. To make all visible reality dependent on God's Word as the infant suckles the breast was what Puritans imagined, and they did not mince words in saying so. "The whole World is a sucking Infant depending on the Breasts of Divine Providence," Samuel Willard declared in 1691, toward the end of a long tradition.[5] Some sixty years earlier, when Anglicans persisted in retaining some "indifferent" areas where human authority could be exercised, nearly 20,000 Puritans despaired of quickly reforming that "vanity" and moved to a new world to foster their shared fantasy of rebirth and pure dependence.

While several psychological and social explanations are suggested here for Puritanism, my study begins in appreciation of what Puritans could take for granted. Theirs was a more communal society, able to imagine a communal self, at least for purposes of analogy. Theirs was an agrarian society, in many ways more open than our own about bodily matters and bodily metaphors. Puritan imagery expressing ultimate authority is more flexible, both in sex roles and in variety of application, and more intimate than we might expect. A strange, affirming simplicity speaks through what Melville called, in a less benign context, those linked analogies. It is truly, in Peter Laslett's phrase, part of a world we have lost.[6]

My thesis is that unconscious ambivalence about the father's authority, and a broader weakening of traditional norms for male identity, helped energize the Puritan vision. As chapter three suggests, the larger context for ambivalence and paternal anxiety is the various mixed expectations parents had about their children, reflecting expectations and tensions in English society. The vivifying contradictions of Puritan discourse reflect contradictory feelings about the mixture of relatively good mothering and relatively anxious, distant, weak, or repressive fathers. Various levels of mixed expectation helped to intensify ambivalence about the father's authority. Defenses took several interrelated forms, at least six of which became part of Puritan faith and language.

First, Puritans sought, with varying degrees of success, to remold themselves into what we would now call an "obsessive-compulsive" personality, and their religion into obsessive ordering. As Joan Webber has said, what Puritans called self-knowledge was really an anxious and incessant effort to make all one's experiences fit the proper pattern.[7] The self must become God's instrument.

Second, they transformed feelings of guilt, anger, or inadequacy into relentless self-observation of personal sinfulness, often expressed with meticulous detail in diaries. A private language of agonized doubt complements a public language of militant submission.

Third, Puritan theology expressed unconscious ambivalence as opposites.

Fourth, ambivalence about the father's role also led to an overcompensating fantasy of God's all-powerful patriarchy, to be mirrored by the father's role in the family, especially in religious matters. Yet that God is a curiously motherly patriarch to the faithful, and one who has voluntarily allowed himself to be circumscribed by covenants. So, too, the father's authority in the home is at once strengthened and limited by a language of mutual obligations. Clarifying duties, not aggrandizing powers, was their aim. No one can be a tyrant and be saved; everyone must fulfill his calling.

Fifth, personal anxieties were transformed into group certainties through a language that constantly insisted on the primacy of the organic whole, the interdependent subordination of parts. Christ was the head; the saints were the body. Collectively they suckled at spiritual milk. Everyone's "mindes and hearts" must be "mortified by mutuall consent of subjection one to another," wrote Thomas Hooker in *A survey of the summe of Church Discipline*; "every part is subject to the whole." As he phrases it earlier, "The power is in the whole firstly, but each part knowes his rank."[8]

Finally, Puritan sermons, largely through imagery and analogy, encouraged a shared fantasy that Freud has named the "Family Romance": a wish that one can be born (or reborn) of higher parents than one actually has. The Puritan version of the Family Romance offered the possibility that sons could rescue the father's authority by being reborn of the greater Father, without a mother's help, and suckled and raised by Him alone.[9]

None of these aspects, taken separately, is unique to Puritanism. Nursing fantasies and Family Romances are common to many if not all religions, though not many people have noticed them in Puritan sermons. There is nothing especially Puritan about infantile imagery, even about feeling oneself in the womb of the Father or sucking at his breasts. All of that is in the Bible, explicitly or allegorically. The same imagery shapes the poetic meditations of St. John of the Cross on

Canticles. Witty Elizabethan Anglicans like Thomas Playfere enjoyed saying just what John Cotton proclaimed in his title for "Boston Babes": "The two breasts of the Church are the two testaments; out of which we that are the children of the church, suck the pure milke of the word of God."[10]

The difference is that St. John of the Cross is imagining a meditative individual bliss, while the Puritans sought a pattern of collective rebirth. More subtly, Reverend Playfere was at least as interested in his eloquent, comforting, flowing succession of images as in the truth of the simile. His pleasant associational style is meant to evoke the unity of the Testaments, as "one wheele is within another," not to assert group identity within a strict frame of authority. His style is deliberately playful rather than explicative. Where he smoothly moves on to other images as he preaches to his king, the Puritans delighted only in unadorned repetition to prove their more pure dependence. Their use of the simile shows their hunger for comprehensive patterns as much as a hunger for more specifically regressive pleasures.

Perhaps the search for pattern indicates that there is something more uniquely Puritan about the obsessive style, especially the strict adherence to biblical authority in all things. For hostile contemporaries their "precise" view of the Word served to label them Precisianists, before the equally hostile label of Puritan took hold. Even to list some basic attributes of the obsessive style, described more fully in chapter four, shows obvious points of similarity to Puritanism: a preoccupation with shoulds, a compulsive patterning, fear of dirt and impurity, pleasure in rigid and repetitive order, a continual citing of external authority, calls for achieving self-esteem through dedicated work, uncomfortableness or disgust with festive play or self-assertion for its own sake, a mechanical tone, a zeal for exact distinctions, unremitting concern with one's flaws, stubbornness, an absence of humor. Puritans took public pleasure in the preeminent genre of shoulds—the sermon— and waged relentless war on the genre of plays, as chapter one describes. All their literature, even meditative poems, is couched in a language of instruction, to oneself or to others. They delighted in the endless elaboration of biblical truths, explained with a dogged multiplicity of firstlies and fifthlies. "The awfull trueth contained in this text, will be the better seen, by resolving it into four propositions," said John Norton.[11] What might make us laugh made them attend. They also thrived on simple similes, interchangeable from "reason" to "reason," preacher to preacher, year to year, almost century to century. Where Anglicans tended to enjoy originality and eloquence of expression, or a deft classical allusion, the Puritan "plain style" was meant to oppose vanity. The minister could not be a breast of God one day and have an ear for Plato the next. If sermons were to persuade proud sinners toward voluntary submission in a reborn company of the faithful, ministers had to show the way in their own speech. To state it too simply, Anglicans offered a complex language of meditative deference; Puritans, a straightforward language of collective dependence.

The difference was always one of degree and emphasis. Almost any given Puritan thought or image can be found in an Anglican tract, though probably more in passing. Yet not until the 1650s did Puritans develop a genre, the spiritual narrative, that described conversion to the expected pattern from the individual's point of view. Theirs was less the "eloquent I" than the militant We.[12] They forswore a supple prose that could produce the flowing, merging ecstasy of Thomas Traherne's *Centuries of Meditation* for strictly ordered prose structured by a form and vision wholly other than oneself. Self-emptying, not microcosmic fulfillment, pleased them, because it pleased their God. And Puritan sermon styles reflected a shared passion for self-emptying obedience in their relatively inflexible application of God's pattern.

Yet many other sects, then as now, have spoken with equally obsessive zeal. Many had and have the same subordination of self to whole, the same punctuation of prose with a holy text, the same mania for precise distinctions, the same humorless interchangeability of voices, the same concern for pure authority. Besides, in other respects most Puritans did not share traits we consider obsessive, and many were not obsessive in any sense. Most Puritans were eminently decisive, they had no trouble resisting authority, they showed a great gift for practical compromise and common sense, and they were deeply offended by mindless ritualizing, which in fact brought on Puritan protests in the first place. Though William Prynne, Michael Wigglesworth, and Cotton Mather seem on the far end of neurosis at times, even they had a clear sense of how the world worked. If anything, those three seem more hysterical than obsessive.

It is true that people thought Puritans too serious. Yet there was wit as well as healthy acknowledgment of sexuality among the faithful, if tending too much to wordplay for our taste. Puritans shared with Elizabethan dramatists a passion for puns, finding providential meanings in the coincidental sounds of words. There was also a striking variety of voices among them, as chapter six describes for American plain stylists. Thomas Hooker, for instance, speaks with self-dramatizing exuberance, confidence, and flashes of humor that belie the stereotypical pattern. As one of many responses to the tensions of the age, the language of Puritanism shares obsessive aspects with other faiths and accommodates many nonobsessive voices of its own.

What *is* uniquely Puritan, at least for its time, is the awkward intensity of the combination. How could such intimate and regressive similes be framed in such rigid, repetitive patterning? Anglicans were more self-indulgent in their prose, yet more patriarchal in their statements about worldly authority. Though they shared the allegorical interpretation of Canticles with Puritans, they did not develop the fantasy of nursing at the heavenly Father to anything like the repetitive seriousness of Puritan ministers, nor were they at such pains to locate the reward at the end of a scrupulously delineated process of self-transformation.

As several scholars have said, Puritanism differs more in intensity than in belief from other available modes of Protestant experience, and there were several degrees of intensity within the faith as well.[13] Yet my study claims more: that the Puritan experience can profitably be examined as a confluence of two contradictory modes of literary expression—nursing fantasies and obsessive styles. Each satisfied various needs among a wide variety of people, and the combination satisfied them more. There were also nursing styles, most notably in John Cotton's sermons, and obsessive fantasies. In fact, chapter four argues that most Puritans were not themselves obsessed but *wished* to be so, in part to make the father's role secure, and more basically to fulfill their own desire for dependent identity. That wish became tangibly embodied in sermon style and in the first-generation patriarchal family in New England.

Puritan language is most striking in the doubleness of its appeal. It looks both ways: to radical voluntarism, yet to utter submission; to absolute authority, yet to limited authority, defined as duties more than powers and constrained by mutual obligation from God on down; to God the father, yet to God as mother; to the Word as strict law, yet to the Word as spiritual milk; to the self filled with filth as lustful pride or anger, yet to the self reborn of the Father in infantile ecstasy or collectively married to Christ in virgin purity. The wish to be obsessively dependent allayed more complicated, and contradictory, anxieties. A polarized and formalized style of fidelity to the Bible satisfies the wish in one way; interchangeable fantasies of regressive transformation from self to chosen people satisfy it in another.

Puritan language was therefore patriarchal, yet not patriarchal. The fantasy of nursing at the father would seem to call for a steady diet of Isaiah 49.23, which imagines a time when kings shall be "nursing

fathers" to their people. Yet Anglicans cited the text much more frequently. Anglicans strengthened patriarchal rhetoric as a justification
for the microcosmic authority of kings and bishops on earth.[14] Puritans
strengthened the father's role in several practical ways, making him a
surrogate minister in the home. He was responsible for morning and
evening prayers, for catechizing the children after the sermon, for governing his wife and ruling his "little commonwealth." Puritan language
also emphasizes the high status, indeed the holiness, of assiduously following a calling. But Puritans scrupulously denied that fathers or
princes had any right to act in their own name alone. They reconstituted the father's authority as an image for all authority on earth and
in heaven, but in a frame of voluntary mutual expectations, not involuntary submission to arbitrary fatherhood for its own sake.

Puritans were eager to resist the tyrannous ego in any form, male
or female, in the court, the church, the family, or the heart. Whether as
willful king, brutal husband, persecuting archbishop, or secret sinner,
proud authority must be humbled to God's commands. Everyone must
be ruled. God himself had voluntarily bound himself to man's salvation
through the covenants; on that, not on kings, one could depend. As
Thomas Hooker declared in his *A survey of the summe of Church
Discipline,* "God is the father of all the family in heaven and earth.
Christ the Head and Redeemer, the holy Ghost the comforter." Elders
are not thought of as fathers or grandfathers, he says, because they do
not beget their flocks. Unlike bishops, they are elected by their congregations. Each church is "Democraticall" concerning the people;
"Aristocraticall" concerning the elders, but only "Monarchicall" concerning Christ. God is the only true nursing father, as Christ is the only
spiritual monarch, and even so, the faithful must become subjects
voluntarily, not as slaves.[15]

At one level Puritans shied away from Isaiah's image of nursing
fathers because their princes so obviously were not. Occasionally one
finds the reference in early writers such as Henry Bullinger. In later
times the citation is made wistfully, if at all. Hundreds of Puritan pages
explicating the Fifth Commandment, which for them as for Anglicans
implied deference to social authority as well as to parents, pass without
a whisper of Isaiah.[16] At another level, as Thomas Hooker and Samuel
Willard both took care to say, "father" cannot apply to earthly rulers
because, precisely speaking, they do not beget their subjects, as elders
do not beget their congregations. Willard goes so far as to say that God
himself should be called Father only in his disciplining role, not in his
essence.[17] More is at issue here than an obsession with distinctions.

Puritans believed in locating earthly religious authority collectively with the congregations, who elected ministers just as the faithful elected magistrates. Bishops were a form of popery. Yet again, their language looks both ways: to radical democracy, and to absolute obedience to a heavenly patriarch whose pattern can be glimpsed in good kings, magistrates, and fathers, wherever they can be found.

Again, the crucial difference is one of emphasis. Anglican sermons also condemn vanity, and Anglican marriage tracts also preach the husband's lordship on earth yet obedience to God. But where Anglicans tend toward a language of microcosmic earthly authority, taking pleasure in nursing at the king's will or the minister's individual style, Puritans tend toward a language of clear egalitarian obligations and heavenly dependence, maximizing duties and minimizing powers, securing identity as roles within a communal organism rather than inflating a hierarchy of persons. God and family meant more; kingdom meant less. Everything was stripped of awe and ceremony. The very word "church" ceased to mean a building, which as only a "meeting house" was spare and unadorned. A church was simply a body of the faithful, because nothing should be sacred but a group of people devoutly and directly nursing at God's Word.[18] For them God was the only pure Father, and earth-bound surrogates should nurse doubts, hopes, and obligations as much as underlings.

One can already see some of the paradoxes and contradictions near the surface of "plain" Puritan prose. Making a virtue of anxiety, it was a language uncomfortable with any human certainty. It made doubt a surer sign of salvation than Arminian righteousness or the Quakers' inner light. It made struggle a necessity, security a sign of sin. "Father" in Puritan usage was a word intimating God himself, yet associated with constraints on earth and female imagery in heaven. If the Elizabethan age was, among other things, a celebration of the unbounded self marching in triumph through Persepolis, Puritans suspected the unbounded self in all its forms, and the suspicion extended to language itself. As a typical Puritan treatise on the family begins, their writing is "not garnished with eloquence, nor full of great cunning nor beautified . . . neither is it stuffed with subtill questions and arguments, nor indited with Rhetoricall and eloquent style" like those made more "for boasting and vaine-glorysake, than for any desire to edifie, and to doe others good." The plain style reflects Puritan disgust at self-centeredness. Appropriately, the first published sermon delivered in New England, in 1621, was Robert Cushman's *The Sin and Danger of Self-Love*.[19] To "doe others good" in God's name was the characteristic

Puritan obligation. One's role in the group required the transformation of personal feeling into duty. If self-centered introspection and patriarchal repression became Puritan legacies, long after the original impulse toward holy communities obedient to the Father's Word had lost its purity, that was because the doubleness of Puritan discourse had ceased to satisfy a new set of conflicts in a new world.

———————————————

My study is not primarily a comparative one, though chapters two and three are in part more detailed attempts to locate Puritanism among competing styles of faith and doubt. The larger aim is to explore some of the psychological and social dynamics that made Puritan language so intensely satisfying to believers for a historical moment lasting 200 years. Though ambivalence is my focus, it is not the only source for the Puritan sense of feeling small in themselves yet militant together in the service of an infinite God. Nor is fatherhood the only role in their rhetoric of callings or among their similes for faith. I emphasize these two concepts, as I do Puritan mothering, because their interconnections have not been highlighted before, and because of my conviction that political, economic, theological, and social sources of Puritanism are profoundly related to family dynamics.

I do not mean conscious ambivalence, in the popular sense of indecisiveness about choices. The Puritans were very decisive; how else could they have come to America? They were also very clear-headed about priorities, values, and goals. Rather, I mean unconscious ambivalence as Freud adopted the term: opposing feelings about the same object.[20] What seems to be conscious clarity can be unconscious mixture, if one looks more closely at what the Puritans loved and hated. They loved God and hated the Pope. They loved the breast of God, his Word or minister, and hated the Catholic whore, priests and liturgy. In reading Puritan sermons one becomes numbed to the reflex adjectives and oppositions, and most scholars have simply ascribed the dichotomizing to Ramist instruction. Yet clearly there is a polarizing fantasy at work. They especially hated those who allowed "things indifferent," or "mixed fellowships, and other pollutions" into a world so clearly structured by God versus Satan.[21] They loved the good father, who is given a good mother's attributes; they hated the bad father, who is given a bad woman's attributes. Some have seen these oppositions as a stage in the history of ideas, or an indirect way of getting at the king, or simple sexism, or the gross simplifications of newly literate minds. To join psychology with social history offers a more complex frame for explaining the emotional sources of Puritan rhetoric.

Puritan family tracts were especially concerned that parents check their tender feelings, at least after the child reached the age of reason, and "break the will" of their children, as recent social historians have emphasized.[22] Many tracts connected childhood discipline to later readiness for conversion. As we shall see, the few examples of actual practice before the eighteenth century tell a different story. Yet Puritan theology does encourage an overtly broken will as a first step toward submission to an infinitely powerful and parental God. A mixture of empathy and rage, projected onto the Godhead, is one source for Puritan language.

Equally as important, however, the anxious father and zealous mother must share the psychoanalytic stage with the repressed child as sources for Puritan fervor. Society broke fathers in these times far less lovingly than fathers tried to break their children. The son's perception of paternal weakness, anxiety, and failure is a major theme in the few detailed accounts we have of childhood. And "tender mothering" was also strongly urged by Puritans.

My approach here is more post-Freudian than Freudian and looks as much to interpersonal as to intrapsychic perspectives. My emphasis on interdependent motives points outward to the family and social forces rather than inward to reductively universal desires. It differs from traditional Freudian orientations in three ways.

First, Puritans were not moved by any one motive. They did not simply want to kill their fathers and marry their mothers, or the reverse, though either fantasy can be found. Resentment cannot be so easily dislodged from affection when the object of mixed feelings structures one's world. "Father," for instance, is as complicated a word as the varied emotions it evoked in Puritan minds. It connotes a role model as well as a disciplinarian, a guide to the world of work as well as an affectionate or stern face by the bedside. Especially in the early seventeenth century, when the role of father—as distinct from worker— was so much more primary in the family and community than it is in postindustrial society, any one of his aspects could provoke contrary emotions. To reduce his impact to the repression of parricidal feelings mocks the variety of ways that a father can give rise to varied feelings.[23] It slights the complicated feelings of empathy and guilt that could come to an older child who sees even the harshest father diminished, confused, and anxious in a changing world. And it avoids altogether the mutual dependence between father and son.

Second, the family must be put in the context of larger historical changes. Richard Bushman, Emory Elliott, Philip Greven, and others have studied in detail the patriarchal nature of the American Puritan family.[24] Many English Puritans no doubt also grew up in similar families, facing fairly conventional Oedipal problems that Puritan theology helped to resolve. What interests me more, however, is that for those few Puritans whose lives we know in detail, strong fathers are more a wish than a fact. There was great stress on male roles as England began its slow transition from a peasant to a mercantile economy, especially in the counties where Puritanism took root. It has often been pointed out that Puritans were conspicuously on the edge of economic change: weavers, small tradesmen, "the middle sort" in areas whose economies were very sensitive to the winds of trade.[25] Chapter two explores the various conflicts between ambition and submission that such changes fostered.

Puritanism, in my view, was one of the first ambivalent responses to the threatened erosion of village, agrarian, patriarchal norms within the family. The Puritan impulse has several psychological sources, among them what Freudians would say is a covert rebellion against tyrannical fathers. Yet Puritanism is also what Freudians call a reaction formation. Rebelling against stern fathers may have helped give confidence to more radical Puritans in their political attacks. But perhaps more centrally, Puritan faith offers a response to an equally unconscious perception that one's father needed support, was weak, was losing his "calling" in a strange new world. More broadly, many nonfamilial disruptions brought on feelings of self-doubt and anxiety, even of inward pollution, in ways basic to the age as well as to Puritanism.[26] The father's role in particular had to be propped up, by exaggerated filial respect and a language of mutual obligation on earth to a sheltering patriarch in heaven. Accounts of various childhoods, by Thomas Shepard, Ralph Josselin, Oliver Heywood, and others hint that at least some Puritan fathers were failures in their sons' eyes. America became a land where the fantasy of old-time village patriarchy, perhaps never more than a fantasy, could be made flesh in daily life.

The Thomas Hookers and Peter Bulkeleys seem to have wanted peace and scope for their faith and authority. But for the John Cottons, even the Thomas Shepards, and for many other Puritans perplexed by new religious choices and new economic risks, preaching God's eternal and unchangeable authority may have eased many anxieties about male roles and generational conflicts. Guilt over hostile impulses toward a strong father, or a strong father-God, was certainly one component of Puritanism, though it is very significant that children from patently patriarchal homes in New England did not have conversion experiences with anything like the intensity of their fathers. Patriarchy may have been the result, not the cause, of ambivalence and anxiety. Puritans may have been satisfied by a language of the pure father because it spoke to a historical moment at which, in retrospect, we can see the father's family role begin to decline and his work cease to be agrarian. These ambivalences, and these defenses, are in any case not universal. They have historical roots in the various and changing social functions of the family.

My third divergence from Freudian norms has to do with evidence. Ordinarily one would look to biography or to extensive records of audience response to Puritan preaching for psychoanalytic interpretation. Chapter two attempts to make use of what biographical data there are, especially on the early childhood of various Puritan figures. We find various orphans, parental deaths, unsuccessful fathers, distraught or hysterical mothers. At the simplest level, as so many have said, Puritanism was a dream of order that allayed conflict at every stage of a believer's life.[27] But we can find these life stories in any religious sect, at any historical moment. We can also find Puritans, perhaps the majority of them, who seem to have led calm and fruitful lives, in no way distinguished from fellow Englishmen except through their religion. Both the skimpy nature of personal records and the permanent muteness of the vast majority of Puritans make it unlikely that we will ever have enough information for more than peripheral, individual speculation.

A somewhat more promising biographical route is to look at child-rearing practices in the aggregate. Psychoanalytic theory suggests, for instance, that adult Family Romance fantasies arise from unresolved conflicts at the anal as well as the Oedipal stages of growth.[28] What we know about Puritan child rearing does not entirely contradict psychoanalytic theory, though the data are slight. In *A Little Commonwealth*, for instance, John Demos uses Erik Erikson's neo-Freudian model of the stages of growth to show how the children of Plymouth had to suppress not their sexuality so much as their anger. At first, Demos finds, these children were loved, held, warmed, and breast-fed by their mothers. In fact, Puritans placed exceptional stress on breast-feeding and infant care in general.[29] The ordinary Puritan child does not seem to have suffered the most elemental conflicts in basic trust and tensions in the mother-child bond that today's theories connect to autism, schizophrenia, and complete personality dysfunction. Nor does Puritanism show many histories of such personal breakdowns, though depression for months at a time was not rare.

Rather, Demos finds Puritan conflicts located at the second stage of growth, where, in Erikson's terms, the child's struggle for "autonomy" from parental discipline can lead to "shame and doubt" if parents do not encourage independence. The outcome seems to fit Puritans well. As Cotton Mather approvingly said of John Ward, "Of young persons, he would himself give this advice: 'Whatever you do, be sure to maintain shame in them; for if that be once gone, there is no hope that they'll ever come to good.' "[30] Erikson avoids labels like anality, which has come to connote a stage of bodily development rather than parental expectations that induce feelings about the body. But the explicit use of anal imagery in Puritan writings—sin as filth, dung, excrement—provides indirect support for Demos's analysis, as does the frequent call for shame and self-abasement. The prevalence of the obsessive character in Puritan prescriptions for behavior is another indicator, since one of psychoanalysis' most lasting contributions has been to correlate obsessive-compulsive behavior with anality.

Oral or anal fantasies are only the mind's way of managing more complicated feelings about parental influence. They are reductive defenses, mental acts done to preserve a sense of self while the behavioral defenses of shame and deference gain parental approval. By emphasizing the wish for autonomy, Erikson's theory slights interpersonal needs, though he has helpfully moved psychoanalytic criticism beyond the jargon of id, ego, and superego. Puritanism has less to do with dung than with discipline, though pollution imagery is obviously central to its language, and Puritanism has more to do with healthy mutuality and shared purpose than contemporary theories of autonomy allow.

At the third stage, the time of more sustained and overt Oedipal rebellion against the father (as Freud says), where "initiative" struggles with "guilt" (Erikson's revision), the Puritan father is said to clamp down an iron hand. Obedience to parents is now the preeminent virtue. "And surely there is in all children," pastor John Robinson wrote, "a stubbornness, and stoutness of mind arising from natural pride, which must, in the first place, be broken and beaten down; . . . lest . . . the tender sprigs grow to that stiffness, that they will rather break than bow."[31] To "bow" that "stiffness," with the Freudian overtones of father castrating son, is also the first step recommended later on for religious conversion. Sometimes one is not quite sure who is doing the bowing, as parents struggle to redeem their children's souls. Here is Cotton Mather's advice, no doubt reflecting his own practice at home: "But, besides your *Family Prayers, O Parents*, why should you not now and then, take one capable *Child* after another, alone before the

Lord? Carry the *Child* with you, into your *Secret Chambers*; make the *Child* kneel down by you, while you present it unto the Lord, and Implore His Blessing upon it. Let the *Child,* hear the Groans, & see the Tears, and be a witness of the Agonies, wherewith you are *Travailing* for the Salvation of it. The *Children* will never Forget what you do; It will have a marvellous Force upon them." Despite, or perhaps because of, the "marvellous Force" of parents groaning and crying before their crouching child, Mather suggests that the children are likely to hold their parents and religion in contempt still, unless parents have been able to "*watch* all opportunities, to be instilling your *Instructions* into the Souls of your little Folks . . . They are *narrow-mouth'd* Vessels, and things must be *drop after drop* instill'd into them."[32] But Mather's instructions are taken from Puritanism at the turn of the eighteenth century, when some parents were enacting extreme versions of the obsessive style. For earlier Puritans, a more moderate discipline went hand in hand with instruction, and tract after tract counsels the necessity of keeping a caring mean between excessive discipline and too much love.

Shortly after the age of five, children are dressed in adult clothing and made to work like little men and women. What Freud called "identification" with parental roles and expectations is now at least visibly complete. The clearly negative associations with pride, stubbornness, and stiffness imply some repression of anger as well as male sexual assertiveness and encourage children to define themselves through familial reverence. Finally, as teen-agers, an age again associated with autonomy and rebellion, Puritan children were often tamed by being farmed out to other families, for the double purpose of apprenticeship and more impersonal discipline.[33]

This theory is neat and perhaps even partly true. Anger at the father is repressed into self-hatred, while overt patriarchal dependence is exalted. Yet despite the enticing parallels between these discoveries about Puritan child rearing and Freudian theory, the theory can be questioned, and the evidence is almost entirely from advice, not behavior. Demos is not writing of a mainstream Puritan village but of Plymouth, a separatist colony whose inhabitants had more humble and provincial origins than the Puritans of Massachusetts Bay and were far less compromising in their conscious theology. Pastor Robinson, who was in Holland when he wrote his remarks about child rearing, never observed American theory or practice firsthand. The practice of farming out children to other families during what we now call adolescence was widespread throughout all classes in England at that time, to one Italian observer's dismay.[34] Moreover, Demos establishes the idea that the child's will was broken between the ages of one and two entirely from Eriksonian theory, not Puritan evidence. But the main reservation has to be the lack of data. Chapter three develops my hypothesis that Puritan child-rearing patterns were mixed, yet it too is based more on what people were told to do than on what they did. Children simply did not interest adult observers then as they do now, and we will very likely never have the hard data necessary to do more than speculate.[35]

So biography, and records of child rearing in theory and practice, can encourage but not fully substantiate a psychoanalytic approach. Unfortunately, the major development in psychoanalytic criticism of the last ten years—the analysis of audience response—is of even less help. Norman Holland's model of literary response cannot be used for Puritan sermons, nor can David Bleich's reader associations, because there are only fragmentary records of audience response, and none of associations to affective reaction.[36] Sermons were often published long after they were spoken, and until the 1670s American ministers usually published in London.[37] Social historians will want a more direct correlation between fantasy and behavior, but again the problem of data is overwhelming. We have no "free associations" of ministers or congregations to base strict psychoanalytic interpretation on. Diaries will mention that so-and-so spoke on such-and-such, but nothing more. Except in the case of election day sermons or sermons preached about specific crises, the Word's impact on daily behavior remains obscure. We could follow Harold Bloom's lead and treat Anne Hutchinson's New England career as a case of "misreading" John Cotton, but at the cost of misreading Puritanism as her experience.

Instead, what we do have are contradictions like the following. In *Religion and the Decline of Magic*, Keith Thomas recounts the story of the sixty-year-old man who all his life had attended sermons, twice on Sundays and often during the week. As a contemporary text has it, on his deathbed he answered his minister thus: " 'Being demanded what he thought of God, he answers that he was a good old man; and what of Christ, that he was a towardly young youth; and of his soul, that it was a great bone in his body; and what should become of his soul after he was dead, that if he had done well he should be put into a pleasant green meadow.' " The despairing teller of this story continued, " 'But, my brethren, be assured this man is not alone; there be many a hundred in his case who come to church and hear much, haply a hundred and fifty sermons in a year; yet at year's end are as much the better for all, as the pillars of the church against which they lean, or the pews wherein they sit.' "[38] As Thomas notes, many ministers said that half their parish did not know the Lord's Prayer or the Ten Commandments.

Yet such a story does lead us to one of the most widespread, manifest, and clear audience responses to Puritan sermons: the taking of notes. Just as the minister strove to make himself a conduit for God's milk, removing his proud self from the process, so his audience was encouraged to jot down the minister's points without any irrelevant sinful commentary of their own. Most American sermons, in fact, were published from congregational notes, not from ministerial drafts. What strikes anyone about a Puritan sermon is how mechanically organized it is, with doctrine, reasons, uses, each with heads and subheads. Though they did not intend the pun, ministers wanted to make sure that the head led the heart. In that way the memory of God's word would be so clear that no wayward impulse could upset the heavenly order. In short, Puritan audiences quite consciously squashed affective associations.

That response itself, a psychoanalyst might say, indicates a great deal about Puritan repression. A nonresponse could reveal the need to keep responses down. But even so, what were the feelings being kept in check? Were they anger, fear, desire, emulation, emptiness, depression, anxiety, joy? And why did other Puritans counsel the heart to lead the head? For answer, all we have at hand are the extraordinarily faithful and minute notes of extraordinarily patterned and organized sermons. Puritans were more consciously concerned with instructing the minds of the faithful than expressing the complex emotions of faith.

What remains are sparse and fragmentary, almost random accounts of the utter despair that a good sermon could induce. In *The Real Christian* (1670), Giles Firmin noted disapprovingly that Thomas Shepard had often brought simple folk to excessive despondency. One man "told me he had a Maid-servant who was very godly, and reading of that particular in Mr. Shepherd's Book, which I opposed, she was so cast down and fell into such troubles that all the Christians that came to her could not quiet her spirit. . . . I have met with several Persons who . . . could not be resolved that ever their faith was true because of that which he had written."[39] But like even the best biographies, diaries, and spiritual autobiographies, these passages are sparse in associations and imagery.

Neither biography nor audience response can therefore give access to the complexity of Puritan motives and feelings that psychoanalytic theory suggests may be there. We are left with the language of faith itself. Since the usual sources of direct psychoanalytic insight—biography, private therapy sessions, associations—are not available, especially for early childhood, I use literary expression, citing other evidence where appropriate.

Literature can bear the burden of this scrutiny because it plays a central role in any literate society. It manages a group's repressed feelings. Through form, fantasy, and style, it encourages its audience to share what would disrupt society if expressed as behavior. Of course this is not literature's only function. But it will be the focus of this study. Freud's own theories have been a major barrier to an integrated perception of literature, since he so rigidly polarized conflict and defense, latent and manifest content. Though Freud was fascinated by art and literature, it has taken post-Freudian analysts and critics—especially Erikson and Jack Spector—to show how literature can be distinguished from other forms of writing by the various and complex ways that it becomes a self-referential system, fusing manifest and latent content into appropriate form.[40]

Such a perspective also allows us to consider why Puritan literature is often so bad, and mostly so dead. Puritans shared with Freud's theories a conscious distrust, and an unconscious fear, of the mixed feelings that can be transformed into form and style. Accordingly, Puritan literature is primarily a literature of polarization, repetition, and reversal: defenses that manage feeling more by blocking than by transforming its sources. Modern readers frequently have the response to Puritan sermons that one scholar had to Puritan family manuals, that to read one is to read them all.[41] But contemporary audiences were avid to hear the Word again and again and again. Given the structured comfort of fixed order, whether in William Perkins's codification of sermon form or in conventional rhyme schemes and lugubrious acrostics, the faithful could dream regressive dreams of heavenly union with mothering fathers. Their fantasies were legitimized by the Bible. Propped by mechanical form and God's unchanging content, Puritan literature, which consisted largely of sermons and instructional tracts, could encourage its audience toward shared fantasy, though rarely toward the complexities of voice and conflict present in great literature.

———————•—•———————

Puritan language was a first, polarized, ambivalent response to several large historical changes: the movement from theater to the novel as the major literary genre; the change from an aristocratic to a middle-class audience for literature; the transformation of the patriarchal family in an agrarian village setting to the modern middle-class family whose father works away from home and whose mother raises the children; the shift of loyalties from the village to the nation-state; the even more basic shift from an oral to a literary culture. Both sides of all these changes are embedded in the ambivalent resolutions of the Puritan sermon. The sermon embodies within its oral form the new, mobile, transitional self, ambitious, skeptical of all earthly authority, with no trappings but a portable Bible and an improvable mind. This "radical" side of Puritanism has been sufficiently emphasized. Yet the language of Puritanism also embodies abject deference to the supreme patriarch, a fantasy of group submission rather than individual ambition, a congregational theology that in many ways preserved agrarian village norms, and a thoroughgoing denial of any complexity in human emotion.[42]

The greatest liberty taken with psychoanalytic methodology in this study is to use literature to apply psychoanalytic theory to social psychology. My emphasis is on shared emotions and defenses, not on individual repression. Psychology has been used to study Puritanism in two quite distinct ways: first, from the standpoint of sexual repression; second, and more fruitfully, as an example of the internalization of authority. Even today, in popular usage, "Puritan" still connotes prurient sexual repressiveness.[43] In academic circles, Puritanism tends to be more associated with the Protestant ethic, although in some respects the hypothesis of internalized authority manifested as hard work and postponed pleasure is compatible with the Freudian hypothesis that superego formation and father identification resolve Oedipal conflicts.[44] My own view, at least of the earlier Puritans, finds more ambivalence at every level, though the language of New England sons comes closer to a model of guilt and internalization. Beyond that, Puritanism demands psychological interpretation in ways more positive than an analysis of internalization and repression allow.

Puritans themselves were preoccupied with motivation and the mind. Their concern with rebirth rather than birth, which made them so impatient with details of sinful childhood, reflected a wish. As the most scrupulous New England Puritans from Shepard to Edwards admitted to themselves, being reborn was a state experienced rarely if at all. Though they tried to make rebirth a matter of verifiable social expectation through a public account of conversion, at least for males, they knew that there was no ready proof for the experience of grace.

Thus they reached for every image available in biblical authority and common experience to make their wishes seem more real than the real. There, in the sermon literature, we find passionate fantasy governed by strict order. Recent interpretations have brought out more conscious fears of personal loss, death, identity crisis, disorder, conflict with neighbors, and other interpersonal crises.[45] More traditional interpretations have stayed within the frame of intellectual or biblical exegesis. My emphasis is on the overdetermined quality of the experience, the various conscious and unconscious appeals of Puritan language, and the central role of literature in articulating shared emotions.

Puritans perceived, quite accurately, that the family and community needed support in an age of threatening social mobility. Fantasies of the greater Father, or of the Family Romance, encouraged them to reconstitute the family on traditional terms while also subordinating themselves to membership in voluntary groups, like the village or church. Attendance at sermons mirrored many aspects of their voluntary group faith in the Word. Their fantasies and wishes were not simply neurotic or escapist, though they certainly had reactionary aspects.[46] Nor did they arise simply from repressive child rearing. In fact, it might be more accurate to say that Puritan concepts of child rearing arose from the power of these fantasies to stabilize and structure their lives. Most of our evidence for Puritan repressiveness at a very early age comes from evangelical families in the eighteenth century in New England, where shared wishes for heavenly patriarchy had become earthly patriarchy, and the insecurities of early Puritans had become sure parental righteousness.

Psychoanalysis, like Puritanism, is an inferential discipline. Where Puritans found God in his visible "providences" and the Bible, Freud's discoveries of unconscious mental processes depended on indirect evidence like dreams, associations, and adult behavior intimating childhood conflicts. Like too many Freudians, who have tended to encapsulate themselves in the language of their master, Puritans—as William Carlos Williams once said—surrounded themselves with "the jargon of God, . . . as with a palisade."[47] Psychoanalysis shares with Puritanism the attempt to see the invisible through the visible, even when the visible, like the New England coast, seems rather barren. Mindful of my distance from both experiences, I have tried to avoid the psychoanalytic tendency, so similar to Puritan analyses of the conversion process, to pile on abstract intrapsychic distinctions, whether between id, ego, and superego or between primary and secondary processes.

My focus is on the interrelationships of social conflicts with private fantasies. Yet finally my speculations about Puritan ambivalences do remain inferential hypotheses, depending on the retroactive application of a still developing modern theory to a rather clannish group who would regard such intellectual forays with astonished disapproval.

One other note about method. Though exploring several aspects of psychoanalytic theory, the book does not venture into structuralism. While a structuralist approach may ultimately be complementary, it seems opposed at present. Literary structuralists tend to assume that language lives in a world of its own and that criticism should rewrite its texts. Psychoanalytic structuralists, especially Jacques Lacan, rewrite Freud as patriarchal in the extreme, without any attempt to come to terms with pre-Oedipal experiences of mothering. Social structuralists tend to remove the self from social process, which for them is patterns engendering patterns. Where structuralists speak of conventions and linguistic roots, sometimes with a tone of playful narcissism and often with the claim that language is a self-generating system, my concern is with literature as a transformational mirror for social history, especially for shared feelings. However, if structuralists tend to overlook some central social functions of literature, I have tried to be equally wary of the "form is defense" equation of some psychoanalytic critics.[48] Form, like style, both manages and mirrors, in specific ways inseparable from the historical moment of the genre.

Feeling has only recently been given the weight in Puritan studies that it deserves.[49] Some could say this study only psychologizes about private individuals who happened to be in positions of authority; or indeed that it takes for shared fantasies what ought to be seen as male techniques of social conditioning. Clearly there was incipient class, group, and generational conflict. But in England as well as New England there was a broad consensus about the necessity for patriarchy, class distinctions, village bonds, and theological modes of discourse. The problem of audience became acute in America by the 1670s, and various "myths of declension" were developed to explain away the ministers' less central community role.[50] But for English Puritans and the first generation of American immigrants, those men with gentry backgrounds or Cambridge educations were expected to assume authority, and at no point did conflicts between mercantile and farming interests overthrow the status differentials. The persistence of traditional respect and traditional social order is part of the emotional needs that Puritan sermons spoke to.

Let me return to the intimacies evoked by Puritan preaching. John Cotton compared the "publick Worship of God" to "the bed of loves: where, 1. Christ embraceth the souls of his people, and casteth into their hearts the immortal seed of his Word, and Spirit, *Gal.* 4.19. 2. The Church conceiveth and bringeth forth fruits to Christ."[51] In two breaths his listeners heard themselves compared to women being impregnated and babies being born, all legitimized by the text of Galatians and the minister's authority. Cotton continues, "And looke what affection is between Husband and Wife, hath there been the like affection in your soules towards the Lord Jesus Christ? Have you a strong and hearty desire to meet him in the bed of loves, when ever you come to the Congregation, and desire you to have the seeds of his grace shed abroad in your hearts, and bring forth the fruits of grace to him, and desire that you may be for him, and for none other?" Let no one say that Puritanism represses desire. Here the minister casts himself as Pandarus and calls forth his congregation's most private sexual and familial experiences to awaken public conviction. The overt connection of these experiences, the open intercourse between private sexuality and public faith, the direct questions demanding strong affections, remain vivid. More broadly, the Puritan sense of rebirth, family, and community was the positive side of a group fantasy that helped them transform private conflicts into public wishes. Sometimes, as Freud discovered with hysterics, it is a mistake to take what people say as literally so. Rather, to see the fantasy in what Puritans took for gospel truth can reveal how a people attained mastery of themselves and their world.

Dreams are not literature, and fantasy is not art. Dreams assume the presence of the dreamer's projected self; literature must continuously seduce our involvement. But literature does act as a clarifying mirror for the common feelings of its audience.[52] To the modern reader a Puritan sermon seems formulaic, dogma ridden, smelling of texts and bile. But in the 1630s and 1640s, to a small band of people huddling into small villages on an alien coast, and for sixty years or more before, the experience of hearing a man speak traditions of paternal and familial authority in similes that bound the Word of the cosmic Father to their own ordinary knowledge was more than a powerful weekly goad. It was more than a way of feeling special. It changed conflict into order; it secured identity and community; it offered a vision of exemplary survival.

Chapter One

Why Did Puritans Hate Stage Plays?

In 1576 Richard Burbage constructed the first London building intended only for plays. In 1642, Parliament passed an ordinance declaring stage plays unfit for the times. The intervening sixty-six years witnessed both the greatness of the Elizabethan and Jacobean theater and the rise of Puritanism as a broad-based social movement.

These two modes of social expression are usually seen in opposition to each other, even by contemporary writers. Ben Jonson satirized the hypocritical moral rigidity of Zeal-of-the-Land Busy in *Bartholomew Fair,* while the Puritan William Prynne had his ears cropped in 1634 after (perhaps) slandering the queen's taste for acting. In explaining and often apologizing for the unrelenting vendetta carried on by Puritans against the stage, modern historians point to the blatant social abuses connected with theaters. Puritan attacks focus on themes like idleness, crime, whoring, money changing, and other audience vices, not on specific thematic analyses of plays. "It was to the acting profession and the theater that the Puritans objected, not to the plays themselves," an early scholar concludes.[1] Roving companies of players disregarded town injunctions in times of disease, thus bringing the plague. Moreover, Anglicans and Catholics often voiced the same criticisms, although one scholar has said that the Puritan attack on stage plays was one of only two distinctively new Puritan themes—the other being their attack on Machiavellian politics.[2]

As social criticism, the attack on the theater was widely shared. Yet one cannot miss the special ferocity of Puritan prose and the malicious pleasure of Elizabethan responses. William Prynne and Philip Stubbes hated *everything* about the theater. Most modern readers have found their arguments comic or dismissed their tracts as the language of zealous, neurotic extremists.

My thesis is more sympathetic: the Puritans saw themselves in what they hated. They did not wish simply to differentiate their busy zeal from the idleness of the rabble, or banish the representation of vice, or follow the Bible's dictates, or attack the king indirectly. Nor is it only a case of incipient bourgeois morality proclaiming new concepts of truth and art.[3] These explanations fail to account for the hysterical overkill in Puritan tone. One reason will not do; they must find twenty, each supported by ancient "fathers" and punctuated by gratuitous expostulations. The stridency of so many interchangeable reasons does not come simply from opposition, or from the compulsion to show off one's reading that so afflicts Cotton Mather in the waning years of Puritanism. It comes from fear of similarity. The theater, in its social and literary form, mirrored aspects of themselves that most threatened their identity as Puritans.

As a social form, the theater mirrored everything the Puritan did not want to be: idle, lower class, spendthrift, disorderly, womanizing. In the world view of the faithful, the theater encouraged the lazy rich and the lazy poor while mocking the strivings of the middle sort. In the wide-ranging set of key concepts clustering around Puritan views of the Elizabethan and Jacobean stage, "whoredom" becomes the most frequently used code word for worldly taint of any kind. Above all, whoredom connoted mixture, and the negative associations with mixture say much about the Puritan habit of mind. Along with the conscious connection of stage plays to idleness and excess, there are more unconscious associations with women, filth, and feeling itself. Those who wished to "purify" themselves from the jumble of fears and desires natural to a time of rapid change needed a form offering more secure defenses, less flexible management of feeling.

Such a perspective can suggest some of the reasons, both conscious and unconscious, for Puritan attacks on the theater. Their need to polarize ambivalence and to make authority secure was profound. The polarities extend to their method of argument: strict dependence on the external authority of the Bible and classical writings, with associational clusters designed to intensify the opposition between virtue and vice. These associations, like Freudian dream associations, reveal Puritan feelings as well as logic. More broadly, the theater and the sermon were two major genres that reveal their conflicted seventeenth-century world more when set side by side than when taken separately for the whole.

———————————•—•———————————

Why did Puritans say they hated stage plays? We might begin with the language of the 1642 parliamentary resolution. The ordinance connected plays with public sports and contrasted both with "humiliation": "Whereas public sports do not agree well with public calamities nor public stage plays with the seasons of humiliation . . . it is therefore thought fit and ordained by the Lords and Commons in this Parliament that while these sad causes and set times of humiliation continue, public stage plays shall cease and be forborne."[4] "Calamity," "humiliation," and "sad causes" contrast with "plays" and "sports." In time of war, when social conflict is so visible, the reigning emotion should be guilt, not pleasure. This reaction to conflict is typically Puritan. Whereas the conventional Elizabethan notion of the theater declared that plays held the mirror up to nature in all its variety, Puritans responded to social mixture or conflict with a frame of oppositions: pleasure and humiliation, play and work, sport and calamity.

Puritan religious dramas were put on through the 1570s, and writers did not generally condemn acting until the end of James I's reign. Even into the 1630s, Puritans like John Milton were staging masques, and at least two of the most notorious Puritan attacks on the theater, by "Martin Marprelate" and William Prynne, made exuberant use of dramatic conventions. Nevertheless, as early as 1572 we can find some Puritans taking it for granted that the stage is the devil's plaything, though the first attacks tend to be more moderate and restrained. In that year John Field's *A View of popish Abuses* connects a nonpreaching ministry with the theater: "For bare reading of the word, and single service saying, is bare feeding; yea it is as evil as playing upon a stage, and worse too, for players yet learn their parts without book, and these, a many of them can scarcely read within book."[5] Preaching must be "feeding," not "bare reading." Puritans placed on language new demands for nourishment and guidance. Words that merely delighted merited at best contempt, and if one's Puritanism was of the "hotter" variety, censorship.

Most simply, Puritans distrusted plays because the Bible told them to. In *The Englishe Catechisme* (1623) John Mayer said that plays were wrong for two reasons: boys dressed like women (Deut. 22.4), and sins were acted for pleasure (Eph. 4.3-4). For William Perkins, plays were not "lawful" because "they are nothing else but representation of the vices and misdemeanors of men in the world." Perkins also cites the issue of women's clothes: "Again, it is unseemly that a man should put on the person, behavior, and habit of a woman, as it is also for a woman to put on the person, behavior, and habit of a man, though it be but for an hour. The law of God forbids both (Deut. xxii.3)."[6] Only "profitable" and lawful recreation can be permitted.

Plays were also connected to uncleanliness, carnality, plurality, and other manifestations of "unprofitable" behavior. In *The Anatomie of Abuses* (1583), Philip Stubbes found plays bad not in themselves but because they took people from the Sabbath "to Theaters and unclean assemblies, to ydleness, unthriftynes, whordome, wantonnes, drunkennes and what not."[7] Attendance at sermons was constantly contrasted with going to the theater as appropriate Sabbath behavior. In the either/or of the Puritan mind, sermons were holy and, in John Rainold's words, "all Plaies, as carnall, be obscene and ridiculous."[8] Then too, the contrast between sermons and plays reflects an equally pervasive contrast between work and idleness. "Love not mirth and pastime," wrote Robert Cleaver and John Dod in an aside to their family instructions, "for they have oft occasion of expences. Againe, they cause losse of time and neglect of businesse at home." Dudley Fenner's *Lawfull and Unlawfull Recreations* (1587) states that all recreation must lead to the glory of God or the profit of man, and that the pagan origins of stage plays, the transvestism of the actors, and the early Fathers' objections assure the unlawfulness of the theater, which makes people "slouthfull and idle to all goode workes." He also railed against "the outward fashion" and the practice of "fayning the outward shewes which are used in playes."[9]

Riotous behavior and fighting brought special Puritan condemnation. Tracts often associate theatrical performances with unrestrained and fractious passions. Even as late as Jeremy Collier, "discipline" denotes what the sinful stage undermines. *A Short View of the Immorality and Profaneness of the English Stage* (1688) asserts that the stage is "the most effective means to baffle the force of discipline, to emasculate people's spirits and debauch their manners. . . . What disappointments of parents, what confusion in families, and what beggary in estates have been hence occasioned?"[10] Discipline, profit, moderation, and family virtue promote right behavior. The stage induces excess and discord.

Other Puritan tracts adduce still more reasons to be wary of stage plays. For the reformed playwright Stephen Gosson, plays had turned a hardy and courageous people into self-indulgent pleasure seekers: "Our wrastling at armes is turned to wallowing in ladies lappes." For Richard Rogers, the players themselves are "unprofitable caterpillers" who are "burdensome and chargeable to others." Edmund Rudierde, who exulted over the death of Christopher Marlowe, described how players "bewitch idle eares with foolish vanities . . . making fooles laugh at sinne and wickednesse."[11] Richard Baxter lists fifteen objections to contemporary plays, and his special concern for the effect of their language on the young shows in other writings where he recommends fit literature: "The true History of exemplary Lives, is a pleasant and profitable recreation to young persons; and may secretly work them to a liking of Godliness and value of good men, which is the beginning of saving Grace: O how much better work is it, than Cards, Dice, Revels, Stage-Plays, Romances or idle Chat."[12]

The list of reasons could go on; what is important is how many there are. They are generated not so much by the rightness of each one but by the structure of oppositions so habitual to the Puritan outlook. Young men are faced with a world that offers, in Baxter's terms, "good men" and bad. On the good side stand lives whose value rests not in their unique achievements but in their exemplary role. The scriptures proclaim the unity of God's working world, while a sinful plurality of vices challenges God's union. Ambition, vanity, sexuality, lies, anger, idleness, conflict—in short, the unchecked self in worldly panoply—are the fearful images associated with stage plays. The "play" of sinful emotions is rhetorically represented by unstructured, unranked, interchangeable lists. Opposed is the disciplined path of reason, work, and submission to God's word. There can be no "occasional" middle ground, not even on the day of rest. One must always strive to bring one's feelings in line with God's models.

The polarizations were not new. Many Christians since St. Augustine had opposed drama, and Augustine himself argued that "the delicate vanity of stage plays" was the main reason Rome had been sacked. Like the Puritans, he connected plays to self-indulgence, uncleanness, luxury, plagues, idolatry, dishonesty, and filth. Again like the Puritans, he opposed them to sermons, self-abasement, and the "pure solemnities of Christ, where both sexes are so honestly distinguished by their several places; . . . where the holy doctrine of God's word is read from an eminent place." Unlike the Puritans, however, the attack on stage plays which threads through the first four books of his *City of God* is part of a larger attack on pagan gods, who are really devils demanding the plays in their honor. Though Augustine railed against poets who "presented the figments of their own lusts and fancies . . . as the guilt of the gods, and therefore of imitable examples," he was more concerned with banishing the gods themselves. One can argue for points

of similarity between the sense of disorder and anxiety in those bar-
barian days and the Puritan response to another world turning upside
down, but there are obvious differences as well. The important point is
that the Puritan critique was one intense aspect of a general language
of condemnation gaining assent at various times and places, for various
interconnected reasons.[13]

At one level, the Puritan assault fits the classic model of the *arriviste*:
those just in from the provinces or just up from the peasantry who
want to make absolutely clear how respectable they are by vehemently
denouncing their origins. In place of traditional definitions of the self
through inheritance and fixed social status, Puritans exalted the "calling," one's self defined through work and faith. Such definition permitted fixed earthly inequality while encouraging the fantasy of
heavenly equality and spiritual mobility through grace. If earthly
mobility results from hard work, ambition could also be encouraged.
Hedged in by dutiful respect to an invisible superior, the Puritan could
feel self-respect beyond his village purview. He was paradoxically
given a secure role, yet encouraged to dream great dreams. Stage plays
called forth such endless Puritan protest in part because they posed a
threat to that narrow road toward self-definition.

At another level, however, the Puritan polarities indicate more than
the first stage of the struggle to achieve middle-class values. Underneath a fairly conscious set of oppositions lies a more profound rhetorical opposition: God and the first fathers vie with images of tainted
women for the possession of young men's loyalties. Several of the
longer Puritan tracts indulge both sides of this fantasy—the endless
quotation of first fathers and the obsessive hostility to whores—at great
length. The issue of men wearing women's clothes especially exercised
Puritan prose writers. It is not enough to explain the inordinate attention Puritans gave to this phenomenon by saying the Bible decreed
otherwise, though reliance on God's word fits into the fantasy of
opposition.

Stubbes's *Anatomie of Abuses* richly embroiders the conventional
Puritan polarities with rhetoric hostile to women. Though most of his
book is taken up with other things, notably the wickedness of contemporary dress, chapter eleven says that stage plays and interludes
abuse the Sabbath and "the blessed word of GOD," which "is to be
handled reverently, gravely, and sagely, . . . and not scoffingly, flout-
ingly, and jibingly, as it is among stages." For Stubbes irreverence in
tone constitutes direct disobedience to authority, and as stage plays
encourage that tone they must be condemned. Vanity is of the Devil;

reverence is of God. There can be no mixture: "Intermingle not his blessed word with such prophane vanities," which "are quite contrarie to the Word of grace, and sucked out of the Devills teats to nourish us in idolatrie, hethenrie, and sinne."[14]

The reader is not allowed to miss that striking image of the "Devills teats," or the opposition between God the pure Father and the mother-devil. Stubbes repeats that idleness is "the Mother of vice" and later declares dancing is just as evil as stage plays, for "it sprang from the teates of the Devils brest, from whence all mischeef els dooth flow." Many citations from church fathers buttress his rather Manichean sense of the world, with God's sermons opposed to the devil's plays. How can it be that churches are empty and theaters are full? In his mind, the answer has to do with the same flouting tone, the same disrespect for authority, the same unleashed sexuality, that mark the devil's handiwork. Though he invokes the usual comparisons, he gives special attention to sexual innuendo: "Marke the flocking and running to Theaters & curtens, daylie and hourely, night and daye, tyme and tyde, to see Playes and Enterludes; where such wanton gestures, such bawdie speaches, such laughing and fleering, such kissing and bussing, such clipping and culling, Suche winckinge and glancinge of wanton eyes, and the like, is used, as is wonderfull to behold."[15] His list of vices taught by plays includes rebellion against princes and the deflowering of maids or "honest wives" as well as idleness, falsehood, murder, pride, jesting, and the like. The metaphor of the devil's breast succinctly states the source of such sinful variety.

Stubbes is so matter of fact about these metaphors that the modern reader easily forgets their origin in fantasy. The Bible sanctions many of the polarities and most of the imagery. But there is far more mentioned in the Bible than is dreamt of in Puritan philosophy. The association of a rebellious, sneering stage with idleness, sexuality, and the devil's breast brings together some basic male anxieties of the period, at least from a struggling yeoman's or artisan's perspective: the temptation to sink back into the seasonal rhythms of the agrarian village, the temptation to yield to sexual impulse rather than strive for family order and future gain, and the temptation to voice anger at aristocratic authority. Stage plays seemed to encourage all these impulses. Puritan theology offered controls that rearranged potentially negative energy into socially useful habits of work while offering fantasies of male authority—invisible, to be sure, but magnified and hierarchic, with the minister as the visible "breast of God" that nurtures order.

To take these metaphors for essential Puritan truths may be mak-

ing too much of a man described even by his contemporaries as
"narrow-sould." Thomas Nashe's response to the *Anatomie* seized on
Stubbes's transparent sexual anxieties; he claimed that Stubbes had
tried to convert a widow by attempting to "put a newe spirite into her
by carnall copulation, and so engraft her into the fellowshippe of the
faithfull."[16] (Nashe adds injury to insult by noting that the widow refused.) But Stubbes differs from other Puritan stage antagonists more
in his intemperate tone than in his basic outlook. The frame of mind
that allowed Nashe to perpetrate his witty outrage was a frame that
encouraged mixture—of spiritual and carnal, man and woman. Like the
best of Elizabethan theater, Nashe is attuned to the ways that conflict
can undermine order. That sort of mental agility, and disrespect, might
let loose in an occasional and anonymous "Martin Marprelate," but not
in the public voice of Puritanism. Rather, Stubbes rails against "this
cursed common wealth, where sinfull simplicitye pufte uppe with pride
of singularity, seekes to perverte the name and method of magistracy."[17]

In *The Overthrow of Stage-Playes* (1599), the more cultured John
Rainolds begins by contrasting pleasure with work. "The vanity and
unlawfulnesse of Plaies and Enterludes" bring such scenes as "many
leaving their houses and sundry necessary duties unperfourmed, yea
not sparing the very Sabath itselfe." Such people shirk work and family
only "to the mainetenance of their pleasures, or to nouzle themselves in
their vanities."[18] The idle self is the devil's plaything, and Rainolds
underlines the dangers of individual freedom with a metaphor of
prostitution. When his debating opponent argues that the stage is
acceptable because it is voluntary and free, Rainolds replies, "By
which kind of reasoning one might conclude likewise, that sith by the
scripture a woman taking mony for prostituting her body to men is
infamous: therefore she is not so, who doth it freely." Despite his
apparently dispassionate reliance on law and the dense citations of
classical texts, Rainolds shares with Stubbes hostility to female sexuality, and the association of women with pride, lust, ostentation, and
theatrical performance.

Rainolds also emphasizes the problem of men dressing in women's
clothes. Where Stubbes speaks in grand metaphors of the devil's breast,
Rainolds speaks more specifically of the "adulterous lewdnesse" of this
"filthie and monstrous" practice. He imagines "what sparkles of lust to
that vice the putting of womans attire on men may kindle in uncleane
affections," and to the argument that "it is not any apparell, but the
mind, that makes a man blame-worthy," he responds with several pages
on the wantonness of women's roles. However, he is careful to rule his

passion by the authorities, even to the extent of allowing some men to put on women's clothes "for the performance of necessary duties." As a good logician, he will always be governed by "the Scriptures, Fathers, or forraign writers by which I confirmed the major of mine argument." Yet the issue of women's clothes keeps returning, along with other concerns about wantonness in the theater: "What further yet, to incest?" he cries to his friend. "My speech was too mincing, when I named bawderie." While invoking Aristotle and Plutarch, he proves that plays seduce women into adultery and worse.[19] Despite his greater sophistication and allusive range, Rainolds uses the same Puritan framework of opposition between reverence for dead spiritual fathers and the variety of sins associated with vanity, sexuality, and women.

The most notorious of Puritan tracts against the stage has too often been ridiculed, not read. William Prynne's *Histrio-mastix* (1633), "that quaint, dumpy little volume of some eleven hundred pages," as Elbert Thompson has said, was only one in an extraordinary array of publications, resembling Cotton Mather's in bulk and style, that has caused his recent biographer to call him "the most prolific writer of the seventeenth century." Other historians have said worse. One speaks of his "pathological" egotism; another agrees that he was an "extremist" and "pathological"; two more refer to him as "paranoid" and dismiss *Histrio-mastix* as "trivial and fanatical vituperation."[20] Though he seems pathological to modern readers, his works were undeniably popular in their day. His biographer even terms him a moderate, at least in the 1626–1640 period, despite the fact that a few passages in *Histrio-mastix* seem indirectly to libel the queen. What stands out now, however, is not Prynne's relatively trivial attack on women actors at the time the queen happened to be performing in a masque, but "the hysterical, sex-ridden repressions" that run through the whole of his text.[21]

Prynne's lengthy title sets the conventional quasi-Manichean frame for his argument. It declares in part "That popular Stage-playes (the very Pompes of the Divell which we renounce in Baptisme, if we beleeve the Fathers) are sinful, heathenish, lewde, ungodly Spectacles." The devil, with "Pompes" and "Spectacles," opposes the holy renunciations of "the Fathers"; and the self's exhibitionistic display implicitly contrasts with obedience. As Prynne later puts it, rather nicely: "Alas what folly is it in you, to purchase with a penny damnation to your selves? Why seeke you after sinne as after a blanket? None delights in those Spectacles, but such as would bee made Spectacles" (p. 540).

Yet Prynne's title also takes the form of a stage play: *Histrio-mastix: the Players Scourge, or, Actors Tragedie*. The text is divided into six "acts" or basic reasons to be against plays, subdivided into scenes, and complete with chorus. Though he accuses "the very forme of acting Playes . . . to be nought else but grosse hypocrisie" (p. 156), with everything *"counterfeited, feined, dissembled; nothing really or sincerely acted,"* his structure displays what he condemns. Perhaps he believed that as long as the actor (Prynne) speaks with a sincere voice, there is nothing inherently wrong with the form. Nevertheless, it is striking that Rainolds chooses to structure his ideas as a debate and Prynne chooses the play form itself, seemingly with no sense of the irony involved. Like Martin Marprelate, Prynne zestfully mimics the object of his scorn, probably with no more conscious motive than to beard the lion in its den. Such imitation is one of the more conscious aspects of the theatrical side of Puritanism.

Prynne throughout his text is preoccupied by the practice of men wearing women's clothes. As he says in "Act 5 Scena Tertia," effeminacy must result, for "must not our owne experience beare witnesse of the invirillity of Play-acting? May we not daily see our Players metamorphosed into women on the Stage, not only by putting on the female robes, but likewise the effeminate gestures . . . yea, of the most petulant, unchaste, insinuating strumpets, that either Italy or the world affords?" How can Christians so "debase their noble sexe?", he continues, "thus purposely, yea, affectedly, to unman, unchristian, uncreate themselves, if I may so speake, and to make themselves, as it were, neither men nor women, but Monsters, (*a sin as bad, nay worse than any adultery, offering a kinde of violence to Gods owne worke*)."[22]

For Prynne to say that putting on women's clothes is worse than adultery shows how fearful he is of the threat to traditional images of manhood. He obsessively returns to the theme of effeminacy as the most frightening evil of stage plays and invests conventional Puritan polarities with his own special call to virility. Even in one of his dedications, "To the Christian Reader," he rails against "that effeminate mixt Dancing, Dicing, Stage-playes, lascivious Pictures, wanton Fashions, Face-painting, Health-drinking, Long haire, Love-lockes, Periwigs, womens curling, powldring and cutting of their haire, Bonefires, New-yeares-gifts, May-games, amorous Pastoralls, lascivious effeminate Musicke, excessive laughter."[23] In Prynne's world view, the evil plurality of the world's pomp and spectacles is most visibly represented by the "violence to Gods owne worke" of having men behave like women on the stage. The implied contrast makes God, and the first fathers quoted so often, stand for the traditional patriarchal manhood so threatened by contemporary behavior.

His disgust extends well beyond the stage, even to hair styles. He mentions "what a noble Earle of this Kingdome in his late dangerous sicknesse" said to forswear "his effeminate fantastique Love-Lock; that he sensibly perceived it to be but a cord of vanity, by which he had given the Divell holdfast to leade him captive at his pleasure; who would never let goe his holdfast of him as long as hee nourished this unlovely Bush." To connect vanity, women, the devil, and "this unlovely Bush" has unconscious as well as conscious implications of hostility toward women. These connotations are reinforced later, in his attack on "our overgrowne Lock-wearers, and frizle-pated men-women," when Prynne italicizes, "But how unseemely a thing is it for a man to do womanish workes? Therefore also may they bring forth children, therefore may they travell of child-birth, who crispe their haire like women." Long hair in women "is a glory to her, for her haire is given her for a covering"—for her shame. Women who act like men also incur Prynne's condemnation: "So our English Gentlewomen, (as if they all intended, to turne men outright and weare the Breeches, or to become Popish Nonnes) are now growne so farre past shame, past modesty, grace and nature, as to clip their haire like men with Lockes and foretops, and to make this Whorish cut, the very guise and fashion of the times, to the eternall infamy of their sex, their Nation, and the great scandall of religion." Unnatural mixture of sex roles, whether by men or women, is "filthy." Effeminacy, he says later, leads to "amorous beastly purposes" "which my Inke is not blacke enough to discypher."[24]

It is hard to tell whether the mixture, the sexuality, the lust, or the threat to manhood most energizes Prynne's apoplectic prose. The frequency and length of his returns to the issue of effeminate dress seem to rank that preoccupation highest. Nearly one hundred pages (pp. 167–261) are spent cataloguing the horrors of effeminacy. The theme is often interspersed in other attacks; he asserts, for instance, that actors make spectators effeminate.[25] He returns for another diatribe against women's apparel on pp. 877–890, and he regularly connects effeminacy with pomp, vanity, rich dress, and lust. While he finds some "Academicall" plays "tollerable, if not lawfull," because they eliminate "Wantonnesse, or Effeminacy," "Womans Part" and "Dalliance," "Womans apparell, or any sumptuous, or costly attire," the most acceptable plays are "very rare, and seldome Acted; and that for the most part in the Latine tongue, for utterance, and learning sake alone; not for any gaine of money, or vaine-glory."[26]

Much of this language clearly reflects Prynne's personal problem with sexuality. At the very start he tells his readers that in his early youth he had been personally acquainted with plays and players (p. 4) and recounts several tales of how friends were debauched. One can presume that he indulged in his share of "unlawful" behavior as well. *Histrio-mastix* can be interpreted as a thousand pages of guilt for youthful sexual peccadilloes, especially as his several dedications stress the dangers awaiting the innocent young. A long passage toward the middle reflects these preoccupations:

> Doe not your owne hearts experimentally informe you, that there are many sinfull swarmes *and flames of lust,* many lewde unchaste affections oft kindled in your brests *by the very acting, sight, and hearing of lascivious Stage-playes?* Doe not the wanton gestures; the amorous kisses, complements, and salutes; the meretricious songs and speeches; the lascivious whorish Actions; the beautiful faces; the ravishing Musicke, the flexanimous enticements, the witty obscenities, the rhetoricall passages, the adulterous representations, with al the other fomentations of uncleanesse in the Play-house . . . even raise a tempest of unchaste affections; yea kindle a very hell of lusts within your soules? . . . Doe not they fraught *your eyes,* your eares, your hearts *with filthy objects, so that they cannot cease from sinne?* Have they not caused you to looke upon Whores and Strumpets, upon beautiful comely women with a lustfull eye, *and so to commit, if not actuall, yet contemplative adultery with them in your hearts, either more or lesse?* If you deny all this, your own *consciences,* together with all the forerecited Fathers, . . . will presently convince you of a lie.[27]

Given that few if any women were on stage, the passage is obviously fantasy ridden. Of all the Puritan writings that have come down to us, only Michael Wigglesworth's diary is so charged with anxious sexuality. Whether feeling guilty for youthful sins or in terror of his present desires, Prynne presents in excess the language we associate with the worst aspects of Puritanism. It encourages the stereotypes of neurosis and repression.

If chastisement of lust were the only basis of his attack, we could comfortably join in modern critical dismissals of him. But Prynne's even more severe strictures against effeminacy strike an odd, contradictory note. How can a man feel guilty for being lustful and womanish at the same time? Here Prynne's personal fear of sexual impulses joins with the more general fear of threats to traditional manhood. It is not enough to label Prynne as hysterical. His anxieties are implicit in the dualistic Puritan frame, and in some respects he voices the fears more clearly than most because his own lack of self-control is so close to the surface of his prose. His symbols of sex-role confusion—the long hair, the men in women's clothes—speak implicitly of the breakdown of traditional religious and paternal authority. In his excess, Prynne says what others only hint at: the fears of mixture and disrupted male identity.

Any kind of contact with woman at all, Prynne seems to think, whether through lust or effeminacy, will emasculate a man. At the end of *Bartholomew Fair*, Ben Jonson's players convert a Prynne-like Zeal-of-the-Land Busy from the belief that plays are "an abomination; for the male, among you, putteth on the apparel of the female, and the female of the male," by lifting up the garments of the sexless puppets. "I am changed," Busy humbly responds, "and will become a beholder with you." That castration of body and argument may have been just a hostile joke to Jonson, but it would have threatened the basis of Prynne's faith. Busy's playful "change," like theatrical transformation itself, mirrors everything that Puritans were in reaction against, and what they turned to sermons to preserve.

The topos of the "woman on top" was widespread throughout Europe at this time, and fears of female dominance were sometimes associated with transvestism.[28] Yet Prynne's fears are not of the strong woman but of men weakening themselves. Shakespeare's Antony is similarly weakened by his love, and *Antony and Cleopatra* has a far more richly embroidered sense of the same polarities: Rome and Egypt, male work and female dalliance, war and love. But Shakespeare shows the good and evil on each side and finally tips his scales toward love, even knowing the worst. Puritan polarities are rigid and judgmental by comparison. Prynne's cries against "our effeminate *overgrowne Yongsters,* and blasphemous Ruffians, *who breath out nothing but oathes,* . . . our impudent, brazen-faced *Man-woman Monsters*" (pp. 514–515) go no further in investigating female aspects of manly pursuits. The image is simply repeated to the end of time as a horrifying specter of mixed identity.

Prynne differs from writers like Rainolds and Stubbes not so much in his language of sexuality, though he accentuates issues of effeminacy while the others emphasize law and industry, but more in his massive repetitiveness, and an occasional highlighting of parent-child differences. Prynne also differs in more directly confronting the threats to the Puritan frame of oppositions. Both stage plays and negative female imagery became useful short-hand notations for the evils opposing

God's work. In *Histrio-mastix,* however, the language of female contamination is associated not just with sexuality but with the overthrow
of maleness itself. Prynne expresses the consequences of mixture and
conflict more vividly than any other Puritan writer on stage matters, as
he does the necessity for unswerving obedience to the image of the first
fathers.

--------•—•--------

What strikes the modern reader about Puritan objections to the
theater is the endless belaboring of the same oppositions, not the
freshness of new voices. It is not great literature, especially when
compared to the glories of Elizabethan and Jacobean theatrical language. What has been sacrificed is the uniqueness of voice, the complex
juxtapositions of high and low, the braggadocio, the mirrors for variety
and conflict. Puritans deliberately asked less of literature than a complex mimesis, yet they wanted more as well. Why did they seek the
guidebook, the sermon, the moral exemplum? Why did they crave
literature that exercised theological reason rather than articulating the
range of human feeling? Why did they shy away from visual and aural
spectacle and ask of simple words what before could only be intimated
by ritualistic ceremony? Why were their minds so animated by a solitary man interpreting the Bible, so disturbed by men in women's
clothes? A different kind of self-expectation is at work here, expressed
through a different literature. We must look to social contexts to find
its sources.

As many historians have said, Puritanism drew its greatest strength
from those areas on the fringes of the new commerce. Small tradesmen,
especially weavers, yeomen of various sorts, a few gentry, but rarely
the large merchant, the aristocrat, or the peasant, were the new faith's
primary constituency. Anxiety and uncertainty of purpose attended
social change at this time, and recent historians have begun to speak
of these problems in their great regional complexity.[29] That Puritan
tracts often seem so rigid, so repetitive, so polarized, and such third-
rate literature, testifies to the need for fixed bearings in moving toward
a new way of being in the world. The movement from an agrarian
village economy to a national economy of trade would transform
neighbors into strangers, take fathers away from the home to work, and
generate a new ethic of ambition and self-help.[30]

Even in the reorientation from reforming church administration to
more broadly engaging the ordinary people, a change of tactics in the
1590s that transformed short-term failure into long-term success,

Puritans never lost sight of the necessity *not* to go to excess, *not* to separate, *not* to challenge earthly authority except in the name of higher authority. Most modern commentators have ascribed that habit of mind to political deftness, in an age where direct confrontation with the crown over even the most trivial issues could lead to mutilations or worse.[31] But the issue seems to have been more fraught with emotional complexity. What most appalled Puritans was indifference, the assertion of worldly rulers that there were things on earth indifferent to heaven or hell. Everyone must agree that God was directly offended by the most transient stage play, or the grossest forms of devilish conflict and toleration would follow. To the extent that rulers would not accept their place in this subordination of the visible to the invisible, they were whores along with the rest—even the queen.[32]

Puritans compromised in their behavior to preserve rather than destroy traditional modes of authority. In psychoanalytic terms, Puritanism has rightly been called a reaction formation. Yet it was also a rationalization of the new order. Their ready change of constituency from court to people in the 1590s indicates how their sense of rulers depended on a larger construct. In part the Puritans already had a glimmering of the revolutionary democratic idea that government depends on the consent of the governed. Patrick Collinson has remarked on how often the congregations led their hesitant ministers to greater purity, greater purpose, and Robert Pope has found the same phenomenon in American Puritanism.[33] But the ground for consent was clearly fixed in the Puritan mind: a fantasy of invisible male authority to which all on earth must conform or be cast out. The radical polarization of perspectives so transparent in the rhetoric of a Stubbes or a Prynne transfixed everything, the stage or the king, in the perspective not only of righteousness but of a new sense of human roles: dualistic, not just hierarchic, either justifying God or enacting the devil's will.

A structure of polarities and the fantasy of the pure father, not incipient democracy and antiauthoritarian behavior, governed Puritan ambivalences. Milton's lines denouncing the Presbyterians state the boundary that the faithful would refuse to cross:

> . . . you have thrown off your prelate Lord
> And with stiff vows renounced his liturgy
> To seize the widowed whore plurality
> From them whose sin ye invied, not abhorred
>
> . . . .
> New presbyter is but old priest writ large.[34]

The fame of that last analogy has obscured its meaning: that the democratic Presbyterian philosophy has embraced "the widowed whore plurality," with father dead, not purified. The attack on the stage reflects similar preoccupations, if not the same genius for formal expression. "Stiff vows" should remain. The rest is contamination.

Reason, logic, and order were not simply products of a Ramist education. They expressed masculinity and a masculine God. Feeling, conversely, connoted femininity, sin, excess. In this respect the two major forms of popular discourse, the sermon and the stage, were inverse models of each other. As Samuel Willard observed long afterward, speaking of God's Word, "Romances and Play-books will but stir up your carnal Lusts, but this will help to suppress them."[35] The stage encouraged self, the sermon aided subordination. The stage offered women and pleasures, the sermon spoke of male authority and duties. Where plays embodied carnal transience, associated with bodies and females, the sermon explicated permanent truths, associated with order and fathers.

That both these forms were extraordinarily, even uniquely, popular from 1590 to 1640 is no historical accident. "Gadding to sermons" vied with gadding to plays not just for Sunday sociability but for the articulation of a country's divided identity. Every Puritan writer pointed out the opposition; the choice between play or sermon signified the way one lived. Entertainment of feelings warred with discipline of the mind. That the Puritans expressed the conflict as a war indicates how threatening stage plays were to their world view, how intolerant their defense.

To bring authority into the heart, not to express mixed feelings toward authority, was the sermon's ostensible function. Even the "plain style" satisfied the Puritan dislike of mixture. William Perkins, in calling for a "plaine, perspicuous, and evident" ministry of the Word, wrote: "That kinde of preaching is to be blamed in which there is used a mixed kinde of variety of languages, before the unlearned . . . in this kinde of preaching wee doe not paint Christ, but . . . our owne selves." Elsewhere he railed against the "scraping and patching together of the unprofitable Pompe of a selfe-Sermon."[36] Instead of pomp, self, mixture, and unprofitable activity, the sermon should express the voluntary subordination of self. The minister's role was to explicate the Bible, not his own opinions, in the clear and unambiguous "doctrine-reasons-uses" form that Perkins codified. Both in form and in explication, pure authority was sustained and communicated. Where plays showed disruptive plurality, the father quietly "called" through his sermons.

Yet of course many Puritan sermons were as belligerent, as dramatic, as any other aspect of English life at this time. William Haller has pointed to the various ways that sermons portrayed the faithful as actors in a universal drama, "the grand outlines of which they all knew," and often Puritans responded more to the "dramatic violence" of tracts like *Histrio-mastix* than to the reasoned explications of the Bible.[37] What drama joined, however—the high and low plots, high and low speech, high and low audience—, the sermon tore asunder. Where clarity prevailed, and elect and reprobate were clearly demarcated in opposition to each other, combat could be righteously pursued. Drama embodied the spirit of the age. But Puritans could allow themselves dramatic experience only in forms that also encouraged strict self-control.

We should not be surprised that Elizabethan theater expresses the basic conflicts that gave rise to Puritanism better than do the writers we have been discussing. Shakespeare explores the consequences of corrupted patriarchy in *Hamlet*, and other Shakespeare heroes reflect conflicts shared by Puritans. Macbeth, Kenneth Burke notes, is the "Faustian man," without the Puritan deflection of ambition into group will and God's preservation. Christopher Hill has sketched the conflict of values in *King Lear* as Edmund's egotism and manipulation opposed to loyalty, inheritance, family. Shakespeare contrasts an ethic that calls for God to "stand up for bastards" with a society of degree, yet degree contaminated by the traditional offenses of feudal royalty.[38] And *The Tempest*, in many ways, articulates the ambivalence toward authority and the flexibility of emotion so fearful to the Puritan mind.

Prospero is a magical God, "a wond'red father." Yet he is also "distempered," capricious, arbitrary, forgetful, even weak. The world of his island, as befits a Puritan frame, is seemingly polarized into the free and the enslaved, the good and the wicked, the pure father Prospero and the whoremother Sycorax. Yet the play fuses and reconciles where Puritans would separate. It allows Caliban to express justified rage as well as unjustified incestuous desire. It presents the redeeming powers not so much of an infirm human God as of transforming natural processes—the "sea-change" that reunites father and son. Nor is the play preoccupied so much with ambition and the triumph of the faithful as with the ironies of self-discovery, questions of rightful authority, and the ways that death punctures life's pretensions. We are quietly offered the possibility that "dream" means illusion, not a new world. Shakespeare's mature acceptance of self-limitation, of compromise, and of the mixture between human evil and human good in every inhabitant of those cloud-capped towers is utterly foreign to Puritanism, though it fits well with a more traditional sense of Christian redemptiveness.[39]

Prospero's abandonment of his art, so in keeping with Puritan demands, happens for reasons Puritans could never allow themselves to understand. Unlike Antonio, a slave to ambition, he is able to give up his fixed passions, the hate and rage that imprison Sycorax and Caliban in the earth. His beloved daughter is given to Ferdinand. Where the Puritans are rigidly filial in their demands for the pure and constant father, Shakespeare allows fathers to speak for themselves, even to seek longingly for sons, without the burden of purity and magic invested in them by children who wish them to be both Gods and dead. In his first scene Prospero worries that his child isn't listening. Alonso is wracked with a father's grief. We see Prospero finally accepting death and supplicating his audience, having relinquished the props of higher authority.

Such a change from fixed powers to free yet needy spirit may have been more unconsciously threatening to Puritans than all the idlers in England, though we have nothing to tell us so beyond the constant call for an omnipotent father-God and purified earthly rule. Antony, Hamlet, Macbeth, Lear, Prospero: all five are kinglike, yet fall toward self-knowledge beyond their social roles. Shakespeare gives their feelings richly sympathetic voice. His broader espousal of traditional aristocratic values, or at least virtues, allows him to present these men at moments of personal weakness and general social conflict, and still provide insight into ambivalence and personal anxiety not accessible through Puritan literature except in abstract theological terms.

That kind of theater may have been too honest for the Puritans. It showed fathers who are weak. It exposed fantasies that are illusions. It enacted the changes that every human rigidity must undergo. It presented angers and desires that can be transformed but never wholly dismissed. For those visions of mixture, flexibility, and limitation—for such a merely *human* world—Puritans could tolerate no forgiveness.

Chapter Two

Ambivalence in an
Age of Dislocation

The language of polarity described in the previous chapter expresses one group's rigid yet conflicted responses to a society with changing values. The next two chapters digress from questions of language to discuss English backgrounds for the American Puritan emigration.

Two new interpretations emerge from familiar material. First, Puritan ambivalence may have had to do not only with repressed anger at strong patriarchs but also with the perception of fathers' weaknesses. Sons *could* advance, and fathers *did* fail in adapting to a new world of trade. Among other satisfactions, Puritanism may have offered a complex set of interrelated defenses transforming ambition, guilt, and identification into a dream of the pure father. Second, as chapter three suggests, the doubleness of Puritan language also expresses the mixed self-expectations arising from good though demanding mothering coupled with reserved or anxious fathering.

This chapter looks more closely at social changes affecting "the middle sort." After briefly locating ambivalent Puritan responses within a larger context of change, confusion, and anxiety, I describe four relationships between fathers and sons, as found in a life of John Cotton, the autobiography of Thomas Shepard, and the diaries of Ralph Josselin and Oliver Heywood. All four were English Puritan divines, though Cotton and Shepard moved to America.

The Middle Sort

New England Puritans came from a world in which large-scale changes were disrupting traditional social authority, leading eventually to the assassination of the king. A hundred years earlier, England had experienced five different official religious directions in the period between 1530 and the 1563 Convocation: Henry VIII's Catholicism, his break with the Pope, Edward VI's radical Protestantism, Mary's attempt to restore Papal Catholicism, and Elizabeth's conservative Protestant course. At one point ministers who had just been allowed to marry had to give up their wives. By the early decades of the seventeenth century far more than religion was in confusion. Urbanization, unemployment, ideological polarization, and the nomadic wanderings of many displaced splinter groups accompanied inflation and apparent overpopulation. After the queen's death, central authority was inept or intransigent, and the stability of village life was beginning to weaken. In the hundred years from 1540 to 1640, more than eighty percent of those working the land abandoned their native villages. A host of social factors led to a great profusion of anxious behavior, including alcoholism, Bible clutching, gadding to sermons, transient sects, and emigration.[1]

Radical visions of social change were beginning to force their way into the public affairs of the emerging nation-state. In the face of so many conflicts, emigration became attractive, especially for those directly persecuted by Archbishop Laud. But persecution is not enough to account for the unprecedented exodus from England. Almost two percent of all Englishmen left their country between 1620 and 1642. Nearly 60,000 crossed the Atlantic to America and the Caribbean. By various estimates, at least 18,000 English settlers were in New England by 1643, 14,000 in Massachusetts alone. More than ninety ministers came over in the 1630s. As Carl Bridenbaugh notes, this was an extraordinary effort for "a stay-at-home folk, enamored of the smoke of their own chimneys."[2]

Puritans, despite the economic and social ties that distinguished them from the down and out, proved more willing than most to transplant themselves to distant shores. They stood in loyal opposition to established authority. Some were yeomen; more were just struggling to rise from yeoman status to more individuated artisan occupations or to become tradesmen. Others were gentry on fixed incomes whose worth was declining because of inflation and whose political loyalties were torn between their villages and their centralizing king. Puritanism's stronghold was in southeastern England, where long traditions of heresy had been fueled in the 1620s by sudden, inexplicable depressions, especially in the weaving industry. Unemployed weavers rioted in 1629. Although Puritanism may not have been closely linked to urban centers in Elizabeth's reign, it was clearly connected to the clothing occupations as well as to dissent. As Richard Baxter defined his side retrospectively, "On the side of Parliament were the smaller part (as some thought) of the gentry in most of the countries and the greatest part of the Tradesmen and Freeholders, and the Middle sort of men; especially in those corporations and countries which depend on Cloathing and such Manufactures."[3]

Recent studies have confirmed the idea that Puritanism was concentrated in market towns.[4] Unemployment mixed with sudden success; ambition rubbed shoulders with failure. Though most of the rural population was excluded from employment in the clothing industry by a 1563 statute that restricted apprenticeship to the sons of forty-shilling freeholders, it was still the largest industry in England, often subject to instability and crisis, and its competitive practices were the cutting edge of a new ethic at variance with the established order of hierarchy, monopoly, and degree.[5] There was not much doubt about Puritanism's broad appeal. England's most published author from 1548 to 1650 was Calvin.[6]

Few aristocrats or indigents were attracted to this ethic of hard work and hard believing. It drew its constituency from what Baxter and others called "the middle sort." The emigration to Massachusetts was remarkably homogeneous throughout the decade of the 1630s: all of English stock, with four counties predominating; the first settlers from country villages, with a shift toward incorporated boroughs after 1634 but a pronounced small-village emphasis throughout; a preponderance of families, usually nuclear, with a fairly equal balance of men and women. Puritanism had a special appeal for those believing in a just, contractual God who would reward hard work and frugality with prosperity and punish sloth with failure. "It was too cold and intellectually complicated for the lower classes," M. M. Knappen has aptly summarized, "and a creed which might set a lord on the penitent stool before an entire congregation was no religion for a gentleman."[7] Arbitrary popes, kings, or bishops would no longer do, and faith in intangible economic "invisible hands" had not yet been invented. To keep confidence in themselves, while not giving way to rebellion, in a country rewarding their work with low status, religious persecution, and unemployment, Puritans looked to a God not only just but absolutely powerful, who was radically disjunct from this world, and who might provide special providences for his special people.

Uprooted from agrarian life, Puritan weavers and artisans had not yet found new institutions to give them stability and identity, new language to voice their problems. What they may have had in common, as David Hall suggests, "was their perception that the gentry as a class looked down upon them."[8] Resentment certainly helped bring on the first Puritan protests against ostentatious vestments, pomp, and ritual in the Anglican service. Puritans looked to themselves yet distrusted themselves; to their families and village values, yet only to a visible village of saints; and most unequivocally to their Bible and ministers, for a sense of purpose, meaning, and direction. Many who emigrated to America continued to list themselves as weavers, in quiet pride at their English status, though they had long since abandoned that trade for farming in the service of their God.[9]

Choosing to remold themselves and their religion at the same time, Puritans found in theology a way to vent their opposition while augmenting their status. They wanted to purify the conspicuous deference of Anglican ritual—no aristocratic display for them—but they also wanted power, not poverty. Unlike the Separatists, Puritans aimed at reform and rule. Their official title was "Non-Separating Congregationalism," and their congregations included adherents of high rank as well as laborers. Robert Cleaver's A Godlye Form of Household Government, written with John Dod (1621), seems to be addressed to the well to do: it counsels those who can "live by their lands" not to be idle and especially urges women not to "sit downe and cap a stoole" but always to be supervising the servants in working or learning. The dedicatory epistle, as with several other Puritan tracts, is addressed to aristocratic patrons, and the sins constantly rebuked are idleness and spending.[10] Yet nearly every family except the poorest had servants, and most Puritan tracts are deliberately pitched to the ordinary needs of an ordinary congregation.

In fact one of the most distinctive Puritan features is an emphasis on the communal fellowship of visible saints. Where Anglicans tended to emphasize both hierarchic order and human reason, Puritans unequivocally stressed man's depravity and God's sovereignty. Yet Anglicans tended toward a passive, deferential reverence, even in claiming a unity of church and state, whereas Puritans constantly worked for local organization and local participation as the center of religious practice. Pessimistic about the self, they were extraordinarily optimistic about the group. One Puritan defender, William Bradshaw, took the idea of group authority to a playful extreme. His English Puritanisme (1605) offers a congregationalist disavowal of the zeal—more Protestant than Puritan—for destroying stained glass windows and ceremonial "trinkets" left over from Catholic ritual. Bradshaw encourages the aristocrats to have in their churches all the ornaments and trappings they desire.

They can have silver fonts and ivory communion tables; their beautiful cups "may be of beaten gould sett about with Diamonds," their ministers may be "clothed in silke & velvet"—as long as each congregation "will maintaine them in that manner" without taxing anybody else.[11] His call for no ostentation without representation does not seem to have taken hold. But the tongue-in-cheek impossibility reveals the widening gulf dividing state religion from local communities of visible saints who demanded that their ministers preach to them of God, not play master of ceremonies for the sacraments.

Puritans were the most aggressive, self-confident, and self-demanding of all this "mechanic class"—as well as the most self-doubting and insecure, a contradiction that theology transformed into strength. They were capable of holy violence, yet had a genius for compromise. As with their mixture of personal anxiety and concerted activism, hotheads and compromisers were not simply two clear divisions within the faith, but faces of each Puritan as well. All over Europe, the small property owners and provincial folk who gravitated to Calvinism felt at sea in strange social disruptions. Yet Calvinism also appealed to the pride of calling in brash young artisans whose nontraditional crafts had high status and security in their communities.[12] English Puritanism shows a similar mixture of appeals, though with a decided push toward transforming dissatisfaction and anxiety into local participatory structures. If a preacher could not find a parish, or was denied one, a group of sympathetic parishioners might give him a "lectureship," licensed by the Church but paid for by the laity, who demanded understanding more than wit, education more than ritualistic submission. If preachers were trained badly, Puritans would organize their own covert training schools.[13] But their opposition always claimed to stay within the law, while professing obedience to a higher law. The doctrine of the elect allowed loyal opposition to convey superior status.

Resentment is not quite the word to describe this institutionalized ambivalence toward social authority. Puritans vied with other sects not to overthrow but to preserve a more pure authority. To "purify" is in one sense a euphemism for hostility. But it is also a cry for better authority, for fathers and ministers with uncompromising fidelity to the greater father's Word, at a time when state religious policy was conspicuously compromised and vacillating. A Jacobean clergyman described the sermon hunger of the age in phrases that indicate the need for visible traditions of authority: "The frequency of sermons seems most necessary in cities and great towns, that their inhabitants, who . . . see for the most part but the works of men, may daily hear

God speaking unto them: whereas such as are conversant in the fields and woods continually contemplate the works of God."[14] Personal disruption often underlay the ambivalent cry for purified fatherhood, and feelings of loss, disorder, and confusion complicated simple resentment.

Even those sympathetic to the cause sometimes wondered whether Puritans were activated by "a contentious spirit under the name of conscience," as Bullinger warned from the continent in the mid-1560s, or by the spirit of pure authority.[15] Here as with most aspects of their faith, Puritans were in the middle. Where aristocrats could nakedly flaunt personal ambition, or the poor could seize theologies that legitimated rebellion with little personal cost, the Puritans avoided direct social expressions of ambition, anger, and separation. Instead, personal ambition became group ambition for the reform of established authority.[16] The source of reward moved upward from the court to God. Though in many respects Puritans accepted in more restrained form the patriarchal Anglican vision of rank and earthly degree, their emphasis on family mutuality and voluntary subordination had the effect of intensifying access to the father, at home as well as in religious fantasy. The major Puritan institutions of church and family encouraged men to model social authority on the father's role. To have direct access to the father's word became the Puritan restatement of the highest earthly ambition. Anyone, no matter how ordinary, could apply himself to that task.

Securing the father's authority, both local and cosmic, was central to the Puritan mission. Many have commented on how family based the Puritan faith was, and how that emphasis differentiated Puritans from other emigrant groups. Far from being the harbinger of individualism that we can see in retrospect, this faith struggled to transform personal ambition into group loyalty, with the family as a "little commonwealth" under the father's rule. William Perkins decried "the impietie of the Roman religion" because "it puts downe the authority of the father: for it ratifieth clandestine contracts" by allowing children to marry without parental consent.[17] Preachers often spoke directly to the head of the household, even gave the husband semiministerial authority to educate the family in religious matters. However, Puritan writers took care to say that obedience to the father, like faith in God, must be voluntary, not coerced. In that sense individual decisions, freely made, were to lead to patriarchal order. That dilemma is at the heart of the Puritan compromise between ambition and the purified father.

One should not be surprised to find a great deal of antiauthoritarian behavior barely held in check by the Puritan language of faith. In "an age that regarded religious dissent as the other face of sedition," as Roger B. Manning has said, Puritanism attracted its share of pugnacious activists.[18] Many early Puritans came to social consciousness during the Marian burnings, or during the various oppressions of bishops and archbishops. The Martin Marprelate tracts of 1588–89, though disavowed by the sober-minded Puritan mainstream, attracted great popularity because of their violent personal attacks on the Anglican establishment. Even some of the most established Puritans were remarkably free about criticizing their queen, as early as the 1570s. Edward Dering, preaching directly to Queen Elizabeth in February of 1570, caustically condemned her indifference to the "whoredoms" of the priesthood: "And yet you in the meanwhile that all these whoredoms are committed, you at whose hands God will require it, you sit still and are careless, let men do as they list. It toucheth not belike your commonwealth, and therefore you are so well contented to let all alone. The Lord increase the gifts of His Holy Spirit in you." For that he was silenced, though the sermon was soon printed and had eight printings in the next ten years.[19]

Such talk set the battle lines squarely. Concern for the kingdom of righteousness must govern political concern for the commonwealth. Puritans were clear about who had to obey whom. John Field's public prayer for the queen asserted, "Teach her to be humble under thy hand, to kiss the rod, and to profit under thy corrections, which tho hast or shall hereafter in mercy lay upon her. Teach her to hearken unto thy word, and to be ruled by it, as by the only rule and square, both of her life and government." In 1576 Peter Wentworth's parliamentary speech directly attacked the queen's "great fault" in opposing the people's freedom of speech, in words so strong that he was stopped before he could finish and sent to the Tower by judgment of the Speaker. Other Puritans expressed an antiauthoritarian strain through actions as well as words, even through assassination attempts on the nobility. No wonder the queen's final speech to Parliament in 1585, with her genius for balance, equally condemns Romanists and "newfangledness": "And of the latter, I must pronounce them dangerous to a kingly rule: to have every man, according to his own censure, to make a doom of the validity and privity of his prince's government, with a common veil and cover of God's word, whose followers must not be judged but by a private man's exposition."[20]

It is not enough to explain the antiauthoritarian strain in Puritanism as the work of an intransigent faction. The point is that each side felt

the other was antiauthoritarian. Each invoked what it considered
ultimate authority, earthly or heavenly, to condemn the other. The war
was between a fantasy of pure authority and the realities of civil
compromise, not just between civil order and what the queen called
"a private man's exposition." In a remarkable dialogue between Bishop
Grindal and some Puritan prisoners in June of 1567, for instance,
Grindal claims the right of kings to do "things which God neither
commandeth nor forbideth, and they are of the middle sort, and are
things indifferent. And such things princes have authority to order, or
to command." There is the classic argument of the Elizabethan *via
media.* To which his jailed debaters rejoin:

> PRISONERS: — Prove that, said one. Where find you that? said another.
> BISHOP GRINDAL: — I have talked with many men, and yet I never saw
> any behave themselves so unreverently before magistrates.
>
> . . . .
>
> JOHN SMITH: — How can you prove that indifferent, which is abom-
> inable?
>
> . . . .
>
> BISHOP GRINDAL: — See how you be against indifferent things, which
> may be borne withal for order and obedience sake.[21]

The spirit of "Prove that!" confronts the spirit of "Bear that for order
and obedience sake," and even the fact of being in jail does not mit-
igate the "unreverent" appeal of these men to higher authority. The
final irony here is that when Grindal became archbishop in the next
decade, his Puritan sympathies led him to write an unprecedented
letter to the queen refusing to carry out an order and asserting God's
primacy over her rule. For that he was ignored until his death five
years later.[22]

"To authorise an untruth, by a Toleration of State," Nathaniel Ward
would later write from America, "is to build a Sconce against the walls
of Heaven, to batter God out of his Chaire." Puritan confidence in
God's absolute rule often led them to chide the great. "Great Polititians
are like children," declared Thomas Shepard, "always standing on
their heads and shaking their heels against Heaven; these think
Religion to be but a piece of policy, to keep people in awe."[23] These
familiar materials show the importance of a fantasy of pure authority
among the motives that impelled Puritan behavior and suggest that the
more intransigent Puritans may have been directly expressing what
moderates like Richard Sibbes held back for (genuine) "order and
obedience sake."

It was uncontaminated authority, not personal freedom, that every Puritan wanted. Their anger at the state was justified, not only by Elizabeth's spirit of pragmatic balance but also by the disastrous condition of the mostly nonpreaching clergy. As Sir Thomas Wilson said, the wings of the clergy are "well clipped of late by courtiers and noblemen, and some quite cut away, both feather, flesh and bone."[24] Yet ambivalence about established authority rarely led to either aggression or subservience. The lawyer John Stubbs was characteristically Puritan, if a bit extreme, in his expression of loyal opposition: as his hand was being severed for behavior contrary to state interests, he waved his hat with the other hand and shouted a heartfelt "God Save Queen Elizabeth!" He meant it, too, in both senses.

In short, Puritans transformed ambition as well as ambivalence in several ways: into a sense of group mission, into a desire to purify established structures of authority, and into a personal sense of calling that gave everyone a stable place in the working world and equality before God. In some respects there definitely were "marked antihierarchical and anti-clerical tendencies," as Patrick Collinson notes. From the beginning, the people led their leaders in demanding purity, not compromise.[25] It is true, as John Winthrop would later claim in his diary, that "the elders had great power in the people's hearts . . . and indeed the people themselves, generally, through the churches, were of that understanding and moderation, as they would be easily guided in their way by any rule from scripture or sound reason." But the rest of his entry talks of mutinies, abuse of liberty, and "dangerous and groundless jealousies of the magistrates." What those in authority, both Anglican and Puritan, interpreted as sedition, lay Puritans might have interpreted as scriptural expectation. "And what is pride," Samuel Willard concluded in 1692, "but an overweening opinion of ones self, which makes him think himself too good for his duty. . . . And this is resembled by the pride of an upstart Minister, who thinks himself too good for his People, and so neglects his care of them."[26] The key to all the contradictory charges and countercharges is the heightened demand on authority in the real world to match the responsive authority of absolutist fantasy. From England to New England, the fantasy of pure authority held by lay Puritans tended to remain absolute, even while their ministers were so often urging accommodation.

Contradictions shaped much of Puritanism. There was an antinomian or Quaker strain, and an antiauthoritarian impulse, constantly seeking expression as claims for direct access to the Father and as demands for unpolluted authority.[27] Most Puritans were more comfortable with doubt than with assurance, however, and many clung with equal fervor to the rules set forth by the Bible and to mechanical forms of intellectual thought as ways of limiting emotional excess. What seems to us like contradictory demands for external law or unmediated grace were two sides of the same quest for absolute authority.

To understand some of the psychological sources for Puritanism, we must venture into what little we know of filial relations at this time. In many ways the New England experiment, like so much subsequent American history, was an attempt to impose shared fantasy on social realities. In this case, the need was to secure the father's authority at various levels within a larger frame of group purity and submission. But the contradictions followed hard upon, indeed were the essence of the Puritan dream, as the first generation of emigrants quickly discovered.

Fathers and Sons

> ALBANY: How have you known the
> miseries of your father?
> EDGAR: By nursing them, my lord.
> *King Lear,* V,iii
>
> My dear father hath been battered
> with anxious thoughts in this per-
> plexing state now this 13 yeares.
> Oliver Heywood, *Diaries*[28]

Henry VIII broke with the Catholic faith because he wanted a son. He placed his royal dream of earthly patrilinear authority over the continuity of God's heavenly kingdom. Just over a century later, England's king was killed. Between a father's wish to continue his line and the fact of social parricide, Puritanism took form.

Most discussion of father-son relations in England at this time has focused on the aristocracy, and on the problem of younger sons. Several historians have suggested a connection between social alienation and younger sons, between the rise of mercantile innovation and the exclusion of those sons from inheriting their fathers' estates, or between younger sons and the "aspiring mind" of Elizabethan England.[29] Hugh Latimer also noted, as early as 1549, that the aristocrats were not anxious to see their sons, oldest or younger, become ministers: "There be none now but great men's sons in colleges, and their fathers look not to have them preachers."[30] These fragments and suggestions do not lead very far into the inward turmoil of the middle sort, except to indicate aristocratic disdain for ministers whom Puritans wanted to revere. By implication, however, the problem of younger sons, even among the aristocracy, highlights the larger problem of advancement and preferment. Access to the center of power was extraordinarily restricted at that time. The social fact of exclusion may have encouraged imagining alternative routes to authority.

Yet that tells us nothing of why Puritans would shape a theology of voluntary obedience to absolute heavenly patriarchy. Moreover, the dream of the pure father, like Anglican political theories of patriarchy, may well have been more the father's dream than the son's.[31] Henry dreamed of a son to confer vicarious immortality upon himself—yet Mary and Elizabeth carried on the kingdom. Elizabethan theater is alive with ambition and revenge, and yet also with Lear and Prospero, querulously unsure of the loyalty of their children, helplessly dependent at the end, and very, very mortal. Paternal, aristocratic empathies, at least when articulated by a yeoman's son from Stratford, indirectly express shared feelings about the father's authority. But we must look more straightforwardly at the relations of particular fathers to particular sons before these hints of paternal weakness and paternal dreams can be partly corroborated.

Of the major Puritan figures who emigrated to America, only John Cotton and Thomas Shepard have left any record of their early family life. The little we know about Cotton's upbringing suggests paternal weakness. In an elegiac reminiscence on Cotton's death, *Abel Being Dead yet speaketh* (1658), John Norton recalls, "This Providence is here remarkable concerning him, That whereas his Father, (whose Calling was towards the Law) had not many Clients that made use of his Advice in Law-matters before, it pleased God after his Son's going to *Cambridge* to bless him with great Practice, so that he was very able to keep him there, and to allow him liberal maintenance: Insomuch that this blessed man hath been heard to say, *God kept me in the University.*" Even in flush times, Cotton subsisted on fellowships for much of his time there.[32] When we recall that Cotton entered college at thirteen, we can surmise that Roland Cotton may have seemed ineffectual to him as a child, at least in the world of work. Though the passage is obviously skimpy, it also indicates that when success came to the lawyer, his son thanked God rather than his father.

We know nothing else of John's childhood, so these remarks are at best speculative. We do know, however, that Cotton was the great compromiser, never allowing anger to show and always looking beyond himself for authority. "He was a Person of great Modesty and Good Nature," noted Daniel Neal in his early *History of New-England,* "and tho' he was often affronted by angry Men, he never expressed any Resentments." In fact, several stories testify to his penchant for agreeing with men who accosted him with snide remarks. Larzer Ziff's intellectual biography cites several instances where more politically astute members of his congregation at old Boston took the place of their studious minister in potentially dangerous negotiations. In his letter to the bishop of Lincoln in 1633, Cotton seems to accept the bishop's major criticism of him, "that wherein I have most seemed to your Lordship to fail, to wit, in not discerning Christian liberty to practise some commands of authority in some circumstances."[33] Always the mediator and intellectual, Cotton encouraged precise distinctions but never extremes. His theory of grace proved dangerous in the antinomian controversy, and to his confusion abetted extremists, precisely because of his advocacy that no man has authority, not even the literal words of the Bible or the best works of the faithful, unless the spirit of God moves in him. Human authority is utterly weak; God's is utterly strong.

Whether Cotton was more uneasy with his own anger or with the wrath of his superiors is not clear. But his God is a remarkable transformation of his father's occupation, and perhaps of his weaknesses. Cotton made of his God a greater and more constant lawyer. After the failure of his preaching in the antinomian affair, he became ever more strict in the legalistic interpretation of the Bible, which had been congenial to him from the start. One of his major tasks after arriving in the new world was to write a code of laws derived from God's Word. Though the code proved socially unworkable, the effort indicates his extraordinarily disciplined submission to a law beyond this world. His ecstatic, almost masochistic yielding to the personal God embodied in that law provoked Roger Williams to their famous "Bloudy Tenent" interchange.[34] As Cotton always made sure there were "many Clients" for his advice and preaching, so he may have found in the Puritan God a stronger father, whom he could obey and love, submitting his conflicted feelings to the pure authority of God's Word.

Inferring childhood conflicts from adult personality, despite Freud's practice, can be like trying to score a touchdown without the ball. The only intimate descriptions we have of Puritan childhoods come from adult memories. But at least Thomas Shepard's autobiography gives his childhood in some detail. As Shepard notes, his father was deeply religious. The Northamptonshire grocer even moved to another town just to be under "a stirring ministry." "My father was a wise, prudent man, the peacemaker of the place," Shepard recalls. The man also had a quiet sense of humor. Since his son had been born on November 5, 1605, "that very hour of the day wherein the Parliament should have been blown up by Popish priests," the father named his boy Thomas, "because, he said, I would hardly *believe* that ever any such wickedness should be attempted by men against so religious and good [a] Parliament."[35]

When Shepard describes his mother, we begin to understand why he remembers his father as "the peacemaker of the place":

> I do well remember my father, and have some little remembrance of my mother. . . . My mother was a woman much afflicted in conscience, sometimes even unto distraction of mind; yet was sweetly recovered again before she died. I being the youngest, she did bear exceeding great love to me, and made many prayers for me; but she died when I was about four years old, and my father lived, and married a second wife, now dwelling in the same town, of whom he begat two children, Samuel and Elizabeth, and died when I was about ten years of age.

Young Thomas began life as the youngest child of a peaceful father and a "distracted" woman who loved her baby passionately and then died. She was replaced by another woman who, in Shepard's account, "did let me see the difference between my own mother and a stepmother. She did seem not to love me, but incensed my father often against me; it may be that it was justly also, for my childishness." Shepard's mild self-judgment could also mean that the situation was worse than he presents it.

In fact, another event did disturb his taut relationship with his first mother: the plague, which came down upon the village when he was three. "I being the youngest, and best beloved of my mother, was sent away the day the plague broke out." He never saw his mother again. Even his grandparents, with whom he lived until the plague abated, neglected him. After his father died, the situation grew more difficult. The wicked stepmother—it seems almost too much like a fairy tale— continued to bring him up, mainly for his inherited portion of one hundred pounds. Finally his eldest brother made a deal with her to get young Thomas out of her hands. "And so I lived with this my eldest brother, who showed much love unto me, and unto whom I owe much; for him God made to be both father and mother to me."

This is the preacher who was so implacably serene that Jonathan Edwards took him for a model. If any Puritan was among the elect, contemporaries agreed, it was Shepard, and of all the New England divines before Edwards, Shepard had the most closely reasoned and unambiguous doctrinal emphasis. Yet his childhood shows great disruption and emotional disarray. As Michael McGiffert observes, Puritanism served him as a refuge from emotional disorder and supplied him with a consistent father-God to pacify his feelings about the kind father who had betrayed him, by marrying again, by being so "incensed" with the boy, and by dying when Thomas was ten.[36] His unconscious ambivalences were intensified by what we can conjecture must have been feelings of loving, hating, even being overwhelmed by mothers who would love, hate, and seemingly desert in return. Shepard's background gave powerful impetus to his dream of a strong and peaceful religious father, and his memory of a loving brother who was "both father and mother to me" is strikingly like his later portrait of God himself: "He is the God who took me up when my own mother died, who loved me, and when my stepmother cared not for me, and when lastly my father also died and forsook me, when I was young and little and could take no care for myself."[37]

Shepard's imagery expressing God is often transparently a call for the sheltering father. As he writes in his 1642 journal, "our strength to hold Christ is like the child's holding of the father, soon weak and falls." A month later he notes, "I saw also how legal righteousness makes us servants and how faith makes us sons." His greatest fear is of separation from God, a feeling that he often associates with despair and sin, while he expresses feelings of union in ecstatic language: he felt himself "covered with God as with a cloud"; he would "roll upon Christ" and "lie by him and lie at him" for hours. He even thought his journey to America was a kind of resurrection, Lazarus-like, being allowed by God to "live among God's people as one come out from the dead, to his praise."[38] This is a classic Family Romance fantasy: ambivalence and separation anxiety leading to a dream of rebirth in the family of God, a loving, stable father. And so he was converted, after a period when, as Shepard says with his usual forthrightness, he was dead drunk at Cambridge.

It would be too simple to say that theology was his way of defending against childhood trauma. Rather, Puritanism reinforced his fragile bond with his calm, distant father, without that father's unaccountable penchant for anger, death, and distracted wives. God the father was Shepard's father purified of changeable responses to his son, just as Shepard wished himself purified of the distracted depressions with which his journal abounds. Having achieved unambiguous identification with the purified father's voice, at least in public, Shepard could speak for God with calm disengagement from man and his puny motives. He was the most Calvinist of first-generation Puritans, and sometimes the most "soul-ravishing" too. Winthrop's journal speaks of a man who killed himself after "being wounded in conscience at a sermon of Mr. Shepard's." Where most others, especially Cotton, allowed and expressed more conflicted feelings about patriarchy, Shepard was always clear. As he said in the midst of the antinomian controversy, "We must not bring rules to men, but men to rules."[39]

Shepard's basic theme is that "the Lord was strong in my weakness." McGiffert speaks of Shepard's two selves, the sufferer and the observer, the Dimmesdale and the Chillingworth, one in anguish, the other almost godlike in its masterful tone.[40] In one instance he can speak of "my widow-like separation and disunion from my Husband and my God," or his "wound, which was but skinned over before, of secret atheism and unbelief." Yet he can also say, "I have seen God himself and have been ravished to behold him," or "I also began to see, nay, feel, God in fire, meat, every providence, and that his many providences and creatures are but God's hands and fingers whereby he takes hold of me."[41]

Toward the end of his life, when his beloved second wife died in childbirth, his faith seemed almost to shatter once more, in ways that recall his mixture of feelings when his mother died. "This affliction was very heavy to me, for in it the Lord seemed to withdraw his tender care for me and mine which he graciously manifested by my dear wife; also refused to hear prayer when I did think he would have harkened." His repetition of "also" continues, mutely accusing a suddenly changeable father: God took her away in her prime "when she might have lived to have glorified the Lord long"; God threatened others of his family with death. "But I am the Lord's, and he may do with me what he will," Shepard declares. Yet again he returns to his grief, unable to withhold blame: "He did teach me to prize a little grace gained by a cross as a sufficient recompense for all outward losses. But this loss was very great." Another list recalls many specific memories of her goodness, reiterating the greatness of his loss and the implicit littleness of God's response. He ambiguously concludes: "Thus

God hath visited and scourged me for my sins and sought to wean me from this world, but I have ever found it a difficult thing to profit even but a little by the sorest and sharpest afflictions."[42]

These pages are very moving, not least in the way his unstoppable suffering exposes the fragility of his faith. His love for his wife clearly tends to outstrip his love for God: "When her fever first began (by taking some cold) she told me so, that we should love exceedingly together because we should not live long together." The intensity of his bond evokes his first love, his passionate, distracted mother, who also loved him exceedingly and did not "live long together" with her child. One senses in Shepard's mature grief the needs for mothering, bonding, shelter, that lay underneath his identification with a calm father-God, and that may have broken through here as well as in his double self.

But for public display, Shepard's tone was entirely masterful, paternally sure rather than maternally passionate. The dream of the pure father gave structure to these nearly unmanageable feelings. Like Benjamin Franklin's memoirs, his autobiography takes a fatherly voice from the start, since it is cast as a direct appeal to his son and namesake. His purpose in writing, he says, is to tell his son "of God's great kindness to him," and he opens with an account to "you" of the melodramatic events of young Thomas's birth. In an unconscious echo of his own infancy, Shepard evokes a situation where the mother is on the verge of death and only the father can protect the child. An earlier son named Thomas had died, and now the Shepards were hiding from persecution when one day his pregnant first wife fell down stairs with "you" inside. Twice Shepard emphasizes, in identical words, "Oh, remember, my son, to know and love this God that here did pity and spare thee in thy mother's womb a second time!"

His son was safely born on April 5, 1635, and after an eleven-week sail to New England, during which God several times saved the Shepards from crises, young Thomas was baptized at last early in 1536, to Shepard's great relief. Indeed, his relief at the baptism seems oddly greater than his grief at the mother's death, which followed hard upon. Her death becomes a means of instructing his son in the virtues of gratitude and faithfulness: "if tho shalt turn rebel against God and forsake God," then "all thy mother's prayers, tears, and death to be a swift witness against thee at the great day." As if to make sure his son gets the message, Shepard reiterates the drama of his son's delivery later in the autobiography, with more detail. Again his worry about getting the child baptized seems more important than his concern for his wife, and again the greater father's protection is what sustains and saves. To have "the child under God's precious ordinances," on land at last, contents him, though this wife died of consumption.[43]

The father saves; the mother exposes the child to conflict, danger, fear. That at least is the conscious message Shepard seeks to give his son. By telling the story twice, Shepard reinforces his expectation of filial gratitude to God and warns of the guilt associated with rebellion or indifference. More unconsciously, Shepard's need to repeat the anxious situation evokes many more ambivalent emotions, repeating as it does his early childhood trauma, though now with a conspicuous lack of attachment to the woman who died.

What I wish to call attention to again is the fear of paternal weakness. Shepard's faith is a slender reed in these winds of familial passion. Moreover, the form of his autobiography conveys a father's faith to a son who may or may not believe. Shepard's dream of the pure father is the fantasy of a man who has tried to deny his complex filial feelings for a simpler identification with the father's voice. The anxiety breaks through, though, in his need to repeat, in his need for the son's gratitude, and in a structure of crisis after crisis resolved only by God's deliverance.[44]

Taken by itself, Shepard's autobiography yields psychological insights no more certain than the speculations about John Cotton's childhood, though the text is more rich in its connections. My theories leap from assumption to inference: the assumption that one's early feelings about parents have a great deal to do with one's adult beliefs, and the inference that Shepard felt various ambivalences about both his father and his mother that indirectly surface in his prose. In particular, both Cotton and Shepard, for very different reasons, felt the need to magnify a somewhat weak father-image into a cosmic constancy. The hypothesis cannot be proven, at least with the materials we have. But it can be partly corroborated by paying close attention to literary form and imagery, and by examining at least two other private records, the only Puritan diaries that extensively describe fatherhood: those of Ralph Josselin and Oliver Heywood, both English Puritan clergymen. With Josselin, we discover even more unmistakably that within the conventional preaching of patriarchy lived a man who loved his children so much that his anxious discipline could rarely stand firm.

Josselin, born in 1617, was the child of a wealthy yeoman who gradually lost an £800 inheritance by bad farming and died intestate when his son was nineteen. His mother had died in 1624, when the boy was seven. Even as a child Ralph had emulated ministers, and his decision to "bee a scholler" was helped along by his sense that the estate might well go to a stepmother if his father remarried. Since his father did remarry, when Josselin was fourteen or fifteen, his resolve to be a minister was set: "Therefore I desird to bee a scholler; so should I make the better shift if from home, & bee able to live of my selfe by Gods blessing."[45]

Here are familiar contours: a change of mothers, a failed or ineffectual father, and an early dedication to the faith. Josselin recalls his stepmother in words quite like Shepard's: "Though my father loved me exceedingly and my mother in law, though I hope an honest woman, yett was of a somewhat sowre spirit, yett I remember not that I ever caused any debate or division betwixt them for any thing, though I was sensible of her disrespect in somethings toward mee." The three "thoughs" and two "yets" tell the story of restrained anger and hurt.[46]

Young Josselin married in 1640, when he was twenty-three, and his bride of nineteen began producing children—ten in all, five of whom died. As Alan Macfarlane points out, Josselin seems not to have lived up to the patriarchal ideal for Puritan and Elizabethan families. Where the conventional picture of family life demands the children's deference, Josselin's children made their own marriage choices, sometimes without parental approval. Josselin also showed an interest in his daughters, especially after their marriages, at least equal to his interest in his sons. In one instance a daughter rejected a man of whom her parents had approved, simply because he was "not loving."

Josselin's eldest son was delicate and sickly, dying at twenty-nine. At his death Josselin writes of "my eldest sonne Thomas and my most deare child. . . . He was my hope, but some yeares I have feared his life." Yet the saga of his stormy relations with the next oldest son, John, who was seven years younger, shows how Josselin was incapable of withdrawing love from a child who seemed the opposite of "my hope" in every respect.

As Josselin's editor says, John's life seems to have been "a violent attempt to attract to himself the love and concern that were likely to have been centred on his ailing elder brother." "High and proud," Josselin called him. He misbehaved, swore, even robbed the family till. Yet one wonders whether it was love that John failed to get, or the loving discipline that Puritans so often prescribed. Still living at home in his twenties, the son seems to have done everything he could to precipitate being disowned. The father threatened it; John conformed for a month, then relapsed. Finally father Josselin laid down the law and wrote in his diary: "John declared for his disobedience no son; I should allow him nothing except he tooke himself to bee a servant; yet if he would depart and live in service orderly I would allow him £10 yearly; if he so walkt as to become God's son, I would yett own him for mine."

Amazingly, the stern pronouncement was never carried out. John remained at home for another five years. Moreover, at the age of thirty John suddenly married, not only without his parents' consent but even without their knowledge. As Josselin records, "John married unknown to me; God pardon his errors." Yet still he lived on at home! Five months later the son finally left his parents to set up his own life. Despite all these strains, when Josselin died the bulk of his estate went to John, who was a "gent" by 1691, and when John died he asked for his body to be buried "as neer my brother Thomas as can be."

There are deep waters here, and our splashes of conjecture simply confirm their depths. John's motives, even his behavior, remain mute to us. It is clear, however, that as a father Josselin continually placed love above discipline, protectiveness above censure, despite all the Puritan strictures to join those modes of parental authority. We have no way of knowing whether his fatherly behavior was the essence of Christian charity or human gutlessness. But whatever he was, he does not seem to have been aloof. The death of one of his children causes him to record in his diary, "Oh, when I returne home, Oh my childe that met me, hugged me, is dead." As Alan Macfarlane concludes, "If Josselin is typical, Puritan fathers were less austere and less able to exert control of their children than some historians would have us believe."[47]

When we couple Josselin's behavior to his children with the failure of Josselin's farmer father, the possibility of paternal weakness as one of the sources of Puritanism becomes more plausible. Faith supplied the father, and the self-image, that life did not. Josselin, as Macfarlane remarks, was "a confused and anxious man, his imagination troubled in all aspects of his life." The diary records constant guilt, constant self-abasement before God the stern father. One entry, for February 23, 1648, notes in grief that God took away his son because Josselin played chess too much and was therefore away from God. Macfarlane thinks that in some respects Josselin's frequent expressions of spiritual pain were cohesive, not disruptive; he was happy in his unhappiness. But the incongruity between his own need for a punishing father and his inability to punish his children suggests that his dream of a pure, powerful father was only a dream. "In all shakings God is the same," Josselin wrote in 1659. The shakings of his life began with the decline in his father's wealth, and every child seems to have jarred the patri-archal image further.[48]

Several American Puritans, notably Cotton Mather and Samuel Sewall, have left diaries recording similar paternal feelings for their children. In one measles epidemic in 1713 Mather's wife and three of his children died within less than two weeks. First his "consort," "my dear, dear, dear Friend expired"; then "my little *Jerusha*," "little *Eleazar*," and last "little *Martha*." He was especially grief-striken over "my lovely *Jerusha*," less than three years old. "Lord, I am oppressed; undertake for me!" he cries. His feelings belie some recent hypotheses that Puritans tended to be distant from their children because of high infant mortality rates. As Mather records in his *Magnalia*, Samuel Danforth's 1659 sermon at the funeral of his three young children shows the same intensity of grief. "My heart was indeed somewhat set upon my *children*, especially the eldest," Danforth declares; "it pierceth my very heart to call to remembrance the voice of my dear children, calling, 'father, father!' a voice not now heard." But for God, he concludes, "my heart truly would be consum'd, and would even dye within me."[49]

Mather's defense was characteristically Puritan. Like Danforth and Josselin, he rested his troubles on the Lord. More extravagantly, he also transforms his private grief into public example. Less than a day after his beloved Jerusha's death, he tells himself that "it will be a great Service unto my Flock, for me to exemplify a patient Submission to the Will of God, under many and heavy Trials, and a most fruitful Improvement of my Crosses."[50] Mather's son "Cresy," named after Increase Mather, proved his greatest cross, flouting him in every way. Yet just as Josselin turned toward John, so Cotton never withdrew his love.

Samuel Sewall's diary, though calm and reserved by comparison, records his frustrating attempts to find the right calling for his son. When the boy cries out at the idea of being apprenticed to a Mr. Checkly, Sewall does not seem to consider asserting a father's arbitrary authority. Instead he agonizes for some time and finally puts him with a Mr. Wilkins.[51] Sewall is in no sense a weak father. Yet once again a loving concern clearly takes priority over authority for its own sake.

However, the diaries of Mather and Sewall come from a later time and a different continent. A more substantial corroboration of paternal weakness as well as loving concern can be found in the diaries of Oliver Heywood (1629–1702), a Puritan minister in Yorkshire. Sincere, extraordinarily detailed, and resolutely pedestrian, Heywood's accounts of his daily activities are objective even about himself. As a child, he says, he was slow at school, "which was a discouragement to masters and parents." When he finally met with a good teacher he was "set back at first for the better regulating of my reading english." As he adds, "I am conscious of more dulness and weaknes in my intellectuals then I think most are." Yet he has a good memory, he affirms, and the diaries certainly prove it.[52] He is especially good about remembering details of his parents' lives and characters for a family history that introduces the diaries.

Richard, his father, cuts a particularly vivid figure. Although Richard's own father was a carpenter, he was brought up to be a weaver of fustians, "the trade of that country." Marrying when he was nineteen, Richard found the early adult years perilously hard, in part because he had contracted for a friend's debt, "wherby he was often forced to skulk in holes and flee, they removed one year from his house to the walk-mill at water-side, for secrecy and security, but it was a sad and afflictive year." Their first-born son died, only a year old. As Oliver says, "they fared bare, and workt hard, and were often put to shifts." So far the story is a conventional Puritan model for hard work, though told with uncommon pungency. Richard finally began to prosper at fustians and was even involved in trade with London by the time Oliver arrived: "They got out of debt about the time I was born as I have oft heard my mother relate . . . he grew to a considerable estate, and things succeeded comfortably far beyond expectation." Oliver takes more than a page to list his father's financial accomplishments in those years.

Then once again, as Oliver reached maturity, Richard's fortunes began to slide. After the children were educated, "his intanglements and troubles in the world returned again upon him in his old age, . . . the fustian trade failed him." The cause, Oliver says, was that even though his father owned a walk-mill, he "began to have an itching mind to be dealing with wollen-cloath, which was an imployment wherin he had not been versed." Richard fell into large debts, though he could not understand how; "he hath often told me, he knew how he bought, and how he sold, and was confident he got abundance of mony, and yet he says also that it went faster then it came, he saw it, but could not tell how to help it."

Oliver's explanation is properly Puritan. In part relatives were wasteful with Richard's money, in part his father was old, but "I look principally at the hand of god, . . . possibly my father, my dear and honoured father sinned in changing his calling, in too eager pursuit of the world, in unfaithful dealing in not keeping his word." Since 1662 his father's fortunes had been reversed, and now "my dear father hath been battered with anxious thoughts in this perplexing state now this 13 yeares." That same year, Oliver observes, he and other Puritan ministers were battered with the Act of Uniformity.

It is not enough for Oliver just to mention his father's failures. All the humiliating details must also be set down. "I must confesse tis matter of admiration to me to consider how strangely he hath been secured out of prison, in many eminent dangers, and how he hath had a way of escape found out in many desperate cases past the power of man to help him in, and yet god hath brought him off." That Richard stayed out of prison is cause to admire God, not his father. Oliver is quite clear about blaming Richard for deserting his calling and doing some dirty deals. There is no attempt to excuse him, and no attempt to revere his patriarchal authority, though the narrative does make Richard's financial anxieties "parallel" to Oliver's role as a nonconformist minister not allowed a public calling. There, however, the difficulties are caused by polluted worldly authority, not Oliver's own sins. The overriding tone is of a son's clear-eyed judgment in God's name.

We can imagine a certain unconscious pleasure in Oliver's instructing Richard about his sins. As Oliver says, "He hath had many days of fasting and prayer, wherin I have discerned some kindly workings of humiliation, and self-condemning confessions." We can also suspect a similar pleasure in setting down Richard's business failures, the suits against him, the two arrests, in more lingering detail than his father's earlier financial achievements. But these are post-Freudian thoughts. Oliver's point is simply to show how God rewards those who stick to their callings and punishes those who indulge worldly vanities. More striking than the scrupulously recorded details is a sense of aloof distance. Oliver has disengaged himself from his father to take up with a much stronger and more unchanging authority.

The family history also attends to Richard as a religious controversialist. In 1647 Richard was excommunicated "for contempt . . . because as they said he laught them to scorn, for having naturally a smiling countenance." His wife begged him to make peace, but he refused. Richard was finally readmitted to his church after appealing all the way up to the provincial assembly.

The issue was simply that he had disobeyed a new rule established by the local elders, who now required communicants to present a leaden ticket. The rule roused Richard to indignant protest. Though he won and was readmitted, the local church apparently tried to save face by claiming he had therefore submitted, so "he never joyned with them at the Lords supper afterwards but was entertained at Cockey and all places about." Most important for us, the incident reveals profound division between a resolute father and a mother eager to allay bad feelings: "The controversy was hot begot much bad blood many animositys amongst good people in that society . . . so that it became a very heavy burden to the spirit of my dear mother, who was all for love and peace, and was willing to have yeelded to any thing rather then have contended, but he stood upon his own integrity." Oliver does not take sides, at least overtly. Yet we can sense his distance from Richard's contentious "integrity," his sympathy with his mother's loving spirit of accommodation to those "good people."

"But," Oliver concludes, "these things were long agoe, and forgotten, and I hope buryed and forgiven." Not content with unburying them once, he brings them to life a second time fifty pages later (pp. 78–81), where he notes that the elders had singled Richard out because they "judged him as the chief Ringleader." He also brings up yet another account of Richard's financial difficulties when he was seventy-nine years old. And twice he tells the story of Richard's death in 1677, at the age of either eighty-one or eighty-two, with the same curious note of filial concern yet unsentimental distance. As he says, "Seldome hath my heart been in such a melting frame." Yet he left his dying father a week before, preached in several places, and was told of the death by messenger.

Nor did he preach the funeral sermon, though Oliver did try to ascertain his father's age by checking town records on the following Monday. He found the relevant pages torn out. Even at the end, he seems more the objective chronicler than the revering son. Oliver adds that another son, Nathaniel, had visited Richard "and was longer with him then he had been above 20 yeeres." When Oliver's diary comes to the weeks of February and March, 1677, his father's decline and death pass without a word. Neither is Richard's death recorded in the Event Book for 1676–77.[53]

Oliver was very much his mother's son, as my next chapter describes. His account of Richard is all business; his account of his mother is all religion and love. While he writes at length of his mother's hours on her deathbed in 1657, he simply observes after his father's death that Richard "bore all his troubles with an invincible spirit." The second version of Richard's troubles concludes with a longer and more balanced portrait: "R H was a man of excellent natural parts, large ca-

pacity, tenacious memory, of a plodding head, always contriving something, . . . naturally very chearfull of an affable, sociable, loving
temper."[54] But God, not Richard, is Oliver's spiritual father now.

A long meditation for March 15, 1674, three years before Richard's
death, earnestly struggles toward the conventional Puritan language
for being reborn. Because he was born of the body, Oliver has "an
absolute necessity of a new birth and of regeneration: . . . the sinful
shameful nakednes of my precious soule" has to be clothed, and washed
of blood, by the Lord and only by the Lord, as his parents had clothed
and washed his naked newborn body. "I tooke god for my father, and
he took me for his adopted son," the forty-four-year-old minister recalls.
"I am baptized into one body with thy faithfull members, oh let me
have an assimilation to them."[55]

In the four volumes of Heywood's diary and memoirs, so attentively
edited and published by a nineteenth-century admirer, Richard's portrait stands out. The uniformly plodding, conventional prose has other
redeeming moments of honestly observed detail, but not many. As
roving preacher Oliver is often pleased with "large auditories" and
finds that a temptation. On August 5, 1677, for instance, he chides
himself for being puffed up after a good sermon, though his chiding
soon takes a more worldly turn: "Oh what a wretch am I, that can
be so soon swelled with popular applause, Lord pardon me—and for
all that admiration not all those people at that rich place bestowed so
much as a penny on me, except one woman (once a house-fellow with
me) that gave me half-a crown."[56] This glimmer of human truth is rare.
Most of his more serious worries about himself are concerned with his
feelings of inadequacy in helping others, or with the little white lies
he tells to avoid conflict. Year after year passes in shallow repetition of
conventional Puritan patterns of introspection and daily life.

On the other hand, Oliver was clearly a devoted, even passionately
attached father in his own right. While Richard is dying in 1676–77,
the diary is filled with fears for his two sons, away on travels. There are
long statements of Oliver's fears and love, and intense pleas to God for
their safety. He would be happy to have them no richer, with no
worldly preferments, so long as they remain alive and faithful to God's
word: "Lord, leave them not to conforme to ceremonys, or turn
formalists or persecutors of thy people." He hopes they will be
preachers and vows to give God a day of thanksgiving every year if
that happens. "Lord, I hope my heart is serious in this solemne vow."
On May 11 he gives thanks for his sons' safe return from Scotland,
noting that he had made May 9 an entire day of thanksgiving to God;

"from hence I am incouraged to consecrate my two sons, (my all) to thee."

His father's death goes unremarked in the midst of growing happiness over the sons' choice of a religious calling. Unlike Ralph Josselin, Oliver is eminently rewarded: soon they are both ministers too. A dream he jots down shows the depth of his worry and affection, even after his hopes are met. "21 Jan 6 77 at night after I was gone to bed, at my first sleep, I had a terrible dream concerning my son John, that he was fallen to the study of magick or the black art and that he had books of that sort, and that he plaid some tricks in my sight,—I was so affrighted that I wakened, fell a sweating, trembling."[57] Even more than in Josselin's diary, a father's feelings come across with an urgency of anxious affection.

A major difference from the other lives we have been considering is that Heywood also shows respect amounting to reverence for a new father on earth: Mr. Angier, "the peer of preachers in these northern countys" and the father of his first wife. Oliver seems to have liked the father more than the daughter, at least at first, though he grew passionately attached to her by the time she died in 1661, only six years after their marriage. By then he had taken to calling Mr. Angier "my father," and many subsequent entries refer to him as father. In 1673, for instance, long after his first wife's death, a briefly noted visit to "my ancient father being sick" sharply contrasts with several lengthy accounts of visits to "my dear and reverend father Angier and mother," times at which his heart always "melted." As early as 1657, when Oliver's beloved mother was dying, he "therfore called my father Angier hastily to her," though Mr. Angier's attentions were brisk: "He askt her if she understood, she answered yes, very well, he told her he must leave her, I am more sorry, sd she, he replyed, I have committed you into the hands of your father, and necessary occasions cal me away, having stayed here beyond my intentions, thus they parted with sweet expressions of mutual affection." She died "an houre or two" later.[58] Father Angier seems to have been the dominant presence in her mind as well as her son's, aside from God, even though Richard must have been present.

Oliver's later years are rather more successful than his father's, despite his nonconformity. By volume three the diary has tapered off into a relatively settled complacency. In 1695 his "Self-Reflections" linger not on faults but on happinesses, of which his connection with Father Angier is high on the list: "that I should be a publick preacher above 44 yeares, . . . marry famous Mr. Angiers daughter, print so many bookes, injoy so many comforts of life, bring up two sons to be ministers build a chappel." Four years later his self-reflections center on the state of his health, not of his soul: "The case is thus with me— My wind grows exceeding short, any little motion puts me out of order." Yet he is not sick, he sleeps well, he can still travel and preach "as long and as loud as ever." Moreover, fifth on the list of satisfactions is his second wife: "5 I have a sweet comfortable wife that takes great care of me, provides sack, and yoke of egge every morning and all other conveniences." Sixth on the list is his income, and seventh is God. Frequently counting his blessings, and occasionally noting he is "rarely" at home, he happily lives out his days before dying in 1702, well into his seventy-fourth year.[59]

Heywood's diaries support the possibility that weak fathers were an important element in Puritan lives. Oliver looks to God and Father Angier for strength, not to Richard. Yet as with Shepard and Josselin, we are reading an adult's memories. No doubt there are unconscious dynamics at work in the son's portrait of his father as a silly and beleaguered man. Yet Richard could have appeared as the epitome of zestful, friendly exuberance to a young boy, especially since those were the father's most flourishing years. The searing division between mother and father over Richard's religious intransigence did not happen until Oliver was in his late teens. And whatever the paternal weakness in his background, Oliver seems to have become a strong and loving father to two sons who turned out exactly as he wished. Once again the facts are too slim to go beyond speculation.

Clearly, however, the fathers in these few detailed private records are not the patriarchs attributed to the Puritans, either by recent historians or by their own public instructions. Their failures and their caring loom much larger than their discipline.

Other Puritans had less conflicted beginnings, and a firmer sense of fatherhood, to be sure. Some may have been spurred toward Puritanism by distaste for their fathers' wheeling and dealing and compromising at court. John Wilson, minister to the Boston church of which John Cotton was lecturer, had Archbishop Grindal in his background and a life of preferment ahead of him when he forsook the Anglican hierarchy for nonconformity. John Winthrop came of gentry stock, though reversals in the clothing industry during the 1620s severely depleted his family's income.[60] Arthur Golding's father was a large landholder in Essex and for a time influential at court.[61] Many more Puritans no doubt found apt role models for holiness in the home. English yeomen in general leaned toward Puritanism, since it expressed village virtues. Thomas

Hooker was the son of a Puritan overseer of landed property. Richard Baxter's father, though not a Puritan, got a reputation for Puritanism in the 1630s simply by reading the Bible on Sundays rather than playing village games.[62] No one set of motives or conflicts led to Puritanism, whose strength always lay in its ability to transform a multiplicity of problems with authority into greater authority.

Nevertheless, it is striking that in those case histories offering any detail, so often weakness, absence, and conflict hover about the father's image. John Preston was fatherless at twelve, in modest circumstances. William Ames was orphaned "quite young." In the next century the father of evangelist George Whitefield died when the boy was two.[63] Lawrence Chaderton, in rejecting his father's Catholicism, not only lost the various lands his prosperous and worldly father intended to settle on him, but occasioned his father's celebrated letter as well: "Dear Laurence, if you will renounce a new sect which you have joined you may expect all the happiness which the care of an indulgent father can secure you; otherwise I enclose a shilling to buy a wallet with. Go and beg for your living. Farewell!"[64]

Hugh Peter, by his own account the "son of considerable Parents," lost his mother the year he was born. His father remarried within the next two years, and his childhood seems to have passed in relative affluence, though his family suffered financial losses at sea just as Hugh was preparing to enter college. Peter later said that his father "lived in straitened circumstances after about 1612," when the boy would have been fourteen. A highly energetic and very orthodox Puritan, who helped develop the New England fisheries during his emigration and later represented the Massachusetts Bay Colony at the English court, he was deeply involved in the opposition to Anne Hutchinson in America, and his active promotion of the rebellion against King Charles led to his execution for regicide in 1660. Like so many other Puritans, his outward contentiousness at times masked severe depressions, which occasionally lasted a whole season. As his biographer says, Peter was plagued with a cycle of illness followed by periods of strong energy, and the illnesses "sometimes so strangely affected his mind with severe melancholia that for days at a time he would be delirious and rave like a madman."[65] His wife, whom he left in America, went insane. No clear connection exists between his spiritual oscillations and his early childhood. Yet certainly his orthodoxy coexisted with deep mental disquiet, in ways that Thomas Shepard more strictly controlled.

Another life history, Sir Harry Vane's, involves such overt conflict between father and son that at one point Parliament passed a public motion commanding the two to be friends. Vane's father was an expedient courtier, while his mother was noted for her "communal piety." Both parents were Anglicans, and young Vane's refusal to kneel for the sacrament precipitated an angry confrontation with Archbishop Laud as well as a separation from his father. Vane seems to have been in revolt from his fifteenth year, when he rebelled against school forms and constraints. In a contemporary history of the period, the earl of Clarendon cites the Vanes as his prime example of the "unnatural antipathy" between parents and children, noting that a privy councilor had to send his son to the world's wilderness just because Vane would not kneel for the sacrament. In America, Vane's advocacy of Anne Hutchinson's cause continued to stir up social waters; he then went back to England, where he betrayed secret papers of his father to a rival faction, incurring an "ague" in the process. It was at this point that Parliament passed its motion about their friendship. The father died in 1655, "terminating a strangely uneasy and ambivalent relationship," his biographers observe, and Vane lost his head on the scaffold in 1662, as retribution for what his father's papers betrayed.[66]

Perhaps, to speculate further, the more stormy relations between strong fathers and sons led sons to adopt antinomian perspectives, while the Puritan sons of weaker fathers tended toward orthodoxy. Anne Hutchinson's own father was "the magnetic center of her universe," Emery Battis has said, and "her love and fear of that ardent man" may have had a great deal to do with her heretical abdication from doubt into the certainty that God spoke to her directly.[67] Roger Williams's similar sense of certitude may bear some relation to what he ambiguously described in a 1632 letter to John Winthrop: "Myself a child in everything, though in Christ called, and persecuted in and out of my father's house these twenty years."[68] Certainly the complex relationship to a powerful mother that helped generate John Wesley's faith is not found in the background of any early Puritan for whom we have records, though the zealous mothers of Increase Mather and George Whitefield may show some similarities.[69]

What can be said with more assurance is that, in those Puritans for whom we have the most detailed records, the public rhetoric of patriarchy is belied by private feelings of need and weakness, on the part of both fathers and sons. As Richard Baxter implied, the Puritan call for fatherhood may have had as much to do with the fathers' need for love as with the sons' need for strength. "I saw that he that will be loved, must love; and he that rather chooseth to be more *feared* than *loved*, must expect to be hated, or loved but diminutively: And he that will have *Children,* must be a *Father:* and he that will be a Tyrant must be contented with Slaves."[70] The center of Puritanism is ambivalence, at several levels: the need for strong fathers, the need to limit their strength; resentment of the social compromises eroding the father's proper authority, yet resentment of tyrannical or corrupt authority; sons expressing ambition, yet needing identity; fathers commanding reverence, yet needing love. The dream of the pure father is a fantasy common to all Puritans, to resolve conflicts that seem progressively more complicated, the more we know of their lives.

Chapter Three

Mixed Expectations:
Tender Mothers and
Grave Governors

> Here, Hamlet, take my napkin, rub
> thy brows;
> The queen carouses to thy fortune,
> Hamlet.
>
> *Hamlet,* V,2

Change of any kind brings threatened values to consciousness, and in the early seventeenth century many English writers were preoccupied with affirming the well-ordered patriarchal family. In particular, a remarkable surge of books offering family advice indicates a new and vigorous attention to raising the young. Children were thought of as both more and less than little adults, some of our current theories to the contrary, and Puritans were especially sensitive to parental responsibilities.[1]

Their special concern shows most obviously in a simple fact: most of the family-advice books were written by Puritans. Anglican treatises on the family are much less frequent. Moreover, where Anglican treatises tend to mention children only in passing, urging conventional hierarchic discipline, Puritans emphasized parental as well as marital duties. More oriented toward mutuality within hierarchy, their treatises are at the very least a frontal attack on the settled tradition of parental indifference and brutality, analogous to their attack on husbands who were brutal or indifferent to their wives. As Robert Cleaver said, "Spare not to bee inamored with her, and rather have too high an opinion of her, then too meane." In an age accustomed to violence, both domestic and social, Puritans were adamant about the necessity for love as the shaping motive for all acts of authority. As two recent scholars conclude, "It is impossible to overestimate the sense of human responsibility which pervaded the genuine Puritan home of the seventeenth century."[2]

Proper love meant, first of all, proper discipline. Puritans and Anglicans alike looked to the family to stabilize a society in the midst of crisis and change. Part of the concern was social. In a society essentially without police, the family was the basic instrument for supervision.[3] But the concern was also spiritual. A breakdown in family rule indicates a dereliction of God's order. Rebellious children meant sinful parents. Fathers and mothers have "disordered and disobedient children," said the Puritan Richard Greenham, "because they have been disobedient children to the Lord and disordered to their parents when they were young." Parents who disobey the duties described in *A Godlye Form of Household Government*, its authors begin, will find that God's wrath is shown "in punishing disobedience with disobedience." Control of one's child, conversely, is an outward sign of one's own inward conversion to obedience. In practice, Greenham declared, behavior speaks louder than words: "Experience teacheth us that children like or mislike more by countenance, gesture, and behavior than by any rule, doctrine, precept, or instruction whatsoever . . . let them so go untaught and they will grow so headstrong that they will sooner be broken than bended. And sure it is that one stripe or two words will do more good to a child in the beginning than a hundred stripes afterward."[4]

The call for "one stripe or two words" has been misinterpreted, I think, as evidence for the harshness of most parents. For Puritans, at least, it is more accurate to lean the other way. Their advice was especially meant for those parents who were so loving they could not bear to administer any discipline at all. "But such is the fond and too much cockering affection of some parents towards their children," John Dod and Robert Cleaver said in *A Godlye Form of Household Government*, "that there is more need in these dayes, to teach and admonish them, not to love them too much, than to persuade them to love them. For *Davids darling* was *Davids traytor*." Puritans characteristically reinterpreted biblical injunctions to lay on the rod as meaning instruction mixed with occasional physical punishment. They also and emphatically reiterated that brutality was far worse than "cockering," bad as that was. After chiding excessively indulgent parents, William Gouge takes care to say that parents who are too severe "of the two are the more unnaturall parents."[5]

The family is "a little commonwealth," as William Perkins said and so many others loved to repeat. In the commonwealth as in the home, a proper balance leads to loving rule: no tyranny and no abdication. Puritans incessantly urged the middle course between too much harshness and too much cockering. "Lordliness" and "familiarite," declared Dod and Cleaver, are both "unmeet," though like Gouge these authors were especially concerned to counsel "patience and wisdom" as the keys to "keepe thee from immoderate anger." Parents must be neither "too austere" nor "too remisse," Gouge advised, since "the one extreme of *remissenesse*" and "the other extreme of *rigour* and cruelty" will provoke children to willfulness or wrath, not love. The welfare of the whole social order depends on everyone following that "mean."[6]

These arguments are well known. Puritan family tracts have been a major source for recent research into the social history of the English family. I emphasize Puritan love, however, because others have concluded that Puritan child rearing consisted primarily of breaking the will. Michael Walzer and Lawrence Stone, to name the most influential, find anxiety, rigid self-control, and harsh patriarchal upbringing almost everywhere they look. Philip Greven, with somewhat more justice I think, finds zealous evangelical families in New England breaking the will of children as young as ten to fifteen months, especially in the eighteenth century, although he wrongly claims the pattern is constant over a 200-year period, while contrasting it with another constant pattern of moderation. Part of my purpose is to correct their surprisingly nineteenth-century picture of Puritan repressiveness.[7]

My aim is to show what seems to me a distinct division of roles and stages in Puritan child rearing. The mother was expected to be loving, even too loving, to the very young child. When the child reached the age of instruction, before nine or ten, the father's more distant governance was expected to check the mother's tenderness and slowly bring the child to God's authority.

William Gouge outlines the stages most clearly, in *Of Domesticall Duties* (1622), with Dod's and Cleaver's *A Godlye Form of Household Government* (1621) the most comprehensive Puritan family tract. Infancy, he said, lasts through baptism and nursing. Childhood lasts until apprenticeship, usually about fourteen. "The child-hood of a childe is reckoned from the time that it beginneth to be of any discretion and understanding, till it be placed forth." In his summary he puts infancy and childhood together: "Childhood from his birth to 14 yeeres. Youth from 14 to 25. Man-age from 25 to 50. Old age from thence until his death."[8]

At each stage parents have clearly defined duties. When a child is born, Gouge says, "it is in the swadling bands, and remaineth a sucking childe." Here "the care especially lieth upon the mother," who was vigorously urged by every Puritan tract to breast-feed. "How can a mother better expresse her love to her young babe, then by letting it sucke of her owne breasts?" Gouge argues. Otherwise her nipples would be only "for ostentation." Breast-fed babies are freer from diseases, cleaner, less likely to die, and nobody in the Bible ever puts her children to nurse. The last of his twenty-three reasons, "which daily experience confirmeth," is that children suckled by their own mothers "prosper best. Mothers are most tender over them, and cannot indure to let them lie crying out, without taking them up and stilling them, as nurses will let them crie and crie againe, if they be about any businesse of their owne."[9]

Other writers also assert the mother's crucial responsibility to breast-feed. Dod and Cleaver make it her first duty and mock "these dainty half-mothers" who avoid the task; "the sweet name of Mother . . . full of incredible love" is gained in large part by breast-feeding, at least if one judges by the much greater attention given to it than to any other of her duties. As Gouge says, "this is the most proper worke of her speciall calling." In *The Doctrine of Superiority* (1609), Robert Pricke more generally defines a mother's responsibility as "a tender care of noursing & bringing them up in their yonger & more tender yeares." Tender mothers and tender children go together. Mothers should not be surprised if children deny them later in life, ran the warnings, when they deny children the breast early in life. Strange milk would lead to strange manners. Some even advised mothers that nursing was more important than intercourse, holding a job, or avoiding pain or inconvenience.[10]

In some respects the advice seems to fit a sexist pattern of men over-riding women's complaints about a painful task. Yet Puritans piled up the reasons not so much to quell female objections as to convince balky husbands. Though a husband who absolutely refuses to let his wife nurse must be obeyed, Gouge says reluctantly after his first twenty-three reasons, he continues with six more to drive the fault home. Clearly God's authority should count for more than a husband's pleasures. Therefore it has to be the husband's special duty at this stage to submit, since "husbands for the most part are the cause that their wives nurse not their owne children." Husbands also have the duties of humoring her "longing" in pregnancy, sympathizing with "the screekes and out-cries" at birth—"the greatest paine that ordinarily is endured by any for the time; none know it so well as they that feel it"—and putting up with the inconvenience at night, just as wives have to sacrifice their beauty to God's ordinance. But of all these, Gouge says, letting the wife nurse is most important. If husbands did encourage it, "where one mother now nurseth her childe, twenty would doe it."

Gouge's figure of one in twenty, though probably hyperbolic, indicates the wide gap between preaching and practice. We should not confuse Puritan talk with maternal behavior. Yet his preaching also indicates how attentive Puritans were to issues of good mothering, defined as tender and nurturing, from the earliest age.[11] The Puritan emphasis—greater than in non-Puritan tracts—on breast-feeding in particular and tender mothering in general probably reflects a *relatively* greater emphasis in behavior as well, especially since Puritans argue from the Bible and "daily experience" quite interchangeably.

In the early years the mother remains in charge, though governed by her husband. Various studies have shown that child rearing in general at this time was more nurturing and less strict than in our own time, with nursing up to eighteen months or two years, only a gradual weaning after that, and little training in cleanliness.[12] For older children the mother was expected to mix some instruction with her tenderness. St. Paul "would have them to sucke in religion, if not with their mothers milke," writes Cleaver in his *Briefe Explanation,* "yet shortly after as-soone as they are capable of it." But the husband is clearly in charge of what religious instruction does go on.

He is the surrogate minister, "the wives head," "A King, a Priest, & a Prophet," like Christ at the head of the church or the head over the body, "a man, the ruler and governour of the house, and of his wife, . . . not onely a ruler, but as it were a little King, and Lord of all." As the two most frequent comparisons said, the husband is like the head to the body or Christ to the church, though with the same final limits to his authority. In Robert Bolton's words, "Man is the womans head, Christ is mans head, God is Christs head." Robert Pricke said more comprehensively, "for although the authoritie of Parents be great: yet the authoritie of God is greater."[13]

The inflated metaphors of high social position speak more to securing patriarchal attitudes than to constraining family behavior of women and children. As provider, the husband was expected to be away from home. Lists of his duties invariably center on his worldly calling and his grave carriage. Though the wife is told to let him "rule all the household, especially outward affaires," she is given a clear and "special" charge over home management. Just as she should never indulge in "molestation" of her husband's business, say Dod and Cleaver, so the husband should never "account her a foole, by medling with her small houshold affaires." His only domestic task, beyond generally supervising his wife's duties, is to bring a sense of God's authority to the children and servants, specifically through morning and evening prayers and catechizing. The wife may officiate at home religious observances, say the books, but only in his absence, with his permission, or in case of his madness, sickness, or "blockish" incompetence.[14]

"Everie husband and head of a Family, is as it were, a Priest and Pastour in his owne house," Robert Bolton declared. No Puritan would have questioned the thought, which was basic to the congregational ideal. The wife is at most a "help" to his spiritual rule. The husband's particular duty is to correct the children and teach godliness, said Dod and Cleaver. The wife's duty is simply to "further godlinesse" by being an "example to her houshold of all ready submission." At most she should "helpe her husband in spying out the evils that are breeding, that by his wisdome they may be prevented or cured."[15] By implication the husband should be the regular disciplinarian as well.

Yet mothering imagery often goes with the "spirituall food" fed young children bite by bite through daily catechizing, "as skillful nurses and mothers doe in feeding Infants." (That Gouge puts nurses first, despite all his reasons for the mother breast-feeding, is another indicator of actual practice.) As Henry Smith put it, the master of the house should be "longing to teach his knowledge as a Nurse to emptie her breasts." Serious efforts to "break the will," which all the books urged, seem to have been aimed at children almost in their teens. Then the father's "correction" or "instruction" is expected to dominate. Parents "are not to correct them being infants, and very small, in the measure which aggreeth to them when they are further growne," Robert Pricke advised.[16]

Dod and Cleaver urge parents to begin instruction before "ten or twelve yeares old," if only by example, taking advantage of the children's "apish imitation" which will make them "doe apishly good." Gouge tells parents to instruct children early; why else, he asks, would noble children of twelve and fourteen be "of more understanding" than "poore and meane mens children at 17 or 18"?[17] Children between the ages of three and seven, advised *The Child-Bearers Cabinet* (1652), "are to be educated gently and kindly, not to be severely reprehended, chidden, or beaten, for by that means they may be made throughout their whole life after too timorous, or too much terrified, astonished, and sotted." Anne Bradstreet, in moralizing about her English childhood for her children, recalled her own spiritual change at about six or seven: "In my young years about 6. or 7. as I take it I began to make conscience of my wayes, and what I knew was sinful, as lying, disobedience to parents, etc., I avoided it. If at any time I was overtaken with ye like evills, it was a great Trouble. I could not rest 'till by prayer I had confest it unto God. I was also troubled at ye neglect of Private Dutyes tho: too often tardy that way." We can infer from this variety of evidence that until children of the middle sort reached seven, the age fixed by Aristotle for the beginnings of reason, they were still allowed their original sin, their glimmers of good sense, their "apish" pliability, and their tender mothers for themselves and their siblings, at least between morning and evening prayers. When Gouge lists the four central needs of childhood, all equally important, they are food, apparel, good health, and—not religion, but—recreation.[18]

Not that mothers never wielded the rod, or never disciplined unruly four year olds. Of course they did. My argument is more relative and contextual: that expectations for mothers raising young children differed strikingly from expectations for fathers governing older children. There were mutual duties at every stage, the books note; parents should be mutually loving, respectful, and godly above all. Nevertheless, the precepts and practical examples make it clear that good mothers were tender, and so were young children; good fathers were grave, and so were good older children.

These parental expectations were not unique to Puritanism, though here as elsewhere Puritans were much more intense, caring, and serious. An eighteenth-century letter from Lord Chesterfield to his son shows a sudden transition in parental expectation, here located exactly at the ninth birthday: "This is the last letter I shall write to you as a little boy, for tomorrow you will attain your ninth year, so that for the future I shall treat you as a youth. . . . No more levity. Childish toys and playthings must be thrown aside, and your mind directed to serious objects." Puritans tended to be at once more demanding and more loving than this letter, which fits just as well into the older aristocratic tradition of relative indifference to the child's early years. As John Aubrey summed it up, "In those dayes, fathers were not acquainted with their children." My point is that, within a new frame of caring, fathers and mothers were asked to express the same intensity of love in very different ways.[19]

Tender mothers were good, but too much of a good thing was bad.

In fact, excessively loving mothers existed in sufficient numbers to be a real problem, at least for Puritans, who often singled out the issue. Gouge chastises indulgent parents who "cannot endure to heare their children cry: . . . Mothers for the most part offend herein." For Cleaver in *Briefe Explanation*, "very often the mothers by too much indulgence and fondness are meanes of their childrens vices." "In cockering, mothers doe more offend," observe Dod and Cleaver, "and specially those that have but few children." Their *Godlye Form of Household Government* makes plain the distinction between tenderness and excess, as well as that between the mother's early tender role and the father's later instructing role. "For even as a childe cockered and made a wanton by the mother, will bee more untractable when the father will seeke to bend him to good: so on the other side, a child wisely trained up by the mother in the young yeares, will be the earlier brought to goodnesse by the fathers godly care." While agreeing, Gouge takes care to add that cruel parents are much worse.[20] The point was to keep a loving mean, not to be meanly loving.

The stages were not quite so cut and dried as my summary makes them out to be, or as some of the quotations imply. Nor were parental roles so strictly opposed in theory. Throughout childhood, Puritan tracts preach, both parents must share the duties of instruction and discipline. Their advice stresses shared responsibilities much more than do comparable Anglican tracts, and in much more detail. But the examples from "daily experience" reveal the actual differences between mothering and fathering even as their counsel urges mutuality. The mother is relatively near, the father is relatively far away.

Every Puritan reiterates that the husband provides and guides; the wife's duties are "subjection" and household management. Whatever their joint duties, as Gouge says, in practice early childhood is "mothers peculiar care." The Bible makes the man "a governour over child, mother, and all." But experience shows a mother's more lasting influence. "Home experience confirmeth as much: for if father and mother be of diverse religions, most of the children will follow the mother. For while children are young, their mother is most in their sight: she feedeth, she apparelleth them, she tendeth them when they are not well, . . . so as what they learne in their younger yeeres, commonly they learne of their mothers." The father expresses his love as "wholesome precepts," Cleaver says in his *Briefe Explanation*, while the mother's love is "knit" with the child's, heart to heart. Dod and Cleaver sympathetically relate how tenuous the bond between father and children can be: "The father doth labour and taketh paine for his children, but the children seldome labor or take paines for their fathers, and oftentimes are sent to inhabit and dwell in other mens houses, whereby in a manner it appeareth, that their streight and fast society doth dissolve and breake." But husbands, like children, can count on love from their wives, who never go away and may "neither change house nor bed."[21]

Much Puritan advice was simpler: check your emotions and chide the child. There was at least one simple reason for this restraint, David Stannard has argued: too many children died young. Yet Puritans lived relatively longer than others, especially in America, where men who survived childhood lived to seventy, and women lived almost as long. Infant mortality was only one in ten, less than half the average for the preindustrial world. In the midst of relatively good nourishment and relatively little disease, the problem seems to have been too much loving, not too little. William Whately, an Old England preacher, advised parents to say to themselves, "Let me take heed therefore that I do not overlove him, that I do not cocker him, and as it were mar and kill his soul by over-cherishing his body. If we find ourselves apt to over-prize and over-love our children, we must moderate those passions by such meditations, and if we find ourselves apt to over-grieve for their death, we must tell ourselves, 'Ah, might not their lives have proved much more bitter to me than their death can?' "[22]

There, I believe, is the real context for the frequent admonitions not to love uncritically. At every age excessive loving was seen as a greater problem than excessive harshness, as Dod and Cleaver said.[23] But for older children in particular, too much love was bad. Although love in the early years is natural, even encouraged, love in the later years is dangerous. In fact, a deliberate withdrawal of affection is advised at just about the time that father's instructional role becomes primary. According to Dod and Cleaver, "wisdome requireth" that parents "somewhat dissemble and hide their love, (specially to those children that be of some reasonable discretion) lest they should take boldnesse thereupon, to doe what they list."[24]

The real Puritan fear seems to have been not of children dying but of rebellious teen-agers. John Bunyan summed up the two stages of childhood in the first couplet of "Upon the Disobedient Child":

> CHILDREN, when little, how do they delight us!
> When they grow bigger, they begin to fright us.

Bunyan seems to mean adolescents, who "reckon they are masters" and heed the "wanton."[25] In earlier times, feisty adolescents seem to have been encouraged, not repressed. All across Europe they were given responsibility for staging charivaris and village festivals, where they could mock their elders in various ways that criticized the social order while venting community tensions.[26] But Puritans quashed all that. Their rhetoric of authority is directed against exactly the playful or riotous youthful impudence most sanctioned by village festivities.

Yet paradoxically, Puritan theology let young children be the original sinners that they could not be when older. They were not yet a threat to authority. In similar ways, the assumption that women were emotionally weak allowed mothers to express strong and tender affections openly and consistently. Puritan theology encouraged mothers to be, as D. W. Winnicott has prescribed for our own time, "good enough,"[27] while putting anxious responsibility on the father for calling his wife, children, and servants to stricter account.

Puritans justified a division of roles, as they did everything else, by the Bible. Cleaver cites David 4.3, "For I was the sonne of my father, tender and only beloved in the sight of my mother," to show the mother's tender affections, the father's wiser distance. Several writers explicated the various biblical instances of breast-feeding as implying a mother's necessary care in other respects. Of course the Bible was also ransacked to show the man's right to govern. And there is little overt differentiation of parental roles after the early years. Robert Pricke offers five biblical citations in arguing the necessity of honoring both parents equally in their mutual calling.

Nevertheless, Pricke's explication of his Fifth Commandment theme sets forth the difference even in denying it. Honor is due both parents, he says, "to prevent and meete with the corruption and partiality of children, who otherwise would either contemne the Mother, and yeeld all honour and dutie to the Father, by reason of his principalitie: or els because the Mother doth beare them, nourish them, and is most tenderly affected toward them, would be wholy addicted unto her, excluding and making no account of the Father."[28] Without God's commandment, children would "yeeld" honor to the father, an oddly grudging verb, because of his "principalitie." But Pricke notes three reasons why children would naturally honor their mother. Foremost, his language implies, is that they would be "wholy addicted unto her" because she "is most tenderly affected toward them."

One would think that Puritan role divisions would lead inevitably to an exaggerated rhetoric of repressive patriarchy for older sons. But

Puritan counsel is conspicuously less repressive than its biblical sources. Puritans preach that fathers must be "tender" too, though grave, in governing both wife and children. A woman is "a weake and fraile vessell," notes Robert Pricke, as well as a gift from God; "therefore men are to deale with them in a tender and charie manner: as men deale with glasses, and with tender vessels that are brittle." That image can be found in non-Puritan tracts as well. But Puritans meant the tenderness more than the glass.[29] Robert Cleaver explicates Proverbs 13.1, "A wise son hears his father's instruction," to mean "a godly and prudent child of either sex" hears the rebukes of "a most tender father." Cleaver even goes so far as to recast Proverbs 13.24 ("He that spareth his rod, hateth his sonne: but hee that loveth him, chasteneth him betime") so that loving speech rather than simple physical punishment is encouraged: "so that the sentence may thus be well englished: He that loveth him hasteneth chastisement, and instruction to him . . . sometimes stripes with admonitions, and alwaies admonitions with stripes." Cleaver emphasizes the mildness, lenity, and kindness of the father's instruction.[30]

Of course no one should be too tender. As Gouge says, punning, "Tending Children too cockishly, maketh them too long children, and too tender." Yet Gouge also defines "an husband-like gravity" as mild and loving speech, forbearance, yielding, and provident care, like Christ's of his church. A magistrate, said Pricke, "may not be proud and haughtie, but behave himselfe in a lowly, sweete, and loving manner towards his subjects, as a father toward his children."[31] Anglicans would be more likely to reverse the comparison, in the interest of lordliness.

Even more surprising is the Puritans' lessened patriarchal emphasis as a whole. Role divisions were encouraged, since everyone must have a particular calling. But in talking of child care after infancy Puritans almost always say "parents," not "fathers," even when the Bible's language is explicitly male. Many explications of Proverbs apply fatherhood to mothers as well, or simply say that "father" signifies "parents." The abundant distinctions made by Puritans to justify man's superiority over women have much more to do with the roles of husband and wife than with child rearing.

I don't mean to say Puritans were egalitarian, even in that one respect. As I have said, their language always looks both ways. Certainly Puritans defined family duties along traditional patriarchal lines, often with an exaggerated sense of strict hierarchy. Milton's famous formulation in book four of *Paradise Lost*, "He for God only, she for

God in him," is close to the common view, though it omits the shared responsibility Puritans always strove for as well. According to the separatist John Robinson, "Many common graces and good things are requisite both for husband and wife, but more especially the Lord requires in the man love and wisdom; and in the woman subjection." For Dod and Cleaver, the husband's fundamental duties are to love his wife, not be cruel to her, and live discreetly with her; the wife's duties are submission and managing the household. Gouge, citing Ephesians 5.23, makes the husband's basic duty "Love" and the wife's "Feare," though he hastens to redefine fear as loving obedience. While the husband should give his wife the right to govern maids, the kitchen, and her "huswiferie," Dod and Cleaver insist that he is lord within the house and lay the blame on him if anything goes wrong. "For the blame of all discord is commonly laid on him that is chiefe."[32]

Authority, as always in Puritan discourse, does not confer pride of place but only responsibility. Nevertheless, responsibility is finally patriarchal. The "wise husband shall never set himselfe so farre in love, that he forget that he is a man, the ruler and governour of the house, and of his wife," say Dod and Cleaver. A husband's aberrations have to do with deviance from loving authority, says Gouge, either in despising his wife, behaving as a "Stoic" without affection, showing tyranny or rash anger or excessive strictness, or commanding unlawful things. A wife, correspondingly, errs in deviating from submission, either by ambition, conceit, "A stout standing on her own will," "Discontent at her husband's estate," or the like.[33] The instances could be multiplied a hundredfold.

Yet the accent on love and instruction, not fear and control, always predominates. "The best rule that a man may hold and practise with his wife, to guard and governe her," Dod and Cleaver advise, "is to admonish her often, and to give her good instructions, to reprehend her seldome, never to lay violent hands on her." "Her cheekes are made for thy lippes, and not for thy fistes," Henry Smith more wittily argued. "Husbands must holde their handes and wives their tungs."[34] The Puritan repetition of patriarchal supremacy both frames and contradicts their equally repetitive call for mutual duties and love.

A rhetorical strategy of implicit polarity, like the polarities in Puritan attacks against stage plays, resolves the contradictions. Yet the strategy shows some of the strains shaping and subverting their exaggerated patriarchal decrees. While husbands are associated with lordship, priesthood, the head, and public dominance, wives are associated with the body, emotions, and private tenderness. These polarities obviously speak to child rearing as well. In public, man is masterful, and woman is weak. Yet her weakness is what most endears her to husbands and children. In fact, emotional weakness is what makes her loving and loved, just as the convert gains God's love through abasing his "head" and becoming utterly low.

Husbands' public mastery is only too clear. Women were not even allowed to speak in church, partly because of the Bible and more because of their weakness. John Cotton said simply that "for women, God hath expressly forbidden them all place of speech and power in the church, 1 Cor. xiv, 34 and 1 Tim. ii, 11, 12, unless it be to join with the rest of the church, in singing forth the public praises of the Lord. . . . The female sex, and nonage, fall short of some power, which Christ has given to the brotherhood . . . I suffer not a woman to teach, nor to usurp authority over the man, but to be in silence." Thomas Hooker disagreed with the biblical argument, at least in the abstract. Women may speak, he said, not as teachers but "when their speeches argue *subjection,* and so suit with their sexes." Yet their own incapacity justifies taking the required public expressions of saving grace in private, "because we find it by experience, the feeblenesse of some, their shamefac't modesty and melanchollick fearfulnesse is such, that they are not able to express themselves in the face of a Congregation." Hooker concludes that it is best to do for all what is "necessary for some."[35] The experience of women's "feeblenesse," not the Bible, is his real guide.

Only among extremists like the Quakers, of course, were women unrestrained. Puritans shared with the age a contempt for contentious or disloyal wives, an idealization of the "quiet, undisturbed and impassionate" woman.[36] Yet in the privacy of the home Puritans encouraged many female responsibilities denied in public. What seems like patriarchal hierarchy was actually a practical division of labor. The wife, writes Robert Bolton, has "her more proper and particular charge, houshold affaires, and businesses within doore, as they say." Dod and Cleaver list the divided duties: "The duty of the husband is to travell abroad, to seek living: and the wives dutie is to keepe the house. The duty of the husband is to get money and provision: and of the wives, not vainely to spend it. The dutie of the husband is to deale with many men: and of the wife, to talke with few. The dutie of the husband is, to be intermedling: and the wife, to be solitarie and withdrawne."[37]

Patriarchy and mutuality seem harmoniously wedded, then, and not only in a polarity of public and private. Head and body are equally pervasive associations. Here too Puritans establish a frame of hierarchic governance. The husband is "the wives head," Robert Pricke said, as Christ heads the church. He has "more sharpenesse and quickenesse of witte: with greater insight & forecast then the woman." Robert Bolton said more broadly that "the husband, by the benefit of a more manly body, tempered with naturall fitnesse for the soule to worke more nobly in; doth, or ought ordinarily outgoe the wife in largenesse of understanding, height of courage, staiednesse of resolution, moderation of his passions, dexterity to manage business." Bolton even goes so far, in one now notorious passage, as to desex the wife in proving both male dominance *and* equality: "His wife hath as noble a soule as himselfe. *Soules have no Sexes*, as *Ambrose* saith. In the better part they are both men."[38]

Yet Bolton's hierarchic frame encourages mutuality, even interchangeability. "Nay, and if it were possible for you to change bodies," he continues, "hers would worke as manlily in thine, and thine as womanly in hers." Dod and Cleaver do not take the idea of interchangeability quite so far. "A beautifull body is such a one as is of right forme and shape, meet, and of strength to beare children, and governe an house; . . . But in the mind (which is judged to be the man) consist the true lineaments and properties of fairenesse."[39] The body, as female, is most beautiful when most useful in the home. The mind, as male, has the "true lineaments" of fair governance. Few Puritans denied that women also had minds, though probably less capacious ones.

As elsewhere in the language of Puritanism, the governors must be governed and polarities balanced at the mean. Husbands beating their wives, says Gouge, are *"heads too heady."* In no case, he emphasizes, may a husband beat his wife, except "if a wife waxe so mannish, or rather mad," as to beat him. Paul Baynes more abstractly warned William Ames, "Beware of a strong head and a cold heart." And Gouge urges earlier that just as the church was not worthy of love yet Christ made her worthy, so wives, even "though they bee no way worthy of love, yet they must love them." He acknowledges that "it is not simply in the husband's power" to make a bad wife lovable, as it is in Christ's. Yet he counsels husbands to take "another patterne" from Ephesians 5.28, and love such women as you do your own bodies.[40]

Mixture within polarity was therefore a strategy separating male and female, public and private, head and body, lord and subject, yet yoking them together, not only as stable family roles but as personal identity. It encouraged male and female equality as well as patriarchy. The language also encouraged a very flexible rhetoric of gender associations within each saint, man or woman. That flexibility was used to express conversion experiences as well, while marriage was proclaimed as at once patriarchal and a fellowship of equal "yoke-fellows" or "help-meets."

Yet finally the associations do come down to male strength, female weakness. Puritans considered strong and tender emotions to be another sign of women's unfitness for authority, even while showing how apt those emotions are for authority over young children. That is a paradox we can see much better than they could. Unchecked emotions were very threatening to Puritan men, for various reasons explored in previous chapters. To be full of feelings, except for God, was associated with anxiety as well as with worldly lusts. To be "weak" meant not having control. Women, however, were allowed their enthusiasms. For Richard Sibbes, the notion was conventional that women were weak through feeling too intensely, while men were strong in their grave restraint. Indeed, female susceptibility to feelings often leads to greater spiritual openness because of God's joy in human weakness: "For the most part women have sweet affections to religion, and therein they oft goe beyond men. The reason is, Religion is especially seated in the affections: And they have sweet and strong affections. Likewise they are subject to weaknesse, and God delights to shew his strength in weaknesse. And thirdly, especially child-bearing women bring others into this world with danger of their own, therefore they are forced to a nearer communion with God, because so many children as they bring forth, they are in peril of their lives."[41] Although Sibbes couples anxiety and feelings in his reasons for being religious, his prose tames them, as much by giving them to women as by briskly setting them down in the Puritan one-two-three step.

It was not that women had no wit at all. As Dod and Cleaver said, "Women are as men are, reasonable creatures, and have flexible wits both to good and evill." The point is their greater weakness, not their obdurate wickedness. Puritans were quick to condemn female stubbornness. Yet they were curiously tolerant of female failings. Especially when expressed as too much love for their children, weakness is a practical reality of life more than a sin to be corrected. Cotton Mather voices a long tradition in *A Family Well-Ordered* (1699), when he assumes "Fondness, and Weakness" in mothers who are too loving: "Oftentimes the *Fathers* have the Wisdom to keep up their Authority, and keep themselves above the *Contempt* of their *Children*. But the *Mothers* do more frequently by their Fondness, and Weakness, bring upon themselves, the *Contempt* of their *Children*, and Lay themselves Low, by many Impertinencies." When Cleaver explicates "A wise son maketh a glad Father; but a foolish son is a heaviness to his mother" (Prov. 10.1), he first says the parental terms are interchangeable. Then he adds, "Yet it is not without cause that the mother is rather put in the latter clause, then the father: for that sex is the weaker, and more impatient of such a crosse: and usually contemptuous children be bolder to contemne the mother then the father." After citing examples from the Bible, notably Rebecca's troubles with Esau, Cleaver repeats: "And very often the mothers by too much indulgence and fondness are meanes of their childrens vices."[42] His tone is as much one of stating "usual" practice as of accusing people of correctable vices.

Elsewhere in *Briefe Explanation*, while explicating Proverbs 15–20, Cleaver reiterates that "mother" and "father" are interchangeable words and yet appropriately divided. A foolish son "sheweth contempt to mother and father, but especially to the mother, because hee presumeth to be more bold with her, and because his state commonly doth lesse depend upon her." To single out the son's calculations of estate is another sign that teen-aged children were the real problem. A mother's love in the earlier years, though perhaps dangerous in bending the twig toward willfulness, is not associated with full-grown rebellion. Most Puritans said it was natural, if regrettable, for women's excessive emotions to lead to too much mother-love. All the more reason for a loving male governance, not cruel condemnation. In the midst of their long argument for breast-feeding, Dod and Cleaver note that "step mothers doe more often offend" in valuing their natural children higher, because "their affections be stronger than mens, and many times over-rule them." And one of Gouge's last proofs that husbands should rule wives is that "women are for the most part prone to pranke up their children above their husbands place and calling." Therefore they must be governed.[43] The more tender love women have, the more husbands must be gravely restrained to keep their families well ordered, their children well disciplined, and their God well pleased.

Of course women were no weaker then than now. They wielded the rod, they ran the house, they sometimes ran the business despite all the advice books; and as Gouge's agonized preface to *Of Domesticall Duties* shows, they rose up in successful protest when he first said a wife could not dispose of family goods without her husband's consent. Gouge now hastens to add exception upon exception to the biblical injunction, since it was obviously the sticking point for his congregation. Certainly not the wife's own goods, he says, or even strictly family goods; you don't have to have "expresse consent," and it doesn't apply to "such Husbands as are impotent, or farre and long absent." Besides, he continues, I was only talking about extreme cases, and in any case it's the husband's duty not to go to extremes. After all, "he ought to make her a joynt Governour of the Family with himselfe." One can feel Gouge's anxiety seeping through his prose, especially since he concludes, "This just Apologie I have beene forced to make, that I might not ever be judged (as some have censured me) an *hater of women*."[44]

A rare instance—the only one I have found—speaks of fear associated with mothers raising young children: "Feare of the rod compelleth children to stand in awe of their mother in her fresh yeeres," Robert Cleaver declares, but only fear of God and a good conscience "worketh reverence towards her, when they stand in no bodily feare of her, or have no need of her." The more usual emphasis on need and tenderness, in Cleaver's own writings and elsewhere, shows that the mother was not expected to demand the kind of "awe" from her children that the father should have. Cleaver himself implies the husband should be the disciplinarian.[45] Nevertheless, the mother could inspire awe when she wanted to.

Not only were women not weak in any objective sense, at least in the home, but the various instances of anxious fathers described in the last chapter suggest reality may have been running the other way. Exaggerated yet circumscribed images of lordliness, a rhetoric of polarity and rigid repetitiveness, associations of feared aspects of oneself with weakness and women, emphasis on male restraint and the male mind's governance of female emotions, the separation of "head" from "body," all evoke a language of male anxiety more than of female deficiency. If women were not allowed to be masterful, they nevertheless were given practical charge of the home as well as relatively unambiguous scope for strong emotions. Since men were not allowed to be dependent, they were given no scope for their own range of emotional needs except in religion, whose language expresses dependence with unrestrained female and infantile imagery. In some respects, I am suggesting, Puritans paradoxically allowed women a kind of strength in weakness that was denied to men, because they so feared their own weakness.[46]

I have overstated the case, since Puritanism transforms more than one kind of psychological energy. But the suggestion could help to explain why Puritanism attracted so many women at the same time that it eased male anxieties with fantasies at once patriarchal and submissive.

———————————•◆•———————————

There are differences between Puritan tracts, as between Puritans. In particular, Daniel Rogers's *Matrimoniall Honour* (1642) is harsh, patriarchal, and rigid compared to other Puritan writings. Most important, though perhaps not surprising for a book focusing only on marriage, Rogers hardly mentions children at all. He remarks in passing how bad some couples are who "bring up their brats to all filthinesse of manners," and he notes, again in passing, that the "care and maintenance" of children is one of the duties of marriage. Where Gouge offers nearly thirty reasons for breast-feeding, Rogers makes it a small part of housework, necessary if unpleasant. The "subject wife . . . seekes not brests in her husbands purse, but in her owne bosome." Egotism is his main concern; some lazy wives "shift off this worke carelessly, and commit their babes to strangers, as if they were too good to nurse them, when as yet their breasts are full, and their bodies strong." The thought is similar, but to include it with housework rather than treat it as a special calling, as Gouge does, is very different. Immediately returning to household management, Rogers concludes that husbands should give "double affection" to wives who really work hard. Later he again briefly urges the duty to breast-feed, unless the wife is unable, though he adds that "no one duty of many (I know) is lesse practiced."[47]

Only one aspect of child rearing is treated with any vehemence: the necessity for parental consent to marriage. Rogers warns that early familiarity makes "children grow so sawcy and effeminated" that they might not even worry about asking for consent. His only particular criticism of too-loving parents is that they may show excessive love or ambition for their eldest child. A concern with primogeniture is part of his larger concern with money matters, which take up a major part of the text. A crucial issue in child rearing, for him, is to make sure parents let children marry for love more than for dowries. Above all, parents should never depend on their children in old age.[48] Throughout, his focus is on the needs of parents, not children. In the table of contents children merit not a word.

Rogers's relative indifference to children contrasts sharply with the other Puritan tracts. Also, his division of labor is much more clear-cut. Husbands should never have to be bothered with young children except when berating or beating them: "She crosses not her husband in any labor, and education of children, she traynes and instructs the tender fry (fittest for her hand) till meeter for his oversight: joins with him in his reproofes and corrections, . . . holdes not his hand from due stroakes, but bares their skin with delight, to his fatherly stripes."[49] Though other Puritans divide duties along the same lines, their instructions are much more tender in tone as well as more mutual in doctrine. At least as important, they clearly and simply urge more attentiveness to children.

The diminishment of child rearing, as a task fit only for the wife, is part of a larger diminishment of the wife's role and a magnification of the husband's. A wife is basically, as Rogers says several times, a "drudge." She should keep "the complaints and trouble of children" from her husband as much as she can, just as she should keep the trivialities of housework to herself. Her first two duties, subjection and helpfulness, make her "a good drudge." Her last duty, that of "Gracefulness," makes her "a good wife." By gracefulness he means she must be "amiable" and "pleasing" at all times, even when feeling sick. "Home hath her heart. She hath worke enough within doores, and dwells most within her selfe. She like the snaile, carrieth her house alway upon her backe."[50]

The husband, on the other hand, has "Gods image" shining through him. Rogers loves to repeat that thought. A good man has "the image of God shining in his understanding and behavior"; therefore "he must be her eye to see by, her hand to worke, her foote to walke with, to discerne things, and persons, how they differ." "He resembleth after a sort, God himselfe, whom *Paul* calls the Father upon whom all the families of the earth depend, and are called by his name." Wives may instruct children in religion too, Rogers allows. Otherwise they would be "good for nothing but drudgery." She should be a wife, not a slave, he says. But she should also utterly submit to her husband in everything not expressly contrary to God's will, even if she doesn't love him, because "in him may shee beholde yet more manifest steppes of Gods image then in her selfe. . . . In the man shines out more authority, government, forecast, soveraignty, then in the woman." However grossly deficient the man's personal character may be, she has to submit to that image with love, as do his children. Conversely, whatever he permits, his children may do. In particular, they can marry "if the father consent and the mother onely be obstinate."[51] From first to last the wife's subjection is absolute.

In large part Rogers's differences probably have to do with his own personality and time of life. He was in his sixties when he wrote *Matrimoniall Honour,* and his deceased wife apparently had had the reputation of being "a shrew." More basically, he seems to have been more classically obsessive than most early Puritans. As the *Dictionary of National Biography* recounts, "Rogers was of a morose and sombre temperament, and his creed was severely Calvinistic."[52] Even in little things, Rogers shows an authoritarian rigidity and a niggling attention to detail. Puritans and Anglicans alike, for instance, counseled moderation in sexual passion between husband and wife. Dod and Cleaver censure those who attempt "lascivious excess" in the marriage bed "by admitting all things," and Robert Bolton warns that "immodest or immoderate abuse of the marriage" will lead to "miscariages, barrennesse, bad children" as rewards "for such secret sensuall exorbitancies and excesse." "Marriage is rather a fellowship of dearest amity, then disordered love," he concludes. While agreeing with the holiness of moderated pleasures, Rogers slights the usual Puritan emphasis on fellowship. He is intent on setting the limits more exactly. As he says, "once weekly or thrice monethly" may not be a rule for everyone, but if Plato can advise that for heathens, then Christians, especially those "in yeares," "should rather aim at being under the line, then above it." Even most Puritans were not that precise.[53]

His title proclaims the ideal of "Matrimoniall Honour" as marriage's highest purpose. Since honor implies deference, wifely subjection leads to the "dignity" of both spouses. Helpless submission to an obstinately bad father or husband, he is fond of saying, is the "crosse" children and wives have to bear. True, a husband should indulge his wife, so long as she remains "modest," and should let her have the "trifles." Since she is "a thing naturally framed to tendernesse," he should be "tender" of her soul. But the honor of both is maintained by her absolute obedience.[54]

Rogers bends the traditional language of social respect and deference, unmixed with mutuality or even strong feeling, to the most obsessive kind of Puritanism. Though he often counsels love, the word slides into obedience on one hand and rather shallow pleasure on the other. "Reade the Canticles," he says. But instead of a disquisition on the ecstatic happiness found at the breasts of the Word or in Christ's marriage bed, we find him taking Solomon's song of love to mean a

man's basking in pure deference: "See how shee pleases her selfe in
his comely proportions, attire, gestures! . . . how shee depends
wholly upon his becke and countenance."[55] The love emerging from
such dependence is truly no more than an "inward complacence" in
each other, at least from his point of view.

It is all a matter of emphasis. But the different emphases do matter.
Furthermore, Rogers explains women's weakness by her descent from
Eve. Despite Milton's example, Puritans did not usually focus on Eve.
Samuel Willard's *Compleat Body of Divinity* makes Adam the princi-
pal cause of sin for both men and women, and at no point in Willard's
lengthy explication of marriage duties does he ever invoke Eve to
justify inequality. Indeed, he scrupulously avoids her in making his
case for tender joint duties and mutual respect.[56] For Rogers, however,
the whole reason for woman's subjection consists in her descent from
Eve. She is the chief sinner, while man, coming from Adam, is the
glory of God. In fact Rogers finds two reasons for weakness in Eve's
story. First, Adam was created perfect, and Eve was not. Second, "her
sin still augmented her inequality." "Remember, thy sexe is crazy,
ever since Eve sinned."[57] An external form, not an inward state, is both
the justification and the end of woman's estate in marriage.

There are many varieties within Puritanism, in short, as within
Anglicanism, especially as a more severe patriarchy took hold in New
England and ideas of reasonable self-interest began to influence
Anglican thought. One popular treatise of a New England divine was
Thomas Cobbett's *A Fruitfull and Usefull Discourse Touching the
Honour due from Children to Parents, and the duty of Parents towards
their Children* . . . (1654), published in England two years later.
Cobbett takes the usual Puritan course of saying God's Fatherhood is
in both parents. However, his advice leans much more heavily on
compelling reverent obedience than on giving love. As he says, "being
too fond of your children, or too familiar with them at sometimes at
least, & not keeping constantly your due distance; such fondness and
familiarity breeds and causeth contempt & irreverence in children."
The thought is conventional, but not the adverbs. He is more rigid in
his censure of familiarity even "sometimes at least," or his insistence
on "constantly" keeping distance. Cobbett also notes that the New
England practice of putting young children to work in the fields makes
honor to parents all the more necessary, since children, "poring too
much upon what they do for their Parents, and not seriously weighing
what their Parents have done for them, they slight them in their
hearts." Attuned to resentment more than to tenderness, Cobbett's

rigorously divided and subdivided text, with its seven inward and seven outward signs of reverence, shows a more inflexible preoccupation with control than we find earlier in Gouge or in Dod and Cleaver, or even in Rogers, who is occasionally playful. In many respects Cobbett's concern with strict obedience resembles Rogers's, though he gives much more attention to children. Tender-hearted mothers are all very well, he says. But "better unborn (almost) than untaught."[58]

On the other hand, the tone of the Anglican Bishop Fleetwood's *Relative Duties of Parents and Children, Husbands and Wives, Masters and Servants* (1705) emphasizes the self-interest of "reasonable creatures," not strict obedience for honor's sake. Parental love, he says, "is greatly heightned and improv'd in Reasonable Creatures, by the hopes of deriving some Comfort, Credit, or Advantage from their Children: So that although the Parental Love be the most disinterested of all Loves, yet is it truly selfish at the bottom." God in his goodness made this "necessary" love also "easie and delightful to the Parent." Fleetwood is attentive to the special cares of mothers, who "bear all the trouble of their Infancy and Childhood." Although noting the father's superiority "in Natural Strength, in Wisdom, and by God's appointment" as well as by human law, and although observing that scripture makes no distinction between parents as parents, he urges children never to give grief, which "is especially the infirmity and feebleness of Mothers, . . . for every thing that gives them grief, is a sort of disobedience." In rather Puritanical language the bishop declares that every worldly relation has "a Reciprocal duty obliging each party." The wife's obedience, though necessary, is only "a limited Subjection," like that of every inferior, and duties should always be related to "Benefits and Favours." In those respects he accommodates an older Puritan tradition of mutual obligations to new ideas of human reason and self-interest.[59]

But in at least one crucial respect Bishop Fleetwood continues an older Anglican tradition of speaking primarily to parental needs. Centering his instructions almost entirely on duties *to* parents, not of parents, he rarely mentions parental obligations to children. His real priorities are with adult life. The last four of his sixteen sermons are taken up with requirements for women's inward and outward dress.

Almost any point made by Puritan tracts can be found in non-Puritan writings. Becon's *Boke of Matrimony* (1543) defines the husband's lordly duties and the wife's dutiful subjection in terms that continue in faith after faith for 200 years. Becon also said fathers must be gentle and caring in correcting children, to instill love of them as parents, not hatred of them as tyrants. The idea of woman as the weaker vessel was also omnipresent.[60] But Puritans differ in what they choose to emphasize. In particular, Puritan tracts encourage a distinctive intensity of loving in parents, especially in mothers, and a loving gravity of restraint in fathers. They give much more attention to the mother's role in early childhood and recommend her energetic tenderness at least as much as discipline, while strictly limiting the father's lordliness. Many Puritan mothers expressed love with vivid intensity, in religious passion as well as mother-child bonds. Anne Bradstreet's poems, the Winthrop correspondence, and other literature also indicate profound love between husbands and wives.

———————— ·◆· ————————

Chapter two mentioned in passing that Oliver Heywood was very much his mother's son. Heywood's own account intimately connects his mother's love to religious zeal. "She was tenderly affected to the fruit of her wombe," he writes; "the love she bore to our bodys, tho natural, was spirituallized, . . . I may say she travelled in birth again for us til christ was formed in us, and the latter travel was mostly sharper, oh wth what passionate teares and intreatys did she plead for us at the throne of grace?" She never ceased to work on her children: "It was her constant custome when my father was gone to London to make al her children pray. . . . though she was very indulgent to us, yet was she severe and sharp agt sin." There is the key: "very indulgent to us," but "severe and sharp" against sin.

Great love and great expectations are very different things, we know. To Puritans they were the same. The mixed expectations in Puritan households begin by mixing maternal indulgence with maternal demands for right behavior. Mrs. Heywood's tender love, while genuine, was also a relentless solicitation: "She would often have said we must be like Christ or mary, the first was always doing good, the latter always receiving good, she earnestly prest after these patternes." She especially loved I John 2:17, Heywood records, and "would be often repeating instances of the vanity and instability of the world." Though the phrase is a cliche to us, the affairs of her husband reveal how intertwined vanity and instability may have seemed to her and her children. While Richard was making and losing his fortunes, or fighting church elders, Mrs. Heywood was apparently an unflagging helpmeet to the Puritan cause. She ripped down superstitious relics in the parish church and worked to settle godly ministers in adjacent places. Oliver speaks of "her frequent fastings, constant watchings, and dayly teares . . . for she spared not her body in any service to her god." In fact, her distaste for the world was so strong that several years before her death in 1657 she was eager to die: "Two or three yeares before she dyed she was so set upon a desire of dissolution, and being with christ that she had much adoe to silence the workings of her spirit."[61]

It was religion, in many ways, that kept her going. "She intirely loved al godly ministers, . . . she would have put them in her bosome, and was even ravisht wn any of the Lords embassadours came under her roofe." As Heywood adds, "A Reverend divine used to cal her the mother of the Clergy." Her deepest wish for her own children was for them to become ministers, and it is not surprising to see her wish come true; "she saw too of us preachers," Oliver being one. His subsequent passion to see two of his own become preachers, with the same happy result, may show his unconscious identification with her.

Like Oliver, "She was exceeding frequent and fervent in secret prayer . . . with strong crying and teares." In the community she was a humble zealot for the Word; "scarce any publick excercise stated or occasional within many miles but she went to it, she was (as it were) the center of news for knowing the time and place of week-days sermons." Also charitable to a fault, perhaps hastening Richard's business failures, "she often prevailed with my father for work for poore persons in a time of scarcity when others cast them off, tho to his apparent damage and disadvantage," and she was always "an unreconcileable enemy to the Bishops government." Very much unlike her husband, "she was very useful in reconciling differences, and making up breaches, . . . she was so much for peace that she rolled every stone to compasse it." Oliver's diary records many similar instances of his own peacemaking, often achieved by means of little white lies for which he berates himself in private. The close connection between mother and son, in personality, outlook, and affection, concludes with her death in his house, not Richard's. Oliver's wife would appropriately die in the house of her blessed father, the celebrated preacher Father Angier; now Oliver blesses God's providence at the rightness of having his mother die with him.[62]

The son's account of his mother's early childhood gives an almost dominolike picture of tender zealous mothers begetting tender zealous mothers. Born in 1594, Alice experienced a wrenching conversion at nineteen, soon after her mother's death, "for whose death she made excessive sorrow." As Heywood writes, "it broke her heart exceedingly" that her mother had died with an unconverted daughter. A conviction of her heart's "dangerous estate," with feelings of "dreadful guilt" for her sin, led her to isolate herself for days at a time, reading the Bible.

The pattern is conventional for Puritan spiritual narratives, from her time through Jonathan Edwards: "She did afterwards with-draw her selfe into a little out-house near her fathers, and took her bible with her and spent the whole day in reading and praying, self-examining and selfe-judging exercises." She was so much in crisis that everyone worried, even her minister. Crying and groaning, with feelings of utter vileness, she was at last converted by a sermon, appropriately enough on Canticles 2.16, "My beloved is mine and I am his." She later said she never lost assurance after that moment. She married Richard for his "piety and sincerity" and never seems to have lost that assurance, though she must have had a few doubts about Richard's worldly competence from time to time. One of the few pieces of direct advice from Richard Oliver records is to "take short notes of every sermon, and write some faire over for your loving mother."[63]

Unlike his mother, Oliver's first wife, Elizabeth Angier, seems to have experienced no trauma, even though her mother died in 1640 when she was eight. Another "very tender mother" replaced her, and soon the two were even more "knit" to each other. According to Oliver, Elizabeth had a sharp mind and often read the Bible when very young. She never had a clear conversion, to her disappointment, but her holiness was unmistakable. She and her stepmother were "examples to others in that relation of meeknes, endearednes and voluntary condescention," and she herself—very much like Oliver's mother—"always delighted in love and concord, and would never indure anger or contention."[64]

To her father she was always "the mirrour of patience and subjection." Oliver applied for Elizabeth's hand in 1655, after one of his most severe sicknesses. The sickness is not an irrelevant detail, because he seems to have been very much in love with someone else shortly before. An entry in his diary many years later says he was once in love too eagerly, as he puts it, with a "godly yong woman." Elizabeth, who loved him "at the first view," was dreadfully sickly, he says. But "a years interruption, . . . disappointments otherways, her opposition to more probable motions, her constancy to me, my gradual complacency in her, every time more then another," led at last to marriage. It is tempting to speculate on possible connections between Oliver's sickness, his mother's wishes for death at that same time, Elizabeth's similarity to his mother, his need to be taken care of, and his "gradual complacency in her." More apparent is her continued sickliness, her passionate affection for him, and his slowly growing love for her after marriage.

Her body was very little and weak, Oliver writes. Many said she could bear no children. On "the day before our mariage she could scarce abide out of bed," and she was in great pain on the nuptial morning, with "a violent feaver" a fortnight after. Yet not only did she live six years longer, but bore three sons and ran a very efficient household. "She was exceeding prudent and provident in managing the affaires of the family, wch were wholly committed to her oversight and charge." She also showed practical contentment with her station, Oliver recalls. "When I had motions of prefermt, she exprest abundance of selfe-denyall," he adds. In fact, the physical demands on such a frail body are shocking to think of. She had "four several abortions or miscariages of the womb" as well as three sons, "and all this in six years, which untimely births (as phisitians told us) exceedingly weakened her strength and wasted her spirits, and was an occasion of her death."[65]

By that time Oliver, as may be hoped, loved her exceedingly. Even at the last she urged her minister husband toward secret prayer and the church; "if it be but too or three words, said she, yet let jerusalem come into your mind." On her deathbed she voiced ecstatic long prayers, which Oliver notes down, and when she died in May of 1661, in the midst of "publick feares and woeful disasters . . . it was the heaviest personal stroak that ever I experienced." So it must have been even heavier than his mother's death. "Methinkes I am but halfe my selfe without her," he writes two months later.[66]

While dying, Elizabeth had talked of Oliver's second marriage and hoped it would be godly. Oliver records that "she mentioned not onely some characters but persons to me, that she apprehended might be suitable to me and helpful to my children." But he does not marry again for six years, while often visiting her father's and now "my father Angier's house." When he does at last begin to think about "a change of my condition," as he puts it hesitantly on April 12, 1667, his mind is suddenly flooded with thoughts of his wife's grave, "where my dearest friend lives." Oliver feels an overwhelming wish to die himself and "be with my spiritual husband." Again we can speculate on his possible guilt at remarrying and his regressive identification with his mother's similar death wishes long before. But more compelling is the simple enormity of grief, even after six years.

The passage, though lengthy, is worth setting down for its powerful mixture of detailed physical setting and mental dissolution:

> As I came homewards all alone upon Blackstone edge, setting myself seriously to meditate I had strange impressions set upon my spirit concerning death and tho I be now thinking of a change of my condition, and tho it be abundantly to my satisfaction yet I had then strange and strong motions rather to be dissolved and go to Cht, I turned upon the edge, looked over Lancashire, and seemed to take an everlasting farewel of Lanc, and upon a deep sense of the vanity of worldly comforts, and the disappointment therin I was indifferent whether ever I should see that place again where my dearest friend lives, and could rather have desired to be with my spiritual husband—oh, it was a sweet season, seldome is my heart in such a frame as then it was.

Heywood plunges here into an extraordinary depth of feeling, at once blissful and terrifying, conventional and personal, and fully Puritan in its contradictory sense of dying into Christ while keeping a clear eye on place, time, and prospects.[67]

Oliver does marry, of course, a month later, and he notes on June 27 that "I am abundantly satisfied in my gracious yokefellow"—whom the diary does not bother to name, except in a genealogical table that mentions "Abigail" in small print. Elizabeth seems even stronger in death than she was in life, though Oliver passes his later years contented, fat, and happy, so far as he chooses to tell.

At the very least, Heywood's diary presents a vivid picture of two women intensely strong in their weakness. It shows in detail how tender mothering complements, even augments, a zeal to bring children to right religion. Although in less detail, Increase Mather's life shows a similar response to what seems to be a more anxious and fearful mother's equally demanding expectations. The intensity of her deathbed wishes recalls that of Heywood's wife. More inscrutably, Katharine Mather seems to have shared with Heywood's mother and the mother of Thomas Shepard a possessive intimacy with death as fear or wish.

Cotton Mather's *Parentator* (1724), in summarizing his father's youth, says that Increase was much closer to his mother than to his father, though Richard Mather was one of the most notable first-generation ministers in New England. Not much is known of Katharine Mather except that she taught Increase to read. She was "a Woman of Uncommon Devotion," with "Importunate Prayers for this her son," Cotton recounts. We learn that Increase was her youngest child, that he was best in his class at school, and that he very much wanted to satisfy his mother's expectations. As Cotton Mather says of Increase's mother, "She sometimes told her Son, while he was yet scarce more than an *Infant*, but very much her *Darling*, That she desired of the Glorious GOD only two Things on his behalf; the one was, The *Grace* to Fear and Love GOD; the other was, the *Learning* that might Accomplish him to do Service for GOD; . . . *Child*, said she, *If* GOD *make thee a Good Christian and a Good Scholar, thou hast all that ever thy Mother Asked for thee.*"[68] No word here of any expectations from his father, who according to a recent biographer was "a trimmer," too adaptable to be strong, and repeatedly buffeted by rejections and humiliations in his ministry.[69] Once again, a weak father is a thread in the stories of intense conversions.

Increase did his best to be a scholar and a Christian, at least after he was fourteen. "Until I was fourteen years old, I had no love to, nor delight in my books," he wrote, even though—or perhaps because—as his son tells us, his mother "mightily Inculcated the Lesson of Diligence upon him." Her death dramatically reinforced her desires. "When he was about Fifteen Years Old, she died Marvellously Triumphing over the *Fear of Death*, which thro *all her Life* she had been Afraid of; . . . On her Death-Bed, she Earnestly Exhorted him, to Resolve upon Serving of CHRIST in the Work of the *Ministry*: and Advised him often to consider on that Promise, *They who turn many to Righteousness, shall shine as the stars forever and ever*: which left a great impression upon him." Obsessed with her "Fear of Death," his mother must often have contrasted death's terror with the immortality of those stars of righteousness. Not surprisingly, Mather's conversion followed hard upon her death, when he was not yet sixteen. "But in the latter end of that year," Mather's own narrative of his life recalls, "God took away my dear mother, who had so often prayed for me. About which time the Lord broke in upon my conscience with very terrible convictions and awakenings. In the months of March & April, and in the latter end of May, 1655, I was in extremity of anguish and horror in my soul."

Increase now fasted, prayed, shut himself up in his father's study alone, and tried to purge himself of his sins. Strangely, he neglected to tell his father of his throes for a long time. He finally put them down in a letter to Richard in Boston. At last, on an election day, he shut himself into John Norton's study and prayed. The words of his prayer

show him speaking with the voice of a dying female, Esther. Cotton
Mather quotes the heart of his father's conversion account.

> So I came before Him with those Words of *Esther, If I Perish, I Perish.*
> *Yet* (I said) *Lord, if it must be so, I am resolved to Perish at the Feet
> of thy Mercy. It is true, I am a Dog, and indeed unworthy of so much
> as a Crumb; I have been a great Sinner; Yet I am resolved, I will not
> Offend any more, but be Thine, and be Thine only, and be Thine
> forever!* And while I was thus Praying and Pleading, those Words of
> CHRIST were darted into my Mind, *Him that cometh unto me I will
> in no wise Cast out:* Which Promise I Pleaded with the Lord. After that,
> I had some *Comfortable Perswasion.*

He has moved from the words of a dying "Esther" to a comforting
father's promise to a son. Resolving not to "Offend any more," he is
assured of being "in no wise Cast out." Saved from his mother's death,
he could at the same time welcome it and join her in the faith of the
fathers. Norton, his own father, and Jonathan Mitchell then helped
Increase through to firm conviction. Now he could truly "be Thine
forever."[70]

Thwarted rebelliousness lurks here and surfaces in Mather's opposition to his father in the politics of the half-way covenant. According to
Robert Middlekauff, "Increase took a hard line—saying in effect that
he would uphold his father's principles, if his father was incapable of
maintaining them." When Richard died in April 1669, and then his
brother Eleazar, Mather felt a sense of desolation and melancholy,
what he called "the hypochondrical affection" that incapacitated him
until March of the next year, when he began to preach again and also
wrote a life of his father. The sickness could have been connected to
"a vague feeling of guilt," Middlekauff suggests. After all, Increase had
left New England for Old England and had been forced to return to
his father's arena, where he had promptly opposed Richard on a crucial
issue.[71]

Yet ambivalence about his mother could be another plausible source
for the son's behavior. It is not hard to imagine his mixed feelings of
love and fear, identification and abandonment, toward the woman who
so zealously asked for his soul and then died. For the rest of his life
Increase tried to lock himself into a minister's calling and his father's
study, overtly to worship his parents' God, and covertly to shut his
father out; overtly to wish for a death that could take him to his mother
again, and covertly perhaps to escape his mother's possessive intensity.[72] Whatever his unconscious fears, his identification with her seems

as patent as Oliver Heywood's with his mother, at least to the extent that he obsessively fulfilled her expectations while obsessively wanting to die for almost the whole of his long adult life.

The contours of these two lives, at least from a speculative distance, resemble Thomas Shepard's in that a minister's calling resolves similar ambivalences at various levels. The lives support my hypothesis that tender zealous mothers and anxious or distant fathers may be one important source for Puritanism's appeal, even in the midst of early New England patriarchy. They also qualify Puritan rhetoric about tender mothers and grave governors. As chapter two tried to show, the self-restraining patriarch may have been in part an idealized image which helped conceal and resolve paternal weaknesses and anxieties. What Puritans took for the mother's tender nurturance may have encompassed her possessive religious expectation for the child as well.

The foregoing stages of love and expectation can be interpreted in terms of the much more theologically intricate childhood stages of Freud, Erikson, and especially Melanie Klein, whose theories of infantile anxiety, rage, and reparation are very suggestive here. I make some motions toward a psychoanalytic frame in the next two chapters. But there is little evidence about early Puritan childhood dynamics other than what has already been sketched. We do not have the least hint of what would be needed to show, for example, how maternal rejection of aggressive infantile behavior led to emotional arrest in the depressive position or the anal-sadistic phase during the first two years.

Possibly the ultimate sources of Puritan fervor lie there, with all the other sources tributaries to its stream. My own sense is that the human mind is more continuously adaptive, given the absence of severe infantile trauma, and that Puritan mothering was "good enough" to resolve the worst traumas described in Kleinian theory. Puritanism is therefore more appropriately studied as a concentration of many conscious and unconscious factors at many levels of child and adult life. What we can more surely say is that Puritan mothering of infants was probably more caring and responsive than mothering in many other faiths at the time.

Fortunately, my argument does not require so much intricacy, either of evidence or theory. It is too bad that we have only records of advice and brief adult memories of fitting the self to faithful patterns, rather than accurate descriptions of child rearing. That fact may finally make depth psychology of individual lives impossible. But we can see the intensity and contradictions in the basic patterns of Puritan parenting, a more manageable, and perhaps more important, task.

Texts and practice indicate that Puritans were neither simply repressive nor simply loving. Their love was highly attentive and took the form of mixed expectations for both themselves and their children. These mixed self-expectations became part of the stages of growth, since children were given more love in the early, mothering years, and subjected to more strict expectations in their later, father-ruled years.

To unearth details of breast-feeding, which probably was not practiced by a majority of Puritan mothers, or clear parental instructions about cleanliness, which characterized neither child rearing nor adult life, is not crucial for my case, because the more essential questions have to do with consistencies and inconsistencies in parental attitudes.[73] And consistent attitudes, much more than specific incidents unless they are searingly traumatic, are what matter, as our own child-rearing books tell us. That Puritans preached and practiced attentive care while condemning brutality, for instance, is much more important than how frequently they used the rod. Their children were recognized and responded to, perhaps the most basic positive ground of identity. Beyond the fundamental level of parental concern, we have sufficient evidence to make some broad conclusions about parental attitudes.

Psychoanalysis, like Puritanism, tends to reduce complex interpersonal feelings to rather rigid inward levels of health and sickness. Its model of oral and anal stages is untestable with the Puritan materials now available. But the more fundamental interpersonal issue, which in some ways psychoanalytic stage models obscure, is the differences between mothering and fathering, and *within* mothering and fathering. These differences help to give the language of Puritanism such a comprehensive and contradictory appeal.

The Puritan family was sending a pervasive mixed signal to its young: feel nourished and valued, yet feel sinful and ashamed. I have rehearsed the evidence at such length because so many others more expert in social history have concluded that patriarchal breaking of the will is the essence of Puritan psychology. The reality—even the reality of Puritan advice—is less simple. Mixed expectations operate on at least six interrelated levels of rhetoric and reality:

1. Mothers were loving even to excess, yet were zealous about "good" responses, at least in religious matters.

2. Children were probably loved quite unashamedly before the age of reason, but then parents were told to check loving feelings. To be loved then meant to become willful.
3. Mothers were supposed to be tender; fathers were supposed to be grave. Most seem to have adhered to their models, in varying degrees.
4. Mothers had charge of the early years; fathers had charge of the later years.
5. Fathers were said to be strong and govern, yet could not be as expressive or "familiar" as mothers. Mothers were said to submit, yet were apt to be stronger in emotions, household love, and even household authority.
6. Fathers were the earthly analogues for God himself. Yet fathers were often anxious, weak, or failing in their own callings.

The levels are rather arbitrarily separated, and too simply put. Any one or two, however, could lead to feelings of ambivalence. More important is how complementary they are, how confusingly rhetoric and reality mix, and how massively the mixed expectations combine to work on the children. A love and hatred for the self turns inward the more threatening love and hatred felt for the sources of mixed expectations. Though not quite the "double bind" hypothesized by Gregory Bateson as a source for schizophrenia, because an unambiguous love is at the bottom of parental attentiveness, the long-range effect was pervasive ambivalence, especially in sons.[74] Ambivalence, not repressed rage, is the emotion that the double language of Puritanism satisfies.

It was clear what men should be doing. Fathers should discipline any excessive mother-love in themselves and their children. To adopt Erikson's psychological terms, fathers should curb the child's basic trust and self-trust, to bring out a sense of guilt, shame, and sin. Being disciplined to obey the father and his greater Father has usually been taken for the whole of Puritanism, without paying attention to the maternal prelude. Yet the advice-book ideal, though reflected in some American child-rearing accounts, is curiously absent from the detailed lives available, especially from the English diaries of Heywood and Josselin. There and elsewhere we find mixed signals within mixed signals, as the relatively consistent and unambiguously mixed expectation of grave governor and tender mother becomes the more confused reality of weak father and strong mother, or emotionally repressed father and warmhearted mother, or anxious father and zealous mother, or distant father and possessive mother, or tender father and near-crazy mother, or any combination of the above, mixed with sudden death and feelings of abandonment.

Beyond particular confusions, however, there was clearly a difference at least of nuance between mothering and fathering. An intensity of her care, mixing love and expectation, balanced an intensity of his restraint, which mixed love and expectation very differently. Out of various emotional dissonances emerges much of the Puritan orientation toward ambivalence, especially in the male child. Just as neither parent was wholly hateful nor wholly lovable, so their language of faith expresses love and hate together, in a frame simplifying feelings about authority and self into pure discipline and pure nurturance. The simplifying polarities of parental images are partial defenses against more mixed realities. Tender mothers and grave governors, in advice books and in the Puritan God, were as much wish as fact.

Never simply repressive, Puritan theology as well as child rearing therefore encouraged a doubleness in male identity, since at no point was such a degree of grave inward distance expected of girls as of older boys. Girls could follow their mothers in their unambiguous emotional calling, weak as it was said to be and circumscribed as it actually was by men. Boys had to change from zealous mother-love to zealous self-control under their father's eye. Theological language mirrors the early nurturing and later discipline in the boy's transition from mother to father, while retaining the mother's religious expectations. If the father was himself ambivalent about controlling his son, all the more reason for unambiguously revering a patriarchal God. To imagine that patriarchal God in mothering similes expresses contradictory inward needs as well as conflicted male roles.

The next chapter develops theoretical aspects of Puritan mixed expectations in more detail. A last comparative note concludes my summary here. With child rearing as with other issues, many psychological aspects are not unique to Puritans but reflect conflicts common to the age as a whole. Puritan literature, whether in guidebooks, poetry, or sermons, is in obvious ways more rigid, defensive, and preachy than the great works of the period. Yet Puritanism was one of the longest lasting and most influential attempts at a comprehensive response to issues expressed more directly in major literary writings.

Stage plays, not family guidebooks, offer the most compelling and complex account of mixed expectations at a time of patriarchal disorder, without the ideal parental types imagined by Puritans as stays against confusion. As chapter one described, men wearing women's clothes on stage horrified Puritans, for whom the affront to biblical and patriarchal self-definition was a symbol of more profound fears. I am suggesting now that the Puritan child was actually confronted by mixed signals about male and female roles. A call for pure and loving patriarchy became more intense as its absence became more evident. Shakespeare's plays are the most complex record of this historical moment. And *Hamlet,* his most problematic play, has remained so central to our culture because it so magnificently enacts the anxieties evolving from patriarchy in decline.

Hamlet's search for the woman in himself, like Puritan fantasies of the breast of God, reflects conflicts between the filial role expected of him and the constancy of heart he strives for, in a world where separation into pure fathers and whores was the easy way to identity and group survival. Surrounded by corrupting and corrupted fathers, Hamlet sees loving women give way to paternal commands, and he himself at last yields to the Ghost, as the Puritan child may have felt his mother's love give way to his father's directives. Unlike the Puritans, Hamlet also sees duplicity and falseness in all the fathers, except perhaps his own, and even there his famous delay indicates unconscious perception, not the unconscious guilt ascribed to him by orthodox Freudian interpretations.

Where Puritans retreat to a language of duty and dependence to secure the identities of both son and father, Hamlet looks to a language of feeling. Yet his self-accusations of "whore" reflect a patriarchal view he cannot escape. Not able to get beyond negative images for the woman in himself, he finally accepts the forced triumph of filial duty over sensitivity to his own heart. His stifling is equivalent to suicide, as the language of the last act shows. Though Puritans looked to theology for identity, their cries about whoredom, like Hamlet's hysterical outbursts to Ophelia about nunneries and painted women, are the outer shell of their horror at what the nurtured, loving, and well-loved soul has been corrupted to.[75]

As the next chapter suggests, obsessive styles and nursing fantasies are contradictory Puritan ways of satisfying contradictory needs. Conversion brings sinful selves to a female receptivity, purified of all feelings except desire for the Father and his Son. Yet the differences between Hamlet's search for the woman in himself and the Puritan's desire to be reborn are immense: integrity beyond obedience; the expressive heart, not the self-disciplined and self-denying intellect;

commitment to love and human friendship, not fantasies of emptiness and group subordination to an invisible father. Hamlet never realizes these possibilities. But in depicting Hamlet's failure, Shakespeare portrays more vividly than any assemblage of Puritan tracts the conflicts descending on fathers and sons after the tender early years.

Chapter Four

Obsessive Dependence

Themes

In seventeenth-century England, as *Hamlet* dramatizes, the role of traditional patriarch was becoming a "false self," an outward response to social expectations denying more complex feelings.[1] Paternal falseness is forced on Hamlet and Ophelia in the play, and more loving and confusing parental self-falsifications were visited on Puritan children. Conscious ambivalence toward oneself became an inward sign of more unconscious ambivalence toward parents. On one hand, varying degrees of anxious or resolute parental discipline helped to intensify childhood feelings of smallness and self-doubt. On the other hand, loving parental attentiveness made children feel very much valued, and parental expectations magnified the importance of the child's soul.

The dualisms and intensities of Puritanism reflect a struggle to manage ambivalence through polarization. Yet the struggle itself is what gives Puritanism its distinctive tone. A conscious dedication to anxiety, as a major defense against recognizing ambivalent feelings, is more pervasive and clear than the ambivalent feelings themselves. Puritans are always on the edge, like Oliver Heywood looking over Lancashire. They are always in the middle, while earnestly proclaiming the absence of a middle. Though framed with polarities, their language looks two ways, to soul and body, heaven and earth at once, with a zealous urgency to make the world and the flesh, if not the devil, conform to God's order. Nothing on earth can remain indifferent to the battle. Even their penchant for similes depends on a faith that worldly relations can express God's truths.

Puritans tried to resolve ambivalences about parental and social authority in a fantasy of dependence. With radical pessimism they opposed this world to God's world, while with radical optimism their language finds eternal spiritual patterns in practical daily facts. They dreamed of being changed into women and babies and of finding in the Great Father a mothering protector. They looked to a theological language of strict patterns yet regressive happiness. Since the command to be reborn is taken from the book of John (1.13, 3.3-7) and the imagery from the Song of Solomon, Peter, and elsewhere in the Bible, the very fact of obedience to God's Word helps to induce rebirth, or at least labor pains. Here again, the struggle is at least as important a testimony of salvation as the final spiritual change.

Enormous Puritan energy went into the rhetorical defense of God's omnipotent purity. With the utmost seriousness they reconceived themselves collectively as virgin daughters to prove their heavenly father's virtue. Yet their exaggerated love for God's omniparental powers does not have to be only false hate, as some psychoanalytic writings imply. A need for a secure identity is more basic than rebellious feelings of self-assertion. Anger and assertiveness need a sense of autonomy, which Freud took for granted even in the drives of babies. His theory has proved to be adultomorphic in that respect. Autonomy comes only gradually, through interpersonal support, especially through parental recognition and acceptance of negative impulses. A sense of coherent identity depends on feeling inwardly secure, and that comes, to oversimplify considerably, from being consistently satisfied and responded to from the first days of life, not being ignored or repressed except when conforming to a parent's needs.

Ambivalence and an inability to tolerate the negative side of ambivalence naturally follow from being intensely loved and intensely molded at the same time, especially when two parents care for the child so differently. How can a child unequivocally resent an attentive father's discipline, even though feeling robbed of a mother's love, when the father's love is crucial to his own social and personal sense of identity? Indeed, Puritan rhetoric of tender mothers and grave governors puts an ideal face on more contradictory, more anxious, and perhaps even more loving parental realities. In many ways ambivalence is not only the child's feelings of love and hate but the inward mirror of the several parental faces turned to the child. The more divergent the faces, the more contradictory the child's sense of himself, and the more fearful unacceptable feelings become with the absence of unambiguous security.

Psychological resolution for Puritans was the opposite of autonomy: loving or anxious submission, with resentment buried in identification and need. To secure feelings of inward coherence, Puritans found a continuous parental response available only in God's language of callings, his special concern for them, his wrath at their faults, and his sheltering "bosom" of forgiveness for repentance. Little of that theology, taken by itself, is distinctively Puritan. As a structure of feeling it has absorbed many different peoples at many different times, though perhaps for some of the same reasons. The particular Puritan note lies in their tone of anxious intensity as they struggle *toward* theological resolution, especially in their awkward, comprehensive, sometimes involuntarily comic language of polarities.

Anxiety and polarity are the two basic defenses against acknowledging ambivalence. Anxiety diffuses an inward fear of one's own rage.[2] Polarity splits love and hate into opposites. What is oddly special about the Puritans is the tendency of their language to rejoin what has been split and make clear what has been diffused, at least in displaced fashion. Grand spiritual abstractions cohabit with the most prosaic daily events. Rigid patterns, unvarying themes, biblical authority, and repetitive imagery frame interchangeable similes of dependence, rebirth, nursing, and ecstatic sex change. Fixed social roles give unambiguous group stability, while personal transformation through conversion gives unambiguous change. Medieval yet modern, radical yet reactionary, Puritans were constantly striving to be centrist, while as humble reformers of the status quo they were constantly striving for the absolute. In every polarity an anxious struggle to couple earth with heaven is a major feature. If all they could be sure of was anxiety, that was to them a profoundly comforting thought.

A strange sense of contradiction hovers between Puritan certitudes. The conversion experience of self-purification leads to two broad and contradictory fantasies, which are the focus of this chapter. What is now known as the obsessive or obsessional character became the basic role model for the faithful: rigid, repetitive, stubborn, work centered, intolerant of ambiguity or play, obedient to an ultimate authority wholly outside themselves. Yet conversion was also, with equally repetitive explicitness, a Family Romance fantasy: a rebirth into the higher family of God as good father and good mother combined. Fluid personal dependence and an obsession with rules and order seem opposed as expressive styles. Yet they join as two sides of a still more basic fantasy: obsessive dependence on God the loving father.

To adopt Freudian terms for a moment, Puritan fantasies of happiness with God show a pervasive orality, offering the milk of the Gospel, while Puritan prescriptions for ideal behavior emphasize anal traits: purity, thrift, discipline, order, meticulous self-accounting, productivity. Though reductive, the Freudian labels are useful to show the

seeming contradiction here between behavior and fantasy. Paradoxically, Puritan faith encouraged both a strict inward and a strict
outward set of controls, felt as stability, and an extraordinarily supple
readiness for fantasy and group mobility. Here as elsewhere, Puritans
relieved inward conflict by splitting frightening ambivalences into
opposites. Both their oral fantasies and their anal behavior hide ambivalence about authority in exaggerated dependence, and mobility was
also a way of avoiding conflict.

Yet ambivalence returns, even in the act of expressing God's will,
since the Word in Puritan hands is as rigidly patterned as its grace is
fluidly imagined. Indeed, at a more conscious level ambivalence seems
almost to have been prized. At no point could emigrating Puritans let
unrestrained anger against Anglican authority lead them toward
separatism, or unrestrained love of God lead them toward claiming a
direct relationship with the Deity. Even saints had to work within a
language of compromise and persuasion, not of tyrannical human certitude. Puritans passionately held that God's Word, publicly preached,
not rebellious deeds or secret faith, could make the whole human
world be reborn in holiness. They believed in reform by example and
instruction. As Thomas Hooker said, "common sense," not "blinde obedience" to any man's will, should lead people to right rules over "things
indifferent."[3] The paradox of the Puritan middle way lay in their hope
of persuading everyone that there was no middle way.

The Puritan language of contradiction also distinguishes their intellectual arguments. They were relentlessly optimistic pessimists. Unlike
Anglicans, they said man was utterly unable to make righteous choices
with reason alone. Unlike Quakers, they said no man could be granted
an "inner light." Puritans were as much in combat with their own
extremes as with conformity. At times their faith seems oxymoronic.
They were extraordinarily self-confident as they lay in the dust of
their depravity. In emptying themselves of pride and lust, Puritans
exalted their anxiety to a kind of holiness and said honest doubts might
be the surest sign of election. As Edmund Morgan has said, "In order
to be sure one must be unsure."[4]

In highlighting the anxious self, Puritans were not simply theologizing contradictory family dynamics. They were also responding to contradictions around them, as their family books tried to resolve confusions in social roles. A stable world view no longer automatically
conferred meaning. The development of spiritual autobiographies in
mid-seventeenth-century England, especially among Puritans, was part
of a longer development toward individuality as we have come to

know it: having to make choices and know one's own mind in a world more complex and less clear than one's fathers had found it. An increasing self-awareness reflected these social pressures. Yet self-awareness provided a defense for Puritans as well. While acknowledging the individual as anxious and alone, their language defined the self as a set pattern, with stages of conversion to God's unchanging meanings.[5] The assumed fit between role and self had become a fearful question, as Hamlet discovers. Puritans answered the question by making the self God's instrument, through rebirth and obsessive dependence. While exalting the anxious self, their theology articulates anxiety as a kind of shared security.

Puritans did not scrimp in developing defenses to allay emotional discomfort, even if one defense was to increase discomfort. Their social defenses secure identity by defining it in terms of fixed social roles, while their psychological defenses encourage remolding the self with a double language of public obsession and private regression. The major psychological defenses focus on the conversion experience. First, conversion encouraged free expression of separation anxiety, shame, and especially guilt as a necessary prelude to obedient union. Second, the expectation of conversion centered the Puritan attempt to remold character into more productive social behavior, along lines that have obsessive characteristics. Third, the private rewards for self-transformation were expressed as a Family Romance fantasy, to be reborn of the pure, omnipotent, nurturing father.

But a strictly Freudian interpretation of Puritan defenses tends to augment patriarchal fantasies, which are only one side of the faith. The previous chapter argues that mixed expectations, more than Freudian or Kleinian stages, are the right context for understanding Puritan feelings. The obsessive defenses, including a vocabulary of cleanliness and anality, have more to do with responses to social authority, fathering, and maternal discipline than with infantile repression at any particular age. The oral fantasies express a sense of lost mothering more than specific unconscious memories of the breast. More broadly, self-transformations must be seen as responses to social expectation and social conflict.

Here Puritans developed several major group defenses to manage feelings about social tensions as well as more unconscious inward tensions. Foremost was the sense of group mission. Perhaps more enduring has been the sense of town itself, felt almost tribally in New England. Puritans were explicit in restricting expansion away from town centers. Third, Puritanism was a family experience. People worked in families, emigrated as families, took notes on sermons for later family discussion. The family was one of the most basic metaphors for governance both spiritual and secular. Where Anglicans tended to make state authority the justification for family patriarchy, Puritans tended to make family mutuality the model for state governance. It was even the model for the well-regulated soul.

Fourth, at least for the first generation of Puritans in New England, the preacher fulfilled the group role of moral anchor, spiritual guide, and emotional comforter. His sermons were the social highlight of each week and often gave meaning to the town's achievements or backslidings. "The main psychotherapists were the clergy," Keith Thomas has said of the age as a whole.[6] Finally, just as the family became a political instrument of emotional governance and social meaning, so the idea of calling took on political importance in a more diffused sense. It urged the paradox of voluntary submission to a fixed social role, the belief in a divine father who calls, and the expectation that those who accept the call to work may have been elected to more than work, by a Father more sure than any father on earth.

Since these psychological and social defenses are extensively discussed in Puritan studies, some will only be touched on here. My aim is to suggest connections between the conversion experience, obsessive behavior, and Family Romance dynamics. The chapter also looks at some broader connections with the social management of emotion, especially the Puritan move to New England.

A word on words: the term "defense" should not be taken in a negative sense. It signifies adaptive transformation. It is not a one-way street, a blocking of an inward attack, despite Freud's inheritance of the term from such a model, but a reordering of feelings to orient the self toward group expression. There is always some cost in personal repression of unacceptable feelings. The reward is in shared articulation, mutual acknowledgment of mastery as well as partial acknowledgement of need, and a shared feeling of identity.[7]

Obsessive Style and Family Romance

The relationship between Puritanism, obsession, and anality is clearer in theory and imagery than in behavior or child-rearing practices. Contemporary psychoanalytic theory connects what it calls the anal character to obsessional behavior and finds anal dynamics in adult Family Romance fantasies. Puritan theory correspondingly urges social virtues associated with the anal character: thrift, productivity, accumulation, a concern with time and money, a horror of waste, habits of regularity and discipline.[8] Puritans characteristically describe sin with imagery of filth, most powerfully in the poetry of Edward Taylor, who often uses images of dung and excrement to depict his loathsome nature. Equally pervasive oral imagery of food and drink, or imagery of clean clothing, rewards Taylor's soul at the end of many of his poetic meditations. From being "clogged" or "fouled" with desires, he becomes empty, cleansed, clad with "holy robes," and open to the milk of God's promise. Taylor's methodical concern to meditate every six weeks on self-transformation is thoroughly Puritan, and part of the anal character as well, as is the compulsion to repeat fecal imagery, if we follow Freudian theory.

Obsessional states, in various psychoanalytic theories, are unconscious responses to conflicts at the anal stage. Not all obsessionals are "obstinate, orderly, perfectionist, overly punctual, meticulous, parsimonious, and frugal," one recent text finds. But these symptoms tend to characterize the neurosis. "Precisianists," we recall, was the other name for Puritans. Obsessives tend to suppress anger against parents or displace it, often against the self. They tend to have a "raging, tyrannical super-ego," an early psychoanalytic text observes. Feelings are split into exaggerated love for an authority figure and repressed hate, repressed because of the enormous fear of aggressive feelings toward those whose love is all-important. There is also great dread of rejection and abandonment.[9]

The real threat is unacknowledged ambivalence. Because the hate side of ambivalence is so fearful, the hate becomes terrifyingly magnified into omnipotent, apocalyptic destructiveness that must be caged at all costs. Obsessional states are linked with depression and paranoia, but overtly ambivalence is avoided, like ambiguity and often feeling itself, through meticulous precision in work and exasperating repetition compulsions over trivialities. Obsessives tend to be intolerant, unable to accept bad qualities or imperfections, authoritarian even as they seek authority. They seek in repetitive daily rituals to ward off inward dangers, especially guilt and anger, and perhaps to eliminate the onrush of mortality as well.[10]

Not, in short, a happy state, though sometimes a creative one. To follow psychoanalytic language more precisely, in obsessional disorders "the regression of drives is to the anal sadistic level," where there is "increased ambivalence of object relationships" and "bisexual qualities in the drives." The tyrannical superego often leads to religious preoccupations, which are said to reflect the anal stage. "The common concern of obsessional patients with aggressiveness, hostility, uncleanliness, sex and religion are consistent with the anal sadistic idiom and the idea of a conscience or superego fighting against the unwanted drives."[11] Other psychoanalytic studies have connected conversion experiences more generally to the suppression of anger and aggressiveness.[12]

Freud's own view of obsessional neurosis comes to us in detail through his studies of the Rat Man and Dr. Schreber. The Rat Man, who imagined rats boring into an anus, overtly loved his father and could not recall any hostile feelings. Yet Freud discovered unconscious connections between rats, money, and anal erotism, with an even deeper connection between rats and children. The Rat Man's fantasy reversed a wish to give birth, and when Freud made that interpretation the rat delusion stopped. The basic obsessional conflict, Freud concluded, was between the son's desires and the father's punishment, especially the punishment of masturbation. More generally, obsessive patients have repressed infantile hatred after splitting the feeling off from love, so that love seems to be the only feeling. The inhibition of real emotion leads to compulsive doubt and indecisiveness, Freud noted, and therefore to an intellectual focus on the chief human objects of doubt: "paternity, length of life, life after death, and memory." Obsessional acts, though perhaps beginning in "constitutional" causes, are finally an approximation of masturbatory acts prohibited by the father.[13]

Freud's theory has obvious limits, notably in his one-sided emphasis on the father's punishment of autoerotic sexuality. But his more general observations about the splitting and repression of infantile anger are useful, even though he assumes here—as in so many other cases—that the causes are finally intrapsychic, not interpersonal. He goes so far as to praise the Rat Man's father as being "a most excellent man." For Dr. Schreber Freud posits the same fine upstanding father, but sees different and more Puritan obsessional symptoms in the patient: female fantasies of being the bride of God, impelled by homosexual desires for his father. A paranoid defense of "I hate him because he persecutes me" reverses the homosexual wish, expressed in fantasies of apocalypse or of being penetrated by the rays of God as sunlight, nerve fibers, and sperm.

Morton Schatzman has discovered the interpersonal sources for what Freud calls an intrapsychic "father complex." Dr. Schreber's father had written a child-care book that shows in ghastly detail what tortures he had put his little boy through from the child's sixth month: straitjackets, hot and cold water, and the like. Dr. Schreber's imagery of rays and hot-cold sensations unwittingly mirrors his infantile treatment.[14] Nevertheless, even when allowances are made for Freud's idealized portraits of his patients' fathers, the fact remains that obsessional neuroses can reflect infantile internalization of patriarchal repression.

Psychoanalytic studies of Puritanism tend to stop right there. Puritanism is a compulsion neurosis to master fear, Oscar Pfister concludes. For Heije Faber it is, like capitalism, part of the anal phase, with no oral feelings of oneness, or—Pfister again—an "atrophy" of the feminine. What remains are only feelings of control and detachment before a Sovereign Father. Lloyd Warner writes with more impassioned insensitivity of Puritanism as a purely "masculine" religion, an unfortunate onslaught of ascetic rational individualism against the "nonlogical" and feminine species symbols of Catholicism.[15]

The fundamental problem with these spinoffs from Freudian theory, aside from their unquestioned acceptance of masculine and feminine stereotypes, is the assumption of autonomy in infant emotions. Post-Freudian studies of obsession, especially those of Melanie Klein and Harry Stack Sullivan, have gone beyond Freud's intrapsychic attack-defense model to describe the interpersonal needs and vulnerabilities that can block the self's formation. Though Sullivan and Klein differ, they share a sense that obsessional feelings begin not simply with the father's discipline, but with earlier responses to a mother who is at once loving, demanding, and rejecting. Her seemingly contradictory behavior and feelings can become more part of the self than the infant's own impulses.

Klein's major psychoanalytic discovery is the pre-Oedipal superego. It can start to be "introjected" as early as six months, with the first splitting of ambivalence into the fantasy of a "good mother" and a "bad mother." The earlier superego is much more cruel and terrifying than the later internalization of the father. It serves to arouse the baby's anxiety over his destructive impulses. In normal development it slowly lessens from awesome anxiety over inward sadism to a more moral and controllable guilt after the anal-sadistic phase, though the child can still be overwhelmed during that phase by desires "to destroy the inside of the mother's body."

Klein's stages elaborate Freud's oral and anal stages in ways that may seem rather fanciful, even to analysts.[16] However, we do not have to adopt Klein's formula of month by month stages to recognize her insight into infantile feelings of fearful, omnipotent rage. She has found a language to show how obsessive behavior can desperately import a condemning external authority to control bad feelings against a parent needed even more desperately, for a sense of self as well as nurturance. Her theory shows how an obsession with cleanliness does not necessarily have to do with toilet training, nor is it simply a repression of intrapsychic impulses. More profoundly, it involves a displacement of interpersonal rage and need into self-censure, self-purification, and dependence.

Harry Stack Sullivan is less concerned with delineating specific interpersonal family sources and stages. Perhaps for that reason he is more eloquent about the broad feelings of vulnerability to which obsessional behavior speaks. For Sullivan, obsessional states are "obscure power operations directed to the maintenance of control over everything that happens." They begin in "a very early, if not a lifelong, condition of profound insecurity" within people who have been given "an abiding contempt for themselves," usually expressed as an abiding contempt for others. Obsessives have a "quiet grandeur," he says, with "quietly omniscient and omnipotent" or even magical fantasies of being in control. Finding it very hard to admit rage, they are riddled with "oughts" and take out their buried feelings on their own bodies. The "tense belly" so characteristic of obsessionals comes because they "swallow resentment." They can't even express anger in fantasy or dreams. They bury it in their stomach. "One finds in a great many of the more severe obsessional people, as we call them in the vernacular, a great degree of what they call hatred, but what actually, on more close scrutiny, proves to be their shocking vulnerability to almost anybody with whom they are integrated. And the obsessional substitutions which make up such conspicuous and troublesome aspects of their lives are simply all-encompassing attenuations of contact which protect them from their abnormal vulnerability to anxiety." Therefore, Sullivan concludes, obsessional substitutions are only "an outstanding instance of what goes on in the self-system in order to keep something utterly excluded from awareness, so that there is no possibility of its eruption into awareness."[17]

Vulnerability, even more than feelings of rage, is at rock bottom. Vulnerability is what makes rage impossible to tolerate. And vulnerability takes us closer to Puritanism than a one-to-one matching of obsessive characteristics to Puritan theory or practice. It is misleading to see Puritans as only obsessive, or to explain obsessiveness with some variant of anality alone. Both are reductive labels that minimize unconscious ambivalence about authority in weak, partially formed selves which are striving to bring authority into the heart as self-security as well as self-censure.

David Shapiro describes the self-organizing functions of the obsessive style and suggests a persuasive general explanation of its genesis. His *Neurotic Styles* (1965) portrays what Shapiro calls the "obsessive-compulsive style" as a "tension-organizing system," structuring and stabilizing one's sense of self. Though it has many negative characteristics, we should think of the style not just as defensive but as actively organizing the self. In this style, he posits, "affective experience as a whole shrinks . . . life pivots around work activity and certain sorts of subjective experience associated with it." Shapiro sums up the familiar traits: inflexible, rigid, narrowly focused on detail, excessively organized, deliberate, preoccupied with "should," stubborn, concerned with willpower, locked into a social role not as self-actualization but as "a general directive for behavior."

It would be hard to miss parallels with Puritan directives. Overt Puritan hostility to art can be interpreted as part of a broader fear of flexibility and feeling, resolved by the fantasy of paternal discipline opposed to whorish lusts. More mechanical than spontaneous, anxious without rules and even with rules, Puritans search for dogma even as they are obsessed with doubt—all qualities of the obsessive style. As Shapiro says, "Both doubt and dogma rely on the narrowed . . . style of thinking and apprehension of the world characteristic of the obsessive-compulsive." Other styles, especially hysteria, are more directly related to repression. The obsessive-compulsive style comprehensively manages tensions to enable one to survive in a threatening world.[18]

Shapiro's book is descriptive, not explanatory. More recently he has suggested two levels of possible causation.[19] On the surface, obsessions satisfy the self by reducing tension and allaying fears, often at the cost of negating new experience. More fundamentally, obsessions can arise from any number of overdetermined situations. Often the style begins as a response to an autocratic parent. It can also be a response to autocratic authority of any kind—a school system, say—or to prolonged social harassment or economic difficulties. It can even be a response to objective weakness: premature birth or a frail body. The crucial factor, as Sullivan finds, is a feeling of vulnerability. The self needs some aspect of the autocratic authority that is inducing feelings of inferiority.

The more general cause, therefore, is a feeling of smallness in the face of superiority. Freud's Dr. Schreber is the classic case of obsessional neurosis whose genesis lies in the son's repression of rage against repressive patriarchal intrusions. Martin Luther, as Erikson shows, is another whose life reflects all the usual obsessive and anal traits, especially a suppression of rage against his brutal father and a preoccupation with dirt and cleanliness. Often beaten by his father, Luther was made to feel "like some sort of criminal" and saw both God and Christ as wrathful masculine judges of his soul. His mother plays almost no role that Erikson can detect.[20]

Puritans, however, are *not* Dr. Schrebers or Martin Luthers. Nor are they Ben Jonsons or Jonathan Swifts. They have neither the dynamics nor the theological resolutions of a wrathful father-God, nor do they have a predominance of secular sarcasm. Puritan obsessive defenses begin in ambivalence, but in complicated ways that have more to do with need than wrath. Mixed expectations, not brutal repressiveness, are at the source of their fervor. Their energy is optimistic, not negating. Not until the second generation in New England does there develop a more classically obsessive style of bitter ritual accusation. Like the repetition that gives pleasure in so many childhood games, Puritans used the obsessive style—often playfully—as a way of mastering a threatening new world that lacked both outward and inward clarity.[21]

My long theoretical road has circled back to overdetermination, and perhaps to some glimpses of common sense. The feeling of smallness was complicated for Puritans by contrary feelings of being loved and important. Some of the Puritan contradictions follow from their contradictory situation. They were loved far more than classic obsessives seem to be, and their obsessive style is more an energizing wish for structure, authority, and group cohesion than a crippling self-imprisonment. But in several respects their lives, like their families, intensified feelings of vulnerability, and social causes abetted a sense of smallness. As Erikson says of Luther, he solved for others what he could not solve for himself alone, in finding a universal language for his patienthood.

Like Luther, Puritanism comes at a time of expansion, invention, and reckless personal risks in the midst of quickening social change. "In each careless period," Erikson eloquently summarizes, "latent panic only waits for catastrophe . . . to cause a shrinkage in the world image, a kind of chill attacking the sense of identity of large masses."[22] The need to fix one's identity in the language of external authority is a response to social and economic tensions as well as to family dynamics. The obsessive style is very rare in underdeveloped countries.

It usually occurs today among upper- and middle-class patients in advanced industrial countries.[23] It has been correlated, at least in the broad frame of Weber's Protestant ethic, with similar social conditions in developing Japan—"protracted discrepancies between orthodox doctrine and practical accommodations, giving rise to moral tokenism on one hand and moral rigorism on the other."[24]

The overriding result, from whatever variety of psychological and social factors, is always a compulsive rigidity, which manages feelings of smallness by partially identifying with whatever induces those feelings. The weak self becomes an "it," whose desires can be disowned or expressed as negatives, while a new sense of power can be felt in condemning the self with the voice of an internalized superior. That voice is not necessarily the same as a Freudian superego, because it is not necessarily a parent's. But it has the same effect of organizing inward energy while stabilizing identity.

What remains important and valid about psychoanalytic theory is the multiplicity of childhood causes and defenses for a fixed feeling of smallness. Puritanism was not the product of strong patriarchs breaking the child's will, at least at the start. It was a complex response of seeming rigidity to the many forces in England, familial and social, that magnified authority while also bringing authority into anxious, loving, or zealous contradiction with itself. Many aspects of English society encouraged a simplifying response of self-condemnation with the inward voice of an infinitely powerful God.

———•———

Yet the obsessive style is not enough to explain the vigor of Puritanism. Connections between obsessional behavior, anality, suppressed rage against authority, and vulnerability show only one side of Puritan language, which thrives on anxiety and love as well as self-control and accusation. The faith also encouraged regressive fantasies of the soul's union with God. If nurturing mothers and disciplining fathers seemed opposed on earth, or fantasized as an idealized polarity, they were joined in God's multiple functions. God was the pure father controlling a pure mother. A Family Romance fantasy of being reborn of higher parents is the ecstatic private wish expressed in many Puritan writings —much more as wish than fact, as more scrupulous ministers such as Thomas Shepard admitted in their diaries—while in public they struggled to conform to the obsessive pattern, which was also for many of them more wish than fact.

Nothing came naturally to Puritans. Not rebirth, not even obsession. Their wish was for everything to come from God, while they worked for everything as hard as they could. What seems illogical to us was so satisfying to them, because the paradox mirrored the two sides of Puritanism's appeal: obsessive styles and nursing fantasies, joined as obsessive dependence. They were always prescribing patterns for themselves and each other, even down to the names they gave their children: More Fruit, Faint Not, The Lord Is Near, Joy Again, More Trials, Sufficient, and of course Increase, as well as the panoply of biblical prototypes. Their forms, themes, and imagery stayed astonishingly constant for over a hundred years. Yet within the fixed expectations, a rich biblical language of rebirth came more easily to them in public than regression comes today in some private psychoanalytic sessions.

The Family Romance is not just a Puritan fantasy. Many fairy tales speak to the wish to be reborn of superior parents in the story of a peasant child who turns out to be the child of royalty. As Freud summarizes the wish in his essay on "Family Romances": "Indeed the whole effort at replacing the real father by a superior one is only an expression of the child's longing for the happy, vanished days when his father seemed to him the noblest and strongest of men and his mother the dearest and loveliest of women. He is turning away from the father whom he knows today to the father in whom he believed in the earlier years of his childhood; and his phantasy is no more than the expression of a regret that those happy days have gone." More recently, Phyllis Greenacre has applied the fantasy to artistic life and found dynamics more basic than "regret" for a noble father now gone. Family Romance fantasies, she writes, show "a marked degree of ambivalence to the parents, especially due to grossly unresolved oedipal problems. This ambivalence seems reinforced by the ambivalence of the anal period to which good and bad, applied to the self and to the parents, appear like black and white twins in so many relationships." A still more recent study suggests that Family Romance fantasies regulate feelings of self-esteem by transforming shame and humiliation into grandiose ambitions.[25]

Thus many levels of nurturance and discipline, of basic trust and mothering yet of profound ambivalence to authority, find expression in the Puritan faith. What Greenacre calls "the tendency to ambivalence and the splitting of images into good and bad" surface in the Puritan concern for polarities. Their translational effort to be reborn in the imagined family of the Godhead gave God the powers of both father and mother and Christ the image of both son and bridegroom, with the self transformed into a female receptacle for oral and sexual grace. Faith was often expressed with interchangeable imagery of womb-union, nursing, fathering, and female receptivity to insemination, as ministers spoke of helping to give God's seed or milk to contrite hearts.

The more constant fantasy shaping such varied imagery is of God as the one true parent. "We have had our Earthly Fathers," said Samuel Willard, "but they are not the Objects of our Religious Prayers, but God only." We must therefore be "leaning on God's Hand" at every moment. John Norton gave the Family Romance an obsessively precise biblical formulation:

> *Isaac* born of *Sarah* ninety years of age, with whom it now had long ceased to be after the manner of women, *Gen.* 18.11. her womb was dead in respect of conception, *Rom.* 4.19. so as no one would have said that *Sarah* should give children suck, *Gen.* 21.7. *Isaac* (I say) thus born of this *Sarah*, was a Type of the Regeneration and Conversion of the Elect. *Gal.* 4.28,29. As therefore the birth of *Isaac* was not by the strength of Nature, like *Ishmaels* of *Hagar*, but by virtue of the Promise, after a supernatural manner, upon sensibleness of barrenness and impotency to such a birth foregoing thereunto.

Thomas Hooker put the Puritan Family Romance more simply. "We are alive," he said, "as a child taken out of one family and translated into another, even so we are taken out of the houshold of Sathan, and inserted into the family of God; yea into the mysticall body of *Christ.*" In the Puritan version of rebirth, the lost nurturance of a caring mother is translated into the father's strength, to be given back through Christ as bridegroom and ministers or the Bible as breasts of God's milk for his family of saints. The sermon was the major forum for sharing that fantasy. As Hooker puts it in *The Soules Humiliation,* "And though thy father and mother cast thee out of doores, and thy husband tumble thee out of his bed, yet if thou be truly humbled, Christ will be instead of father, and husband, and all comforts to thee. God hath but two thrones, and the humble heart is one."[26] The Puritan dream of being reborn in dependence both contradicts and complements the obsessive style.

———————————•—•———————————

We have come too far on theory rather than evidence. As Freud says of his speculations about Jewish monotheism, it "seems like a dancer balancing on one toe."[27] Advanced psychological speculations about Puritanism can fly in advance of their data, especially since Puritan children had no anal period of cleanliness training, and most babies may have been breast-fed by nurses instead of their mothers, at least in England.

Yet the essentials can be confirmed by what evidence we have. Whatever the source, whether in threats to class boundaries, male and female roles, or family authority, there was obviously conflict with traditional modes of deference in seventeenth-century England. Anxiety and feelings of smallness were also prevalent, especially in the market towns. There were confused, confusing, loving, and demanding mixed expectations in child rearing, both between and within stages. Ambivalent intensities of various kinds, conscious and unconscious, are more characteristic of the minority of Puritan households, as of Puritan prose, than of the more indifferent non-Puritan majority. In retrospect we can see the beginnings of the long shift from the patriarchal family to the postindustrial split in the middle sort, now the middle class, between matriarchal child rearing and male power in the world of work. These were some of the discontents to which Puritanism was such a conflicted first response.

We do not need to reduce nursing fantasies to the lost breast. In fact, that denies the broader associations to mothering, dependence, and tender feelings, even to the self-interchange felt with a tender mother and a tender God. One paradox of our language today is that our nervous titillation at the word "breast" reflects a hypersexualization of its mothering functions. Up to the eighteenth century women could walk about with breasts exposed, even in high society. For Puritans the breast was a natural and common expression of tender mothering, not of voyeuristic sexuality.

Similarly, reducing anal vocabulary to a stage of toilet training denies the whole social range of reference for fecal imagery in that unclean, disordered age. To us "shit" means excretion in the privacy of the bathroom, and more unconscious conformity to parental expectations. Its compartmentalization in a childhood stage is part of a larger set of social expectations having to do with compartmentalized behavior as well as cleanliness. We use the word as a magical invective, to shock, dismiss, or expel anger. For England in the seventeenth century, "dung," "excrement," "pollution," and "befoul" were words meant to express common worldly states, not secrets. They had much more pervasive daily connotations. To locate repression at a particular time is less crucial than to see how Puritan language clarifies mixed feelings. The effort requires a social as well as a psychological interpretation.

Puritanism was a thoroughgoing set of controls, psychological and social, on the ambivalent and ambitious self. Wit in preaching, self-exhibition in the theater, gaudy robes, and Anglican ceremonies aroused visceral disgust in the faithful, to whom any display of man's merits was "high presumption" against God. But Puritanism was an expressive set of transformations as well. To be reborn in godly community, not to erect oneself, was happiness, and Puritans never held back in subjecting erring pride to communal restraint. In New England the state enforced church attendance; it found the hearing of the Word conducive not only to faith but as the laws of Massachusetts said, "also to civill obedience & allegiance unto magistracy." Family disputes were often resolved in public before the congregation, and confessions were encouraged as well (e.g., Samuel Sewall's statement of guilt for the Salem witch trials), as proper ways of resolving conflicts, maintaining discipline, and stabilizing society.[28] But there were extravagant dreams of union attending group restraint. Even the few rituals peculiar to Puritanism, like the Sabbath, had more to do with group affirmation than individual display. It is easy to misinterpret Puritanism as a first manifestation of individualism, in which solitary pilgrims confront their God. Yet it was primarily a group phenomenon, especially in New England. Controls were only the outward side of a collective feeling of mastery, though our more individualistic age has naturally emphasized Puritan repression of the individual. The rest of this chapter tries to show how much more was satisfied by the idea of group translation.

Reborn of the Father

> Of his own will begat he us with the word of truth.
> James 1:18[29]

To acknowledge one's essential sinfulness and God's embracing power was the first step toward being reborn. Chapter five looks more closely at the Puritan language of sin. This section examines the language used to express three key elements of the Puritan Family Romance: God, Christ, and grace, with God the ground of all. Associations are drawn more from New England preachers, since in New England fantasy had more scope. I should add, however, that New England preachers tend to emphasize collective rewards and group identity more than their English counterparts, who are more taken with the idea of solitary pilgrims. As with Anglican preaching, any one image or theme can be found in any given preacher. But there is a relatively greater emphasis, especially in New England, on self-transformation into the purified body of the saints as bride of Christ. Anglicans also preached the necessity to be reborn of God. But their language tends neither to develop stages nor to repeat basic similes within a fixed, comprehensive frame.

"God alone is an happifying object," said Samuel Willard in a 1694 lecture in Boston. Puritan ministers never tired of reiterating that the essence of this "happifying object" was God's power, his order, and his transcendent fatherhood. "The word *Father*," Richard Sibbes declared, "is an epitome of the whole gospel." "Look as it is with a father," Thomas Shepard begins many similes to describe God's care. Shepard characteristically finds God's "deep and frequent desertions" to be more terrifying than wrath and often uses the analogy of parents and children to describe man's state. "Parents that have had rude children have turned them out of doors; they themselves have sent them clothes and money out of pity, but themselves have not been seen, that they might seek for a father's house at last. So when God is angry." John Cotton finds the relation of God to the church like that of a father and virgin daughter: each has powers, God of guidance and the daughter of choice.[30]

Though God can be a wrathful father, he is always just, never arbitrary. "God deals with Man in a way of *Precepts, Promises*, & *Threatnings*, which is a *Moral* Way," says Willard. When Shepard expresses his sense of God's presence more privately, in his diary, his words vividly evoke God as a caring parent who has rescued him from trauma with caressing hands. "Let us carry our selves to the Father," writes Peter Bulkeley, "as children in feare of him, with faith depending upon him, walke before him in child-like obedience." As Thomas Hooker divided the Godhead, "God is the father of all the family in heaven and earth. Christ the Head and Redeemer, the holy Ghost the comforter."[31]

Omnipotence is a major aspect of God as divine father. Light, especially sunlight, and streams, oceans, or fountains are the two most frequent image patterns used to convey his omnipresent energies. As John Norton argued, "for love is nothing else but a reverberation or beating back of Gods beam upon himself, or a return of duty in the sense of mercy." "When a master gives light to his servants," Richard Mather reasoned, "and they do no good therewith, but abuse it to cards, dice, drinking, drunkenness & c.: it is just if he come and take away the light from them, and so they be left in darkness."[32] In his *Farewell Exhortation* (1653) Mather made the simile more extended. "If the Sun should depart out of the world there would be nothing left but dreadfull darkness upon all the Creation, all light being now placed in the Sun: and if the fountain be dryed up or stopped, all the streames must needs fail. In like sort take away the injoyment of God from any soul, and all that is left must needs be nothing worth, but even a lump of vanity & evill." That "lump" of worldliness has a fecal quality made abundantly explicit by other ministers. "As the *Sun* is not defiled by shining upon the most Dirty stinking Places, tho' they Stink the more for it's shining upon them," said Willard, "so God is then *most Holy*, when He is giving of Men up to *Sin*." Sin can be redeemed only by opening oneself to the sluice gates of the divine stream. As Willard observed, "How then should this eggshell comprehend the Ocean?"[33]

Puritan intimacy with God was expressed in more broadly masculine ways as well. As Thomas Hooker said in *The Saints Guide* (1645), "God deales like a Wrastler, first catches hold then comes in, and at last throwes a man upon his back makes him yeeld and confesse, I am the man." Elsewhere, in *The Soules Vocation,* he makes God even more down to earth: "The Brewer he tumbles the barrell of beere and roules it, but [it is] the earth that beares it; so whatsoever trouble is in thy eare, roule it upon the Lord"[34] Hooker often speaks of God in imagery from a broad range of workaday vocations. God is a farmer, an axeman, a captain. Though the more conventional marriage analogy is with Christ as husband, Shepard occasionally makes God a husband as well: "God . . . is like a jealous husband, can bear with many weaknesses, but will have the whole heart." Every male role, both public and intimate, was part of God's protean power, especially those roles that could be similes for God's powers of regularity and authority. For John Norton, citing Romans 9.21–23, "God is that only absolute Potter, having power to dispose of one vessell unto wrath, and of another unto mercy." As Willard said, "God is a God of Order, and not of Confusion."[35]

Yet Cotton and Shepard also stressed God's capacity for maternal shelter and family solace. Dependence is a universal theme. But Shepard and Cotton express dependence in feminine images. Especially in

Shepard's writings, God's powers are to give rebirth and nourishment or to cast out and abandon, more than to thrust, dominate, rage, and destroy. Once the cosmic father's authority is accepted unquestioningly, and once one's lust and pride are overcome, God's omnipotence is felt not as fearful aggression but as blissful union. Aggression is reserved for those who are not saved. God will "wrap thee up in everlasting embracings," said Shepard, who imagined heaven as a place where "there is nothing but a God to suck in, and breathe out, and live unto."[36]

Here is one of many Cotton similes for God's mothering: "Women, if they were not Mothers, would not take such homely offices up, as to cleanse their Children from their filth; why if God were not of the like affection to us, hee would not cleanse us from our filthiness, . . . it is with us as it is with young Infants that would lye in their defilements, if their Mothers did not make them clean, and so would wee even wallow in the defilements of sin, if God did not cleanse us, therefore admire Gods love and mercy towards us." Peter Bulkeley's *Gospel-Covenant* attributes the same office to a nurse: "We are like little babes, who can defile themselves, but would lie in their uncleannes for ever, should not the nurse wash and cleanse them." Shepard, too, notes how natural it is for men to be infants and God to succor in a motherly way: "for a God so pitiful as many times to help without cries, more than a mother with tender bowels."[37] Edward Taylor's poems stress the food and drink of the Lord's Supper, and Cotton draws God's shelter very beautifully in one of his own poems, "A thankful Acknowledgment of God's Providence," reprinted by John Norton after Cotton's death. His poem begins:

> In mothers womb thy fingers did me make,
> And from the womb thou didst me safely take:
> From breast thou hast me nurst my life throughout,
> That I may say I never wanted ought.
>
> In all my meals my table thou hast spread,
> In all my lodgings thou hast [made my] bed:
> Thou hast me clad with changes of array,
> And chang'd my house for better far away.[38]

Here God dispenses a mother's care with fatherly control.

There is an intense quality of wish rather than fear in the Puritan call for a father who can make the sinner feel disgusted with himself, then inseminated as a woman or reborn as a coddled baby. Freudians might say it is a wish-fulfillment defense against castration anxiety and guilt for parricidal impulses. To transform oneself into a virgin, and God into a mother who feeds and tucks in, removes the threat of castration, and changes a desire to get rid of the father into a fantasy of oral dependence on the mother. There is some truth to this interpretation in the age of the patriarchal rod. If one takes further what John Demos has suggested in *A Little Commonwealth,* the practice of Puritan child rearing made the experience of separating from the mother so magnified, the confrontation with the father so awesome, that Puritan theology offered fantasies overtly reversing these feelings, denigrating women and magnifying the father's image, while unconsciously putting the mother in the father's place.

Yet as we have seen, many Puritan lives do not suggest the presence of strong patriarchs. As Freud discovered of female hysterics, tales of being raped by one's father can be wishes, not facts. So here. To dream of a pure father who would tell them what lumps of dung they were partly reflected the gulf between mothering and fathering in English Puritan society. But it also shows a wish for strong and secure parent images. The mixed signals of the Puritan's world were mirrored in the wish for a father who could control the mother's gratifications, while his powers are reimagined in maternal terms of benign dependence rather than repressive rule. Puritans looked to women for an image of humility, feeling, and care. Even staid and sober John Winthrop spends a page in A *Model of Christian Charity* empathizing with Eve as a way of illustrating God's command that everyone "might have need of another." To be "knitt together" beyond selfishness was Winthrop's plea.[39] Female and maternal imagery was just as important as a language of patriarchal authority in persuading Puritans toward group cohesion under God's caring eye.

The idea of the saint's progress from awe at God's wrathful power to union with God's fluids also compresses a realistic sense of the levels of authority in the Puritan child's life. The Puritan God is not a fantasy of bisexuality, since the father's power remains the basis of identity and feeling. But communication from heavenly father to saint, via the Holy Ghost, or Christ, or the Word, or the minister, or communion, is expressed in oral and maternal terms, just as the Puritan child was allowed greater intimacy with his mother while told to feel greater awe of his father. Thomas Hooker makes it clear in the preface to A *survey of the summe of Church-Discipline* (1648) that "truth is the Daughter of time. . . . Only as in other births, so here, the barrennesse and fruitfullnesse of severalages, depend meerly upon Gods good pleasure;

who opens and shuts the womb of truth from bearing, as he sees fit, according to the counsell of his own will." While noting that "earthly minds can not understand heavenly language," Shepard suffuses his attempts to share God's fullness with imagery of tasting, drinking, and eating. "Here is all light in this Sun, and all water in this Sea," he writes in *The Sincere Convert* (1641), "out of whom as out of a Christal fountain, thou shalt drink down all the refined sweetness of all creatures in Heaven and Earth, for ever and ever."[40]

What is most impressive about the Puritan fantasy of God is the range of emotions, from fear to strength to dependence, that it encourages, within a frame transforming many anxieties—about powerlessness, aloneness, sexuality, deprivation, anger, and ambivalence—into gratifications. God was truly the wished-for ground of being. By submitting to the father's power and the mother's love, believers unite with both and discover God similarly united. Father's authority is secured, while remembered infantile tendernesses are resurrected. "God" thus becomes a metaphor for the satisfaction of personal needs and community bonds, while the specter of lonely isolation and inadequacy, or sinful wrath, is driven from the home of the saints to be visited on the unconverted.

As the title of Jonathan Edwards's first major sermon proclaimed, God is "glorified in man's dependency." The idea facilitated an interdependent subordination of self to community. What seems like a legalistic determinism of categories to an outsider was more like a nurturing womb, grounded by providental paternal power, to those who believed.

Once man is ready for conversion, Christ is the agent for God's grace. "Our comfort lyes not in the excellencie of our duties," wrote Peter Bulkeley, "but in our free acceptance of Christ." As Shepard said in his diary for March 22, 1643, "by my vileness I may understand Christ's glory. As I am void of grace, he is full."[41]

Puritans defined themselves as those who are striving to be wholly reborn in Christ as persons and married to Christ as churches. "By Puritanes," said Robert Bolton, "then I meane only such, as JESUS CHRIST his owne mouth stileth so, *John* 13.10 and 15.3. . . . whom the powerfull worke of the Word hath regenerated, and possessed with purity of heart, holinesse of affections, and unspottednesse of life." Christ is variously portrayed as the head to the church's body, the husband to the church (Eph. 5.32), the tree to which believers are in-grafted (Rom. 11.17–24), and the cornerstone or foundation of God's building (Matt. 7.25, 16.18; 1 Pet. 2.4,5). These images have in com-mon a personal transformation into union, dependence, and group identity. And love, above all, is the key. "Love is impulsive and con-straining," wrote the English Puritan John Robotham; "it hath a sweet kind of violence to draw out all the affections of the soule unto Christ."[42]

Not surprisingly, the Son shares his Father's imagery. "It is certain," wrote Samuel Willard in *The Fountain Opened* (1700), "that all men in their natural state, are in a perishing condition, being cut off from the fountain of living waters; there is no recovering of it again, and life by it, but in and by Christ, in whom it is stored." Willard empha-sizes elsewhere, in *A Brief Discourse of Justification*, that "you can do nothing for your selves by your own strength, but you are in sence of your utter impotency, to be looking to and waiting upon God in Christ, for his Spirit and Grace." God and Christ together are a fantasy of mutual dependence between consenting adults. "If the world be but five thousand and odde years old," asks an imaginary questioner in John Cotton's *A Practical Commentary . . . upon the First Epistle Generall of John* (1656), "what did God so many years before?" Cotton replies confidently, for both Father and Son,

> Ans.   1.   They nourished, delighted, and solaced each other.
>   2   God ordained Christ to be a nourisher, and solacer of his Church.

God's ordination of Christ makes the Son, as Shepard put it, a "medi-ator between God and my soul, as one in a pit, a mid-man, holds both him below and him above."[43] The experience of being "held," "nour-ished," and "solaced" defines what Christ can do for the faithful, while heaven adds "delight." Christ offers a vision of ecstatic transforma-tional union, expressed with the customary Puritan intensity of oral and sexual imagery.

God also can be imagined as husband, which means mutual com-mitment to a covenant. "When a man taketh a wife into the covenant of marriage with him," says Peter Bulkeley, "what ever he is, he is wholly hers; he gives himselfe and that which he hath to her; so when the mighty God of heaven and earth taketh his people into covenant with him, he is an husband to them, and marryes them to himselfe."

But Puritan language for Christ as husband is more intimate and sensual. In a Whitmanesque moment Samuel Willard asked if anyone could not want "to ly all night in the bosom of Christ, and have his left hand underneath his head, and his right hand imbracing of him?" Holy embraces were also evoked in imagery of eating and being eaten. "So, take the Word; that Communicates Christ to the eare," Thomas Hooker cries with his usual vigor in *The Souls Humiliation,* "cut the meate, and let not the Lord Christ goe whole from the Table, and no man looke after him, fill your hungry Soules with Christ."[44] It was a convention to declare the glory of being "swallowed up" in Christ. As the pure act of self-transformation, the Son embodies and intensifies God's maternal gifts with God's steady paternity.

Ernest Jones has given the experience of Christ an orthodox Oedipal interpretation in his classic essay, "A Psychoanalytic Study of the Holy Ghost." In his view of Christianity, the Son

> attains greatness, including final possession of the Mother and recon-
> ciliation with the Father, only after undergoing the extremity of
> humiliation together with a symbolic castration and death. A similar
> path is laid down for every follower of Jesus, salvation being purchased
> at the price of gentleness, humility, and submission to the Father's
> will. . . . Object-love for the Mother is replaced by a regression to
> the original identification with her, so that incest is avoided and the
> Father pacified; further the opportunity is given of winning the
> Father's love by the adoption of a feminine attitude towards him.
> Peace of mind is purchased by means of a change in heart in the
> direction of a change in sex.[45]

Jones's interpretation emphasizes Oedipal incest wishes and conflict with the father, while ignoring more ambivalent infantile memories of mothering, expressed as oral gratification and oral fears of being separated or devoured. Puritan writings do not linger on the "humilia-tion" of Christ as Anglican writings do until the second generation in New England. They emphasize his glorification and rewards. More-over, the dream of pure union between father and son is as much a fantasy of fathers as of sons. But Jones is right to stress the process of regression, and especially the change in sex. For the Puritans, the change was really one from whore to virgin, for both men and women.

The most pervasive simile for Christ's role made him the bridegroom for the collective saints. As Shepard said, "He will exceedingly comfort thee; and look as it is with tender husbands, then they comfort most when most sorrows betide them [you?]; for who could endure his

wife should be always drooping?" Or again, Shepard frequently makes
the comparison of bride and bridegroom in his long explication of the
parable of the virgins waiting to receive their Lord: "A woman may
be espoused to another, and yet she may be sometimes not ready to
meet him; her foul apparel is on. . . . you ought to be in a continual
readiness to clasp the Lord in your arms, and to lay your heads in his
bosom in heaven." Marriage and feeding are Shepard's two central
metaphors; one cannot be married to the world and married to Christ,
no matter how fair the world's aspect seems. "Now, a man is married
to the law, when he crowds for ease into the bosom of it," he says,
speaking of those who find proof that they are saved by the covenant
of works, but "no man that is married to the Law, but his fig leaves
ever cover some nakedness; all the duties ever brood some lust." But
to be married to Christ, Shepard reiterates, requires constancy and
self-discipline, which he expresses as preparing oneself to feed at
God's breast in the sermon:

> But now to spend Saturday night, and all the whole sabbath day
> mourning, in trimming the Lamp, and in getting oyl to the heart, to
> meet the Bridegroom the next day; and so meet him in the Word,
> and there to tremble at the voice of God, and suck the breast while
> it is open; and when the word is done, to go aside privately, and
> there to chew upon the word, there to lament with tears all the vain
> thoughts in duties, deadness in *hearing*—this is hard, because this is
> the power of godliness.[46]

One can imagine Shepard raising his voice suddenly to make sure his
congregation woke up to that *"hearing"*—by which, Romans 10.17 says,
faith comes.

John Cotton also emphasized Christ as purifying bridegroom. "We
were Harlots, running a whoring after our pleasures and profits; What
a depth of love is it for God to offer us his Christ, his onely Son in
marriage; what manner of love is this?" Cotton also loves to imagine
physical analogues for the Word's effects. "This is the effect of upright
Answers, men kisse his lips; but God kissing a mans lips, is the cause
of mans answering upright words; his breathing into our mouths a
right answer, maketh us speake accordingly." His homoeroticism here
is strong, even if mothering is just below the surface of his father-son
dreams.

We should remember, as Shepard tells us, that the ecstasy described
is only a metaphor. It helps to lift the Puritan from the world and to
make the Father and his holy Son comprehensible in worldly terms,

not to reduce faith to worldly pleasures. "Never was husband and loving wife so familiar one with another," Shepard says in *The Sound Believer,* "as the Lord Jesus will be (not carnally and in an earthly manner) but in a most heavenly, glorious, yet gracious manner with all his saints." Occasionally Puritans even reverse the comparison and use it to instruct actual husbands, as Dod and Cleaver put it, "that thy wife shall be unto thee, as the Church, and thou unto her as Christ."[47] Christ as Word is the lynchpin of the Puritan effort to bring literal and spiritual relations into a comprehensive linguistic frame. The reversable, interchangeable, yet fixed similes for Christ show the same mutuality within dependence that we have seen in Puritan marriage tracts.

Second-generation New England ministers, especially Increase Mather and Edward Taylor, put Christ's Godhead at the center of their faith. Emory Elliott's *Power in the Pulpit* suggests that from 1660 to the 1690s there was "the exchange of one dominant archetype —the image of the angry and wrathful God the Father—to another archetype—the figure of the gentle, loving, and protective Christ."[48] Elliott misstates the first generation's imagery of wrathful patriarchy, as I have tried to show. But he is certainly right to see the sons focusing on the Son. For the first generation, the images of Christ are more varied. Thomas Hooker even dared think of Christ as a bride waiting for the saint's choosing. For Shepard and Cotton, Christ was a fusion of son, bridegroom, and oral pleasures, all willed by the father's benign promise. Heaven is "no other happiness," says Shepard, than this: "now when laid in the bosom of Christ, when sucking the breasts of the grace of Christ, when you can go no farther, though thou wert in heaven, for there is no other happiness there; now sit still contented." Christ, Grace, and infant reborn are at last one, wrapped in the "swaddling-clouts" of God's ordinances.[49]

———— •—• ————

The Bible, the ministers, meditation, and all the acts of preparation and contrition were central to the Puritan faith, but they remained only forms. Grace was the content available in those forms. To receive grace, the sinner has to take the feminine posture for Christ the bridegroom. More crucial than the simile of intercourse in the marriage comparisons, however, is the fantasy of its fruition: the self's rebirth. This transformation, Alan Simpson has said, is the essence of the Puritan way. Samuel Willard, precisely delineating the stages of holiness, declared that God is a judge until he adopts his saints, and only then does he reveal himself as Father to help his chosen toward sanctification, when saints are "renewed in the whole man after the Image of God, and are enabled more and more to dye unto Sin, and live unto Righteousness." "First, the Father elects," said Peter Bulkeley; "then the Sonne redeems; and lastly the Spirit sanctifies."[50]

The true convert begins with complete self-abasement before the Father. As John Winthrop described his own experience, God "laid mee lower in myne owne eyes than at any time before, and shewed mee the emptines of all my guifts and parts, left mee neither power nor will, so as I became a weaned child." Such an experience leads the sinner to a new womb. For Shepard, there is "nothing more stirring than faith in a true Christian, because he lives by it, yet it is very little known; as children in the wombe, that know not that navel-string by which they principally live."[51] That birth will not come without much labor. "For can a child be born, where there never was any travailing paines?" asks Richard Mather, whose *Farewell Exhortation* continues, "Can there be a crop of corn at harvest, where the ground was never plowed, nor broken up? Is not the way to Canaan through the wilderness? doubtles through the wilderness you must go, if ever you will come to Canaan." Yet once the sinner fights down the wish to get something for nothing, he will find Christ waiting for him. "Grace goes directly to Christ," said Cotton in *The Way of Life*, "as a childe new borne goes to the mothers breast, and never leaves crying till it be laid there." As Shepard cried to recalcitrant believers, "Why, you see, and taste, and sip of this love, but you feed not heartily, abundantly, on it." Cotton explicates John 7:37–39 to show how pervasively grace can irradiate one's new life: "Running streames of the Spirit shall ever be flowing from a beleeving soule; he shall have a spring of grace in his soule, that shall ever be like a running river cleansing his heart and way, and making him fruitfull in all places, cooling and refreshing his owne and others soules with the experience of Gods favour to him in Christ."[52] Rebirth makes one flow with God's pure fluids. The self can feel stamped in the father's image and filled with the son's love.

However, the saint never knows these feelings in and for himself. Puritans from Shepard to Jonathan Edwards took great pains to prove that evil always resides in the private will. Rather, grace transforms the sinner only as he becomes a member of a group, the elect. This group is described with the two metaphors most familiar to Puritans, the family and the body. Christ is the head, and the elect are the limbs and torso, or Christ is the bridegroom-husband, and the church is the bride. There is a strong component of surrender, even masochism, in this conversion process. But there is also an ecstasy of fantasized union and reunion, through a purified body and family. "You love Christ, you say," noted Thomas Hooker in *The Christians Two chiefe Lessons*, "but you hate his members because they are hypocrites; tush, that is a fancy; can a man say, I love your head well, and yet would chop off your armes?"[53]

The Puritan fantasy of conversion contradicts the Freudian myth of the primal horde.[54] Instead of warring among themselves and then uniting to castrate and kill the father, these sons erect the father to absolute authority and give themselves a homoerotic wish fulfillment of cooperative submission. Earthly fathers must submit as well, except as they too exercise pure authority. Otherwise, like the king and the pope, they become contaminated by worldly institutions, which are compared to the proud sexuality of unruled whore-mothers. These dreams are more than defenses. And their satisfactions have as much to do with a secure knowledge of fixed stages as with anticipation of ultimate union.

The double language of Puritanism sets up a strict ladder of progress: from election, before the world began, to sinfulness, when the soul has a duty to be active in seeking salvation, to vocation, compared to the circumcision of the heart (Deut. 30.6), when "the infant is generated in a moment" and the soul becomes passive, to justification and adoption, when God accepts saints as persons and sons, to sanctification and glorification after death. While the stages impart the comfort of a fixed pattern, the ultimate fantasy evokes union and fluidity, when the soul is not "clogged" by the body's senses. As John Norton said in his *Orthodox Evangelist*, "the Body is of the Earth, the Soul is immediately from God."[55] Puritans dreamed of a spiritual time of mutual permeability, when self is nothing and union is all, and everyone will speak mentally, through pure will, as angels do, or vocally "when they please," said Norton, "probably in the Hebrew tongue." "How many of God's people daily," Shepard wondered, "knowing their work of vocation and glory, ascend from these lower stairs of the Lord's ladder to the highest of election, and there are swallowed up with eternal wonderment, filling their hearts with that joy and peace, that the weak tabernacle of flesh and blood can not bear the weight of that glory long." Now they are truly children of God, Willard said, and can cry "Abba Father, Rom. 8.15."[56]

"All his hewings and hammerings of you," said Shepard, "nay, his knocking you to pieces, and new melting and new casting of you, it is that you may be vessels of his glorious grace, that you may be able to live in the air of God's grace, to suck in and breathe out grace." Heaven is the place where infantile ecstasy is manifest. As Shepard declares elsewhere in his *Parable of Ten Virgins,* the saints "look to the riches of God's grace, to the freeness and riches of the Lord's promise, and hang there, and plead that, and suck that breast." Even more than Cotton, Shepard is especially eloquent about blissful feelings of being mothered by a comprehensive father: "Now thou art in the very lap of love, wrapped up in it, when here thy heart rests." In heaven, Willard imagines, the soul will be received by Christ "with widened arms . . . and with the most tender Embraces, lodge it in his Bosom, and thereby give it the feeling Assurances of His Everlasting Love." As Shepard says so often, heaven is endless communion with God, and "this communion shall be chiefly in sucking out the sweet of all God's love, past, present, and to come."[57] These were the dreams that circumscribed the minds and hearts of the faithful, especially in New England.

"Flying to the American Strand"

> And truly, my reason for my self
> and others to go [to America], was
> meerly not to offend Authority in
> that difference of Judgment.
>
> Hugh Peter[58]

To counter the contamination of authority without rebelling, Puritans set themselves up as examples on a public stage on a new continent. With extraordinary communal fervor, anxious Englishmen became patriarchal Americans. One irony is that Puritan contradictions thereby became all the more apparent. A more enduring irony is that in pursuit of a dream of pure dependence, they moved to a land where ambition could be more expansively rewarded than ever before.

There were good economic reasons for the Massachusetts Bay Colony to survive. It had joint-stock sponsorship and more frequent shipping from England, the first relief ship arriving in February 1631. Although over 200 people had died that winter, other colonies had had far worse luck and had waited far longer for ships from England. The colony also had good initial relations with the Indians, who had just been laid low by diseases imported by previous immigrants, and England's growing need for trade kept the struggling settlements in touch with the mother country.[59] But there were many more reasons for the colony to fail—obvious ones like death, isolation, failure of nerve. None of the traditional institutions for social stability crossed the water—no army, no landed aristocracy, no accepted order of status except as voluntary deference. Yet as Stephen Foster has said, even the massive Indian wars of the 1670s left New England stable, while much milder Indian threats in Virginia at that time brought Bacon's Rebellion and the collapse of the colony's governing institutions.[60]

Social bonding for theological purposes, more than economics, brought the Puritan experiment through its crises, even as it brought on some crises. Those who wanted economic reward could move to the Netherlands, where Calvinism was already the state religion. New England Puritans wanted more. As Foster concludes, they substituted "radical voluntarism for most of the customary engines of social coercion of early modern Europe," even though voluntarism contradicted the Puritan belief in subordination, which itself had no institutional base.[61] The contradiction, in my view, was essential to Puritan ideology. Puritans could never conceive of the self the way we do: isolated, individualist, anomic, filled with separable desires, complex personal histories, and uncertain futures. What to us is the norm was to them the essence of sin. In fact, their reaction against the forces precipitating such separate identities helped drive them to New England. "Members are in *subordination*, Wolves and Cancers are in *opposition* to the Head," Hooker summed up. But the head must grow from the body. Cotton Mather's 1690 election sermon, after Massachusetts had at last rid itself of hated Governor Andros, recalled the basic issues for a new generation: "We came into the *Wilderness*, because we would quietly worship God, without that *Episcopacy*, that *Common-Prayer*, and those unwarrantable ceremonies, . . . we came because we would have our Posterity settled under the pure and full *Dispensations* of the Gospel, defended by *Rulers that should be of our selves, and Governours that should proceed from the midst of us*." As Hooker says, "mutuall ingagement" must be the ground of mutual power, in all things.[62]

The Puritan view of the whole was insistently organic and positive, not mechanical as modern views tend to be. Visible saints would never have dismissed group participation as being "just a cog in the machine." That phrase comes from postindustrial values. The ideal Puritan self must be wholly changed from sinful separation to group union. One must accept subordinating part to whole just as—one of their incessant similes—a part of the body is not the whole body. One must further accept the subordination of part to part in the natural order of "callings." In a great variety of ways the New England emigrants intensified a sense of group: by emigrating in families, by requiring everyone to live near a town center, by keeping sons at home, by enforcing the social rituals of the Sabbath and the sermon, by giving the vote to church members only, by defining themselves as the chosen people. Group motivation, not individual achievement, guided their success. America seemed to be the place for holy communities to thrive.

New England seemed like heaven to those staying behind in fractious England. Robert Bolton says as much when speaking of those who want to get to heaven without preparation. "It is even as if one should busie himselfe much, and boast what he will do in New-England when he comes thither; and yet (poore man) he hath neither ship nor money, nor meanes, nor knowledge of the way, nor provision before-hand for his comfortable planting there."[63] As ever, the Puritan mixes practical advice with grand designs, of which New England is meant to be the heavenly end. Of course an emphasis on work and productivity after arrival helped to ensure that end.

Here Puritan strictures about calling ensured that attitudes toward work would be framed by respect for authority. Calling originally meant a summons to the priesthood; Calvin defined it more broadly as the proper use of God's gifts. Yet his definition shows the new anxieties: "The Lord commands every one of us, in all the actions of life, to regard his vocation. For he knows with what great inquietude the human mind is inflamed." Calling thus regulates feelings. Duty, productiveness, and all the other outward signs of submission to community needs were at least as important to the Puritan emphasis on work as the aggressive individualism commonly attributed to the Protestant ethic. Work itself, not acquisition, characterized the successful community member.[64]

Ambivalence toward the self helped to induce such strong reliance on habits of work and community. John Cotton put the issue squarely: "Diligence in a mans calling, and trustiness and faithfulnesse are comely things in Christians. A well-girt Christian the Lord wil keepe, that men shall not see his nakednesse; though in many things he may faile and be ashamed, yet the Lord keepes him that men see not his nakednesse." Puritans sought refuge from fears of failure, nakedness, and shame, not only in New England, but in a collective fantasy of industrious expectancy, with outside authority providing stability, purpose, and controls, even down to the inward voice characterizing the obsessive style. Ambivalence toward social and familial authority was thrust onto the self.[65] Here too, emigration offered the promise of collective self-realization.

In New England, Christopher Hill has said, "the full theoretical consequences latent in puritan teaching were drawn out."[66] But New England Puritans were more than an extension of their English counterparts. They tended to have more internalized conflicts, more opportunity for institutionalizing contradictory desires, more community orientation, more unity of church and state, more emphasis on patriarchal social authority, and more expectations of collective purity. Group mobilization, like the translation of self into God's elect, avoided conflict as much as it promised unity. Less contentious than the Puritans who would soon turn revolutionary, often more "Brahmin" in being sure of their abilities to govern themselves individually and collectively, with more emotional and economic wherewithal—as Bolton intimates—to take passage to a new continent, they chose to make dignified if surreptitious exits rather than accept compromise or foster rebellion. The journey to America was the passage from fractious selves to a vision of patriarchal community.

American Puritanism's use of its two major literary forms, the sermon and the spiritual narrative, enacts the same transformation of the isolated self into the "tribe."[67] Its major social form, New England towns, was obviously tribal. Kenneth Lockridge has called these towns "peasant utopias," and Timothy Breen has shown their roots in the English village.[68] As always, there were contradictions. Small, voluntary groups, whether in churches or towns, were expected to join in ideological uniformity. Governors would be elected by the people yet rule by God's ordinance. Men should obey their callings yet find a partial measure of grace in material grain. Separated from England, yet claiming exemplary union, American Puritans from the beginning were a "People of Paradox," even as their literature tolerated no ambiguity.

Unlike English Puritans, who speedily accepted toleration and often chastised their American brethren for being so intolerant in the 1640s and 1650s, New England Puritans went through intricate theological convolutions to avoid even the appearance of what Milton called "the widowed whore plurality." Not only did they prohibit dissent through communal authoritarianism and banishment of dissenters, they also held to a more strict fidelity to the Bible. Conflict or tension of any kind was taken as a sign of town sinfulness. Within ten years the New Englanders had even institutionalized the inward essence of their faith, the conversion experience, as a public process: a spoken account of one's spiritual change became a requirement for church membership, stated in public by men, in private by women. They were newcomers to the original Augustinian vision, and they rigorously adhered to the forms. More uniquely, they tried to give a rigid social pattern to their most fundamental inward needs.

Subsequent popular traditions, as well as many scholars, have reduced these complexities to inward anxieties and outward vindictiveness. Hawthorne built the coffin; Mencken nailed down the lid. But tensions between anxious self and stable community in many ways allowed personal anxiety to be voiced, while transforming conflicted feelings into group security. Those who trace a straight line from seventeenth-century Puritanism through the Protestant ethic into nineteenth-century individualism miss the central family and community thrust of the American Puritan emigration and undervalue the power of a language of voluntary dependence.

By the eighteenth century, open lands to the west and the promise of gentry status to the wealthy had encouraged a reversion to more English models of overt rewards. Class resentment against the establishment, so variously refracted into the Puritan movement, had been largely dispersed by the ease of mobility on a vast continent, to surface suddenly in revivals or finally in revolution. But the legacies of Puritanism were not restricted to the insular family, the New England town, and the close rein on sexual, artistic, and emotional expression. A preoccupation with things spiritual as well as material, a concern with group betterment rather than individual success, a preoccupation with mastering one's self as well as one's environment: these aspects remained, long after a provincial tradesman's world had split the Puritan experiment into its disparate elements.

For a moment in history, a moment lasting 200 years, ambition, community, and dreams of a pure nurturing father seemed to coalesce. New England began with that hope. That so many conflicts could be subsumed in the expectation of order for so long was the transient genius of Puritanism.

Chapter Five

Breasts of God,
Whores of the Heart

> What, shall I fall by a woman?
> Shall I fall by the worst?
> Thomas Shepard[1]

This chapter develops relationships among Puritan polarities, Family Romance fantasies, and female imagery at more length. I also suggest some differences between England and New England in child rearing and female roles. In bringing fantasy to life, as I have said, New England Puritans become more group oriented and patriarchal, in language and behavior. To take language first, we turn to expressive similes for the Word and sin in the New England sermon, whose astonishing success as the major forum for public identity reflects its ability to satisfy divergent needs: for intellectual control and clarity, for strong fathers and good mothering, for social order and group bonds, for self-discipline and self-transformation. While stabilizing community controls, the sermon genre helped to voice mixed inward feelings as public instruction and private delight.

Puritan sermons appear to be paradigms of the obsessive style. They offer compulsive patterns of external order, rigid arrangements of "doctrine, reasons, and uses" in a thicket of numbers and quotations, with no space for private opinion or loose feelings. They call for patriarchal deference, invoke the one true text continuously, endlessly repeat their litany of "shoulds," and take minute care to make precise distinctions within a grand either-or frame of polarity. Yet Puritan sermons are at the same time capacious, supple, and vivid in their similes, with a practical sense of social roles. The double appeal of Puritan language is nowhere more expansively set than in the flexibility of sermon imagery speaking through the rigidity of sermon form.

Puritan imagery associated with the Word and sin, and more variously with the minister's role, polarizes female functions. Good mothering contends with contaminated whores. The opposition provides some indirect support for theories advanced in chapter three about "good enough" mothering, though the scarce evidence available on American child rearing also tends to support a widely shared sense that New England fathers were sterner than English fathers.[2] Pervasive opposition of virgin brides and breasts of God on the one hand, whorish lusts and aggressive women on the other, might seem to indicate profound separation anxiety and fears of being abandoned by one's mother, since a fantasy of the good mother and the bad mother is the first defense against fear and rage during the most dependent stage of infancy.

However, sermon imagery does not often reflect bad mothering, even in displaced form. Negative oral imagery of "devouring" hell is not prominent until the second generation of New England ministers, notably in Increase Mather's jeremiads. There are very few similes of "mutilating mothers," supposedly the most terrifying infantile fear.[3] Neither are there many images of oral deprivation, terrifying mouths or teeth, or rapacious animals, all of which characterize unresolved infantile trauma. Nor does Puritan language show schizophrenic dissociations. It is both obsessively ordered and very much connected to practical realities. Only Mather and, to a much lesser degree, Thomas Shepard, both of whom seem to have had mothers more possessive than tender, turn occasionally to images of murdering mothers to make their points.

In fact, the most vivid image of a murdering mother I have found is in Shepard, who also has the most ecstatic language of suckling. The passage's truculence toward the woman is as shocking as the incident he records and shows both the ferocity of his female imagery and his plea for self-translation. It is from *Parable of the Ten Virgins*: "In this country, a woman killed her child, and she said when she did it, her child smiled upon her. Wilt thou kick Christ's love now when he smiles upon thee? Afterward she repented, but it was too late. Women, when they have a mind to some other, murder their husbands; but if known, burned they must be. But wilt thou have him and love him alone? O, if persuaded to this, then happy forever! Let this day be the beginning of eternal glory to thy soul, and the God of peace be with thee."[4] But until the second generation in New England, the primary indictment of woman is as "whore." That image, as in *Hamlet*, suggests some unconscious displacing of feelings about the father's impurities onto the "weaker vessel." It also suggests Oedipal or later resentment for the loss of the mother's undivided affection, and it more overtly pictures female pride and aggressiveness as the image of sinful human will. But it does not call into question the image of tender mothers so often invoked by Puritan family guidebooks. Only her sexuality is condemned.

While the Puritan Family Romance extravagantly indulges dreams of rebirth and suckling at a mothering father, imagery associated with sin connects babies, the self, excrement, and the mother's sexuality. The connections reflect a variety of suppressed concerns about the self as well as resentments at both the father and mother. The negative self is located in the mother's imagined whorishness and the body's filth. Anxiety over incestuous desires and more adult sexual nervousness are also projected onto the weaker vessel. But as mother, her functions remain unthreatening, indeed the essence of God's rewards.

Despite the obvious sexism of fantasizing that the father is in charge of all the mother's virtues, first-generation American Puritanism perhaps unwittingly fostered assertive energies in women's behavior as well as dependent female fantasies in men. Anne Bradstreet's poetry, Anne Hutchinson's heresies, Mary Dyer's Quaker attraction to the Puritan flame, the later incidence of witches, and especially the great variety of ordinary women mastering homes, farms, Indians, and the wilderness all reflect a rich spectrum of practical as well as religious female purposefulness. Though several women do seem to have been driven mad by their circumstances, the Puritan rhetoric of whoredom does not appear to have been nearly as incapacitating to women as we might suppose. Here as elsewhere, Puritan polarities can be seen as contradictory appeals when examined in detail.

Sermon and Minister

"Puritan life, in the New England theory," Perry Miller has said, "was centered upon a corporate and communal ceremony, upon the oral delivery of a lecture."[5] In the early years of the Massachusetts colony people were so sermon hungry, as the phrase had it, that they would go two or three times a week, "to the great neglect of their affairs," John Winthrop wrote in his diary on December 3, 1639. The focus for this ceremony was the minister, who had to "drive a match" between the sinner and Christ. He had to be forceful, even threatening, to bring his congregation to a sense of the insufficiency of their lives without God. As Thomas Hooker confidently declared, "For the word of God [i.e., reading the Bible] is powerful to prepare you for the Lord; but the minister must hew your hearts, and hack them, he must frame and fashion your souls before they can be prepared."[6]

The preacher had to speak from the heart himself: from memory, not from manuscript, William Perkins decreed. He also had to have experienced a valid conversion to preach conversion, somewhat like our contemporary requirement for psychoanalysts. God's Word had to be the sole ground for preaching, with no extraneous views or private interpretations. Speaking from memory or perhaps notes encouraged a clear format of simple order, authoritative argument, and practical uses. The minister's aim throughout was not to exercise his subtlety or wit but to change behavior toward rebirth in God. As John Norton began his *Orthodox Evangelist,* "What hath my soul longed, or labored for more, after your birth in Christ, then that you should be, not only Babes, but men."[7]

None of that is peculiar to New England Puritanism. At the end of the seventeenth century Richard Baxter defined Puritans as those who had "a suspicion of all that is Ceremonious in Gods Service, and of all which they find not warrant for in Scripture, and a greater inclination to a rational convincing way of Preaching and Prayers, than to the written Forms of Words, which are to be read in Churches. And they are greatly taken with a Preacher that speaketh to them in a familiar natural Language and exhorteth them as if it were for their Lives." Selected by their congregations, not by bishops, ministers earned their pay and authority by forceful fidelity to God's Word alone. As Hooker put it, "I am a poor ambassador sent from God to do his message unto you; and although I be low, yet my message is from above."[8]

Most studies of the Puritan sermon, especially as it was preached in New England, have emphasized its intellectual rigor, plain style, judgmental tendencies, and fidelity to the Bible. Sermons not only served what Freud would call the superego functions of Puritan society, they also encouraged mental toughness, a faith in larger patterns to make meaning of their chaotic lives, and a variety of community bonds. They served for news, guidance, and what one scholar calls "adult continuing education."[9] But conversion was obviously the most important aim. Puritans on both sides of the Atlantic argued with Augustinian fervor that, as one early English preacher put it, no one had ever been "converted by hearing stories or fables of poets."[10] Art that delights rather than instructs tends to erect false gods.

Sermon hunger was acute in many social groups throughout seventeenth-century England, and we should not overstate as unique the Puritan preoccupation with preaching. Nor was the seeming rigidity of Perkins's "doctrine-reasons-uses" format and the "party badge" of the plain style really set until the 1620s.[11] The early history of Puritanism shows flexibility, variety, and moderation in styles as well as politics. Not until emigrating to New England could Puritans institutionalize their uncompromised fantasies as social facts. But from the beginning, Puritans differed from Anglicans in stressing the importance of the sermon. It replaced readings and church ritual as the primary focus for the public experience of God's truth. Though Puritan preachers were scrupulous to say sermons could only prepare souls for faith and confirm souls in sanctification, not effect God's own work of transformation, preachers were also adamant about the sermon's crucial role in helping to bring on the soul's readiness and perseverence.

Tender mothering was therefore not an immediate aim of Puritan prose. Soothing words could deaden possibilities for conversion. Besides, real comfort was available only in scriptures. As Samuel Willard said, naming the three parts of the mind, scriptures satisfy "all the ends of Religion. Sometimes to inform the understanding: Sometimes to engage the will: and sometimes to move upon the affections." A disciplined understanding must rule both the will and the affections. In practice, however, since ministers were the Word's agents, they could bring God's soothing comfort to the feelings, especially by use of a plain style communicating God's truths in earthly images just as Christ did. If "the promise is the mouth of Christ," John Norton wrote, then "faith is the mouth of the soul," and a lifelong kiss often begins in the hearing of the Word.[12]

Consciously, the parenting functions of Puritan sermons therefore evoked a father's discipline, though with frequent similes intimating a mother's nourishment. An intellectual control of feelings is one obvious effect of a form that encourages lengthy logical rigor, not emotional display or sprawl. Congregations sat for up to two hours listening to God's familiar instructions repeated in the familiar format.[13] Quite unabashedly, sermons were meant to be repressive, at least of carnal feelings, and just as Freudians define the superego as the internalized father, so John Norton said that "conscience is Gods vice-gerent in the soul."[14] Sermons and religious instruction in the home were the main agents for setting up the vice-gerent's rule. Comfort was an afterthought in Charles Chauncy's instructions to a young minister in 1665: "Explain the words of your text clearly; bring clear proof of parallel scriptures; let your reasons be Scripture-reasons; but be most in application, which is spent in five uses, refutation of error, information of the truth, correction of manners, exhortation and instruction in righteousness. All of which you find in 2 Tim. iii. 16,17. And there is a fifth use, viz: of comfort, 1 Cor. xiv. 3."[15] While the minister was a resident teacher, intellectual, interpreter, and shepherd of souls—what Samuel Stone, speaking of the Congregational church government, called "a speaking *Aristocracy* in the face of a silent *Democracy*"—he also explicitly fulfilled a father's role. For the English Puritan Robert Pricke, ministers "are called *Spirituall Fathers,* because they begette and change men anewe." Thomas Hooker took as doctrine in a 1626 English sermon that "the ministers of God should be as fathers to the people" and should act therefore with appropriate "staidness and gravity" to deserve the "loving subjection" of their congregations.[16]

Yet ministers often called themselves breasts of God, and milk imagery was interchangeably dispensed among several theological roles: the minister, the Word, and God's promises. Thomas Shepard explains the parable of the ten virgins in allegorical terms by defining ministers as "those that sell" God's promises, or breasts.[17] Several interpretations of "Canticles" (the Song of Solomon) by Increase Mather and John Cotton interpret the woman's breasts as "ministers from whom they may receive the sincere milk of the Word," and Thomas Shepard expresses the power of the spoken word in similar imagery: "Dish milk and slit milk may convey some nourishment, but breast milk hath spirit going with it; good books may be blessed, but there is not that spirit in them as in lively dispensations of the gospel by ministers themselves."[18] His lengthy set of sermons on the parable of ten virgins has imagery of feeding on almost every page.

At one level these interpretations reflect the Puritan preoccupation with breast-feeding the young. To imagine the minister as both father and breast reconciles in fantasy the opposition between the father's discipline and the mother's nurturance. But at another level what is most striking is not the overt regressiveness but the almost playful flexibility of roles available to the faithful. The fantasy of rebirth liberated a wonderfully polymorphous, and to our eyes even perverse, set of redefined identities. As the Word flowed, so did their reborn selves, from one quick simile to another. So a minister could be in one breath a father, in another a breast, and in another a Pandarus (or John Alden) wooing virgins for Christ: "And truly it is the main work of the ministry to woo for Christ, and so to present chaste virgins to Christ," said Thomas Shepard, who defined "virgins" as "such churches, or members of churches, as are divorced from all other lovers, and matched only to Jesus Christ."

Taking their similes literally misses the point. Breast imagery from the Bible is not used to mean breasts in Puritan discourse. The only such use I have found is in Robert Cleaver's *Briefe Explanation,* where he interprets "let her breasts satisfie thee at all times" to mean, let "her presence, and personage, and the use of her body *satisfie thee,* as well delight thine eyes, and otherwise suffice, as the milke of the mothers breasts doth content the appetite of the infant."[19] Ordinarily Puritans took breasts to mean churches or ministers. The fantasy was of trans-formation and infantile dependence, not of marital foreplay. Fathers can have breasts, men can be virgins, words can be pure once more. To be reborn is to become unstuck from selfish desires, as holy lan-guage becomes unstuck from the world. More unconsciously, the mes-sage of Puritan sermons is: once father has been heeded, mother becomes available again. In that process the minister shows the way.

A multiplicity of roles, not a strict masculine self-image, denotes the successful preacher, within his one calling. As Hooker said, he could not be a magistrate. Flexibility in fantasy must be rigorous self-applica-tion in practice. In fact, whenever possible, the minister's functions should be divided in two. The teacher defines and expounds faith and doctrine, while the pastor shows the nature of sin and hypocrisy. Though the offices are equal, the duties are separate. In fantasy too, John Cotton strictly limited the minister's role in declaring that the bride (church) herself must accept Christ and subjugate herself to him; "which she may do effectually, whether ministers be present and assistant or no." But his similes for explaining these distinctions rein-force the basic match-making allegory for the minister's function: "The Church as it is the house of God; so it is also the spouse of Christ: ministers are the friend of the bridegroom, and of the bride. The ministers have done their work in preparing the bride for the bride-groom; as also in ministering to her when she is married. But in be-trothing her to Christ, the bride in that work, must herself profess her own acceptance of the Lord Jesus, and subjection to Him."[20] In all these roles, some sense of receptive feminine virtue is crucial to being prepared for conversion.

For one sixteenth-century Puritan, the minister is "a Father to beget us with the immortal seed of the word, a Mother to nourish us up in the same." Like those who experienced saving grace in his congrega-tion, the minister welcomed the profusion of self-abandoning identities. To call himself a breast of God makes him most intimately a vessel for God's omniparental powers. Thomas Hooker vividly describes such rapture: "Oh yes, saith the soule, me thinks I see the Ministers face still, and when he came to such a point and such a passage, good Lord, mee thought I was in heaven; could words, and reasons, and sentences have done it? No surely, the Spirit of grace was there, and my heart did close with the same: the stomack receives not meat, as the dish or vessell doth, but the stomack doth receive it, and is fastened to it, and hath the sweetnesse of it, and is made one with it."[21] At such a pitch, ministers reached for all three Freudian levels of food, cleanliness, and sexuality to describe being emptied of self and filled with God.

It is possible that preachers were simply inducing their bench-bound listeners to link regressive bliss with good habits of attention. A more orthodox Freudian interpretation would finally find homosexual fantasies of nursing at the penis and being raped by the father, along lines congenial to Dr. Schreber. But since the father is himself transformed into a good mother, a sexual interpretation would miss the powerful needs for self-abandoning dependence that lead both fathers and sons to imagery of breasts and food. Female imagery provided a transformational vocabulary satisfying desires for dependence while denying ambivalence in fantasies of regressive union. At the same time the imagery ostensibly enhanced structures of community roles and male authority that New England Puritans were so zealous to preserve.

The Word

While flexibility of roles characterizes imagery associated with the Puritan ministry, the Word is more emphatically associated with dependence and transformation, as milk and seed. Rebirth brings the two image clusters together. God as pure Father, begotten through "understanding himself from Eternity" as John Norton explained, begot the Son as pure Word (1 John 1.14, 5.7). Therefore by the pure Word Puritans are made. As Shepard said, "Give children milk in the dish, they cry still; they must have it from the mother, and there suck; so 2 Pet. i. 2,3." Either book of the Bible, like any good minister, could be a breast; I have already cited the title of John Cotton's catechism for children, *Spiritual Milk for Boston Babes In either England. Drawn out of the Breasts of both Testaments for their souls nourishment.* The Word is also sperm. "Looke as it is with seed that is cast into the wombe of a woman," Hooker declares in *The Soules Vocation,* "the seed is enough to beget some fruit; but if the wombe be a miscarrying wombe, it comes to nothing: so it is betweene the stirring of the Word in the heart of a poore Saint, and in the heart of an Hypocrite."[22]

Of course Puritans were not alone in wanting to return to God's Word. The effort characterizes the Reformation as a whole. In contrast to the Quakers, Puritans were "low and legal" in their interpretation of the precise path. Where the Quakers made spirit primary, Puritans meant God's law when they said the Word. They were careful to say that God, not the Bible, is the only proper object of faith. "But though we ought to reverence the blessed Bible above all other books," said Increase Mather, "yet we may not worship it, but the author of it only." Their emphasis on reason and conscience, not on irradiated sense perceptions, always kept enthusiasms restrained. When Willard says the Word is "compared to a Seed that is sown in us, and produceth such fruit" as a new birth (James 1.18) and new growth (1 Pet. 2.2), he adds that whenever hearing or reading the word, *It is our Duty at such a time, to set a strict guard on our Senses.*"[23]

Not only do Puritans use more food imagery while Quakers focus almost exclusively on seed metaphors, but perhaps even more important, Quaker language tends to obliterate the distinction between the metaphoric and the literal. Puritans always show their scaffolding.[24] They state that they are making a comparison and place the simile in a clear frame of ordered argument. Rarely do they use metaphors, so common is the simile formulation of "as" or "like as to," or "may be compared to." Rarely are similes extended for longer than a sentence. The usual course is to pile them up, not drag one out. Puritan style sets bounds to metaphoric fantasies even in the act of making them. The effect is to modulate what might in Thomas Traherne's Anglican hands be an ecstasy of merging into a restrained happiness of joined parts. The father's roles, not the mother's nourishment, set the tone. Puritanism is a language neither of Anglican deference nor of Quaker mysticism, both of which bring out the "I" in opposite ways. It is a language changing "I" into "we," a nursing collective in a logical pattern. In a group perspective, associations to the Word take on an intensity of tender mothering only within a secure frame of paternal control. For Shepard there is "nothing more stirring than faith in a true Christian, because he lives by it, yet it is very little known; as children in the wombe, that know not that navel-string by which they principally live." "In the hearing of the Word," wrote John Cotton in his *Commentary on John*, "we are to come like *New born babes, desiring the sincere milk of the Word.*" Both passages quietly affirm a "they" or "we" as the appropriate vehicle for pure childhood desire.[25]

Repetitive Puritan wishes to rediscover the father's authority at the breast suggest some contradictory feelings toward the mother in her natural state, ungoverned by the father's control. "As it is with a woman," Shepard asserts, "that though others do not, yet her husband knows she is fallen in league with some other man, he will be strange to her, and will not do any thing for her." So the affections must love no one but Christ, and the Gertrude-like will must be ruled by the understanding father. Imagery of changeable female affections reflects some unconscious fears of separation and abandonment, not surprising in a fantasy that stresses the absolute necessity of dependence. The more central emotional concern, however, is the mother's loss of proper reverence for her husband.

"That *Mother of Harlots* the Church of Rome," fulminated Increase Mather in a stock phrase, "she has made her self drunk with blood."[26] In the Puritan allegory the elect, or the saint himself, became the Virgin, and the Catholic Church became the whore. Life without a father, even with the best of mothers, exposed children to the Catholic terror. "Doe but cast your eyes abroad," Hooker said in *The Danger of Desertion* (1641), "and there you shall see poore fatherlesse children sending forth their breathes, with feare, crying to their poore helplesse mothers. Step but a little farther, and you shall see the sad wife bemoaning her husband, and that is her misery, that she cannot dye soone enough; and withall she makes funerall Sermons of her children within her selfe, for that the Spaniard may get her little ones, and bring them up in Popery and superstition."[27] To set the pure Word against the Catholic Church helped to clarify Puritan feelings about the mother they were really trying to purify: the Anglican faith. John Cotton's celebrated dispute with Roger Williams over "The Bloudy Tenent" centers on Williams's accusation that the Church of England was a daughter of whorish Catholicism, not part of the true Church. Cotton rejoined: "Did ever the holy Scripture call any Church an Whore, that worshipped the true God, onely in the Name of Jesus, and depended on him alone for righteousnesse and salvation? Is it not the part of a base childe, or at least, a base part of a childe, to call his Mother whore, who bred him, and bred him to know no other Father but her lawfull Husband, the Lord Jesus Christ?" To see the Church of England as a good though errant mother was an intrinsic part of the Puritan refusal of separatism. "And here, *O England,*" wrote Peter Bulkeley in *The Gospel-Covenant* (1651), "my deare Native Countrey (whose wombe bare me, whose breasts nourished me, and in whose arms I should desire to dye,) give eare to one of thy children, which dearly loveth thee."

The appeal was politic, of course, yet heartfelt—two basic strands of Puritan discourse. For the first generation, their English mother is more helpless than whorish, and more whorish than the blood-drunk vampire conventionally invoked by Mather in the jeremiad.[28] The similes show empathy, need, and optimism about reforming her, not rage and fear of her devouring powers. The accusation of whore reflects some unconscious guilt and anger at the loss of tender mothering, to be sure. But it does not reflect fear of the mother's possessing or rejecting powers. She may stand for ego, pride, lust, or contamination, but not for danger to babies. The Puritan task was to set the family right again by reforming this proud woman. If not by immediate seizure, then by far-off example, they wanted to recall her from her snobbish citified ways to become once again the conduit for the Father's Gospel fountain.

It was not just a lack of printing facilities that led most early New England ministers to publish their sermons in London. These children wanted their mother purified by returning her to their father's bed. Simultaneously, the father became pure by being returned to the children through the mother's breast. More simply, they attributed all her powers and virtues to the Father's Word.

Sin

Why should grown men want to be feminine and infantile in fantasy, while intensifying the trappings of patriarchy in New England? Why should they have treated Anne Hutchinson and the witches so badly, while imagining themselves as brides of Christ or breasts of God? Such fantasies can satisfy when the self seems jammed with contradictory feelings. Metaphors of being emptied of sin, guilt, lust, and filth, and of being filled with God's grace, recur throughout Puritan writings. A language of obsessive dependence encouraged saints to project inward contradictions onto a dualistic universe, even onto the Godhead, while reconceiving themselves as infants again. The unconverted self collects images of excrement, abandonment, lust, anger, and female sexuality.[29]

Most Puritan preachers express the feeling of sin simply as filth, self-loathing, isolation, or whoring after the world. "For Sin, which all the children of men are naturally guilty of," said Willard in *A Brief Discourse of Justification* (1686), "had separated between God and man, and all mankind was for Sin under a severe threatning: so that they had no hold of God at all, but were quite knockt off from any such thing." Willard's characteristic imagery for sin has to do with disorder, anger, and filth. Thomas Shepard put it more personally in his diary for May 23, 1641: "On the Sabbath . . . I came to a serious consideration what sins were between God and me that eclipsed his love?" The impulse to religion itself, said Shepard, comes from self-disgust and the fear of being seen and judged alone rather than being absorbed into God's community. "Every man must have some religion, some fig-leaves to hide their nakedness."[30] Pervasive imagery of disease, war, and disorder used to express the essence of sin comes to root in the sense of being alone with one's self-loathing.

Loneliness carries unconscious associations of separation anxiety. In psychoanalytic terms, separation anxiety is an infantile feeling of being abandoned by one's mother.[31] Puritan cosmology recast separation anxiety as both wish and fear: the fear of being separate from God's light and fluids, and the wish to be separate from oneself, at least one's sinning self, and the nonelect. However, ministers said that the father's, not the mother's, abandonment is what creates anxiety. "All these vile sins are but the running over of the scum and filth that is within," Willard said. "Original sin is the mother, and this is the fruitful progeny of it."[32] There is clearly some unconscious separation trauma at the center of Shepard's imagery. But the more conventional Puritan pattern is to connect sin not to the mother's absence but to her presence when unguided by the father's hand.

Sin is not, therefore, feelings of emptiness, though it can be associated with abandonment. Emptiness is the state of being receptive to God's grace. As Shepard said and Jonathan Edwards would comprehensively reiterate, sin is "resistance." It blocks man's capacity for union with God and leaves the separateness of things as the "perishing condition" of nature. Thomas Hooker is the most Elizabethan in his sense of how God's absence perverts the order of degree. Sin, he said, "crosseth the whol course of Providence, perverts the work of the Creature and defaceth the beautiful frame, and that sweet correspondence and orderly usefulness the Lord first implanted in the order of things; . . . Man was the mean betwixt God and the Creature to convey all good with all the constancy of it, and therefore when Man breaks, Heaven and Earth breaks all asunder, the Conduit being cracked and displaced there can be no conveyance from the Fountain." "Sweet correspondence," which underlies the Puritan reliance on similes, and "orderly usefulness" depend on the "constancy" of man as a conduit for God's good. Sin blocks and breaks the conduit, thus leaving the world a barren and jumbled wilderness. As Hooker said in *The Poor Doubting Christian*, when a man is sinning, "these two things follow. *First*. Stop the Stream of God's Promise, and let down the Sluce against it, so that the Promise cannot enter into us. And 2. *Secondly*. We set open the Stream and Floodgate of Corruption, and make it to run most violently down, and to flood in upon us; and in the end to overwhelm us." "It is a desperate Malignity in the temper of the Stomach," Hooker says elsewhere, "that should turn our Meat and diet into Diseases, the best Cordials and Preservatives into Poysons, so that what in reason is appointed to nourish a man should kill him." For Shepard sin could even more succinctly be compared with a hungering stomach: "For all the reason in the world will never kill a lust, no more than all the reason will persuade the stomach not to hunger. The belly hath no ears."[33]

Yet awareness of sin, not a blameless life, was the precondition for salvation. Shepard lists sins in their natural order of occurrence in a man's life: first bad company, then lust sometimes leading to "self-pollution" (masturbation), then love of the world and the world's goods, then hypocritical pride in spiritual glory, and finally sloth, one's laziness before the task of self-humiliation. Shepard's imagery for sin is even more comprehensive, if possible, than Hooker's; he draws his similes from organic diseases, military disruptions, body malfunctions, dirt and pollution, fire and storms, darkness, death, and separation. Whereas Hooker tends to emphasize disruptions in social order, Shepard is resolutely psychological in his sense of sin as resistance, and all his imagery is meant to make inward evils tangibly felt, as the necessary prelude to the work of purification. Sloth is therefore the last and most dangerous stage in the movement toward self-awareness. "It is not sin, but a privy peace with sin, and a secret quietness in sin, which overthrows Christ's kingdom," Shepard says in his *Parable*. John Cotton agrees: "For if a soul were never yet bruised with sin, and with the sense of sin, he never yet laid hold upon Christ."[34]

The argument reflects the basic Puritan polarity between sinful world and glorious God. The self must be evacuated, because sin is the self's natural desiring essence in Puritan theory. And desire means pollution. As Shepard says parenthetically, "Indeed saints purge not themselves of themselves, for dirty hands will never wash a foul face." And he speaks shortly after of "the great, yet hidden secret sin of the whole world . . . their hungry lustings and dropsy desires after the sweet of the things of this world." Those desires are, in Shepard's recurrent simile, the marriage of a whorish woman with a corrupted husband. The stock Puritan phrase is "a dunghill world," and the proper wife must cleanse herself from its foulness. *Any* desire that does not give God full devotion violates the Second Commandment and indicates the soul's contamination. This is "the great error, most common and dangerous of the whole Christian world," Shepard says, to think that one can embrace the world and Christ at the same time.[35]

"Hence many that know much of Christ feed on their lusts and dunghill delights, because their knowledge feeds them not, fills them not, as fancies do not feed." As Cotton said, interpreting Jeremiah 31:32, let the Lord take a sinner by the hand and be a husband to him, "and let him go on, not in his own strength, but in a depending frame upon Jesus Christ." Or Shepard: "Whatever comes from self, it is ever for self. . . . And so a man makes himself his own god."

Even to desire Christ because one fears damnation or God's wrath indicates that desire, not emptiness, still rules. Shepard was rigorous in stressing the sinfulness of seeking Christ for comfort, not for Christ alone: "If a man close with Christ to remove horror, not sin, and so has not closed with him for his holiness, you never closed with Christ . . . but only for your own ends." A similar realization would later prompt Jonathan Edwards to abandon his famous terrorizing of the sinful soul. Fear leads only to a desire for ease. As Shepard put it, these emotions are like those of "a sick woman that comes to the physician, not to marry her, but to heal her, cure her, and so comfort her. Or, if she doth come to marry him, it is only to satisfy her lust, or to save her from trouble, etc. . . . They close with Christ to make them happy, not to make them holy." With his usual bluntness Shepard is saying that just as a woman who is in "trouble" (i.e., pregnant) may try to get her doctor to marry her, so a sinner may look to Christ for rescue. But neither motive makes a whore a virgin. Any worldly happiness, even the feigning of grace, if it is "pleasing to men . . . is one of the great part of the inward, secret, subtile, spiritual whoredom of the soul."[36]

Anne Hutchinson had the misfortune to become an "objective correlative," in T. S. Eliot's phrase, for women who did not accept dependence on God's allocated duties but asserted a separate and certain connection to the Deity.[37] Shepard devotes several of his sermons in *Parable of the Ten Virgins* to a scornful critique of various heresies, especially the antinomian conviction of certain grace, which to him is just one of many "slothful opinions" by which men can avoid working to abase themselves. Shepard cannot refrain from outrage that a woman should have persuaded so many to this point of view. "What a swarm of strange opinions, which (like flies) have gone to the sores of men's heads and hearts . . . golden dreams of grace . . . that there is no grace in the saints, no grace in Christ, no human nature, no promise to evidence grace, no Law to be a rule to them that have received grace: who would think that ever any should so fall by a simple woman?" In another passage, also preached at the time of the antinomian crisis or shortly thereafter (1636–38), Shepard again says, "(as

Judg. ix.54,) What, shall I fall by a woman? Shall I fall by the worst?"[38]

Other Puritans had similar views of Mrs. Hutchinson. "That wretched *Jezabell*," Peter Bulkeley called her, "who made her selfe a Prophetesse," was as bad as the monks who "have their assurance by revelation . . . it is too low a work for them to descend into themselves, & to examine how it is with them *within*." We can find more comfort in faith and love, he says, "than they shal do in their fancied revelations, and absolute way, neglecting the state of the inward man." Hugh Peter lectured her more directly: "You have stepped out of your place; you have rather been a husband than a wife, and a preacher than a hearer; and a magistrate than a subject, and so you have thought to carry all things in Church and Commonwealth as you would, and have not been humbled for this." "American Jezebel," Winthrop wrote, and added, "*Dux foemina facti*."[39]

Yet Mrs. Hutchinson was only one of several obstreperous women who found scope for unwifely energies in New England's early years. Sarah Keayne was driven out of Boston's First Church for "irregular prophesying mixt Assemblys and for refusing ordinarily to heare in the Churches of Christ." Mary Dyer, a Quaker missionary and earlier a Hutchinson disciple, was martyred in Boston in 1661 after having been thrown out once before. Female "enthusiasts" frequently disrupted the decorum of ordered religion in New England. Puritan Englishwomen too had always had a reputation for zeal, as we can see in the history of Oliver Heywood's mother. In America women were given more rights, more respect, and more responsibility, a recent study has claimed.[40] On the other hand, America also drove several women crazy. Anne Yale Hopkins, according to Winthrop's diary, went insane because she wrote books, none of which have survived, instead of keeping to a housewife's calling. Sarah Hutchinson is another who lost her mind and was pictured as an erratic intellectual woman by an intolerant male world.[41]

What seems like simple sexism is part of the more paradoxical polarities of the Puritan Family Romance. Insofar as women were pure mothers accepting subjugation to the pure Father, they were exalted in fantasy and given great range for their emotional and assertive energies in daily life. Insofar as they struggled toward more various intellectual and nonmothering identities, they were seen as willful. Yet Puritan theology seems to have fostered female assertiveness, verbally at first, more flagrantly later on, especially in the naked Quaker women marching to assert their defiance in the 1650s, and of course the witches, most of whom were female, in the latter half of the century. These breakdowns of expected social roles indicate by their intensity and by the excessive reaction of male authorities a diminished ability of Puritanism to hold together contrary energies. We can imagine, as a reaction, growing severity in the pressures on homespun Ophelias to conform.

Thomas Shepard in particular frequently compares sinful feelings to a wife out of control. Christ, as a husband, will not give everything to us now, because "give some women their will, and you give them your lives, and loss of all; so here." Like a proper husband, he says, Christ must be "Lord in my house." As a bridegroom, he says earlier, Christ can transform his spouse's deformities into beauty, and we must mourn "as widows without him." Shepard is unrelenting in his use of female analogies for sinners imprisoned in their desires. "As some women, because God does not feed so liberally their sweet tooth, their lickerish longings, build them ceiled houses . . . nothing can please them, neither husband, servants, ministers, nor God's ordinances." These women are the epitome of self-absorption. They serve as an appropriate simile for "the secret meaning" of the hypocrite's account of conversion: "Why, the secret meaning is, I pray admire me," and you can tell because the word "myself ever comes in."[42]

Yet the same values that equated unmaternal women with sinful selfishness also gave rise to England's first good female poet, and the only good poet in first-generation New England. Just as Anne Bradstreet kept to a balanced submission in her life, her best poems express both a genuine love for her husband, family, and God, and an ironic consciousness of how her role as mother and wife conflicts with her attempts to be a poet as well. Her extraordinary images for her struggle to write poetry reflect a Puritan's proper self-loathing. Yet they also more covertly reflect a spunky woman's perceptions of the box made for her by men, even down to the smoothly metered and rhymed lines asked of her by classical "DuBartas" traditions. Like Hamlet, she understood how inextricably embedded she was in her time, yet how ardent were the demands of her inward voice. Puritan society gave her a frame and a language for her self-perceptions, even while constricting her. As she wrote in "The Prologue,"

> I am obnoxious to each carping tongue
> Who says my hand a needle better fits,
> A poet's pen all scorn I should thus wrong,
> For such despite they cast on female wits:
> If what I do prove well, it won't advance,
> They'll say it's stol'n, or else it was by chance.

The stanza roundly asserts an "I am" against the expectations of her culture. Yet the rest of the poem speaks equally strongly of "My foolish, broken, blemished Muse," her "weak or wounded brain," "defect," and "This mean and unrefined ore of mine."[43]

The stance is partly conventional, and the structure of her argument leads some modern readers to find irony or anger rather than ambivalence toward herself. Other poems, however, speak vividly of the "ill-formed offspring of my feeble brain," ambiguously showing how playful she could be with the convention of poem as child ("My rambling brat") yet how sincerely Puritan were her artistic self-accusations of weakness. Woman; artist; fancy; self-loathing—these were the contradictory coordinates of her self-consciousness given to her by Puritan rhetoric. For Puritan preachers, the coordinates were properly one, not contradictory. Women, art, fancy, and self-loathing were all associated with sin, except as woman became virgin bride and tender mother.

In arguing that saints should touch defiled people with reproofs rather than defiling themselves by separating, John Cotton translates 2 Corinthians 7.1 ("let us cleanse ourselves from all filthiness of the flesh and spirit") as "It is good for a man not to touch a woman. If so be a man touch a strange woman, so as to be familiar to plead for her, and to connive with her, this man is defiled; and if I now touch this man so as to be familiar with him, and to keep fellowship with him, I am also defiled." The image of woman begins the chain of defilement, because woman connotes whorish lust and self-love. As Shepard observes, "There is never an unsound heart in the world; but as they say of witches, they have some familiar that sucks them, so they have some lust that is beloved of them." But the image of a sheltering mother ends the chain of purification. So Shepard dreams of Christ: "Never to go away from under his wing, out of his bleeding bosom of love and endless and unspeakable compassions no more."[44]

Sin is often and explicitly represented by the natural mother. She is responsible for the fleshly nature of the flesh; the father, for the spiritual possibilities of the soul. Cotton made clear the necessity for "the blood and spirit of the Son of God" to wash away "the sinfull uncleannesse of our natures, from our Mothers wombe; . . . we are borne in the goare blood of sinfull defilements, and therefore God hath provided the blood of Christ, to wash and cleanse us from our Mothers womb, Col. 2.11, 12. so that Christ, by his blood and Spirit, cleanses us from the sinfull nature of our flesh." His equation of sin, flesh, and mother, like the worldliness that Puritans saw in the Anglican church, became a reflex in the rhetoric of purification. In proportion as the saint identifies with the virgin, he attributes his flesh to the mother. "The sin of thine heart or nature is the cause, the womb," wrote Shepard, "that contains, breeds, brings forth, suckels all the liter, all the troop of sins that are in thy life." Thomas Hooker cried out in *The Soules Vocation,* "Mine owne base heart, it is the mother and breeder of all these sinnes." Elsewhere Hooker makes the analogy more plain speaking: "When a woman that is with child strongly longs after something, she doth minde that thing: How? her mind is continually upon it, her eie, her heart, her fancie, her thoughts, her whole self, as it were, is taken up with it. Thus is it with those that have sin alive in them." Even in more playful intellectual manipulations, the weaker sex came in for scorn. *"Humanum est errare,"* noted Edward Taylor in his sermons on the Lord's Supper. "It is proper to men while here to be mistaken, though it be *per accidens*: our conclusions are syllogistical: these always are births teemed out of the womb of the weaker sex, and therefore are not above a possibility of being mistakes."[45]

So Thomas Shepard says: "What is the end of the mother in laying wormwood and gall upon her breast, but that the child, by tasting the bitterness of it, might be weaned, and have his stomach and will turned from it? what is the end of fear and sorrow, but by this to turn away the soul from sin?" Later in *The Sound Believer,* Shepard makes the connection even more graphic: "When the soul sees that all its righteousness is a menstruous cloth, polluted with sin . . . it begins to cry out, How can I stand or appear before him with such continual pollutions."[46]

The image of self-pollution is more than masturbatory, though references to the sinner's "tinderbox" in Puritan writings have masturbatory overtones, and Shepard elsewhere has a specific indictment of that uncleanness: "It may be God keeps him from the act of whoredom, but wanton looks, lascivious thoughts, speculative uncleanness, self-pollution, (which he commits when the candles are out, and none but God sees,) . . . Scholars of Westminster have been detected from twelve to fourteen years of age to live in this sin."[47] But the real sin is the pleasure in self that blocks emptying oneself for the father's will. Willful wife, or mother giving birth, or whore, are synonyms for sinful selfishness, and any identification with the mother, if at the father's expense, calls forth massive self-recrimination. Thomas Hooker summed up both the temptation and the resolution in *The Unbeleevers Preparing for Christ* (1638): "There are many thinke that

they brought grace into the world with them, and that they had grace
from their mothers belly; aske them when did you receive grace, when
did you receive faith, they will answer, they beleeved ever since they
were borne, they had faith ever since they can remember; a great many
poore ignorant soules thinke that grace came into the world with them;
No, no, be not deceived, faith commeth by hearing, faith is the gift of
God." As William Haller has said, there were no Rousseaus in the
pulpits of New England.[48]

Connections between sin, desiring self, whore, and conceiving
mother are characteristically expressed with anal rather than sexual
associations. Puritans purged themselves of sexual or aggressive feelings by expressing them in images of filth, disgust, and shame. To
Hooker, in *The Christians Two chiefe Lessons*, "the heart of man by
nature is a sinke of abhominations, the very imaginations evill, and that
continually: it breaths forth nothing but uncleannesse, hatred, selfe-
love, worldlinesse, with whole swarms of evil thoughts: it is evill, and
wholly evill, even in all the corners of the will, understanding, memory,
affections, full of corruption, over-spread with the leprosie of sinne."
John Cotton asks "why is sin so loathsome," and answers, "Because it is
that which comes naturally from man corrupt, it is the naturall issue of
corrupt nature, therefore loathsome; the excrements of a clean person
is loathsome, much more of a corrupt, . . . if a child should lye in its
dung, or if we should, we would think we were unfit for civill company,
yet such are wee, as long as wee lye in sin unpardoned." He then compares sin to diarrhea. "Wee would bee ashamed to come into company
with defiled bodyes, wee should not say it is our infirmity or a loosenesse
wee are subject to, we have our spirituall loosenesse from God, from
prayer, from our callings, from holy duties, this is a loathsome thing to
pretend loosenesse or infirmity in filthy things, therefore let us take
shame to our selves, and strive for cleansing, *Psal.* 51.7."[49] For Puritans, there was a strange and deeply felt connection between excrement and babies. One came from a proud body, the other from
the mother's sexuality. Sin therefore comes from both. By dismissing
the mother's body as a more general simile for the flesh, one's own body
could be purified and made virgin, ready for the Lord to enter.

In one aspect of Puritan theory, children were born as filthy bundles
of original sin. "Stained from birth with Adam's sinful fact," Anne
Bradstreet said in a poem about childhood, "Thence I began to sin as
soon as act." As with sin and mother, adult images of childhood evoke an
acute and shameful consciousness of body, for which anal imagery was

the conventional formulation. Bradstreet's sense of how ugly, painful, and physical childhood could be is more surprising to us, if equally conventional.

> What grippes of wind mine infancy did pain,
> What tortures I in breeding teeth sustain?[50]

Yet these are retrospective fantasies of adults, not children's actuality. The language of anality for original sin uses babies as a central association. But in practice, Puritans were loving and tolerant of young children until well past the Oedipal stage. Moreover, language used to describe children is much more deliberately flexible and optimistic than language using infants as metaphors for sin.

Though writers often say children are born with evil in their hearts, they are at least as ready to say children "are like narrow mouth'd vessels," ready to receive good or evil drop by drop, or like young twigs, ready to be bent toward right or wrong attitudes. For Peter Bulkeley parents are the ones really responsible for abetting or diminishing sin in their young, either by "letting them grow like wilde plants, or rather like the wilde asse-colt which snuffs up the winde at her pleasure," or by raising them to be "made like the polished Saphirs, and as the carved stones of the Temple." Robert Pricke in England said that "there lieth in the heart of the child such a bundell or sea of naughtines, as wil bring him to utter destruction, if it be not diminished: or at the leastwise restrained." However, just a few sentences before he finds that "a childe is as a neue vessel, which not onely doth easily receive good liquor, but doth a long time retaine and keepe the favor thereof."[51] Puritan language used children as goads to parents, and several psychoanalytically oriented social historians have seen adult projection in every facet of Puritan child rearing. Even so, the language of advice is much more ambivalently tempered toward children as vessels than the language of comparisons for sin.[52]

Dung, semen, and babies had the same negative associations for Puritans as art and other human products. They are emanations of the desiring will; therefore they have to be cleansed, restrained, then transformed and purified so that God's image can speak truly, as spiritual semen to virgins or milk to babies. The infamous Puritan emphasis on infant depravity and strict childhood discipline—actually more Calvinist than Puritan—shows one side of ambivalent adult self-condemnation, projected onto the child. Yet babies also serve as the central image for regeneration. As in so many other ways, America was the place for Puritan dreams of self-translation to thrive, in their contradictions as well as their intensities.

New England Child Rearing

It is not clear how or, indeed, whether New England child rearing differed from child rearing in the mother country, or elsewhere in Europe. As John Cotton said, one of the chief reasons for emigrating from Holland to New England was that Holland seemed "a place of so great liberty to children, that they could not educate their children, as their parents had educated them: nor could they give them due correction, without reproof and reproach from their neighbors." On the other hand, the separatist William Bradford remarks that in New England parents could be more "tender" than in Holland, where "necessity" forced them to become taskmasters.[53]

In the main, although the same sex-role expectations prevailed, recent studies suggest several important differences. Their cumulative effect was to simplify the confused mixed expectations of Old England's Puritan families into a less ambiguous and less anxious set of attitudes. Broadly speaking, mothers were even more tender to infants, since nearly every woman breast-fed her own children, and fathers were more patriarchal throughout, while the social frame induced security and restriction rather than uncertainty and change.

At least eight differences of relative emphasis have been discerned:

1. There may not have been any swaddling.
2. Mothers, not nurses, usually breast-fed, unless they were sick.
3. Children may have been weaned somewhat earlier, when they were twelve to eighteen months old.
4. Physical controls, such as beating, were used less frequently and ideological controls, especially parental instruction, more frequently. Parental instruction may have begun at an earlier age.
5. There was probably somewhat more maternal discipline.
6. Children dressed as little adults from the age of six, and because life was more agrarian they had to begin working earlier.
7. Group consciousness and group restraints were more prevalent.
8. Childhood play may have been more actively discouraged.

Life in New England was also healthier, as higher longevity and lower infant-mortality rates attest. More generally, New England society reinforced patriarchal norms in language and behavior, giving men much more authority than had been possible in England. An early social historian noted the intense emphasis on family and the characteristic structure of "patriarchal clans." Also, for at least some families the division of duties by sex was more absolute. Increase Mather, for instance, seems to have written, preached, and studied almost every waking hour, giving his family over to his wife. As he wrote to his children, their mother was "a Tender Mother (if there was such an one in the world)," so that Mather "kept close to my study & committed the management of the affairs of the family to her."[54]

Some of these differences are in dispute, notably swaddling, which is simply not mentioned in New England writings.[55] It seems to be highly probable that infants were breast-fed by mothers rather than nurses except in rare cases, even up to the 1790s.[56] Though there is much less evidence for time of weaning, several scattered quotations and the relative frequency of births every two years imply some change, at least of parental expectations. Samuel Sewall notes that one of his children was weaned at eighteen months and one at fourteen months when the "nurse" was sick. Thomas Shepard mentions that his twelve-month-old son had a mouth so sore "he could eat no meat, only suck the breast." Anne Bradstreet observes that "some children are hardly weaned; although the teat be rubbed with wormwood or mustard, they will either wipe it off, or else suck down sweet and bitter together," indicating some parental efforts toward weaning before the child was ready.[57] As always, the problem of evidence is probably insoluble for the earliest childhood years.

For governance, however, there is more evidence, at least in the form of instructions. Self-control is the keynote, though at what age it should begin is unclear. There is no evidence of toilet training in either England until John Locke prescribes it in the 1690s. In both colony and mother country parental expectations of self-discipline in the young child increase as the seventeenth century draws to a close. The language of self-government does not seem to be applied to the very young child in New England until the eighteenth century, however, when the Puritan John Barnard calls for children to be governed and instructed "while they are scarce weaned from the milk or drawn from the Breast," though that may be a conventional formulation. First-generation Puritans are more apt to reflect the seventeenth-century pattern that governance begins at the age of reason. Thomas Hooker says that a child of ten or twelve, "living the life of a beast," cannot "consider the mysteries of life and salvation," and Anne Bradstreet makes the conventional distinction between the father's tender early rule and stricter instruction afterward, at least for physical burdens: "A wise father will not lay a burden on a child of seven years old, which he knows is enough for one of twice his strength, much less will our heavenly father (who knows our mould), lay such afflictions upon his weak children as will crush them to the dust." On the other hand, John Eliot recommends the "gentle rod of the mother," and it may be that mothers were encouraged to discipline more.[58]

American families were clearly more patriarchal in the father's domination of older sons. "Keep them within doors at their book, at some little service," especially on Sunday, said John Barnard in 1737. Contrast that with William Gouge's remark made over one hundred years earlier that "recreation" was one of the four chief needs of childhood.[59] Thomas Cobbett's mid-1650s family-advice book, written in New England, stresses obedience much more than love and urges children to revere their parents in order to master resentment. "Present your Parents so to your minds," he says, "as bearing the image of God's Father-hood, and that also will help your filiall awe and Reverence to them." A simile from New Haven's John Davenport assumes a patriarchal disapproval of play: God sometimes "creates darknesse in the soul; . . . As a father, when he seeth his child doth but play with the candle which he afforded him to work by, takes it from him, and leave him in the dark." Cotton Mather assiduously worked to force a direct parallel between child rearing and religious reverence, with the father acting the part of God. "I first beget in them a high opinion of their father's love to them, and of his being best able to judge, what shall be good for them. Then I make them sensible, tis a folly for them to pretend unto any witt and will of their own . . . my word must be their law. . . . I would never come to give a child a blow; except in case of obstinacy or some gross enormity. To be chased for a while out of my presence I would make to be looked upon, as the sorest punishment in the family." When one of his children died at two years and seven months, the child "made a most edifying end in prayer and praise." In *The Protestant Temperament* Philip Greven cites many eighteenth-century instances of paternal severity and high parental seriousness of expectation for the very young.[60]

No social historian denies that, if only for the first year, as John Demos puts it, "a baby had a relatively tranquil and comfortable time."

The evidence Demos finds for breaking the child's will between one and two years comes entirely from Eriksonian theories of autonomy, not Puritan accounts, though Greven cites some horrifying eighteenth-century instances of infant deprivation in evangelical families. New England practice does seem more severe than earlier behavior, though not to the very young child until the second generation and beyond, when English practice also seems to be moving toward Lockean norms.

The real difference, I suggest, is simply that in New England parents were less anxious and more secure, in their roles as well as in their communities. Yet if mixed expectations for their children seemed less confusing, the basic contradiction between mother's love and father's control thereby became all the more stark. The hypothesis I suggest is that children born and bred of American Puritan families tended to become either more classically obsessive or more overtly rebellious against their parents than their English forebears had been, because the fathers were more patriarchal and less anxious. Conversion experiences, though eagerly expected by parents and children, strikingly declined. The language of American Puritanism expresses these changes in its inability to keep obsessive styles and nursing fantasies together. A rhetoric of accusatory authority and private solace divides the double appeal of Puritan preaching, as chapter seven describes for Increase Mather and Samuel Willard.

The high point of Puritanism therefore occurs in New England's first generation, where earlier anxieties are transformed into a rare vigor of purpose, scope, and certainty. The change from a variety of anxious fathers to a more uniform set of stern patriarchs led eventually to changes in the obsessive style, as my next two chapters describe. The Puritan appeal moves from doubleness to divergence, in themes and imagery, while the frame remains fixed. For the first generation, however, style was indeed the man, quite marvellously so. Recent scholars find the second generation a more important source for American literary beginnings. If that is so, I am tempted to say, so much the worse for American literature. The best first-generation ministers were able to articulate vivid personal intensities as well as shared convictions. No later generation of ministers could speak with such confidence, in a world rapidly growing too complicated for a language of breasts and whores to explain.

Chapter Six

New England Styles:
Diverse Fathers

This chapter is an appreciative account of how unobsessive, diverse, and personal the best first-generation New England Puritans could make the supposed unanimity of the obsessive style. Their faith never became the monolith that they dreamed of or that Perry Miller imagined. The wish was shared more than their practice.[1] While preceding chapters have suggested the range, repetitiveness, and intensity of shared fantasy in Puritanism, to stop there gives a very misleading picture of Puritan language.

Regressive imagery certainly helps to shape New England sermons, but these images are oddly interchangeable with other, nonregressive, images of union through dependence: trees, plants, oceans, fountains, government, the body, marriage, sex, buildings, corporations. It is not so much the individual similes that matter as the fact of their abundance and repetition within a grand polarized frame. Puritans invert their comparisons with remarkable freedom. Family imagery is used to express religious experience, from marriage to babies to parenting; yet religious comparisons are sometimes used to guide family conduct. Breasts can be ministers, God's Word, or God's promises; yet Peter Bulkeley can say, "Keep Christ neare unto us . . . Lay him therefore in our hearts; Let him lie between our breasts, Cant. 1.12."[2] Biblical language and practical experience seem interchangeable to the point of reversibility in Puritan "reasons," even as Puritans proclaim the virtues of precision, rigorous distinctions, and the complete separation of spirit from world.

Puritan similes always point to a frame. Like selves, or individual churches, they exist as separate multiples, yet all are equally subordinate to the Word's order. They are simple, rarely developed at any length. They are interchangeable, none more valid or invalid than any other. The part depends on the whole, not the whole on the part. Their force, like the army of the saints, lies in their numbers, not their individual will. No one regressive simile holds the key. Rather, each calls attention to a larger pattern of polarity within which stages of self-transformation can occur. Group dependence is the end of individual comparison.

So much can be said generally. Yet the more one reads of sermons, the more an individual stamp is clear even in the densest explication. Identity returns, despite the common task of emptying the self. A sense of assertive voice as well as shared fantasy and intellectual order spoke to the needs of New England congregations through interpreting God's Word. It is not just a question of patterns and similes, though we can see differences of emphasis at that level too. The imagery chosen by Thomas Hooker for the experience of rebirth has more to do with fathering, sexuality, order, and worldliness than the female or infantile receptivity of John Cotton's prose, or than Thomas Shepard's taut union of infantile and virgin imagery with strict rules and restraint. Even in prose rhythms and sentence construction a richness of individual voice is apparent, at least in the first generation.

Puritans were not aiming for literary effects. As Owen Watkins says, "When they produced literature they did so in the same way as the British were said to have acquired the Empire—in a fit of absent-mindedness."[3] They wanted "right attitudes and right conduct," not glorious prose. However, that understates the intensity of impact Puritans demanded from their well-ordered words. They did have imperial dreams for the human soul, and God's possession of sinful territory required affecting as well as convincing prose to bring the natives of the heart to voluntary choice rather than mindless slavery. In a deeper sense, New England sermons had profound literary effects as well as consequences, even in what seem to us to be defects. To argue for Puritan styles in the plural, as being more than plain and much more than obsessive while they vivified plain and obsessive conventions, is the purpose of this chapter. Readers can correct my bias toward the first generation of New England preachers with recent sympathetic discussions of the second generation.[4] New England patriarchy itself, I have suggested, began in part as a wishful uniformity; yet its exercise in the early years shows the energetic diversity that a broadly accepted cultural fantasy can liberate, especially in fathers. Though Milton, Marvell, and Bunyan are obviously greater writers, the high point of Puritan language as shared emotional experience comes in New England from 1630 to 1650.

There have been many analyses of Puritan plain style. Just as they were hostile to stained glass because it kept out the light, ministers tried to avoid any ostentatious displays of wit or erudition that kept out the plain truth of the Bible.[5] Partly because of Ramist training, and partly because of more unconscious needs to divide emotional realities into separated, interchangeable parts, the numbered category and the simile remain among the most easily recognizable aspects of Puritan sermon style. Other aspects include the lack of humor, the use of "I" as public exemplum, the reliance on conventional phrases, the long and incremental lists, the pervasive polarities.[6] Jonas Barish, in his analysis of Ben Jonson's Zeal-of-the-Land Busy, describes the excesses of Puritan prose as Jonson perceived them: a reliance on repetition, apposition, cliches, anaphora, and genitive phrases leading to "a narcotic doze . . . a trancelike rhythm that conceals the vacancy of meaning beneath."[7] A vacancy of self, not of meaning, was what was aimed for. In many ways these are the characteristics of the obsessive style, which routinizes emotion by creating a mechanical atmosphere of intellectual exercise rather than emotional expression.[8] Even the most private conversation sounds like a speech to the troops, full of repetitive cadences, melodramatic instances of God's grandeur or personal calls to arms, and emphatic gravity. Such a style speaks as much or more to one's internal audience, the self that has been repressed, as to one's listeners.[9]

Certainly much Puritan preaching, especially of second-rank ministers, sounds like that. But with the best preachers the sermon becomes a vehicle for assertive self as well as empty self. For Thomas Hooker, John Cotton, and Thomas Shepard, personal voice becomes congruent with public rhetoric. In the sermons of two second-generation ministers, Increase Mather and Samuel Willard, as my next chapter suggests, there is a movement toward aloofness in two divergent ways: public accusation and private solace. Where the first generation could affirm themselves, God, and community together, the second generation's proclamation of a ritualized collective self is more obsessively self-denying.

Thomas Hooker, 1586–1647

Thomas Hooker's style, like his vision of social order, shows an Elizabethan brashness. Proportion, order, and harmony are part of his expressive technique, along with a wonderful sense of rhythmic balance. Listen to the lilt in his annotation of a passage from the Bible in *The Application of Redemption*: "This Spiritual Good intended, is the heap of Grace and Happiness, with all those sweet Fruits and Refreshings which are either in preparation to it, or attendants upon it; the whole Estate, and Portion, and Patrimony of a Christian, the Riches & Revenues of the Gospel, what is in Hand, what is in Hope, what in Posession, what in Expectation, the whole Mass and Inventory of those Everlasting Treasuries which are stored up from all Eternity for the welfare of His."[10] When Hooker establishes his rhythms of balanced order, as here, he begs to be read aloud. Everything floats, almost bounces, in apposition, with nouns as the alliterative resting points in the movements toward "those Everlasting Treasuries." The very short phrases, when put together to make up one of Hooker's typically mammoth sentences, give a cumulative effect wholly justifying the Ramist theory that particles, if arranged in their natural order, will form a whole. Here the arrangement also shows the static, well-regulated "nature" behind Hooker's order. From the "heap" to the "Mass," nouns are nudged into relationship only once by the verb, with two peripheral verbs, all variants of "to be." The positioning alone, with the devices of contrast, alliteration, and parallelism, gives harmony to these discrete rewards and desires. When the sinner feels the force of an obvious simile, he cannot help but become a saint.

Elsewhere Hooker balances verbs rather than nouns: "Sometimes the Lord knocketh at the doore, sometimes he pickes the locke, thus every way striving to come in, stands thus knocking, and intreating, exhorting, perswading, he knocks with much patience and long suffering, if any man will but open, here is all the Lord requires, all that he expects and lookes for, the opening of the doore that is all; the doore is the heart, the opening of the doore is the enlarging of the heart to entertaine Christ; if any man will but open now, here is all the Lord desires, hee will come and suppe with that man, and [be] with him."[11] A series of independent verbs and participial actions comes to rest again in the verb "to be," which establishes the correspondence between a common situation and religious truth. No adjectives qualify the force or the balance of either reality. Nor does he try to keep God "above" the drama of picking a lock.

No wonder he has been called, by Sacvan Bercovitch, "New England's finest first-generation stylist."[12] His style is the verbal enactment of the Puritan demand to replace earthly hierarchy by earthly equality (for the saints) under heavenly rule. Born in a tiny village, the son of a Puritan overseer of landed property, Hooker seems to have grown

up with a brash yeoman's confidence.[13] Discovering the witty elegance
of Lyly's ornate antitheses, Hooker took all the snobbery and elegance
out of Lyly's subject material while keeping the knack of balancing
and contrasting states of being, often in an "if-then" or "when-then"
format that gives rhythmic life to conventional phrases:

> for alas what is our life: a bubble, a flower, a shadow, the bubble
> breaks, and the flower fades, and the shadowes pass away, thou art
> not certain thou shalt live til the evening, or if thou doest, how doest
> thou know thou shalt have ability to seek the Lord for mercy? when
> thy brain is grown weak, not able to remember or consider the things
> belonging to thy peace, and when nature is grown so weak it's not able
> to grapple with the difeate, when the daies of sorrow and sickness
> are come upon thee, and thou sayest I have no pleasure in them.

Where Lyly categorizes, Hooker seeks to describe the interaction of
equal essences rather than impose a hierarchy that might separate him
from common people with common experiences. At times he pares
down complexity to an extraordinarily simple balance of short phrases,
here structured by the logic of divine intent: "for what Christ praies
for, that he obtains, *John* 11.22.42. *I know that thou hearest me alwaies*:
but this is not obtained, therefore was not desired, therefore not intended by Christ, therefore for this end our Savior did not lay down
his life, and undertake his sufferings: For what he suffered, for that he
intended, his own end was most serious in his own intention; that he
intended, he desired; that he desired, he obtained: that he obtained
not, he desired not, and that he intended not; therefore for that end
he did not suffer."[14] Hooker's style can be a lullaby of logic.[15]

Along with repetition and balance, the simile is his major rhetorical
device. "You may conceive it by a similitude," he says countless times:
"if a pot be boyling upon the fire, there will a scum arise, but yet they
that are good house-wives, and cleanly, and neat, they watch it, and
as the scum riseth up, they take it off and throw it away . . . Thus is it
with the soul, impuritie will be in the heart." Though Hooker wrote
the most comprehensive and politically mature of first-generation books,
A survey of the summe of Church Discipline, his real love was the
"application" of intellectual truth to the heart. As an early biographer
records, even in England Hooker "would therein so touch the *con-
sciences* of his auditors, that a judicious person would say of him, 'He
was the best at an use that ever he heard.'" "Take hot water into a
windy stomacke the winde will stirre on one side, and the water on
another side, and distemper the stomacke, but let the party take a

little Methridate, the Methridate closing with the stomacke will ease a man, and refresh a man in this kinde: so a good man hath a weake judgement in this kinde, and sometimes a distempered heart, but when the good word of the Lord, the Cordiall water, the Methridate, when that comes . . . If the sermon acts like Methridate, so much the better. The idea was to make the Word as immediate and dramatic as possible. "The soule would be carelesse and secure, will not heare, nor attend," he declares in *The Saints Guide*. "The Lord knockes at the doore of the soule, findes him out behinde the Pillor, awakens him asleep in his Pue."[16]

Like no other New England minister, he respected his audience as potential buyers of God's wares, rather than treating them as hard disobedient hearts. His early success in converting Joan Drake, a modern historian tells us, gave him confidence in preparing sinners for grace, and throughout his life, unlike Cotton, Hooker refused to detach conversion itself from ordinary experience. It was not a mystical flash reserved for the few but a possession that any sincere heart might anticipate.[17] Don't worry about temporary aberrations, he says at one point; "cast a bowl, though there be a rub here and hub there in the way which turn it out, yet it falls upon the bias: so an upright heart." Yet he can also rail against the hypocritical outward show of faith as "a paper wall against cannon shot." He fully understands the plasticity of human motives and therefore has a winning confidence in the ability of men to reorient their feelings toward Christ, while coming down especially hard on those who don't make the effort. "Many are Sermon-sicke, as those that are sea-sicke, exceeding ill at ease, queasie stomacks, while they are on the Sea; yet the same men when they come on land, are as well as ever they were so we have many who in the hearing of the word, seeme to bee much troubled, exceedingly cast downe; yet the same men when comming abroad, they are but acquainted with the ayre of the world, their pangs of sorrow passe away." But his anger at the foul-weather friends is a loving anger, because he knows how easy it is to make the change, as easy as floating: "As in the Art of swimming, hee that will swimme, must plucke his feet from the bottome, and commit himselfe to the streame to beare him up, so must we plucke our hearts from these things below, and them from us."[18]

The ship and the clock, two of Hooker's favorite images for the soul, satisfy his penchant for making the soul into a Ramist collection of interacting parts, a little world functioning in the big world. "For what the oyle is to the wheeles of a clocke, it makes them run glibber, so godlinesse to the soule, when the soule is oyled and annointed therewith, it is fitted to performe any good duty." In *The Soules Vocation* he takes three pages for a protracted trope which presents the soul as a clock with its wheels awry, while grace finally sets everything right. Hooker expressed his sense of the natural relation of microcosm to macrocosm in another favorite image: the body. Everyone must have his fit portion and proportion, he says; "thou that art a finger, shalt have so much grace as befits a finger, and thou that art an hand, thou shalt have so much grace as shall save thee, and is fit for thy place; but another is an arme, and hee shall have more, but all shall have that which is fitting." As usual the thought is conventional, the phrasing brief and pungent. The phrasing is often dramatic, as here: "A man that hath had a bone long out of joynt, and it is now festred, it will make him cry many an *oh*, before it be brought into his right place againe; so it is with a man whose heart is full of filthinesse."[19]

Unlike Cotton and Shepard, Hooker thought in terms of "right place" and social functions. For him, order and location in the whole give identity and security, not individual success. "As it is with a little barke, if it should have a great maine mast, and broad saile cloathes, then instead of carrying it, it would be overthrown by them: therefore men proportion their mast according to their ship or bark." Even sin, that great Puritan conglomerate of sexual self-assertion and excremental separation, offends Hooker most because it disrupts proportion: "To the end therefore that there may be a proportion between the root, and the branches, between the head, and the members, between the elder brother, and the rest of the brethren, between Christ and the people of God, hence it cometh of necessitie, that sin must not have dominion over any of God's people." He also compares sin to a gangrene on the body politic, or a rotten pillar in a house: "When the main pillars begin to rot, and the supporters of the house molder away, there is no supporting of it, but it must be made new, or else it will fall down. As it is in the body natural, so also in the body politic as in the house, so in the estate."[20] A confident proportion governs his similes as well.

Hooker's assiduous attentions to his audience can be accounted for by his sense of part and proportion. He needs conversions to complete the whole, so he speaks to sinners directly. He batters them with similes, he exhorts them, he dramatizes their anxieties and problems, he even dares to speak as God would. Where most New England ministers gave almost all their attention to saints and hypocrites, those already within the covenant, Hooker was "the magnificent exception," as Edmund Morgan says.[21] Hooker himself put the matter squarely: "For my brethren, here is all the quarrell between you and the Minister of God, it all lyeth here, the Lord saith, thou must forsake thy sins, or else I must damn thy soul. For we come for souls when we come to preach, we doe not come here onely to spend an hour, and so an end of the matter." He speaks in his master's place, and in his early sermons he even speaks with his master's voice: "I deal plainly with you and tell you what God hath told me: . . . I must returne an answer to my Master that sent me to night, why speake you not an answer? I must have one. Do you like well of it, would you have England destroyed? . . . God bade me aske, why do you not answer me? I must not stirre without it, I must have it, I am an importunate Embassador."[22] This arrogant metaphor comes very close to the assertion of direct contact with God, for which Anne Hutchinson was exiled. But Hooker knows his audience is with him, because he does not assert an unrestrained intimacy but a proper public role. His is an unquenchable faith in the possibility of a redeemed community, not personal messages of grace.

In Hooker's universe no one had to forswear his humanity to be saved. Other preachers might stress the absolute corruption of the human heart, and Hooker would agree in theory, though in practice he stressed the efficacy of baptism and preaching more than most.[23] His practice also was to study and use the psychology of the average man to convince him that, in his own terms, and for his own good, he should take God for his master.

> The world hath three motives to draw things. Honour, Profit, Pleasure; Now all these are here.
> 1. It is Honourable, a man shall doe as his master doth. . . .
> 2. It is pleasant and comfortable. You shall fare as *Christ* fares, all rost meate, *John* 14. . . .
> 3. The profit that comes by this is better and greater then all other.

Hooker knew perfectly well that "a mans selfe naturally is a God to his soule." But for him sin is something more easily shaken, because less integral to the soul, than it is for Shepard. It is simply a problem in the psychology of wanting possessions: "But how shall we shake off Selfe? here wee are at a plunge, we should doe it, but how may wee? not onely to plucke off our coats, but our shirts too." Hooker even considers the possibility that one can corrupt corruption into being saved. Our hearts are capable, because crooked, of being bribed. "Wee should deale with our hearts as a man would doe with a corrupt Justice, when hee would have him to be on his side, the onely way is to bribe him, though that is sinfull, yet it is good to bribe the corrupt heart with the goodnesse of the promise." Natural motives can be used to prepare oneself for grace. This is the basic premise of Hooker's similes and applications. "As Water-men take the advantage of the tide, so should we learn to take the advantage of our natures."[24]

Hooker had the most exuberant of Puritan imaginations. He knew his people, and yet he loved them (almost) as they were. He went beyond strict theories of infant depravity to work on the middle-aged: "A mans nature in his infancie is like wax that is too soft, and the nature of an old man that also is like wax too hard, but now a middle agged man . . . is most fit for God to put a stamp on." He knew, too, the positive rhythms of the natural soul.

> Learn a similitude from the trees and hearbs of the field, which as they have their spring, wherein they in their glorious hue are comparable to *Salomon* in his royalty, so have they their winter, wherein their sap retireth to the root, the branches seem to be withered, as if they were not the same, no life in them: so is it with the graces of God in mans soule, they have their spring and summer seasons, they have also their winter, wherein they seeme cleane blasted and decayed, as if there were no seeds of grace in their hearts; and as we must not call in question the vegetative power and life that is in plants and hearbs, by reason of the little appearance thereof in the dead time of the yeere, no more must wee make question of the truth of grace in our hearts.[25]

It was a rare Puritan divine who could assure his congregation of the "seeds of grace" already in them. No other preacher would have made such a confident connection with the natural wilderness rather than the Bible, though of course his imagery is generalized on biblical models. Even more remarkable is the assumption grounding not only this simile but Hooker's relation to his audience: that knowledge of natural order can in itself bring man to God.

Hooker was optimistic enough to articulate great faith in the rational understanding guiding natural will. As he says in *The Application of Redemption*, "That alone which my mind judgeth, my Faith embraceth: there is nothing can come to the Wil, but by the Understanding: what the Eye sees not, the Heart affects not. No light comes into this Room, but by this Window." Technically the idea conforms to Perry Miller's discussion of the Puritan concept of mind, though I suspect that Miller derived the theory mostly from Hooker, with references to Elizabethan psychologies. Hooker's style here, as usual, is almost euphuistic in its pattern of balance. But most other ministers condemned man's natural mind, whatever its processes, to the whoredom of Catholic ritual and other sinful manifestations. Hooker's own objection to Catholicism was rather different: "that colliers faith of the Papists, that put out his owne eyes to see by another mans."[26] To him Catholicism deprives man of necessary and intimate contact with daily, visible reality. That alone gives everyone some direct analogues to the truth of God's order.

"You may conceive it by a similitude." The phrase became Hooker's version of a litany. What would later seem like a chasm between sinners and saints, the unredeemed world and the faithful heart, can be leaped over with the flick of a comparison. Structuring each of his similes is the sense that anyone with the least shred of ordinary understanding can be saved. Hooker comes as close as any Puritan to saying, follow your own bent and the Lord will provide. "This is the nature of an Eagle, shee will not goe to catch flies, (that's the nature of the hedge Sparrow,) but shee will prey upon the carkasse. So, this is a good heart that will not prey upon dead duties, but upon the Lord Christ, who is the life of the Soule." In many ways Hooker himself was an eagle among sparrows. He was the man who, a contemporary observed, "while doing his Master's work, would put a king in his pocket." A man with that kind of authority could also keep his similes in line. The natural world is not a metaphoric emanation from God, but it does offer an analogue for God's truth.[27] As such, social order could squelch any antinomian claim to personal intercourse with the Father, in the name of peaceful proportion between nature and God.

Unlike Shepard and Cotton, Hooker does not cast himself as an erotically submissive son. His language expresses a vigorous political order of balanced parts, and he himself was a father to his people in the Father's name. Yet as Frank Shuffelton, his recent biographer, has shown, Hooker's orientation was toward peacemaking and community, not authoritarian power or contentiousness. He was "A Sonne of Thunder, and a shower of Rain," Cotton's poem about him says: a wrathful father and tender mother to his flock, which kept their own hostilities remarkably in check during his fourteen years at Hartford.[28] The historian Daniel Neal describes him in *The History of New-England* (1720): "Mr. *Hooker* was a Son of Thunder in the Pulpit, and having a loud Voice, expressed himself with a great deal of Warmth and Vehemence; his Ministry was adapted chiefly to the awakening of Sinners, and was remarkably blessed that way. His natural Constitution inclined him to Passion, but he was a very great Master of it." Though naturally imperious and wrathful, he mastered himself in part by speaking in the voice of his greater Father. Cotton Mather tells of an incident in which Hooker mistakenly berated a boy, then sought him out to apologize. As Shuffelton says, the incident "shows both Hooker's choleric temper and his overriding commitment to rational charity," as well as his "sensitivity toward children."[29]

Being a "Son of Thunder," Hooker rails most at those who, unlike himself, cannot control anger and oral excess. For him swearers and drunkards are the worst sinners, with adulterers coming in a poor third. "Yet to be an ancient Drunkard, an old blacke mouthed swearer, and ancient Adulterer, . . . the father naught, and the sonne naught" incurs his mightiest wrath. "Hee that hath a plague sore blossoming, hee that hath a tongue belching forth his venome against the Lord of host: he that hath a plague sore of drunkennesse, a plague sore of adultery, then goe farre enough, flie soone enough, the Ale-house is the Pest-house where the plague is, the drunkards are the persons infected." More generally, any oral sickness occasions his biblical vituperation. A hypocrite is like a dog licking vomit, he says; the dog loves it still, though he casts it up, and so the hypocrite "would vomit and confesse his sinnes, and crave mercie, not because he loaths his sinne, but he loathes anguish and horrour of heart, and when that is taken away, he falls to his vomit and base practice." Hooker himself freely accepts the convention that "I am a dog I yield it, yet the dogges lye under the table, that is all I crave and aske, that I may lye under the table and waile for crummes of mercy." But the submission comes more by way of model to his congregation than application to himself. Hypocrites challenge his verbal mastery by not wailing for his crumbs, and he whips them into the kennel with every device: "When the dainties of salvation are distributed, you that are at the lower end of the Table, should thinke with your selves; will the dish never come to the lower end? Oh that the Lord would now guide the Minister, to lay his hand on the sore of this cursed infidelity of mine?"[30]

We have no data from Hooker's early life even for speculating about his personal polarities and projections. All we can say is that his language vigorously expresses the more fathering aspects of Puritan conventions. Anger and oral excess may be associated with mothering for him, but mothers are not a major part of his imagery, and it is more likely that fathering is the locus of his unconscious as well as conscious concerns. His most constant image of control and security is the father guiding the son. Hooker has the utmost confidence that the father exists beyond and within the order of human surroundings. The move to Connecticut, his biographer says, was in part to remove his people from political bickering to become a more holy and loving Christian community, where Hooker's generous faith in the possibility of bringing natural men to God could thrive unhampered by the harsher rhetoric prevailing in the Bay.

At the breakfast table, God will always lend a hand. "A childe that longs for the meat on the table, when his father gives him a peece, hee eats it; his father cuts him another, he eats that too; then his father bids him goe downe; no, but more of that, father, he still begs more of that, and is never content. So it is with a soule that desires grace for grace sake." No mother is here to do the cutting. And no one need give up anything essential to himself to receive the father's help. "Looke as it is with a father, hee sends his childe to the taylors shop, tels him the cloth is bought, the money paid, the suit made for him, onely bids him goe fetch it, and put it on: this is our folly, and it is our misery also, wee either thinke to purchase or to coine grace out of our owne abilities; I tell you no, you must goe to the shop, it is bought and made already, only put on wisedome, and put on sanctification, and it is yours." In fact, the father will be with us whether we want him or not. Hooker expresses the father's presence in dramatic yet intimate images of family life: "When the father is going on in his journey, if the child will not goe on, but stands gaping upon vanity, and when the father calls, he comes not, the onely way is this, the father steps aside behind a bush, and then the child runs and cries, and if he gets his father againe, he forsakes all his trifles, and walkes on more faster and more cheerefully with his father than ever. So when the Lord Jesus Christ . . ."[31] The father-son similes go on, secure in the faith that simply being a sincere human, far from separating us from the Father, makes us analogous to the Son.

In this sense Parrington's celebration of Hooker as the first American democrat does have some validity, not in Hooker's Connecticut polity but in his psychology of analogues. He relinquished stratification, at least in his sermon style, to the one Father who sits in heaven and earth alike. Ironically, however, Hooker's compelling vision of voluntary natural order guided by the Father's voice quickly disintegrated after his death. His congregation split apart. His eldest son refused to return to New England and joined the Church of England at the Restoration, though a young son did become a Puritan minister. Even Hooker's elaborate preparational stages, which triumphed in first-generation theology after the antinomian controversy, gave way to the half-way covenant in the 1660s and 1670s. His magnificent confidence that fathers and sons could be united in holy community proves both the force and the transience of wishful thinking in the New England way.[32]

It would be possible to call Hooker's style patriarchal, at least in contrast to Cotton's more maternal style. Certainly he appropriates the Father's voice for his own awakening purposes much more freely than do the ministers of Massachusetts. But it is really the second-rank ministers, such as Peter Bulkeley, John Norton, John Davenport, John Wilson, and Richard Mather, whose style is more narrowly fixed in a patriarchal mode of legalistic discipline. The conventional Puritan God is a God of law and order, and the conventional obsessive style is correspondingly less supple, more oriented to patriarchal father images, more concerned with rigid duties, rules, and stages. Where orthodox ministers reach for a text or reason, Hooker reaches for a simile. Where they invoke a father's stern judgment, he portrays a father's helping hand. Hooker was eager to open the heart with experiential language, not to enforce conformity with a strict call for reverence, obedience, and self-control. In his life as in his style, he expresses the feelings of a tender father, not a wrathful judge, except to those who could not even perceive how natural a thing it is to be saved.

In some stereotypical sense he shares with mainstream Puritan ministers a certain "masculinity" of style: an emphasis on God's order and fathering, expressed in short phrases, punched home with great vigor and highly dramatic images. Peter Bulkeley, for instance, speaks with tough, assertive short sentences of three to five phrases and often returns to similar father-children analogies. John Davenport frequently uses father-son comparisons, though more harshly than Hooker.[33] While Hooker's language is much more spirited and flexible than the prevailing use of heads and subheads for conventional similes and biblical texts, it remains within the same basic frame. His way of reasoning his hearers to right feelings was a manly way, at least in the thinking of Puritan men. Where Cotton and Shepard variously mix an almost mystical language of rebirth and maternal dependence with an abstract sense of God's rigid laws, Hooker holds to the more orthodox paternal line. Yet he makes the Father extraordinarily attentive, tender, and personal, and the Father's order more a matter of natural acquiescence than rigorous submission. He is also much more alive to the nuances of human psychology. His style may be masculine and patriarchal, but to compare him to a rigid rule maker like John Norton shows how unobsessive Hooker can be within the confines of obsessive conventions. To call him a "Son of Thunder" may finally be right, if we accent the "Son," because Hooker's thunder had exultant sonship as well as fatherhood as its aim.[34] In similes as in themes, he preached the natural heart's comparative readiness to be drawn up by the Father's hand.

John Cotton, 1584–1652

John Cotton's contemporaries thought of him as the most important intellectual figure of the first generation in New England, and Larzer Ziff calls him the best preacher. He had the highest salary; he brought forth the most conversions.[35] For twenty years he was also the great compromiser, trying to keep the troika of Massachusetts, Connecticut, and England on one course while fending off the wolves of Anne Hutchinson and Roger Williams. Hawthorne may well have found his prototype for Arthur Dimmesdale in Cotton's ambiguous relation to Hutchinson's antinomianism. While Hooker concerned himself primarily with application, preparation, and "Church Discipline," Cotton threw himself into the most difficult doctrinal problems. Where Hooker was attuned to natural psychology, Cotton sought perfection in the Word alone. In trying to find and communicate the milk, light, and law of the Bible, he showed an extraordinary tolerance—some called it waffling—for dissident possibilities of personal grace rather than social order. As Shepard wrote in his diary after the antinomian controversy, "Mr. Cotton repents not, but is hid only," while Hooker had "melancholick suspicions."[36]

Though his immersion in theological and personal ambivalence finally yielded to being "hid" in the law in the 1640s, Cotton remains the minister who best illustrates Puritanism's inward discontents. Where Hooker sought group independence, Cotton sought personal dependence. Hooker tried to bring his audience together, inwardly and outwardly, as his Father's representative. His speech, like his God, reveals a man of many parts. Cotton, far more unworldly, wanted to bind himself to the Word. Scriptural devotion allowed Cotton to maintain his renowned restraint, while he could unleash his aggressions, and his contradictory bonds, against the fantasy mother of the Catholic Church. Few Puritan tracts compare with *The Pouring Out of the Seven Vialls* for vituperative intellectual destructiveness.[37] In every other area he advocated submission and obedience to the theocratic ideal.

Cotton was in no sense an initiator. Obedience, not entrepreneurship, differentiates him from Hooker. Norman Grabo has shown how Cotton's opposition to the use of images in art was determined not by reason, which told him that images could help the conversion process by transforming the affections (as Hooker knew), but simply by what God said in the Second Commandment. Unlike other Puritan divines, Cotton does not rationalize about the inherent sinfulness of art. He merely states that he accepts God's decree, unfathomable as it may seem to him. "If thou submittest thy self to God, and puttest thy mouth in the dust, willing to be turned any way, so that he will set thee in a good way: Why, then there is a spirit of love in thee, . . . seeds of light and joy sown, which ere long will sprout forth to thy endlesse comfort."[38] Cotton's lifelong endeavor was to abase his various emotional hungers in hopes of being entered and fed by his heavenly father, even if abasement led to acute suffering. These feelings eventually became part of the process he prescribed for redemption. In some respects his effort resembles Hooker's control over oral excess through paternal order. But Cotton is achingly more needy than Hooker, and therefore much more uncomfortable with anger.

His sermon style reflects an intense transformation of want into possession. Obsessively depending on the Bible for all his perception and sustenance, Cotton persuades through incantatory repetition of simple words from his chosen text. Here, for instance, is his vision of happiness in *Christ the Fountaine of Life* (1651):

> If we have him for our portion, we have enough, therein the soul is fully satisfied, and if we have lost him, we chiefly mourne for that, our chiefest care is to get him; and we mourne most bitterly for want of him, *Zach.* 12.10. and we make it our desire cheifely to have him, and then we truly have him when we so set him up in our hearts, we may affect many earthly blessings and want them, as gold and silver, and friends, and health, and yet want them all, but no man desires Christ thus, but he hath him.

Superficially the same short phrases in the same long sentences characterize Hooker's style. But here, instead of balanced order, we find the ongoing spasms of desire. Motives, not comparisons, are Cotton's specialty. The passage also contains values that counter Hooker's more democratic equality of syntax and parts. There is hierarchy, as in the incantation of "chiefly . . . chiefest . . . cheifely"; there is devaluation of earth's variety for the singleness of heaven; there is an "if-then" logical structure, indicating the hypothetical nature of the reality he seeks; and there is the overwhelming need to "have," not, as in Hooker, to "be." The verb of possession is repeated so often as to become almost hypnotic, a cradle of security rocking his hearers into submission to the vision of their "portion." The short phrases communicate peace more than order, and the incremental repetition of single key words turns the linearity of the sentence into umbilical folds. But peace and security depend on a syntax of exclusion far more elitist than anything conveyed by Hooker's balance of negatives and positives.

Three pages later Cotton expands on his dream of obedience:

> And as it is thus for our obedience in doing his will, so is it for our patience in suffering his will, there is a glorious worship given to Christ in patience, when as if so be it the will of God to call us to suffer, we lay our hands upon our mouthes and sit down, and quiet our selves in this, that it is the will of Christ it should be so, and being for the glory of his name, in the defence of his truth, and from his owne hand, it [scares] us not, we sit down quietly under the hand of Christ as knowing whose hand it is that is upon us, it is a worship of Christ and we debase ourselves to worship him, when we acknowledge that it is no matter what becomes of us so the will of God be done, this is true worship of Christ.[39]

This passage is most compelling not in the equation of obedience with suffering, evoking the original meaning of "passion," nor in the laying of hands upon mouths, evoking more unconscious oral ambivalence. Nor is it Cotton's repetitiousness, which makes us very aware of the length of his sentence by doubling back and omitting most structures of subordination. Rather, perhaps testing our patience in calling for patience, the passage overwhelms the reader with one-syllable words. It should be read aloud to feel how the words of more than one syllable (only 26 out of over 150) receive just enough accent to be resting places in the soft pattering of vocables from one comma to the next, never really stopping, never really having started, awash in the one four-syllable word "obedience." That word inaugurates a succession of long phrases, which perceptibly shorten to the quiet breaths and lowered voice describing how we "quiet ourselves in this," and finally expand again to the longer phrases "acknowledging" the hand that has been laid upon us midway through.

The repetition of simple words and single syllables creates an elementary "primer" tone, appropriate for the man who wrote New England's basic religious text for children. The passage begins at the simplest level, occasionally adding a new concept here, a different emphasis there, in the midst of constant reiteration and return. As in his style, so in his beliefs. Like a good Puritan mother, Cotton constantly tries to return his children to the possession of Christ through obedience.

The words he chooses to reiterate are not just simple and plain. They are also almost invariably taken from his biblical text. Unlike Hooker, he will rarely venture into an image of his own. Rather, he prefers to elaborate an image in the text. In *God's Promise to his Plantations* (1634), Cotton declares as his highest praise of Christ's parables, "For he never fetcheth a comparison from any unlawful thing, to illustrate a thing lawful." Norman Pettit has shown how Cotton's excessive scripturalism, unlike the more pragmatic emphasis of other ministers on preparation, made him susceptible to antinomian influence.[40] Behind strict biblical dependence lies a wish to avoid complicated, ambivalent, or aggressive feelings and become a little child, like the children for whom he wrote *Spiritual Milk for Boston Babes*, sucking at the "two Breasts" of the Bible.

To drink and to suffer were in the same relation for Cotton as obedience and self-abasement, or want and fulfillment: opposite faces of the same need. "And if they be many and great and sore exercises, the greater and deeper your troubles be, the deeper you drink of Christs cup, the more sweete will it bee in the bottome; there is something in the bottome will counter-vaile all; you will finde the blood of Christ in the bottome, and the Spirit of grace, and the presence of God there." If Hooker expressed earthly equality in Lyly's elitist balance, Cotton retained more than a little of the Lylyan hierarchy of essences. But his need for oral submission, not fatherly grandiloquence, led him to hierarchy. As his namesake and grandson, Cotton Mather, recounts of Cotton in the *Magnalia*, "And being asked, why in his latter days he indulged *nocturnal studies* more than formerly, he pleasantly replied, 'Because I love to sweeten my mouth with a piece of Calvin before I go to sleep.'" Such pleasantries were rare in the quiet suffering that suffused him. "You would scarce think a child were living, if it did not cry as soone as it is borne; if still-borne, you take it for dead borne. If thou beest a still-borne Christian, thou art dead borne; if thou hast no wants to tell God of, if yet unlisty to pray."[41] No hint here that prayer could be anything but cries.

Pleading is all. Unlike Hooker, who often "sold" the Lord by stressing how little man had to pay to be saved, Cotton says that we often must give all we have, and more:

And yet thus much I say, that many times without laying out of mony, he cannot be had, without parting with money we cannot get him, the case so stands that sometimes, the holding fast a mans mony lets go the Lord Jesus Christ, . . . because it is hard for a rich man to part with all that he hath, when God calls for it at his hands, so that without mony sometimes Christ cannot be had; And yet for mony he cannot be had, it was on the point of mony, that the Lord Jesus parted with the *Pharisees*, . . . so that sometimes for want of spending of money in a right way, many a man looses the Lord Jesus; so that though Christ cannot be had for money, yet sometimes without expence of mony he cannot be had.[42]

I have omitted just the two references to his text and the brief textual explication. Yet the incantatory surge of "mony" and "had" almost makes us forget that the whole sentence is only a gloss on the Bible—a gloss whose rhetoric is designed to intensify both the necessity and the uncertainty of personal sacrifice.

Cotton resolves the complex relationship between obedience, suffering, and oral desires by his wish to melt, to become tender and feminine for the Lord. As he says, "The will that before was most tough and obstinate, of all the faculties, these torments make it soft and tender . . . the heart is made raw and tender, that look as raw flesh would be against the fire, so the tender raw conscience is anguished with this fire of Gods wrath." Elsewhere in *A Practical Commentary . . . [on] John* he says more succinctly, "so much stiffnesse, so much deadnesse." Even his contemporaries spoke of Cotton's style in terms of fluidity: "Mr. Cotton had such an insinuating and melting way in his preaching," said William Hubbard in his *General History of New England* (1680), "that he would usually carry his very adversary captive after the triumphant chariot of his rhetoric." For Cotton this melting was most urgently desired. "The spirit of Grace lets us see our sins as so many daggers pointing at the heart of Christ, . . . as soone as we see our sins darting against Christ, then will the heart begin to melt, for that we have crucified the Lord of Life and Glory." His similes are often more extended than Hooker's, creating a flowing, circling effect rather than a sense of parts in order. An exceptionally elaborate one takes the commonplace image of the soul as swimmer, to be cleansed in the permeating, womblike waters of grace. When the "loynes" and the affections that reside there are fully drenched, they will at last *"bee girt with a golden girdle"* and, a thousand cubits further, "a man may swimme as fish in the water," girdled with self-immersion.[43]

Unlike Hooker, who sets himself up as the Father's emissary and speaks with the father's authority, Cotton almost always says "we."

In doing so we worship Christ and in worshiping him we have him, but on the other side, if we so look at Christ as we can prefer ten thousand other things before him, and can sit downe quietly without him, if we looke at Christ as a refuse commodity, not worth the cheapening, and we looke at our selves as the great Omegaes of the world, and we would not have our names blemished with seeking after Christ, but have greater businesse then that to looke after, and we wil be our owne carvers; if so, then we do not worship Christ, and then we have him not, and so no redemption by him.

Here again is the "having," the "if-then" logic, the simple connectives of "and" and "but," and the balancing of alternative or hypothetical realities. There is always the chasm between "our selves," the great Omegaes of the world, and the Alpha, Christ. Here also is a more subtle, if narrower sense of the psychology of attitudes than Hooker achieves. Hooker's psychology is dramatic, situational, evoked by a real context. Cotton gives us no drama, no social situation—just the bare motives. He empathizes with men's rationalizations, a process that Hooker slights, believing as he does in rational understanding. Hooker's reality is in the open air, a functioning world of corresponding things and hearts. Cotton's is inside, echoing his own desires and sinfulness: "All these are such as men may be carried to doe from outward respects; they may doe something that one would thinke would argue life, but all the duties they doe by their owne strength is like a Spider, that weaves a webbe out of her owne bowels, we follow not the rule of the Word exactly, but are ever wheeling about to our owne ends."[44] "We" becomes just a spider, and disobedience is like a woman-spider giving birth to sin "out of her owne bowels." Note, too, Cotton's subtle pun on the "ends" from which outward respects issue, and to which they go. Whether as aims, bowels, or death, the ends are all associated with "their owne strength."

Cotton asked to be reborn from more heavenly "bowels." Yet finally it was not so easy to separate himself from the world. His images of the body differ from Hooker's ordered interaction of healthy members and prescriptions for amputation, because no matter how gangrenous the limb, Cotton feels its loss:

In a natural body, if a member be but cut off in a combate, in our hot bloud we misse it not, nor feel the pain, but in cold bloud we find the misse of it, and seek out for help; so in hot contentions betwixt Christians they fall off from one another, they discern no change for the present; but when they begin to look back at former passages, and see what wounds they have made, both joyntly begin to be sensible of pains, and cannot rest till they have taken some course to set the members in joynt again.

That marvellous pun on how "joyntly" Christians begin to be aware of being out of "joynt" reminds us of Hamlet, another punster who knew how out of joint were his times. Cotton shares with Hamlet an ambivalent union and disgust with the body, especially the mother's body, projected onto the world. Norman Grabo perceptively differentiates Cotton's style from Hooker's: "Unlike Thomas Hooker, who sees the soul as a delicate mechanism of mutually related parts, an enormously intricate watchwork, Cotton's view is insistently organic. . . . It leads Cotton into images that are dynamic and malleable or fluid, images of vitality and energy rather than Hooker's images of mechanical force. For Hooker the mind is exercised in perambulating or opening numerous doors, and preaching is most effective when ministers hammer their points home like sturdy carpenters."[45] The whole for Cotton is far more than the sum of interacting or disposable parts. Though both preachers cherish the father's control, Cotton transfixes that control with body imagery that is more ambivalent and regressive than Hooker's confident paternal similes.

Wholeness and organic imagery, to Cotton, carry feminine nuances: *"The onely one of her Mother, the choycest one of her that bare her.* In the Hebrew phrase, the whole is the Mother, the parts are the Members. The true Catholique Church of Christ is the Mother of all Reformed Daughters; and these Daughter Churches that are most chaste and milde, and undefiled, they are best esteemed, and best beloved of the Mother Catholique Church, as comming nearest to her in chastity, innocency, purity, & c." Cotton conceives of his role not just as the father's ambassador but also as the mother's protector and purifier. What can save him from feeling engulfed by the worldly mother his faith warns him against? Only strict obedience to the Father's Word. He even refused to allow his son, named Seaborn because he was born on the passage to New England, to be baptized because there was not yet a properly covenanted congregation. With God's Word firmly planted in his heart, a precarious ambivalence about his mother can surface, not just in attacks on the Catholic Church but in more general terms: "That woman that holds it impossible that her childe should know his Father, is a strumpet; so that Church that holds her children cannot know their Father, is an Harlot, because they worship so many gods, they know not of what seed they be, for if they were begotten of the Seed of the Word, hereby we might conclude, we know that we know him because we keep his Word."[46] What is he saying here? Simply that only if "we keep his Word" can we know that the Father exists at all. Otherwise, the harlot-mother would control her children completely.

Part of his dispute with Roger Williams, in their series of mutual recriminations on "The Bloudy Tenent," centers on whether Cotton called the Anglican Church a daughter of this whore. Williams says he did. Cotton, mastering his ambivalence, says he didn't, in order to keep the body of the "true Church" whole. He could neither deny his mother nor wholly espouse her, so he would strive for the faith that, as he says in *Christ the Fountaine*, "teacheth us not to pray to our Mother, as the Papists doe; nor to our Brethren, and Sisters, as the Papists doe to the Saints and Angels, but only to the Father."[47] Perhaps his virulence against Catholics was the conscious side of his guilt for wanting to pray to his mother "as the Papists doe."

Such reverence for the Father meant more purification of the mother's body, or the self as it identifies with that body, than Roger Williams knew what to do with. Williams, a man with the pure vision of the Father's truth, accused Cotton of "the bloody tenet," namely, the belief that suffering and submission to tyrants are good in themselves. As with Williams's other criticisms, there was truth in his accusations: Cotton's most compelling psychological defenses against his feelings led him precisely in the direction of the bloody tenet, just as his intellect led him part way back to Williams's assertive purity. It was the same ambivalence that made him receptive to Anne Hutchinson's vision of God beyond earthly law.

Cotton's most pervasive defense was masochistic. He cried to God to erase all his needs from his soul. Oral needs, for instance, have to be "cleaned up" into anal purity by transforming housewife into tyrant.

A Scullion in the Kitchin, when he scoures his Pewter, when he first takes it in hand, you would thinke he would quite spoile it, but he but scoures and cleares it up, and makes it more bright than it was before; the end of all is, but to take away the filth, and to make it cleare and bright. And so an Huswife that takes her linning, she Sopes it, and bedawbs it, and it may be defiles it with dung, so as it neither looks nor smels wel, and when she hath done, she rubs it, and buckes it, and wrings it, and in the end all this is but to make it cleane and white; and truly so it is here, when as Tyrants most of all insult over Gods people, and scoure them and lay them in Lee, or Dung, so as the very name of them stinks, yet what is this but to purge them, and to make them white.

This long trope, filled with Cotton's characteristic monosyllables and tripled verbs, has a simple moral: never, never get angry at authority. In *Gods Mercie* he elaborates on the relationship between cleansing from filth and dependence on the father. "This word *washing*, signifies tribulation like water; tribulations are like mire and water mixed together, in which the people of God are afraid they shall sinke downe, and never can recover, untill they beginne to finde there is the blood of Christ in that water, and finding the power of it, their *garments* that were besmeared with afflictions, are so scoured and rubbed off from their own *righteousnesse*, as that they are glad to depend wholy on the righteousnesse of Christ." Faith in the mother's powers of cleansing is stronger with him than with other Puritans. As he defines afflictions themselves in *The Way of Life*, "Faith sees afflictions as *fountaines, and mothers, and increasers of grace and glory: Job* 23. 10. *I shall come out like gold*, more pure, and precious, and solid, and compact then ever before."[48] His fantasy of anal birth through suffering makes pain a requirement for salvation.

In the latter part of Cotton's life, especially after Anne Hutchinson was driven from Massachusetts in 1637 by his own decree, he fled from his inward mixed signals to the law:

> Quest. *What is Sin?*
> Answ. Sin is the transgression of the Law.

The early response in Cotton's Catechism was one of his basic beliefs. After all, his father had been a lawyer, and submission to the father's law, like submission to the magistrates of a theocracy, will bring peace. But no; law, being outward and visible, cannot quite suffice. As Larzer Ziff has said, Cotton "acted as a constant brake to the commonwealth's rush toward legalism and capitalism, insisting time and again on the need to refine all duties by the inner test of the spirit." Too much stress on earthly law opens him to womanish feelings once more. He must make sure that the father's law remains as pure as the Word, secure in heaven alone. Here, where Hooker made a bridge, is a chasm between the visible and the invisible: "Mariners goe not to Sea without an anchor, but perhaps sometimes though they have pitched their anchor in the bottome of the Sea, yet the storms may be so great, that they may be forced to cut the cable; but if thou hast an anchor pitcht in heaven, thou shalt be safe. A woman in childebed may be put to distresse, but hope in heaven wil carry her through."[49] Again the mother identification surfaces, when rooted in a strong father in "heaven."

Cotton's fascination with the law was not specifically theocratic, though a theocracy satisfied his need for submission to strong fathers. Nor was the study of scriptural law a way of indulging himself in his beloved distinctions. Rather, the law represented—as he said many times—"the power of the keys." The power alluded to in Matthew 16.19 is, as Cotton often reminds us, "the power of opening and shutting, binding and loosing." Such power evokes Cotton's need to control the body, particularly the child's power to defecate and the mother's power to give birth. Control, for him, is the greatest of the father's gifts. To hold tight or let go, to open or shut the door, even to open or shut one's mouth, is what can be done in the father's name.

At times Cotton seems to be in such a hodgepodge of ambivalence about female powers that he reaches for almost any external security in the name of self-control. The fear of being allied with the sinful female body drives him into extraordinary intellectual contortions to avoid both guilt and anger. At other times a need for mothering frankly emerges:

> Women, if they were not Mothers, would not take such homely offices up, as to cleanse their Children from their filth; why if God were not of the like affection to us, hee would not cleanse us from our filthiness, . . . if hee did not sweep the Sinck, and scum off the scum of our hearts, it would never bee done; . . . it is with us as it is with young Infants that would lye in their defilements, if their Mothers did not make them clean, and so would wee even wallow in the defilements of sin, if God did not cleanse us, therefore admire Gods love and mercy towards us.[50]

Cotton's "mother hen" side, which usually surfaces only in the lullaby style of his syntax and imagery, here is projected onto God himself.

There *must* be more Father than the law, he says. That is what the Holy Son gave us, himself the Father's gift.

> Under the Law they had but a dark draught of the Image of Christ found in them; but now the fulnesse of time being come, God seeing his children fit to be trusted with a larger measure of grace, he sends forth a spirit of grace into their hearts, and therefore they then called upon God, as God and Lord, and but seldome as Father . . . *Father in the old Testament is a rare expression*; but now scarce any of the

poorest beleevers, but the name of Father is as ready with them, as if all were taught to say, Our Father, and Abba Father: Now the Father looks at us, as come to fulnesse of age.[51]

If there were only law, we would have little knowledge of the Father. So there must be grace, the intangible inward melting and pouring and swallowing that was Cotton's maternal vision of potency. Despite his cry for cleansing, however, and despite the craving for biblical texts and scriptural legalism into which he retreated, his inward image of the lawyer father never quite conquered his more complex, more ambivalent sense of the sinful, powerful female within himself and the world.

Cotton's God remains, like Cotton himself, a mother hen. Cotton's best prose style gives the feeling of a mother tucking a child into bed, or of the child being tucked into the womb of God's spiritual obedience. Larzer Ziff has said of his poetry that "John Cotton's best verse was not emotion recollected in tranquility but emotion tamed by law." But the law that tamed all his words was itself a defense against his mothering needs and fears of his own anger. As Cotton said in *Gods Promise to his Plantations*, "When God wraps us in with his Ordinances, and warms us with the life and power of them, as with wings, there is a Land of Promise."[52] In Cotton's personal Family Romance, the law was like swaddling clothes wrapped around him by a calm and infinitely attentive father. To the degree that he became God's child, he could restrain the feelings of the human child inside him.

Thomas Shepard, 1605–1649

If Hooker's style is masculine or patriarchal, though with uncommon tenderness and flexibility, Cotton's is both maternal and filial. Where Hooker vivifies Puritan conventions of confident fathering and order, Cotton has a more needy, fearful sense of submission to pure mothering law. It seems probable from his style that mother identification shapes his feelings. I suspect he was suppressing anger at the father's authority, which he blamed for his loss of mothering. I also suspect that his fear of his own anger was compounded by guilt over his father's weakness, and perhaps by more profound unconscious rage against his mother as well, for loving others and abandoning his needs. In any case, the language of Puritanism resolved various levels of ambivalence for him by offering a strait gate of self-denial welcoming him to a pure father's tender mothering. Hooker, who is much more tolerant of the self's nasty aspects, is correspondingly more able to transform rage into the father's reasonable if imperious human demands. Hooker can see persons, right up to the Godhead, where Cotton can allow only perfections. It is a remarkable tribute to the capacious nature of Puritanism's rhetorical appeal that two such dissimilar men could speak with its one voice.

Thomas Shepard's life, as I have said, indicates ambivalences more directly connected to his passionately loving mother, who died when he was so young. Though he also seems to share the more conventionally Puritan ambivalence toward betrayals by his peacemaker father and toward nonparental authority, his public themes and private doubts show a much greater degree of separation anxiety than Cotton's sermons. His resolution of personal conflicts within the Puritan frame is a less fluid, more rigorous joining of patriarchal and maternal modes, while his style reveals a self divided between the two contradictory Puritan satisfactions. No one approaches him in the ecstasy of his similes for regressive mothering. Yet he also has no peer in the frightful clarity and disengaged calm of his implacable rules.

Shepard was the man whom Jonathan Edwards chose for a personal exemplum. He was the epitome of the New England way, the purest of all the Puritans. Despite his short life he left a remarkable reputation for rigor and faith. He was the man, everyone agreed, with the truly immaculate soul. Edward Johnson, the rough-hewn militia captain who wrote *Wonder-Working Providence* (1654), spoke with wonder of how "the Speech of a poore weake pale complectioned man" could make grown men cry at the exposure of their sins. In fact Johnson was moved to call Shepard, alone of first-generation divines, "that soule ravishing Minister." A contemporary preface also refers to him as "this soul-melting preacher." Yet Shepard was among the most scholarly and reclusive as well. "He was a Person of great Piety and Industry," Daniel Neal relates, "spending almost all his Time among his Books; . . . his excessive Labours shortned his Life."[53] Meanwhile, Shepard's private diary shows all the anxieties, doubts, and secret atheistic fears that one would never suspect from his lucid and implacable sermons.

Of all the New England preachers before Edwards, Shepard had by far the most closely reasoned and doctrinal emphasis. Where Cotton searched for illumination beyond the law and Hooker emphasized preparation of the sincere heart, Shepard was unremittingly legalistic.[54] It would be too simple to say that legalism was his defense against childhood trauma, since we sense none of the willed masochism, the textbook submission to law, that characterizes Cotton. Rather, the Father's Word became for Shepard a way of dividing himself into what Michael McGiffert has called the observer and the sufferer. From the removed vantage point of the calm Father's heaven, Shepard as observer could look with disengaged contempt on man's puny motives, even on his own. Though he disowned direct influence, he was the most Calvinist of the first generation.[55]

Fully endorsing the doctrine of total depravity, his metaphors link man to the filthy natural world, rarely admitting any thing or creature to God's providence. The total separation of what is man's and the world's from what is God's, often expressed as whore against virgin, makes his doctrines seem much simpler than Cotton's complex identification with natural needs or than Hooker's open acceptance of the natural world as a source of divine analogies. His incessant message is that one cannot embrace the world and Christ at the same time. Those who "close with Christ" to remove bad feelings, not sin, have closed "only for your own ends," and therefore are still sinners filled with self and lust.[56] Shepard wrote to a faintly Arminian friend, "For since I have observed and seen the lamentable ruines of the soul: and seeming graces of many men, by being rockt asleep in a quiet still calm, easie performance of duties; without such awakening temptations and tumults within, which it self complains of: I say since I have observed what a deal of mudd is in the bottom of such standing Pools, and what a deal of filth is in such Moats, which are inwardly at ease, and not emptied from vessel to vessel." Stagnancy, filth, sloth, and natural ease are interchangeable in Shepard's descriptions of the natural man, especially the natural man who thinks he has faith by doing good works. His attacks on the comfortable mind are as vehement as those of a Houyhnhnm looking at Yahoos: "Thy mind is a nest of all the foul Opinions, Heresies, that ever were vented by any man; thy heart is a stinking sinkhole of all Atheism, Sodomy, Blasphemy, Murder, Whoredome, Adultery, Witchcraft, Buggery; so that if thou hast any good thing in thee, it is but as a drop of Rosewater in a boul of poyson; where fallen, it is all corrupted."[57] Elsewhere Shepard often notes the "hardning" quality of the sinful heart.

Shepard throws adjectives of disgust and aggression against "the fruits of a corrupt head, and steams of a dunghill heart." Worms are always biting the hard heart, just as Christ occasionally bites Satan, and Shepard sometimes speaks of hell in images of devouring flames. "God is a consuming fire against thee," he declares in *The Sincere Convert,* "and there is but one paper-wall of thy body between thy soul and eternal flames." A page later we learn that "thou art condemned, and the muffler is before thine eyes, God knows how soon the ladder may be turned, thou hangst but by one rotten twined thread of thy life, over the flames of Hell every hour."[58]

Though Shepard apparently disavowed what Cotton Mather calls "the woful *horrors*" that *The Sincere Convert* caused in its many editions, his implacable tone is characteristic. The heavenly body may have Christ as its head, the faithful as limbs, but the body of natural humanity has been cursed with Adam: "*Adam* was the head of mankind," he says in *The Sincere Convert*, "& all mankind naturally are members of that head." Since Adam was treasonous against God, "the whole body is found guilty, & the whole body must needs suffer; *Adam* was the poysoned root & cistern of all mankind; now the branches & streams being in the root and spring *originally*, they therefore are tainted with the same poysoned principles." Here the body comes close to Shepard's image, quoted earlier, of the "menstruous cloth." Before his fall, Adam had no self at all. He was a pure form for God's image. Afterward, man became messy, heavy, material, full of the resistance that Jonathan Edwards would take from Shepard's theory for the keystone of his own sense of sin. Originally, "in his pure naturals," Adam was "like a white paper fitted immediately to take the impression of *Gods Image*." But the fall put sin on this paper "like a mighty *blot* upon the soul, whereby a man not only wants grace, as the dark ayr doth light, but also *resists grace, Joh.* 14. 17. Hence this resistance must be first taken away, before the Lord introduce his image again."[59]

How to overcome this resistance? First and foremost, through divorce: man's divorce from earth, from himself, from his manhood. Any touch of selfish longings for the world will clog the flight, "as birds in a string may fly high, but when they come to the end of the line they fall down there; and so, though the soul flies to Christ, yet when, indeed, it comes to the end of parting with all, it falls down and falls off from Christ." The least adherence to external security, though it be to the law itself, will destroy one's chances to be saved.[60]

Divorce was also Shepard's intent for his audience. Hooker imagined the congregation as natural souls with natural conflicts which could be reasonably resolved through appeals to common sense. Cotton spoke to sinners as projections of himself or of his feared shadow. Shepard, however, spoke primarily to that one element in his congregation who refused to make the total divorce that his purer Family Romance required: the hypocrites. How to be sincere occupied almost all his sermon time. Sinners he could dismiss out of hand; saints he could commune with as brethren. But hypocrites brought out his own con-

flicted energies, as he tried to separate earth from heaven, whore from
virgin, mother from father.

The intent of a Shepard sermon was therefore not so much to instruct, as with Hooker, or to affect, as with Cotton. He wished to
humble. Hooker and Cotton both developed styles intimating security,
Cotton despite himself. But Shepard tried to unsettle his hypocrites in
every possible way, knowing as he did that the least shred of comfort
would keep them from dependence on the purified father.

> Take heed the Lord find not many of you foolish; take heed you that
> are not so, that in time you grow not secure. You have the pillow of
> peace to lie on, . . . and you have no pinching persecutions to
> awaken you; and if no wrestlings within, look for security there. Folly
> will be the death and bane of some; hence boast not. Security (a sleep-
> ing sickness) will be the disease of others, if the Lord prevent not.
> But I intend not to anchor here, only to set up marks at these flats,
> that you may avoid them, and come not near them.

Hooker's style reflects a balanced order; Cotton chants and croons key
words from his biblical text. But Shepard's style repeats a structure of
commands and exhortations ("Take heed . . . take heed"), interlaced
with simple statements about the way it is. His wonderful metaphoric
twist at the end removes the "anchor" even from the security of having
come to rest at what he has just said. Time and again he returns to the
illusory comfort and ease endemic in resistance: "Like men scorched
with heat, and almost ready to die, the shadow of a tree is now very
comfortable, and therefore there they sit; so these. Or, as men with
scalded arms, they put them in water, which gives them ease, no cure;
but because it gives them ease, there they keep them; so here. Men
have been scalded with wrath; O, now gospel is very sweet, and so are
eased by it, never cured by it." He dramatizes the sinner's inward,
secret colloquy to show the ways men rationalize comfort. Often he
structures his sermons as two voices, the questioning sinner coming up
short against the answering minister, and often he vividly expresses his
congregation's thoughts: "Why, the family is great, children increase
upon me, (and they are so busy and long a dressing on the Lord's day,
that sermon is out before they come,) and we are not called to book
it all day as ministers can, and worldly employments are so many, and
the best are entangled here; and they think this is an excuse. Luke
xiv.18, 19."[61] Hooker says "I," Cotton says "we"; but Shepard says
"me" and "we" only to set up a "they." One brush from the Bible
whisks all these excuses into damnation.

Real divorce from the world must emasculate the sinner. Lust must be lopped off. If the sinner says, "Lust is his limb, he cannot suffer it to be cut off, or be pared," Shepard responds, "If a man hath a wooden leg, he can cut it answerable to his shoe, but if but a limb, he must have his shoe cut answerable to his leg, because it is his limb, no cutting of that less: O, it is dear. So it is with a man that hath a lust after any thing: it is dear." But it must be cut. Adam has to give way to union with Christ.

> Q. *How doth the Spirit make this Union?*
> A. Two waies, first, By cutting off the soul from the old *Adam,* or the wilde Olive Tree, in the work of preparation. *Rom.* 11.23, 24. 2. By putting or ingrafting the soul into the second *Adam,* Christ Jesus, by the work of vocation. *Act.* 26.18.[62]

Images of trees cut on earth or flowering in heaven are often linked with Shepard's pervasive imagery of eating or drinking heavenly fluids. Holy "ingrafting" will gain membership in the elect, with the oral rewards for which the lumpish earthly body hungers in vain.

With all resistance gone, redemption reconstitutes the single separate body into the whole body of the father, at last free from the step-mother world: "None can pluck thee out of Christs hand, neither sin, nor Devil; she were a cruel Mother that would cast her child into the fire; Christ must do so, if thou shouldest go to hell; yea more, if that should be so, he should rend a member from himself, for he is thy head, and thou art one of his members." In expressing a need to trans-form his separated self into the image of the Father, Shepard justifies the Puritan use of similes as "the ground of love," not narcissistic but wholly self-abandoning. As he said in *The Sincere Convert,* "Adams body was the Lanthorn through which holiness like a Lamp burning in his heart, shined; this was Gods Image, by means of which (as it is said in the description) he pleased God: similitude being the ground of love." God may be a narcissist, but man must be no more than a mirror, just as a minister must mirror the Word in his words. To Shepard a similitude was an open vessel, not one of Hooker's correspondences. "As the glass set full against the Sun: receives not only the beams, as all other dark bodies do but the image of the Sun: So the under-standing with open face beholding Christ, is turned into the Image and likeness of Christ."[63]

"For this is God's greatest plot," Shepard said, "to pull all men down, that his Son may be set up." "Faith empties a man so as it makes him the poorest orphan in the world," he observed elsewhere, in yet another statement of the Puritan Family Romance; "now the father can not, will not keep back his portion, but gives it him . . . it is his Son himself he gives to orphan, fatherless, helpless creatures." As orphan, uncontaminated with the mother at last, the child can receive the father's love: "Blessed be God, he will keep our lives as the life of Jacob was knit up, and bound up, in the life of the child." Always, however, the saint must strive to be imprinted with the father rather than with himself, and again associations with polluted females define the desiring self. "Whorish lovers look not after him, but his; his peace to comfort them when in horror and fear, his mercy to save them from eternal flames; but virgins look to him." Self can do nothing; only faith can be the anchor, much like Shepard's description of the anchor that barely saved their ship in the passage to New England, during a storm: "And so we rid it out, yet not without fear of our lives though the anchor stopped the ship, because the cable was let out so far that a little rope held the cable, and the cable the little anchor, and the little anchor the great ship in this great storm."[64]

Those who can "ride out" the world's satisfactions, which "clog the stomach, and glut the soul," can see how the Father in heaven makes small threads into extraordinary art. Whatever his private doubts, Shepard's public voice could assure the faithful that "here our eyes, ears, minds hearts shall be ever ravished with that admirable glory which shines brighter than ten thousand Suns, the very fabrick of it being Gods needle-work (if I may so say) quilted with variety of all flowers, in divers colours, by the exactest art of God himself." The final purity is to become one with God's love, at once the source of all art and all selflessness: "It is a pure love. Others make love for their own ends, but the Lord hath no need of thee, or of thy love." Here, at long last, is comfort and "mercy" for the "fatherless."[65]

Shepard's style reflects his struggle for dependence in the opposition between long, incremental lists of quantities and finitudes, intimating man's sin and God's wrath, and ecstatic oral imagery for God's fullness. "Sweetness" is always associated with Christ, who "only is the procurer and author of all the good that ever thou didst suck out here . . . an infinite good; this cannot be seen in a finite time. . . . He is the delights and bosom love of God himself." Jonathan Edwards shares that imagery for Christ and heavenly rewards. But Shepard, like the early Edwards, spends far more sermon time devising structures and images to make damnation seem inexorable to those who keep some vestige of self. While sweetness and sucking are associated with faith, the sinner is made to feel how his fatal solidity separates him from pure union with Christ's body. Occasionally Shepard reaches for an almost playful single image to describe that feeling: "The least joint in a man's finger united to the soul, hath life of it; but signets, though near to the finger, yet they have no life, and hence no union, and hence no members; so the saints have life, though weak; but unregenerate men (as signets) may be near life, and near the true members of Christ that be quickened, but receive no life." But most of his passages on hypocrisy or sin pile up images in an incremental repetition of resistances, as objects and motives exposed in their naked interchangeability: "Those that are like children born before their time, that have had some sorrow after the Lord, but comforted before it was deep enough; have some desires, but eased with other things before they were satisfied with Christ himself; that have run for a while, but are grown weary before they came half way home, and so sit down in the way; like clocks set slow in the first hour of the day, run slow all the day after. So these set back, and think they are set right, too, run slow all their life after."[66] Here the image of the clock caps a series of comparisons, ending in a bit of wordplay on sitting and being set. But the alliteration leads only to the dismissal of how "slow" these sinners "run," collapsing clock and runner into a dead comfort.

Ordinarily Shepard is not so playful, nor so condensed. His concern is to find a language that mirrors the sinful heart to itself, and he finds that language in the alternation of negatives with positives, "and" with "but":

> It is with most professors, commonly, as it is with a woman that loves her husband, and begins to dress herself, but so much business to do, that she doth it but by starts; hence, call her never so late, she will say she is not yet ready, she has so much to do she can not: so it is here. Or as it is in a house where all things are in a lumber, and many things wrapped up and put into holes; so long as all things be in a lumber, there is no readiness. So many a soul has a heart fit to receive Christ, but all things are in a lumber, in a confusion, out of place and order.

Hooker experienced order as a pleasure in itself. Cotton experienced suffering as a receptivity to infantile grace. Shepard felt both and used both kinds of imagery, but as ways of expressing the Father's peaceful and ordered glory. For the disordered and cumbersome self Shepard showed no pity, only a mirror for the "lumber" of the sinner's secret voices, framed by flat accusation:

Though guilty of more sin, then there be motes in the Sun or Stars in Heaven, though their sins be crimson, and fill Heaven with their cry, and all the earth with their burden, yet they mourn not; never did it one hour together; nay, they cannot do it, because they will not; if you are weary and loaden, where are your unutterable groans? if wounded and bruised, where are your dolorous complaints? if sick, where is your equity for a Physician? if sad, where are your tears in the day, in the night, morning and evening alone by your selves, and in company with others? Oh how great is the wrath of God.[67]

Each phrase is a stale convention. Yet the syntax gives the passage a driving momentum, with two "though" phrases leading to "yet" and five negatives ("not; never . . . nay . . . cannot . . . will not") expressing the negating human will, and then to four "if-where" clauses, the last piling up four prepositional phrases in the predicate to hammer home the falseness of the sinner's rationalizations. The shift midway through from "they" to "you" brings home the falseness of the earlier negations. Then, after all that rhythm of denying their denials, Shepard makes the last phrase a conclusive summing up, a final judgment of God's wrath, its simplicity a dramatic "awakening" from the hydra-headed juggernaut of sin.

Here, as elsewhere, the stock ideas and images get their force from the incremental structure. Whenever Shepard addresses hypocrites, his sermons take on a judgmental tone, rule oriented and aloof. He voices their feelings only to pin them wriggling on God's wall. When he talks of the grace of the Father, however, his style becomes more appositional in its repetitions: "This call is alway sounding in thine ears, *Oh come*, not only because thou feelest holiness in thee, but come, because poor, hungry, empty, naked, lost, blind, cursed, forsaken, full of sin; there is not one moment of the day of grace, but the Lord beseecheth thee to receive his grace, . . . Oh thou tossed with tempests, and not comforted, come unto me and thou shalt find rest to thy soul." When the saint does come to God, Shepard's style evokes his happiness with the lullaby quality of Cotton's best prose, though with his usual parallel constructions:

Therefore you lie down, not sluggishly, but humbly at the feet of God, and contented to have him to be your God, and for ever to be disposed in any thing by God, if he will fulfill his covenant in you, contented to part with any sin, if he will rend it from you, contented to know any truth if he will reveal it to you, contented to do any duty if he will enable you, contented to shine bright with all his glorious graces, if he will create and maintain them in you; contented to bear any evil if he will lay his hand under your head; and thereunto strengthen you.[68]

Six times he urges us to be "contented . . . if" God fills us with himself rather than ourselves. Though perhaps too listlike for a lullaby, too ordered and ordering compared to Cotton's more supple returns of phrase, the passage conveys the same wishes to "lie down" and be "contented" at the Father's feet.

Yet contentment, like the structural connections, begins to disappear into an "if" when looked at too closely. Phrases begin to jar into separate truncations of thought, like the omnipresence of sin and the poverty of faith in the world, whose language he has to speak. The pure father was always more wish than fact, even for Shepard, and at his most honest he can speak of the tenuousness of faith in imagery that evokes his first mother's crazed passion, his father's frail "promise": "It is with faith as with a poor woman that hath a child, and hath nothing in the world to give it, she takes the childe at her back and goeth from door to door, and what she getteth she giveth to the childe; so faith takes the soul, and carrieth it to promise after promise, and what ever she finds there, she gives to the soul."[69] Emptiness lurks there, as Shepard repeatedly discovered in his own life. Even at the end, with the death of his second wife, Shepard's attachment to a woman could not be restrained by remembering how the Lord "sought to wean me from this world" by such afflictions.

No wonder that the greater part of his sermons exposed the needy, greedy self, mirroring Shepard's two voices of resistant sinner and observing or wrathful God. Too honest to be confident in his private faith, he enacted with his public voice a massive self-condemnation, whose prevailing tone, to use a phrase from *The Sincere Convert*, is simply "a bitter lamentation for every natural man."[70]

Chapter Seven

New England Styles:
Divergent Sons

"Fear not enemies without, but your selves at home," Shepard preached. That came true for the second generation of preachers in New England, though with a sense rather different from anyone's original intention. Shared wishes had seemed able for a time to subsume disparate conflicts. But by 1660 the faithful were "in a lumber." Boundary disputes reflected a growing sense of boundaries between groups of people: gentry, lesser gentry, farmers, and servants; ministers and magistrates; the frontier and Boston; and New England and old England.[1] Here was social division of their own making. As Norman Pettit has said, "The settlers were mainly concerned with preserving their freedom and economy, while the clergy struggled to preserve the ritual structure of the churches; and indifference to the inner life became more and more pronounced."[2]

Tensions were present from the first day of settlement, even in outlying villages, as Cotton Mather notes in his *Magnalia:* "I have heard that one of our ministers once preaching to a congregation there, urged them to approve themselves a *religious* people from this consideration, 'that otherwise they would contradict the main end of planting this wilderness;' whereupon a well-known person, then in the assembly, cryed out, 'Sir, you are mistaken: you think you are preaching to the people at the Bay; our *main end* was to *catch fish.*' " That is one of the few audience responses to Puritan preaching on record. Another—my favorite—was discovered by Perry Miller; perusing a copy of Jonathan Mitchell's *Discourse of the Glory to which God hath Called Believers,* he found penned in the margin:

> Some doe Walk & som runn,
> It is for money when all is done.

But more than a simple tussle between religious and economic motives was at stake, even among what Mather's anonymous "person" called "the people at the Bay," though accusations of worldliness are a central theme of preaching after the first two decades. Puritans felt a loss of shared purpose as well. As Ezekiel Rogers wrote to a Charlestown minister in 1657, "We grow worldly every where; methinks I see little godliness, but all in a hurry about the world; every one for himself, little care of public or common good."[3]

The varied Puritan discontents are well known and will not be rehearsed here. Rather, this chapter sketches the effect on sermon styles of a growing sense of alienation in the ministry. For some, patriarchal visions were more invoked in their passing than to confirm the present, since by 1690 probably two-thirds of church members were women.[4] For others, a new style of rational control replaces ecstatic dependence. Puritans were more divided, and in some ways more repressive, after the 1650s, and our stereotypes of them emerge from their rigid responses to a new set of social changes.

Second-generation styles have more to do with guilt than with ambivalence. There is a change from Hooker's semipatriarchal style of order to a divided "masculine" style of wrathful patriarchal accusation and ritualized guilt, especially in Increase Mather's sermons, or Samuel Willard's rational sermons of comfort through obsessive patterning. The feminine or maternal side of first-generation styles becomes reserved for private, alienated solace, apart from the world and the body. We do not find the flexibility, sensitivity to psychology, and tolerance for contradiction characteristic of more capacious and affecting first-generation prose. In short, Puritan language is reduced to two forms of the obsessive style.

Robert Pope has persuasively argued that the incessant talk of "declension" was a ministerial myth. There was a major revival of church membership from 1675 to 1690, despite excessive scrupulosity about qualifications. The famous half-way covenant of 1662 (named so in derision a century later) was approved two years after the English Restoration dashed Puritan hopes for the old country and symbolizes the old generation's awareness of the need to endure through its children rather than through England's purification. Puritanism had always had a strong generational sense. The problem was that an account of one's conversion was a prerequisite for church membership, according to the 1640 requirement, and too few children seemed to be having genuine Puritan experiences. Perhaps, as Pope suggests, they were too sincere and scrupulous to lie. But it is more than odd that the vehemently patriarchal family in New England should have led to so much anxious submissiveness among second-generation preachers, yet not to the radical self-transformation that first-generation fathers had thought was the essence of their faith. At one point the only second-generation member in the First Church of Boston who had professed a conversion experience was the child of John Wilson, the minister.[5] So the half-way covenant went half way by admitting children of the faithful to baptism but not to full participation in communion.

This was a ministerial compromise. Remarkably, Pope discovered, many congregations did not accept it. Just as early English Puritans consistently pushed their ministers toward greater militancy and purity, so the compromise was blocked until the 1670s in nearly every major congregation.[6] Clearly, a gap in generational self-perception and in social status had developed. The ministers wanted children in their self-image, while the children were too honest to assert a radical change in themselves, and lay parents would not compromise their own hard-won purity. The problem also indicates a shift in the relationship of Puritan child rearing to religion. For those brought up in submission to pure fathers, what was there to convert to? Ministers, on the cutting edge of these tensions, found their role changing from voice of a united flock to adjudicator among factions. Or rather, they were less able to indulge their fantasy of a visible flock converting to a model of the pure Father's invisible order.

Here is where Puritanism's divisions became manifest in the contradictions of sermon style. The second generation shows more self-division, more public myth making in the accusatory mode, more merely "rational" versions of orderly comfort, and more private, withdrawn visions of dependence. Other scholars, notably Robert Middlekauff and Sacvan Bercovitch, have argued that the second generation fashioned an optimistic and collective myth of New England or of the prophetic self. In my view, these myths are strident and brittle posturings that were adopted to avoid social and personal conflict, not triumphant legacies of the redemptive private imagination. They were contradictory, even desperate rhetorical solutions to the fundamental problem of sons who had followed the pure Father's calling and found, like Kafka's Hunger Artist, that though they were doing it better than ever, the people seemed to be watching for something else.

The shared energies of Puritan language became less than its parts, not a grandly coherent frame of contradictory satisfactions. There was a growing provincialism, separatism, and self-important isolation in the new rhetorical focus on New England. Earlier Puritans had looked outward as well as inward, with internationalist fervor. Now apocalyptic millennialism, though always a part of Puritan language, focused on the minister as isolated prophet for New England's future. His role was becoming just one among many, after an extraordinary period of primacy, and sermons expressed a flailing self-pity as ritualized attack.

The jeremiad—as Perry Miller called this genre of New England sermon—was the sons' formulaic and impersonal reminder of first-generation greatness and second-generation decay. It was the major development in the New England sermon form, and served to codify a ministerial sense of alienation. These sermons were formal, even condescending, in their equation of external disasters with community sins and often listed the sins of various groups in the congregation in ways that broke down a sense of community even in asserting it. They were not meant to terrify, and not meant to bring on conversions, but only to ritualize guilt. They did not speak of essential depravity but of external events—long hair, comets, and the like. By the end of the 1670s a further change had occurred within the jeremiad form: sermons now spoke to groups alone, especially magistrates, not so much to the people as a whole. Predicted punishment for present misbehavior was the keynote, with the present measured against the purity of a giant patriarchal past.[7]

It was, as several have said, a mutually guilt-relieving fantasy. The sermons turned attention from real social and political conflicts to an abstract moral passivity. Personal feelings of failure and anxiety could be blanketed with a retrospective sense of "mission." A private agony of insufficiency could be transformed, by speaking ever more grandly with the voice of the vanished fathers. Sacvan Bercovitch has found a paradoxical optimism about self and community distinguishing Puritan writers of jeremiads from other users of the form. Yet there is an obvious tone of accusation, impersonality, and absence of shared community except through negatives. While an abstract New Jerusalem continued to be wished for with passionate intensity, self opposed to society becomes the imaginative focus of the optimism. Conflicting imperatives, as Stephen Foster suggests, could be resolved by collective self-accusation.[8] The collectivity is patently ritualistic, a dead husk, while vibrant communion was experienced privately.

In some respects there is a reversal of the usual Puritan split between public affirmation and private doubt. Edward Taylor, a most dull and dogged Westfield minister, wrote extraordinary poems every six weeks, not for his congregation, not even for his friends, but only for God, to help prepare his mind for delivering his sermons. Though the poems brilliantly enact the mind's wishes for conversion, he felt no need to show them to anyone as passionate models for the hope of saving grace. They were not even discovered until 1937. The American tradition of redeeming contaminated society by retreating into solitude begins with the breakup of shared fantasy and shared community into alienated imaginings. We can see the same search for private solace in the public imagery of Increase Mather and Samuel Willard as in the quiet scratchings of Taylor's pen.

"Few churches retain their purity long," Shepard had said; "aged, gray-haired purity is seldom seen."[9] In the face of change, faction, and compromise, the jeremiad asserted the purity of an abstract and vanishing patriarchal past. While ministers like Urian Oakes began the change from grace to gracefulness, developed more fully in the enlightened style of Benjamin Colman, the main thrust of the jeremiad was toward the unaccommodating presence of three related abstractions: fathers, death, and Christ. This new trinity gave ministers the opportunity to cleanse themselves not of their sinful hearts but of their sinful congregations, by expressing purity as compulsive loyalty to the first fathers and incessant rage against the times that contaminated them. Isaiah and Jeremiah, not the Song of Solomon, become more typical sources for Puritan imagery. A divided rhetoric of accusation and rationality becomes as important as the older rhetoric of group dependence and stages of self-transformation. Imagery of hellfire and apocalypse, much more physicality in depictions of death and sin, and use of the body for imagery of grossness and disease rather than order and proportion, complement ministerial fantasies of withdrawal. Indeed, all three abstractions encouraged dreams of escape: into death, into the past, or into the arms of the crucified Son.[10]

Leonard Hoar, for instance, invoked the variety of mortuary experiences in *The Sting of Death and Death Unstung* (1680), two sermons that separate the miseries of dying sinners from the glory of those "that Dye in the Lord." In *The Sincere Convert*, Shepard had recounted ten "stings of death" in barely two pages. Here, Hoar spends an entire sermon on them: "The ordinary way is to rot in the grave. Now this carries a sting with it, to think that worms shall destroy this flesh, *Job.* 19.26. The bowels and the vital parts shall be the Region of vermine. When Joseph is carried out of Egypt, there is nothing but a Coffin of bones: and when you shall seek a Father, or other Relation, or be sought for, there shall be nothing but corruption, an ill favour, or a few dry bones." This in a funeral sermon! Hoar's uncompromising physicality makes the Father into "a few dry bones" and deliberately dramatizes

Joseph's "Coffin of bones" by using the present tense. The rhythms he
sets up are the rhythms of physical accumulation, a macabre version of
the acquisitive spirit. He is death's accountant: "There are many things
fall in a dying hour, there are the pains of death, grievous sickness,
faintness, outward parts grow numme, the eyes sink, the lips quiver
and tremble, the tongue falters, the breath whezeth and draws hard,
the whole face waxeth pale, the heart beats and throbs."[11] The listlike
flavor is endemic to the new generation, without the larger structural
balance, momentum, and sense of the whole characteristic of first-
generation sermons.

Death's twelve stings are all Hoar presents of doctrine before he
heads into uses. He knows his audience is no longer composed of saints,
so he wishes to picture them decomposed. He immerses the sinner in a
visual picture of physical immediacy, with accumulations of data designed to make the hearer lose any sense of pattern in the feeling of
fear and revulsion. Unlike Hooker, he rarely presents a simile to raise
rational convictions. The congregation must wait passively for Hoar to
turn to transfiguration, and he leads, typically, by dragging his slow
negatives along. The soul must be resolutely considered as separate
from the body:

> Ah, should I tell you nothing, and you should [find] no other but your
> souls seperation from your body, can you part with it without a sigh
> or a serious thought? or of your bodyes corruption, though it might be
> wrapped in lead, and entombed in marble, yet in a few days it shall be
> an abhorring and loathing to all living, it shall be a prey to vipers and
> creeping worms of the earth: your carcases and your remembrance
> shall alike rot and perish together. Should I tell you of your sicknesses
> and death-pangs that shall oppress you, and your helpless friends
> standing by, should I shew you your Coffin, your Grave or Tomb, your
> Herse cloath and your Bier; should I tell you of the breaking of your
> purposes.

On and on, with his "I" utterly separate from their bodies, and more
powerful. "Ah but I tell you, it is the wrath of God, the scalding drops
of it, and the fruit of your sin," he concludes, physical to the last, before continuing into his vision of the elect. Finally, in the last two paragraphs, he mentions the lady whose death had occasioned his strictures.
"But since it was not my lot to attend her in her more solemn obsequies
I thus come to lay down these little branches of Bays and Cypress on
her Tomb."[12] The ridiculous artistic touch of those little branches,
intimating the awkward emulation of European high secular culture,

indicates the failure of an integral personal voice to express shared faith. The sense of gross physical decay is what lingers.

In fact there is an odd air of comedy as well as decay rising from second-generation prose, at least to modern readers. The prose is fat with flesh and things, unchecked lists, and repetitions of material realities for invective's sake, without godly shape. While it may have satisfied their needs to expel guilt, the repetitive physicality reveals a breakdown in Puritan language, whose genius had been its ability to harness literal facts to spiritual truths.

A tendency to pun out one's grief is the most obvious instance of involuntary comic elements. Puritans had always anagrammatized death; it was part of their faith that words could order the world's disorder. But New England efforts to make dead founders into enduring monuments are self-conscious about language in very awkward ways. John Norton, for instance, though a first-generation preacher, lingered long enough to write of Anne Bradstreet,

> Her breast was a brave Pallace, a *Broad-street*,
> Where all heroick ample thoughts did meet.[13]

His playful punning has an obsessiveness that reduces loss, grief, and even her identity to a forced fit of syllables. A delight in bringing unlikes together can be a great virtue in puns, as in first-generation similes. It can yoke worldliness to godliness. But not when meanings and feelings are reduced to cleverness for its own sake. Then the minister's status as wordsmith is the major residue.

As Joan Webber says, Puritan language sometimes leads to involuntary comedy by its nature, since a fixed abstract design is constantly replenished with unique particulars.[14] The attempt to make practical experience bespeak higher realities works brilliantly for Puritans when there is an overriding seriousness of tone and an organic tension among levels and parts. The best Puritan prose shows a supple connectedness of body and spirit, even in single images, as in the magnificent snort with which the Elizabethan Puritan John Hooper summed up the Anabaptist belief that Christ had no taint of flesh from his mother's body: "He passed through the Blessed Virgin Mary as saffron doth through a bag." That one line suggests a world view connecting thing to Word, practical to theoretical, and folk wisdom to the Bible, as well as mother to son. But when Puritan language loses control of those tensions, as it does in the second generation in New England, its order tends to become an assemblage of parts. Physicality increases, while obsessive patterns of merely verbal precision, from lugubrious puns to Willard's enormous *Compleat Body of Divinity*, seek to bring everything under intellectual control.

Another, noncomic, manifestation of physicality is a growing pre-occupation with punishment of the body, through death and hellfire. Even mild Samuel Willard, who has received a very good scholarly press lately for his doctrine of happiness, shares the second generation's explicitness about future torments. His 1693 sermon on hell in *A Compleat Body of Divinity* lists the biblical conventions in by then conventional detail, with his usual polarity of negatives and positives. Negative punishments will be the loss of God's mercy, the loss of heaven, the loss of moral goodness, the loss of hope, and the loss of our prayers, since praying for the dead is "antiscriptural." Positive punish-ments are hell's universal torments, the "never dying worm" for souls, the body "plagued with an unquenchable fire" without intermission, the wailings and lamentations in the lake of devouring fire. Citing Isaiah 23.14, Revelations 21.8, and Matthew 25.41, Willard describes the "exquisite" torments, compared to which "those pains of travailing women, of men under the torture of the stone, . . . are but flea-bitings." Even worse, God "will laugh at their calamity," and the roar-ings and blasphemings of sinners will be drowned in the "joyful acclamations" in heaven. It could happen this evening, he concludes, "the flames of the bottomless pit, where you shall be filled brim full in soul and body with the wrath of God" forever and ever, with no emotion for all eternity but helpless hate.[15]

Finally, as Hoar's sermon indicates, the second generation shows a much greater physicality in its rhetorical representation of death. Allan Ludwig's *Graven Images* shows the beginnings of Puritan gravestone iconography at this time, with the ritualized physical representation of death that was also taking place in the jeremiads. There are as yet none of the huge, toothy skulls resting between humped and breastlike wings; they would come after the Great Awakening of the 1740s. But already a paradoxical though muted hope develops that death can liberate the artistic powers through visual images, just as Hoar more flagrantly indulges his flights of rhetorical rot.[16]

If Jonathan Mitchell had lived beyond 1668, David Hall suggests, he could have given the second-generation ministers a strong leader. But his death unleashed faction and ambition. The chief rivals were Increase Mather, who accepted the call to the Second Church of Boston, even though it was "relatively ne'er-do-well," to remain at the center of things, and Samuel Willard, who went to Boston from Groton in 1676. As Hall says, they "were rivals for every honor and position open to the ministry."[17] Their styles show a divergence between harsh accusation in the name of the vanished fathers and the comfort of rational order. Perhaps the split mirrors New England patterns of child rearing by stern patriarchs and tender mothers. More likely, I think, the split is one of ministerial roles, with tender mothering buried in the future rewards available after the body dies.

Increase Mather, 1639–1723

Increase Mather was so named, as his son tells us in *Parentator* (1724), "because of the never-to-be-forgotten *Increase*, of every sort, wherewith GOD favoured the Country, about the time of his Nativity." A heritage of optimism was not the least ironic aspect of the man who spent more than half his life waiting to die. Though his service to the struggling colony included renewal of the charter, though he was president of Harvard College, and though he wrote book after book with unflagging zeal, a death wish set the tone for his life. It was the final refuge for self-obsession.[18] "For many years you have seen and heard his earnest Desires to *go* from you, by the will of God, into his Everlasting Rest," said Benjamin Colman in his eulogy, *The Prophet's Death* (1723). "He often told you from this *Desk*, in the most solemn and affecting manner, of his *Desires to depart*."[19]

Ostensibly the wish came from his perception of the appalling world that had increased around him. Each sermon, Mather used to announce, was his last word on the subject.[20] "I say the Sins, the *Pride*, the *Profaneness*, the *Worldliness*, the general *Security* and *Iniquity* that prevaileth amongst us," he cried in *Heavens Alarm to the World* (1682). Like so many of his sermons, this one takes a natural event, a comet, and moralizes on the impending catastrophes. "Will not the haughty Daughters of Zion, reform their Pride in Apparel? Will they have *the Attire of an Harlot*? Will they lay out their Hair, and wear their false Locks, their Borders, and Towers like *Comets*, about their heads?" His imagery seems arch, but his intent is deadly serious, to show how a self-satisfied world deserves destruction: "Yea, duties of Communion with the Lord are either totally neglected, or slubbered over. Some don't pray in their families above once a day: Why? they have not time, they say. Why not? how is your time taken up? Is it in doing publick service for God or for his people? . . . no, it is because they have not time for their worldly occupations."[21] The old work of preparation, he implies, now has to be done differently: not preparing for grace but for trouble. Men "may be left without excuse if they do not prepare for *the day of trouble*," he declares in a sermon of that name. "Hence then, when every mans hands are upon his loins, and all faces are gathering paleness, it is an ominous sign." Mather's fantasy of apocalyptic destruction begins with the sense—perhaps only a biblical allusion—that "every mans hands are upon his loins."

Mather seems most upset over the sheer number of unbelievers, the "thousands of Wolves and Tygers" that surround his *"little-little flock of Sheep."* The conspicuously Old Testament imagery indicates his deliberate rhetorical insulation from the wolfless and tigerless wilderness that in fact surrounded them. There is trouble among the elect also. "Alas! that Gods Diamonds should be cutting one another," he exclaims.

But the minister has to persevere, unheeded though he may be. He has a better master than the world's rewards. "His Ministry had more of a CHRIST in it, than is usually met withal," said his son in a funeral sermon. Increase frequently stressed that theme. "We may do the most Generous and General Service for our people, & be ill rewarded by an Ungrateful World. But we Serve a better Master then is the Generation whom we Serve, we Serve the Lord Jesus Christ; and he will be sure to reward Whatever Service we have done." In *David Serving His Generation* (1697) Mather even imagines the minister as the central link between generations: "Should there be but one Age in which were no Faithful Ministers of Christ, the whole World would [putrify] for want of this Spiritual Salt by which Generations are preserved from Corruption." Earlier ministers only called themselves matchmakers. But purity has become equivalent to obedience, especially obedience to the fathers. "What was it that our Fathers came in to this Wilderness for? It was pure Conscience to the Second Commandment that brought them hither."[22] As the question was asked more frequently, the answers became more retrospectively self-righteous, with a magnified sense of the father's purity set in a grandiloquent rhetoric of destruction. Like the other highly obsessive Puritans, Mather was busy inventing a father worthy of his enormous self-expectations for obedience and self-denial.

Mather's style reflects a tension between obedience and apocalypse in the fragmentation of his sentences. Short phrases are characteristic of Puritan rhetoric, though the first-generation ministers developed syntactic structures to give brief phrases "affecting" weight in very long sentences. By contrast, Mather's phrases are jackhammer drills into stony pavement, making the same point over and over again. His sentences are often short, and when they do lengthen, they generally hold together by a simple structure of opposites, with very conventional imagery. His repetitive didacticism makes Mather one of the most boring of Puritan sermonists. He unfailingly substitutes querulous cliches for personal vision. His similes become monotonous allegories that transform the literal occasion for his sermon into a permanent expectation of vindictiveness.

> The sky looketh red and lowring, we may therefore fear, that foul weather is at hand: As once that Prophet said, There is a sound of an abundance of Rain, and in the mean-while, *the Heaven was black with Clouds.* Truly so it is at this day, the Heavens are black over our heads. The Clouds begin to gather thick in our Horizon; yea, there is a Cloud of Blood, which begins to drop upon us. When once a Cloud begins to drop, you know that a shower is wont to follow. The Cloud of Blood over our heads begins to drop; there was one drop fell the other day, witness the man that was slain upon the Coasts; the Lord grant that a Shower of Blood may not follow.

The passage is more vindictively hopeful than fearful. Searching for meaning in every event, he grounds his explications either in allegorical interpretations of natural occurrences, as here, or in typological connections to the biblical past. Robert Middlekauff notes Mather's endless absorption with Israel as the model for "chosen people."[23] But either kind of connection shows the strain, the lack of genuine coherence and shared frame of reference. A dogged repetitiveness, without structural momentum, is his main stylistic residue.

Sometimes his metaphor falls over of its own weight: "Such fearful Sights are usually Signs, that those Judgements, which are (as *Tertullian* speaks) *Tonsure humani generis,* God's sharp Razors on Mankind, whereby He doth poll [;] his Sythe, whereby He doth shear down multitudes of sinful Creatures, doe draw near: . . . And it may be, He is declaring to that generation of hairy Scalps, who go on still in their Trespasses, that the day of their Calamity is at hand." "So much Latin is so much flesh in a sermon," the earlier Puritans held. Now Increase Mather loosens the belt of arch secular reference which his son Cotton would entirely burst. Like Cotton, Increase has a predilection for lugubrious metaphor as well as for what Middlekauff calls "the grand smash."[24] The awkwardness of his call to "that generation of hairy Scalps" reveals the human artifice more than God's truth, in Mather's struggle to make the world yield visible signs of God's intent.

Physical destruction has become more imaginable than invisible fathers, and Mather's fantasy of hell is almost gloatingly intense, with fires of wrath devouring the body. At one point he offers a spectacular, if conventional, vision of parents being followed to hell by their cursing children: "O think with your selves, if you that are Parents should any of you perish, and your miserable Children should follow you to Hell, how will they curse you there? If thy Children perish throw thy evil Example, they will follow thee up and down in the ever-burning Lake crying out Woe to us that ever we were born of such Parents that had no grace to teach us the wayes of God, . . . Thus wilt thou hear thine own Children yelling in thine Ears, world without end." Hell is to be hounded eternally by your squalling brats! One can see why he praised his wife so highly for keeping all household matters from his mind. He also associates hell with the devouring orality of a gorging mother, taking his cue from Isaiah 5:14, "Hell hath enlarged her self, and opened her mouth without measure." Aggressive orality extends to the saints, too. "Have we not been like foolish little Birds," he asks in *A Sermon . . . Preached on a Publick Fast* (1682), "pecking at one another, until the great kite be ready to come, and devour one as well as another?"[25] Against the "great kite" of hell, the Godhead as a city of refuge seems even more escapist than the death that Mather longs for.

The unremitting intensity of his destructive fantasies raises questions about Mather's childhood, which were discussed in chapter three. Samuel Willard's imagery of hell does not include devouring or oral anxiety, but focuses on physical pain and feelings of guilt and hate. The roots of Mather's more frenzied and sadistic imagery probably lie undiscoverably embedded in his relationship to his mother, Katharine, who seems to have had such loving and possessive religious expectations for his soul. Increase wanted a *man* up there in heaven, a wrathful God who brings suffering in the shape of a sword: "When lighter Afflictions would not do, the Lord hath made bare his Arm against us, brandishing a glittering Sword, making it bright for the slaughter, yea, & drunk with blood."[26] Yet his wish for a bare-armed God raising a "Sword" becomes identified with a "drunk" violence of devouring and blood. If the language is conventional—part of his dependence on God's Word—his repetitions of the convention indicate his inward frenzy.

For Shepard, a calm and peaceful nursing father could be at once a personal dream and a central part of the culture's shared fantasy. But Mather fused himself with Christ's sufferings, not God's blissful promises. Like his son, he was obsessed with the crucifixion. As Benjamin Colman said in his eulogy, "the first and last Subject and Object of all his *Sermons* and *Prayers* among you, was *Jesus Christ and him crucified.* This only he desired to *know* among you."[27] Feeling abandoned by his people, and perhaps by his mother, Mather turned to the image of the suffering son to chastise himself into holiness, while turning to images of the wrathful God to chastise his flock.[28]

The contrast between Shepard and Mather illustrates what happens when a writer cannot find a language for personal conflicts that is part of community discourse. Where Shepard sought virginal union, and was able to communicate his dream in "heart-melting" imagery, Mather communicates a more abstracted disunion and self-pity. His sermons are simply not in touch with the roots of his faith. They are exercises in self-exculpation only, not shared purpose. As he concludes in *Two Sermons Testifying against the Sin of Drunkenness*, "Therefore if there be any Drunkard that will be a Drunkard still, he shall die in his iniquity: But I have delivered my soul." To "deliver" himself now does not mean being born into the company of the faithful but being separated from a drunken people.

Almost fifty years later, in his introduction to *A Course of Sermons on Early Piety* (1721), Mather was still bewailing the fact that "the very interest of New England seems to be Changed from a Religious to a Worldly Interest." Now, however, even self-delivery had long since proved illusory, and he just cried for the death that could take him away: "*Till He send for me!*—Which, O my GOD and SAVIOUR, I am daily waiting for;—Why is thy Chariot so long in coming? Why tarry the Wheels of thy Chariot!"[29] American literature would find death wishes common to its major figures, but perhaps never with such helpless, ritualized repetition.

Samuel Willard, 1640–1707

Samuel Willard escaped Mather's obsession with death, crucifixion, and a devouring mother-hell by distancing his own similar resolutions of conflicts with authority into legalistic forms and themes of reasonable comfort. Impeccably orthodox and ordered in his public pronouncements on faith and polity, he also voices a more private fantasy of father and child apart from the visible world. Like Mather's obsessive accusations, Willard's obsessive precision of reasons distances his anxieties, while his theme of rational happiness speaks to needs for tenderness, though in scrupulously intellectual terms.

To the public God is visible as a judge, not a father, until God chooses to adopt the saint. "I am under the watchful eye of an all-seeing God," Willard declares in *Impenitent Sinners Warned of their*

Misery And Summoned to Judgment (1698), "who keeps an exact account of all my thoughts, words and deeds, and will certainly in that
day, bring them into open light, and set them in order before me."
Focusing on covenant law, Willard presented God as a reasonable
arbiter, and opposed Mather's call for a colony-wide fast day as a need-
less expense of lamentation and humiliation.[30] He was liberal in his
sense of the possibilities for rational faith. Yet he was also a man of
distances, categories, and rules and saw his God that way: "He doth
not act the part of a Father in this case, who may connive at, pity and
overlook faults and weaknesses in his Child, but of a judge that takes
the Law for his Rule, and *cloaths himself* with *Righteousness* as a
garment."[31] Edward Taylor also made clothing imagery central to his
expression of God's grace. Clean clothes become a central image in the
new generation's language for heavenly happiness.

Willard's sermon structure reflects his legalism. His "openings" usually
place his biblical text in context (who was speaking to whom, where,
when), without attention to internal significance. His sermons do not
so much address a specific audience as state, in a general way, what is
possible and what is not. In his definitions he stresses duties, not
internal states or affections. So he declares in *The Truly Blessed Man*
(1700): "*Guilt is properly an obligation lying upon a sinner to suffer
punishment.*" Much of his sermon time passes in defining and cate-
gorizing, with emphasis on precise distinctions among hierarchies, and
among stages of grace—election, vocation, justification, adoption, sanctification, glorification—rather than on the experience of grace that
diversely enthralled Hooker, Shepard, and Cotton. Willard's differences
from Shepard, the most legalistic of first-generation ministers, are
similar to Coleridge's distinction between the secondary and the primary imagination: Willard has only "that false secondary power of
making distinctions." A typical Willard page contains little evidence
of God the Father dispensing joys and rewards, but much legal bickering about various aspects of the mechanics of salvation. His concern
for territorial rights also lies behind one of his three favorite images:
life as a war, a metaphor he could expand to great length.[32] His other
favorites are light and mechanical order.

In psychological terms, Willard's sermons have aspects of a compulsive ritual to defend against anxiety by setting everything into firm,
categorical, visible order and place. He was the Puritan analogue to
the Freudian second generation's Heinz Hartmann, who refined the
master's ego, id, and superego into so many interlocking compartments.
The Father is thought of not as breast but as judge or restrainer for

"impetuous lusts" and "violence," and "the dread of an after reckoning" is God's best restraint: "When therefore this chain, with which God ties men up, and sets bounds to their violence, is taken off, and men are insensible of any impressions from it, what will not their impetuous lusts make them dare to do?" Willard wants to cover every anxious contingency with a chain of categories. It was symptomatic that his *Compleat Body of Divinity,* a set of his lectures collected posthumously in 1726, was—as his respectful friends say in their preface—"the largest that was ever Printed Here, and the first of Divinity in a *Folio* Volumn." Their pride in the physical object illustrates what Puritans were up against. They had waited eighteen years, "till this growing Country is become now capable of taking off the Impression of so great a Work."[33] The "complete body" seems more impressive to them than the divinity.

Willard's *Compleat Body* is the longest single chore awaiting anyone who ventures into Puritan scholarship. It is methodical in every way, from its systematic explication of text after text in the Shorter Catechism to the once-a-month format for lecturing. Yet the text is not without its virtues. It has none of the hysteria of Prynne's *Histrio-Mastix,* and if lacking in liveliness, at least it is earnest and thoughtful. As his 1726 editors say, "The Language appears to be manly clear & natural, agreeable to his manner of Reasoning, which is regular easy & nervous; and his Words & Phrases exceedingly suited to express his *Ideas,* the great Design of Language." Their emphasis on his language of *"Ideas"* is quite right. Feelings are deliberately slighted. There are almost no similes from practical experience, only from the Bible. In fact there is relatively little imagery at all. Instead Willard offers reasoning and argumentation on biblical themes, developed, divided, and categorized as polarities or stages. He does make one joke, on page 529: "There is a drowsy Opinion of some, who suppose the Soul to fall asleep in the Body" till the last trumpet. But Willard's usual method of awakening his hearers is to reason out the Word to the limits of text and mind. Indeed, he is far more conscious of the limits of earthly language than are first-generation preachers, and those limits constitute one of his major themes.

Willard's first concern, however, is with system. "He was indeed a Recommender of *Divinity-Systems* even to all sorts of Persons," his editors say, "and especially Young Students, in order to Methodize their Enquiries and Conceptions, to keep their Minds from wandering and Inconsistency, and help them to see the Connection and Harmony of divine Truths." Like his God, his preoccupation with intellectual judgment clearly outweighs any flights of fancy; "His Phansy was Copious, tho' not Luxuriant, but most Correct, being Obsequious to the Dictates, and kept under the strict Guard of a well poised Judgment." Willard's quality of assured judgment, the editors conclude, is what made him a "tender Father" to younger ministers. Now readers too can enjoy "his Stile Masculine, not Perplexed, but Easy as well as Strong." Their highest praise for him, in keeping with the role and status expected of second-generation ministers, is that his "Elaborate, Acute and Judicious" discourses "smelt of the Lamp, and had nothing *Mean* in them." What would Thomas Hooker have said to that?

Recent scholars have made a great deal of Willard's emphasis on rational happiness rather than depravity in his definition of human identity. As his first sentence announces, "the Great Thing which all Rational, and Immortal Creatures have to be mostly inquisitive about, is HAPPINESS." Man, he says, "is a Creature that was made capable of Happiness: which no other inferiour Creature, can ever attain unto." Like any good Puritan, he is quick to say that "man is a Dependent Being; his Felicity is out of himself." Willard's end in establishing his theme is to convince the reason that the world has nothing to do with true happiness. His more particular aim is to equate happiness with a hierarchy ascending to pure thought. He is certainly more comforting than most Puritan preachers, and at first glance one would therefore think he continues the rhetoric of tender mothering. But his language of happiness reduces bliss to rationality, not feeling, and places it at the summit of a mind-body hierarchy.

By the end of his third sermon he has thoroughly established the familiar Puritan polarities of vanity, desires, the body, creature comforts, and the world on one side, opposed to real happiness, whose chief end is simply to glorify God. "The Desire of Man, that *Horseleeches Daughter,* is still crying *Give, Give,*: The Bed is too narrow, and the covering too short: The World looks bulky, but it is empty, void and waste. . . . the World is a great Nothing, Prov. 23."[34] To associate desire with a woman in bed, though a biblical convention, is part of his larger dissociation from need and feeling. Only pure reason can come close to glorifying God's much purer understanding. Hooker, Cotton, and Shepard, whatever their differences, would never have so minimized the role of the affections, though Shepard would have spoken with the same strictness.

Willard's intellectuality is uncompromising. "Man is a reasonable Creature, is able to draw inferences from inferences; and our Saviour Christ hath taught us how to argue" (p. 29). Much of his argument has

to do with distinguishing means from ends, with God as the rational
end. Sin means being "separated from his end," through loss of understanding, since "man knock't his head in his fall, and craz'd his understanding, as to divine Truths. It is but a little that he knows of that
Rule. Some broken fragments, & moth-eaten registers, old rusty out-
worn monuments there are; but so imperfect & illegible, that there are
but very few of them, that he can spell out what they mean, and in
others he is mistaken" (p. 15). Willard's language is lively even as he
calls attention to its limits, as he does so often.[35] But it works
better in short bursts than over the long haul. This particular argument,
for instance, is one of five reasons why we cannot get truth from nature.
The fifth reason is divided into two parts, the second of which is divided into three parts. Though his short phrases and strong adjectives
sometimes convey vigor, the overwhelming impression is of intellectual
patterning and division, in keeping with his theme of reasoning about
reason.

The passage also shows Willard's tendency to equate "divine Truths"
with "Rule." God "deals with men, as with Reasonable Creatures, and
hence they must have a Rule to apply themselves to in all things: This
is only God's Word" (p. 21). Rational obedience, not the milk of the
first-generation Gospel, constitutes Willard's idea of dependence. If
the Word is "Logical milk," as he says (p. 32), he stresses the logic.
Faith is "a rational confidence," or a dependence that "requires a discerning or apprehending of the Object," not an utter dependence. We
must understand why we wholly lean on Christ, or else our faith
"would be nothing better than frenzy, if it saw nothing in him for
which it so doth" (p. 23). The first sin, after all, was pride, which is
nothing "but an overweening opinion of ones self, which makes him
think himself too good for his duty" (p. 181).[36]

Willard   preaches entirely to the understanding, which for him is
capable of grasping enough truth to know Christ and be saved.
Through understanding, polarity can be transcended, so that no one
need oppose the creature but "rise higher" and see the whole (p. 129).
Truth is seeing. Truth is "light," he frequently says, especially sunlight.
Truth is "sweet and delectable" food, he says less frequently. Truth is
a compass, a pole star. Above all, "the general nature of Truth consists
in conformity," as opposed to "lies, Romances, and foolish vanities"
(pp. 25, 27), and the major happiness proposed in the *Compleat Body*
is the happiness of a system conforming to itself in all its parts. God's
very existence is proved by "the *harmony* of the whole in all its
parts . . . every wheel in this curious watch moving aright" leads to

faith (p. 38). Man's body, "the setting together of this great *Machine*, the harmonious placing of every piece of it, and that among so many uncountable parts, there is none displaced or useless" (p. 66), proves God's wisdom, just as does his "*Providential management* of the World . . . the keeping of so many wheels, which are in motion, to go regularly, and none of them to mss" (p. 66). The machine image is conventional; his fascination with accountability for every little part is more unusual. Indeed, the typesetter may have been having a little fun by missing on that last word. Regularity is a classic preoccupation of the anal-obsessive character, and Willard's language invokes regularity as one of God's major attributes, even in his basic definition of sin (p. 187) as "any want of Conformity to, or Transgression of the Law of GOD."

Another aspect of obsessive language is a preoccupation with God as wrathful judge. However, Willard is careful to make strict distinctions between God's various roles. Willard's God is one who has chosen to accommodate to human capacities, in roles we can understand. Wrath is a part, in fact the first part, but not the whole. Until the moment of adoption, God is a judge and only a judge, whose characteristics are infinite power and infinite wrath toward sinners who "dishonour" him. He would destroy the whole world, Willard says, before he would "lose the least tittle of his Glory" (p. 74). God is pure law, which commands death for the least sin. Yet if the Anglican God is supposed to be "without body, parts, or passions," as the creed has it, Willard's God seems to be nothing but parts and passions. Just as the judge is about to kill the sinner on the spot, along comes his patience and goodness to soften the blow. "Patience moderates his Anger" at that moment (p. 82), and God contents himself with being an exact accountant. He "keeps an exact register, of *all the individual sins*, secret and open," just as, while the sinner is "in his Mother's belly," God "writes down all his Members in his Books, that there is none of them wanting, none superfluous, and every one in their right shape and place, . . . he gives them a seeing eye, and an hearing ear; it might have been otherwise, and God sometimes orders it so to be" (p. 84).

The high comedy of God as perfect bureaucrat attending to everyone's anatomy is high seriousness to Willard, because his God has to encompass each detail every moment. Not wrath but relentless system for the body's parts and passions, projected onto the world, is the greatest power Willard can imagine. Much more than for first-generation preachers, hierarchy orders the order, and wrath is associated with rebellion against rank.[37] Willard is no Luther or Dr. Schreber. Yet his anal control illustrates the decline of Puritan language into divergent forms of the obsessive style, with rigorous distinction making complementing Increase Mather's fulminations. He is even able to distinguish between kinds of anger, rather nicely too: "There is this difference between *Anger* and *Malice;* Anger being a sudden motion, grows cold upon second thoughts, whereas malice useth deliberation, and gathers strength by consulting" (p. 397). That passage, one of the few to show any awareness of human psychology, is not intended to comprehend God's wrath but to show how the malice of sinners "heightned their wickedness."

On the other hand, God's parts do make kindly motions toward "his Family." When justice would put you in hell, mercy "stept in, and stopt the Execution." Willard enjoys repeating that drama. Wrath is about to push sinners into the ocean of fire when "Grace stept in" with "Ransom" (pp. 86, 88). Polarities of justice and goodness are contained in the Godhead itself, and through Christ mercy slowly triumphs, giving to sinners air, rich tables, overflowing cups, "a soft Bed," rich houses, wives and children, and "all manner of Recreations, Mirth, Musick and Jollity" (p. 86). Here, to collapse several hundred pages of argument, Willard's precise delineation of the stages of salvation is central to his theme of rational happiness. It structures the first two-thirds of his text, before his explication of the Ten Commandments, as he walks his audience through the steps of election, vocation, justification, adoption, sanctification, and glorification. Like Mather and Taylor, Willard puts Christ at the center of his theology of grace, as the essence of God's kindness.

As always, Willard is careful to define roles. Perhaps his language reflects second-generation concerns with more specialized functions and status. The Father, for instance, is only one temporal aspect of the Deity; God "is not Father as he is God, but as he begets the *Son*," just as "a *Man* differs modally from himself considered as a Man, and as a Master, and as a Servant; which though it be but a dark resemblance of this great Truth, yet it is such as God accommodates us with" (p. 98). Willard is more comfortable with Adam as the father of sin than with God as the Father of all, since fatherhood is a matter only of relation, not of essence, as the son's "Relative *Property*" is "to be *Begotten,* and not to Beget" (p. 99). God is a father only as he engenders. Willard's usual language portrays God's other aspects as sun, sovereign, lawgiver, order maker, and perfection. Thus God chooses to become a Father to his saints only on page 489, ten years after Willard began his monthly lectures, when God changes from the role of judge to adopt justified saints into his family.

More probably, Willard's language reflects new patriarchal realities

as well as specialized roles. He defines God's fathering after adoption
with a striking absence of love and tenderness. God will provide, protect, uphold, instruct, help us work, chasten, commend service, overlook infirmities, and make us heirs (pp. 489–490). The list assumes
patriarchal distance, not loving or anxious bonds between New England fathers and sons. Willard's rhetoric of tender love is entirely reserved for the Son, whose role is one of blessed mediation. The Father
without his gift of the Son would be only judgment and wrath. We are
brought to a knowledge of sin by his law. Christ cannot console us
before that awareness; "but know it, as long as you are under the Law,
you are under wrath" (p. 204). Yet only to stress the law will "drive
men to desperation" (p. 190). After proving with obsessive thorough-
ness that Adam's disobedience broke all Ten Commandments (pp. 193–
194), Willard states that sin descends from Adam through the body's
seminal generation, since "Adam in this one act, acted as a publick
person, representing the whole cluster of Mankind" (p. 197). Spending
two sermons on the knotty problem of how Adam's sin is actually
"communicated," he finally confesses ignorance of how it is physically
done, though the moral way is clear (pp. 194–200). All of which makes
us *by nature children of wrath.*[38]

Only Christ was not born of Adam. He was born of the Holy Ghost,
the only man ever exempted. Without Christ we are condemned to
death and wrath, in soul and body. "There is an hand-writing of terror
against you," he says (p. 208). There is no possibility of rationally
comprehending God without Christ, because sin has destroyed God's
image in us—"not only crazed, & weakned, as some would have it, but
there is none of it remaining . . . quite rooted out." Affections then
rise up against reason and become "exorbitant," "the handmaids of the
will" rather than "the feet of the soul" (p. 211). Willard's emphasis on
male generation of sin and its location in the feelings is the other side
of his emphasis on rational happiness. Sin is filth, separation, and especially "*Anomy* . . . a missing the law or rule" (p. 215). It brings
"an iliad of miseries" (p. 225). And since we are under the law, we
face a future only of absolute rewards and absolute punishments, with
punishment the certain end. Heaven is for grace; hell is for justice
(pp. 205, 237). There is no grace available from the human mind,
rational as it is, without Christ, because God—the only permissible
artist—intended the fall "to be a foil on which he would draw in most
lively colours the portraiture of his rich grace" (p. 245). Since Willard
had the mind of an accountant, his first concern when he reaches the
theme of grace is to tote up how many might be among the elect. He

concludes that "there is a fair probability" of escaping hell. Some biblical passages say only a few have made it, but since Judges 14 says a
"kingdom," there ought to be "many ten Thousands," and he suddenly
leaps further to say, "I can assure you that there shall be many millions"
(p. 249). In any case, the elect and the reprobate can rest assured that
God "will gain his glory either *from you* or *upon you*" (p. 257).[39]
Willard even suggests, citing five biblical texts, that God knows each of
his elect by name (p. 265). The frame for his argument is the absolute
dependence on God's freely given grace, without which there is only
wrathful condemnation, because election and reprobation are done
solely for the end of showing God's "two everlasting monuments . . .
viz. *Grace* and *vindictive Justice*." Otherwise they are incomprehen-
sible, he says, because they predate any human acts that might merit
mercy or justice.

In describing Christ as the agent for grace, Willard makes his usual
distinctions among the three offices of priest, king, and prophet, mocking Quakers for nonsensically making lion and lamb other offices. That
is simply not linguistically correct, he says (p. 322). His language for
union with Christ is more flexible, since the Bible allows so many
similes for the spiritual coupling. The best carnal image is vine and
branches, he observes, though images of body, building, temple, and
marriage, "to name no more," can shadow forth how profoundly it is
"a rational union, and is founded, in mutual consent" (p. 430). Characteristically, he avoids more intimate possibilities for a language of
parts and whole. He states several times that a "Synecdochall" language is as close as we can come to God's truths.[40]

Over a hundred pages follow on the stages of redemption, before
and after death. Willard is especially eager to make clear how distinct
justification is from adoption, since in justification God accepts sinners
as a judge, while in adoption God adopts sinners as a father. The vast
polarity between man's sin and God's righteousness then begins to
yield to the image of God in man through sanctification, which is a lifelong battle to be "renewed in the whole man after the Image of
God . . . enabled more and more to dye unto Sin, and live unto
Righteousness" (p. 491). Willard is more concerned with precisely
delineating the slow stages of the battle than with expressing a Cotton-
like ecstasy of absolute rebirth. Though he cites the requisite passages
from John 3.3 and Ephesians 4.24 on being a new man (pp. 497–501),
his language is gradualist. There can be no real happiness on earth,
he says, only in heaven. On earth it is always a "War."

Willard's text seems to mellow as he gets older, though there is little thematic change. Perhaps his point by point explication of the Shorter Catechism also encouraged a shift from wrathful judgment to grace. Yet he continues a tone of assurance into his later explication of the Ten Commandments. God alone can separate and judge, he says; no one else can judge the heart. Ministers in particular must have "*tender love*," because their role is to be "Pastors" or "Shepherds" to their "flock" (p. 636). "They are compared to *tender Mothers*, on the account of their Love to them, 1 Thes. 2.7." However, Willard avoids any mention of ministers as breasts of God in describing ministerial duties, as he avoids infantile language in general. In fact the first mention of Canticles that I noticed is on page 519. His concern is with precise roles, not nursing. Ministers must avoid "*Exotick* or new-fangled Words, (which scarce One of Ten understands)"; they must visit privately, but their main duty is preaching the Gospel. The congregation must give them respect, prayers, and especially "*an Honourable* Maintenance," he emphasizes. We should "Love *them* as our Spiritual Fathers" (pp. 637–641).

In later sermons he is somewhat more free with fathering imagery, thanks to Christ, whose sufferings brought us beyond the Father's wrath. In explicating the first line of the Lord's Prayer, for instance, Willard says that it teaches us to be "as Children to a Father," indeed our only real father, since "Christ . . . stands between an angry God, and sinful Worms, *Eph.* 3.14. *Col.* 1.12." Just as he avoids breast imagery in discussing the minister's role, so he slights rebirth imagery for God's fatherhood in finding language for regeneration. God is a Father, he sums up, "by *eternal Generation*," in his begetting of Adam and Christ, "and by a *gracious Adoption*" of his saints. It is not our first rebirth in dependence but God's subsequent decision to adopt the already born that brings on the work of sanctification. As one would suspect from his preference for rational comprehension over regressive imagery, Willard finds that the word "Father" is meant to convey the same "deference" as children give to fathers (pp. 903–904). That is true "Reverence."

Willard does urge the happiness of God's rewards in all his books, with strong if conventional promises. Justification, he says in *Brief Discourse*, will "exalt you to a glorious Throne, and set a massy Crown of life upon your head; entertain you in the everlasting embraces of his ravishing affection, and make you eternally to swim in bankless, boundless and bottomless Ocean of pleasures, in the presence of God, and of the Lamb; where you shall be filled and run over with fulness of Joyes." The law, and God as judge, remain for the mixed earthly community. Grace, and Christ as the "Ocean of pleasures," await the few who fully accept the covenant. In accepting the law they find more than the law. This vision of Christ's possibility as Son and transformation is as central to Willard as the crucifixion is to Mather. Although much less than in first-generation sermons, oral imagery is occasionally used to express Christ's "light" or knowledge for those who "dwel at the Wel-head of light: while we can scarce see enough to establish our faith and confirm our hope, you are gazing your selves into exstasies, and drinking your fill of pure fountain light . . . refresht with everlasting beams of purest light from the face of Jesus Christ."[41]

Unlike the first generation, whose imagery expressing God's fullness is often in the present tense, Willard characteristically pictures God's fullness as unrevealed until the Day of Judgment. Death is the way to gain access to Christ, and Willard offers death to the saints with some of Mather's fervor: "Never doth the Box of their Sweet Ointments give a better savour, than when the Case is broken: the *Saints* do not go out like a Candle in a stinking Snuff, but they ascend like *Frankincense* or *sweet Incense*, in a cloud of fragrant Smoke." His fantasy is of death as freedom from the body's "Case" so that the soul can become a sweet-smelling invisibility.[42]

We know nothing about Willard's childhood, except that his mother died when he was very young. Yet his language expresses anal aspects of the obsessive style as clearly as Mather's language expresses more wrathful aspects. Imagery of disorder and battles is as close as Willard comes to direct tensions. Rational dependence means strict control of feelings. In heaven, however, Willard's fantasies of happiness at last spill over into sensuousness. Removed from earth, worldly society, and the body, the soul finds a pure home. The *Compleat Body* locates the beginnings of assurance for God's love in sanctification on earth, though assurance properly belongs to glorification, which begins on earth but "*supposeth,* and so is *after* Vocation, Justification, Adoption, and Sanctification" (p. 504). Willard's language is still rational and legal. Only with glorification, not even with sanctification, comes the knowledge of being children of God (1 John 3.2) who can cry Abba Father (Rom. 8.15) and be newborn babes. Willard locates the bliss much later than do first-generation ministers. His first mention of Canticles occurs now, as God "ravishes" the heart. But all real happiness comes after death.

"There is an Inchoate Blessedness, which God's People partake in in this Life," he admits (p. 528), "but Death passeth them over to a yet more glorious State, and makes an inexpressible advance of their Happiness." Then there is no more sin. The soul is received in heaven by Christ, who "shall with widened arms receive it, and with the most tender Embraces, lodge it in his Bosom, and thereby give it the feeling Assurances of His Everlasting Love" (p. 533). This is the first instance of mothering language in the *Compleat Body*, though its intensity makes up for its absence on earth. As befits a patriarch, God the Father receives souls at an awesome remove, after Christ has received them intimately.

Christ is the center of heaven's ecstasy, as son, mother, and spouse. The soul is taken into Christ's chamber, where they make love. "These Visions of Glory cannot be cloathed with humane language" (p. 534). Yet even that happiness is not the greatest, because Christ has also united with the dead bodies of the faithful, which are raised at the resurrection. Willard scoffs at those who say bodies must be created anew; that would "undermine God's Omnipotency" (p. 537). Now the body rejoins the soul without sin, without disease, without deformity, and without mortality. Eternity will be an endless singing and contemplation of God's glory, "and acting Love upon him, and never be tired." The greatest happiness of all, on Judgment Day, is to be *"Openly acknowledged and Acquitted"* (p. 551). Guilt persists to the last, even in Willard's fantasy of ultimate reward. And when they are at last presented by Christ to the distant Father, "what an astonishing Interview will it be" (p. 556).

Though Willard's language is now ecstatic, it maintains its second-generation preoccupation with role and paternal distance. He also shares the second generation's comic excess of physical detail. He ferrets out texts for every one of heaven's attributes. There will be no food, since the sinless bodies have no creature needs. There will be no clothing, since no one will have any shame and heaven has a pleasant climate. No one need sleep, since there is no night (Rev. 21.25), and besides, "Sleep is thought to arise from Fumes engendred by the Nourishment taken, and the exhausion of the Spirits by Labour" (p. 546). There will be no marriage except to Christ, since procreation is no longer necessary. Not only will the soul consummate its marriage to Christ, but it will also have "a wonderful foil" in the unhappiness of sinners down in hell—a vindictive touch, if only a touch.

Another great pleasure will be in possessing heaven itself; here Willard sounds like a tourist guide to an aristocratic resort. Words fail him, he says, to describe the city, the streets, "the wonderful Accommodations," the palace. "True, there will be great Disproportion in Degrees" (p. 557). But as we are wife to Christ, thus honored by his greater glory, so saints "shall then lie in his Bosom, enjoy his Embraces, *know him as they are known* by him, according to their Capacity." At the last reach of happiness, Willard banishes all questions of fatherhood and power to celebrate eternal union with the Son: "He shall, having resigned the Kingdom into his Father's hand, spend his Eternity in their Company," with no "interrupted Caresses" and immediate, not mediate, communion (p. 557).

Willard ends the first part of *Compleat Body* here, with faith's final rewards. The second part describes obedience, which as he says is the second part of religion. Only in heaven does his language of parts and rational happiness loosen into the blissful comfort we have met on earth in first-generation similes. Even here, for Willard, the Father remains a distant judge to the last, while the Son has all the tenderness. And in trying to literalize God's habitation, his imagination never goes beyond God's text. Obsessive to the last, his vision is a reward fit for obsession.

I have presented *A Compleat Body* at such length to show that what seems to be tender comfort to modern readers is actually an atrophy of feeling, an excess of mind. Willard and Mather are two sides of the obsessive style, without the first generation's feeling-filled language of collective dependence to complicate and deepen Puritanism's appeal. In diverse ways their writings indirectly indicate the presence of a more distant, controlled, and repressive patriarchy, with tender mothers more as dream shadows than as equals. Guilt, not need, is the overriding emotion, expressed in Mather as accusation and in Willard as ordered judgment. They also share an identification with Christ crucified and a passion for imagining life after death.

Yet finally Willard offers a more attractive language of faith than Mather. While sharing Mather's separation of Christ from God, Willard's Christ is more sheltering Son than crucified sufferer, and his God is more rational judge than wrathful sword thrower. On the other hand, while similar in his focus on death and Christ's death as the crucial transformation, Willard recreates the Puritan Family Romance without the virgin churches, without the breasts, and without any touch of the messy, contaminated world that energizes Mather's hysteria. Willard's continuing appeal is in his identification—rare in *Compleat Body*—with a small, secretive child.

The Child's Portion is Willard at his best. His style loosens into simple conjunctions, sentences that almost flow in describing how sons can depend on God: "Gods Sons in this life are like little Children, always tripping, and stumbling, and falling, and so weak that they could never get up again but for him: but by reason of his hand that is upon them, his everlasting Arm that is under them, hence if they fall at any time through incogitancy, or by stumbling at any thing that lies in their way." No one but Willard could imagine falling because of "incogitancy." Otherwise the rhetoric seems conventional for the first generation, flowing for Willard. But Willard can imagine this relationship only away from the world and all the law pertaining to the world. Moreover, these children are no longer visible saints: "The reason why the children of God are so little regarded here in the World; it is because the World knows not who they are, nor what they are born unto: Their great Glory for the present is within; outwardly they look like other men, they eat, drink, labour, converse in earthly employments, as others do; the communion which they have with God in all of these, is a secret thing." Perhaps such sentiments justified the half-way covenant on the Roger Williams-like grounds that no one can tell who really believes. But the real wish, I think, is to be dissociated from the dry, dark, restrained world of law, lust, and corruption. "Hence let us do what we may to be hidden in a day of darkness," Willard emphasizes as one of his uses in *The Checkered State of the Gospel Church* (1701).[43]

The future would become darker. But for those who had "the child's portion," a new, secret, and intimate relation to the Father, the community can be tossed aside like a moldering toy when Daddy comes into the room. Death, as with Mather, becomes a natural liberation from the transient duties that life asks of the faithful. In dreaming of this end Willard could write one of the most peaceful passages in Puritan literature.

> And is this the thing I am so much afraid of? Is it this at which my thoughts do so much, start and give back? No, no, I will not fear, but make all the hast I can that I may in due season finish my work, and go home: The World is weary of me, and would gladly part with me; and I am as weary of it, and as willing to leave it: And were it not that I have a little work to do for the glory of my God and Father here, I could be content forthwith to be gone: However, I am willing to tarry on his business, but when my father shal please to call, I will say, Lord, here am I; and in the mean while, I will wait till my chang comes.

It was suitable, in several ambiguous ways, that when Willard died in 1707 Ebenezer Pemberton lauded him not as a spiritual father but "as the *Elder Son* among many Brethren."[44] Never mind the success or failure of the "errand into the wilderness"; never mind whose worldly ambition triumphed, who scoffed or turned away from the preachers. The inward child could still go home. What did it matter if no one knew?

———————•———————

The fathers may have had fantasies of being united with the Son, but too many sons did not have dreams of being pure fathers. Perhaps the New England fathers had become so secure in their patriarchal roles that mixed expectations were no longer compounded with anxiety. A simpler set of obsessive responses to patriarchy and possessiveness defines second-generation styles of faith. A corollary to patriarchal security was that some parents were starting to break their children's wills well before the age of reason, as Philip Greven describes in *The Protestant Temperament*. Or perhaps, as Cotton Mather says in the *Magnalia*, parents had become "out of measure *indulgent* to their children," though Puritans had always sounded that theme. Thomas Cobbett's family guidebook rails against "the arising generation now a daies, too many of them begin to grow so rude and graceless."[45] Rebellion and indifference, not oversubmissiveness, were obviously the greater worries to the elders, whose generational sense had become quite desperate, at least as reflected in rhetoric.

The need of fathers for children in their image, like their need to be welcomed by Christ, both contradicts and supports our image of repressive Puritan patriarchs. Their expectations were now not so much confused as overwhelming, especially in Increase Mather's case, since his mother so pleadingly abetted the patriarchal vision. As Cobbett says in 1656, "What, in an ordinary way, would become of the way of God, of religion, of church, within a few years?" His solution is to train as many young people as possible to be scholars like himself. But his cry goes further: "You are so strangely Metamorphozed from any likeness to your good Parents, or Ancestors." What he has in mind here is long hair.[46] Yet the pain, the anger, and the wishing swirled around that silly symbol because it expressed a generational truth. Not only rebellion but change, autonomy, and physical expressiveness were becoming ways of the world, replacing adherence to the pure father's eternal image of restraint and judgment. Oddly enough, though Puritan discourse becomes more overtly concerned with parental expectations, both Mather and Willard are bent on descrying patterns of order, reward, and punishment, while slighting the work of bringing on conversions through affecting language. The expectation of conversion, so central to first-generation experience that it was institutionalized as public testimony, became a bitter question with the half-way covenant, and finally a lapsed question by the eighteenth century, when Solomon Stoddard made conversion a matter for external sacraments to handle.

I don't mean to say that conversions ceased, or that Puritanism ceased to speak to children. In fact parental expectations for children to fulfill their image joined with an earlier breaking of the will in at least one new way: a spate of conversions by the very young. The reborn child was a last, paradoxical shared fantasy of the faithful, who formerly had said children were bundles of original sin. Children, especially girls, responded by having conversions as early as four years old. Jonathan Edwards discovered a model of holiness in four-year-old Phebe Bartlett, and he married seventeen-year-old Sarah Pierpont four years after writing his moving account of her walking with God in the fields of New Haven. James Janeway's *A Token for Children* (1671), an English collection of stories about children converting and dying young under God's all-seeing eye, was very popular in New England. In some respects the fantasy indicates a greater innocence in parents than in children, as parents intensified and projected wishes for their own purity onto their children rather than adapt to change. Others have seen the fantasy as a way for parents to absolve themselves of guilt for childhood deaths. In any case it was a strange, antinomian expectation for young children to meet God alone, not as rational members of a holy community. The patriarchal hierarchy of obedient subordination, felt so keenly by the second generation, had been reversed, with a girl leading the way, at least in the fathers' fantasies.[47]

It is easy to make much of oppressive parental expectations. Yet the real point is that they were not fulfilled. Slowly, after many struggles, congregations became more loosely covenanted, as the culture began to reward risk taking and expansion more than tight communal deference. Two children can serve to illustrate the failure of paternal expectations. Cotton Mather's eldest son seems to have done all he could to smear his grandfather's name, which he bore. Robert Middlekauff recounts the career of the younger Increase: "He shirked his studies, failed as an apprentice in a countinghouse and as a seaman, and, worst of all, showed little evidence of piety. The distress Cotton Mather felt at these deficiencies became despair when 'an Harlot big with a Bastard' laid 'her Belly' to his 'poor Son Cresy.' " After the boy rejoined a gang that rioted throughout Boston Cotton Mather renounced him—only to take him back, still unrepentant, much as Ralph Josselin had wavered between banishing and loving his son and come down on the side of love. In fact Cotton seems to have loved "Cresy" far more than his dutiful dull son Samuel, who never left the Puritan fold. Perhaps, as Christopher Bollas has suggested, such sons were acting out the parents' repressed wishes. A year after the death of his grandfather, Increase drowned at sea. The gulf between the grandfather's traditions and filial realities had in this case become immeasurable, and the name "Increase" was now ironic in the extreme.[48]

Another unrepentant child was Timothy Root, associated with Jonathan Edwards's parish. Ben Franklin, who shares center stage with Edwards in the next chapter, might have appreciated Timothy's spunk, if not his language. Edwards liked neither. Twenty-two youths had been brought to account by the Northampton fathers for reading "the Young Folks' Bible," subtitled "The Midwife Rightly Instructed." Edwards perhaps hastened his own dismissal by peremptorily reading their names from the pulpit, to the disgrace of their families, though whether he actually read the names is not entirely clear. There is no doubt that a public hearing was held, because Edwards himself took down the proceedings in shorthand. It is a classic drama: the young generation, with its "Bible," confronting the famous minister with pungent language which the minister faithfully transcribed.

Sarah Pierpont Edwards, who as a girl had communed with God in the fields of New Haven and was now the minister's wife, gave the central testimony.

> Sarah Edwards Testified that at the Time of the first sitting of the Committee of this Church, she heard Timothy Root say I won't worship a wig; and on some bodies making answer that some Respect was due to some Persons, he said again I won't worship a wig, repeating, a wig, over many times, as appeared with much of an air of disdain— . . . Timothy Root moved to others to go away, and said to 'em in the Presence of a Considerable number of Persons come we'll go away; do you think I'll be kept here for nothing? and speaking of the Committee said they are nothing but men molded up of a little Dirt. I don't care a Turd, or I don't care a Fart for any of them.[49]

Patriarchal authority was nothing but "a wig," and the language of defecation had been dumped on the fathers.

To some, the situation might have seemed another illustration of the "visible shrink in all Orders of Men among us" that Cotton Mather speaks of in his *Magnalia* (1702), a book written to preserve the images of the first fathers for a generation whose respect, even interest, was slipping away. By the fourth generation, Jonathan Edwards at times

seemed alone in striving to keep the vision of Thomas Shepard alive. As
Loren Baritz has said, "He was so intent on the matter of purging
New England that he quite overlooked the possibility that it would
purge itself of him."[50] Since he had become uncompromising in his up-
holding of the first fathers' purity, Edwards had to be ejected from his
covenanted community: a final ironic statement of lay power over
ministers who did not speak the language they wanted to hear.
Franklin, faced with more overt conflict with his father and brother,
simply moved to Philadelphia. The difference in styles foretells a
different world.

Chapter Eight

Franklin and Edwards

When creatures smile god is under
valeu'd.
                    Michael Wigglesworth

He that lives upon Hope dies farting.
                    Poor Richard[1]

In 1915 Van Wyck Brooks's essay on highbrow and lowbrow attitudes in American life fixed Jonathan Edwards and Benjamin Franklin
as exemplary poles: the spiritual and the material, submission to invisible authority and mastery of visible things, apocalypse and progress, the saved and the useful, holy mission and self-reliance—two
confident voices of a divided age. Actually, as so many have said,
Franklin preserves Puritan values in fundamental ways, bringing into
ordinary commerce what had been reserved for the transcendent.[2] Instead of the Puritan faith in the Word of the good book, Franklin had
an equally salvational faith in the power of words, or books in general.
His autobiography attributes his success to wide reading and a facility
with writing and conversation, which impressed men in high places
when he was still very young. Both Franklin and Edwards assiduously
sought the approval of male authority, though Edwards looked elsewhere than this world. Like the Puritans, Franklin also had a strong
sense of social mission, not for a New Jerusalem in the wilderness but
to improve whatever community he happened to be in. His devotion
to public service as well as to steady success in his business calling is
well within the Puritan tradition.

Moreover, Franklin too records his conversion, in his case to a strict
code of conduct. "Industry" and "frugality" are his saving graces,
though removing him not from spiritual damnation but from his lower-
class beginnings.[3] Both men want to transform themselves into images
of the authority they most admire. Franklin, like Edwards, wishes to be
within the circle of the worldly elect. The *Autobiography* shows his
deliberate change from habits of pride, lust, and argumentation to at

least the appearance of benevolent humility. Though in Puritan terms
Franklin is unrepentently Arminian, with visible usefulness the measure
of all things and with a distaste for all intolerant zealotry, he nevertheless
speaks of work and self-control as a very real form of personal salvation,
perhaps the only form. His *Autobiography* can easily be placed in the
Puritan tradition of spiritual narratives, complete with its accounts of
early sinfulness, failures spiritual and material, contrasts between his
own hard work and the descent of more backsliding friends, and a
hard-won ascent to the well-ordered self among the chosen company.[4]
The end is similar for Franklin and Edwards: to appropriate the voice
of respected authority as one's best self, which then can frame youthful
"errata" with affectionate irony or impersonal dismissal.

A still more basic similarity is that both men quite consciously develop a false self to distance inward conflict with authority. Franklin's
style is centered by a tone of self-parody, implying rational distance
from self-interest, and his characteristic irony depends on the distance
between common sense and passion. Recent studies have shown how
the tone of both his almanac and his political philosophy passed
through stages of transformation, from that of a combative and zestful
upwardly mobile businessman to the mellow didacticism of the 1740s,
and finally to that of public usefulness which also pervades the *Autobiography*. "I always knew him to be a very factious man," David
Hume wrote to Adam Smith. Franklin's "vicious publick attack" on
Thomas Godfrey in 1732 led Godfrey to withdraw his almanac from
Franklin's printing shop, thus forcing Franklin to begin his own at the
last minute.[5] Argumentative, cruel in his wit, and perhaps, as Paul
Conner suggests, resentful and anxious about his social status, Franklin
develops a false self of gentlemanly restraint and self-deprecating
humor by which to distance his earlier tainted place and passions. It
was his last and finest mask. As he said in *Poor Richard Improved*
(1753), "Paintings and Fightings are best seen at a distance," and
Franklin's enduring achievement has been the presentation of his fight
with himself as if it were a painting by another hand.[6] Edwards describes a more complete conversion from sinful pride and guilt to a
rebirth in the Father's name. The difference is that Franklin looks to a
community of worldly interests for self-validation, while Edwards is
content with God alone. Edwards was supremely uninterested in
human approval.

Yet Franklin was obviously not a Puritan. He hated sects and moralistic preaching. Nor was he a materialist. "I would rather have it said,
'He lived usefully,' than 'He died rich,'" he wrote to his mother in

1749. As the letter indicates, he was always more attuned to the regard of others than to his purse. Nor is it enough to say that Franklin was a transitional figure to a more secular age. Edwards and Franklin were born only three years apart, both to large New England Puritan families, and their lives illustrate the conflicts and contradictions in American values at that time. One settled into his father's calling and his grandfather's parish at Northampton until he was forced out of his office in 1750. In every way Edwards expresses the older submissive, patriarchal Puritan values.

Franklin, in contrast, is mercantile to the core. He was unwilling to bend to the brutal passions of his brother and the no-saying of his father, who indentured Ben to his brother at the age of twelve to prevent him from going to sea. The *Autobiography* merely presents that as his first lesson in what is "good, just, and prudent in the Conduct of Life." But Ben's real prudence was to be on the move, inwardly and outwardly. When later conflict with his brother and with Boston authorities proved too much, he simply moved to Philadelphia, forsaking Puritan Boston for perhaps the most hospitable and cosmopolitan center of middle-class ambition in the western world.[7] Here style was the man, and Franklin could reduce the Puritan tradition of allegorical similes to proverbs, the plain style framed only with the authority of common sense. There were few structures in his new world other than those he wanted to organize. Rules and generalizations, like selves, were provisional, so long as shared ideals of rational order and restraint could be kept in view. Franklin's genius for tall tales and hoaxes depends on a keen sensitivity to the preconceptions of his audience, and to the audience he wanted. "Write with the learned, pronounce with the vulgar," Poor Richard said. The implicit ideal was to have a voice so adaptable that everyone could take it for his own. Amiability, not zeal, is proper character, except as zeal for hard work, in the world of merchants and professional men for whom the Addisonian style meant class as well as reason.[8]

There is a Family Romance fantasy at work here too: to be reborn of European cultural models as the courtier in homespun, "mon cher Papa," the *philosophe*. The true home for his false self was the capitals of the great, while his wife, the carpenter's daughter, was left at home for years, never to venture further away from Philadelphia than Woodbridge, New Jersey. But Franklin differs most radically from Edwards in his sense of what it means to be "possessed" with a self re-formed. For Edwards, the dream was to *be* possessed by the Almighty. For Franklin, the dream was to *possess* a self as useful as any other artifact.

Having proved himself, though "remote from the Eye and Advice of my Father," he says in the *Autobiography,* he can say with confidence that "I had therefore a tolerable Character to begin the World with, I valued it properly, and determin'd to preserve it." Character is external from oneself, a tool to be steadily made more serviceable as habits of "abrupt Contradiction, and positive Argumentation" are replaced by the ability to "put on the humble Enquirer and Doubter." Ascending from the "tolerable" and "useful" to the "graceful and easy," Franklin can transform his grasping bourgeois ambition into the retrospective aristocratic yet Puritan cliché of "vanity" and prove his self-transformation by comfortably mocking his pride. In all his playfulness, Franklin speaks of himself from the vast distance of his finest possession: a modest and ingratiating style so well ordered that even self-love has its place, appropriately restrained.[9]

"We hold these truths to be sacred and undeniable," Jefferson had written. Franklin changed the phrase to "self-evident." The change shows both the continuity and the contrast with religious values. It seems only a short step from sacred to self-evident truths, until one makes the most obvious truth an evidencing of the self. Yet the self that Franklin presents for his son William is not one of inward passion. Its pleasures are those of approval, not self-reliance—a curious paradox for the self-made man.[10] Simply by fulfilling the biblical maxim to be *"diligent in his Calling,"* Franklin says in one of his most famous passages, he has also achieved the biblical reward of standing before kings, "for I have stood before five, and even had the honour of sitting down with one, the King of Denmark, to Dinner." The long road to "self-evident" independence has been traveled by accepting the necessary separation between role and inward man.[11] That was one of the separations that Puritan language so arduously strove to reconcile.

Both Franklin and Edwards manage private conflicts with authority by speaking with a stabilizing paternal voice, either that of God or a cultured aristocrat, though Franklin enlists his aristocrat in the common cause of the middle sort against arbitrary authority. Each man splits his identity into a private self, filled with anger and anxiety, and a public self acceptable both to higher authority and, in Franklin's case, to his audience. The dazzling success of his revolutionary writings lies in their simultaneous appeal to English aristocracy and American common sense. That the voices of Franklin and Edwards differ so profoundly, despite their similar resolutions of conflict, indicates the growing divergence between religious and secular forms of authority, not any "high" or "low" attitude toward one's audience. Both men got their first taste of fame from bringing communities into being, one through his almanac, the other through the Great Awakening. Both subsequently withdrew from their excesses, Franklin to a more respectable status and Edwards to God's uncompromising divinity.[12] Edwards's singular lack of success shows his misunderstanding of secular realities in the 1740s; Franklin moved from peak to peak because of his unerring grasp of popular needs.

Each man, in his own way, is a preacher, and they share a certain calmness of inward distancing, at least in print. But the public defense of speaking with patriarchal arrogance was no longer acceptable. Various rebuffs, Franklin notes in the *Autobiography*, "made me soon feel the Impropriety of presenting one's self as the Proposer of any useful Project that might be suppos'd to raise one's Reputation in the smallest degree above that of one's Neighbours. . . . I therefore put my self as much as I could out of sight, and stated it as a Scheme of a *Number of Friends*." Speaking acceptably, in several ways, began Franklin's successes. Friends, not God, now provided appropriate guidelines for putting one's self out of sight. In that sense both Franklin and Edwards struggled toward opposite forms of the self-avoiding self, at least for public consumption. Where Franklin states his self, or "it," as "a Scheme of a *Number of Friends*," Edwards states his self as the scheme of God, with more grandiose humility. As he wrote in his "Personal Narrative," "I cannot bear the thoughts of being no more humble than other Christians. . . . it would be a vile self-exaltation in me, not to be the lowest in humility of all mankind."[13]

———◦———

The first paragraphs of their respective personal narratives offer a more specific set of contrasts between styles.[14] The true Puritan now radically separates his isolated soul from its interpersonal context and seeks a self separate from relations, even separate from its illusion of "delight." The entrepreneur speaks of pleasure, of varied motives and roles, of rising from low to high, and in doing so seduces his readers—especially his own son—by establishing a style of balanced connectives, dependent clauses that artfully conceal the natural self, and negatives presented as positives.

For Franklin the self is defined by interest in a family past. Franklin's "I," so seemingly vain, is a rhetorical construct entirely congruent with the supposed desires of his audience for instruction or family bonds. He slips through at least four roles in the first paragraph—father inquiring about ancestry, successful man speaking to posterity, author correcting his life like a book, and vain talkative old man. The stance that links all these roles is of a man who is aware at every point of what "you" thinks, and styles himself to be acceptable. For Edwards "you" is neither explicit nor implicit, except as he presents a model for conversion. The narrative, written about 1740, some twenty years after his conversion, remained unpublished until after his death.[15] His friends, like the "many" who are deceived with their affections, are dismissed with his earlier feelings, those that he "had" before "I was brought to those new dispositions." The change from active possessing to passively being possessed is crucial to his basic theme: the contrast between delight and grace. Though each speaks of pleasure, Franklin's style tries to augment delight in self-presentation while Edwards sets the reader up for a fall. And of course their respective sense of what "grace" is could not be more different.

Here is Edwards, beginning his "Personal Narrative" with a childhood reminiscence: "I had a variety of concerns and exercises about my soul from my childhood; but had two more remarkable seasons of awakening, before I met with that change by which I was brought to those new dispositions, and that new sense of things, that I have since had." His first sentence, as Daniel Shea points out, sums up the issues in three clauses of ascending importance: concerns, awakening, change.[16] The last clause properly places the earlier "had" in a wholly new frame of being met and being "brought to" a new sense. The repetition of the verb brings home the change, and the three "that" phrases enforce a dependency of "had" upon "met with," as well as recapitulating the triad of clauses. Repetition to reframe desire as submission is one of Edwards's most basic stylistic techniques. "I" appears four times in this one sentence, yet the cumulative effect is not to brag but to assert the change that made "I" give way to "my soul." Where Franklin possesses his character in the world, Edwards moves from a childhood attitude toward the soul as possession to a mature irradiation with a "new sense of things."

He then offers an account of his early "concerns and exercises":

> The first time was when I was a boy, some years before I went to college, at a time of remarkable awakening in my father's congregation, I was then very much affected for many months, and concerned about the things of religion, and my soul's salvation; and was abundant in duties. I used to pray five times a day in secret, and to spend much time in religious talk with other boys; and used to meet with them to pray together. I experienced I know not what kind of delight in religion.

My mind was much engaged in it, and had much selfrighteous pleasure; and it was my delight to abound in religious duties. I with some of my schoolmates joined together, and built a booth in a swamp, in a very retired spot, for a place of prayer. And besides, I had particular secret places of my own in the woods, where I used to retire by myself; and was from time to time much affected.

Repetition of simple words characterizes his style here: delight, retire, abundant-abound, affected, duties, pray, and of course "I," repeated nine times, with "my" recurring seven times. Only one word, "self-righteous," judges his proceedings overtly, though it stands out as the longest. As we shall see, Edwards sets up his repetitions for impersonal exposure in the last two sentences. For now, in the first stage of awakening, the reader too shuttles back and forth between "together" and "secret," wondering whether the children are truly "affected" or just putting on airs. The verbs are simple, with "was" predominating; the structure of each sentence begins with some variant of "I" and a verb of feeling or doing holy acts, with parallel phrases in rather lengthy predicates. The third sentence, by far the shortest (eleven words), indicates an ambiguity in the seeming balance of words and phrases hanging on "I": "I experienced I know not what kind of delight in religion." Later in the narrative Edwards frequently says true holiness is an inexpressibly "sweet" feeling. Adjectives, not predicated "duties," communicate his mature happiness. But here the next sentence frames "I know not what kind of delight" in self-righteousness rather than inexpressibility and repeats "delight" to bind it to "pleasure" and "duties." It is the new self, we realize, that has no knowledge of what the old self knew so delightfully.

The effect of Edwards's balanced repetitions is to transform the security of pleasures and duties into an ambiguous insecurity. "I" becomes partially external to the truth of holiness. The last two sentences of his first paragraph suddenly speak with a judgment that abandons his early self to its falseness: "My affections seemed to be lively and easily moved, and I seemed to be in my element when engaged in religious duties. And I am ready to think, many are deceived with such affections, and such a kind of delight as I then had in religion, and mistake it for grace." Now "seemed" means "deceived," and such delight is for the "many" who look to duties rather than saving grace. His style takes us along the same journey from pleasure to awareness of self-deception. But to follow him means to leap outside of our "I" to impersonal dismissal of inward sufficiency. "My element" must be left behind. The simple past-tense verbs of being and doing are summed up as "seemed," and the last sentence moves to the present tense to make his previous dialogue between "together" and "secret" an irrevocable opposition between plural and singular, the "affections" and "duties" of the "many" and the lone sinful self's experience of "grace." In just one paragraph, Edwards has winnowed the "I" down to that single word, and the worldly reader can follow him only by abandoning a plurality of selves and pleasures for the repetition of a single feeling. His paragraph is an exercise in disconnection.[17]

Franklin, who also begins with "I," expands rather than contracts. By the end of his first paragraph he is ironically thanking God for his own vanity, "among the other Comforts of Life." His style aims to connect, not separate. Indeed, writing to his forty-year-old son William, the snobbish Tory governor of New Jersey whom Franklin had not seen for seven years, the father assiduously courts the son with rhetorical devices that preclude rejection by recalling his childhood and evoking childish self-interest:

> Dear Son,
>   I have ever had a Pleasure in obtaining any little Anecdotes of my Ancestors. You may remember the Enquiries I made among the Remains of my Relations when you were with me in England; and the Journey I took for that purpose. Now imagining it may be equally agreeable to you to know the Circumstances of *my* Life, many of which you are yet unacquainted with; and expecting a Weeks uninterrupted Leisure in my present Country Retirement, I sit down to write them for you.

Pleasure is in possessing, he begins, and "I" is defined as the wish to obtain anecdotes of ancesters. So, by implication, self-interest should induce his son to be interested in Franklin, who reminds his child of the time "when you were with me" and "imagines" that what is agreeable to the father "may be equally agreeable to you." By the time Franklin announces his role as writer, he has thoroughly reversed the roles of son and father. "You" has become the cause for writing: "I" is simply the subject. Franklin justifies his writing about himself by establishing filial parallels that link him with his son in a common interest. Denying their separation in fact and their potential separation in feeling, he changes a negative (Why would you want to know anything about me anyway?) into an "agreeable" expectation of imitation.

The father had reason to be anxious about William's feelings. Born illegitimately of another woman six months before Franklin married

Deborah, William was apparently brought into the Franklin family over Deborah's objections. Franklin forced his wife to raise him, and one can imagine what life was like between son and mother during the long periods when Franklin chose to be away. Since Franklin's beloved legitimate son Francis died of smallpox at the age of four, William was his only male heir. The *Autobiography*, some have said, is an effort to build a bridge of words between them.[18] Yet finally William was a profound disappointment to his father, because he became the false self that Franklin put on. A "thorough courtier," as Benjamin called him, he became a rather foppish loyalist who opposed the Revolution even to the point of being associated with Tory guerrilla raids. The *Autobiography* remains as a covert "appeal" from father to son, midway in their estrangement. Perhaps to illustrate proper paternal respect, Franklin presents a rather idealized portrait of his own father, from whom he had run away just as William had run away as a teen-ager. And the *Autobiography* emphasizes the lean, tough virtues of hard work and thrift in part because of Franklin's sense that his son was becoming a snob.

Thomas Shepard's personal narrative had similarly been addressed to his son, with more explicit calls for the son's salvation. But those two had a God in common. Franklin had to connect through style. To be agreeable was his way of trying to get his son to agree. His appeal ostensibly is to self-interest rationally ordered. But the underlying tricks of style are intended to deflect his son's indifference or hostility and secure his interest. Interpersonal anxiety, not vanity, is concealed behind his definition of "I" as "you."

The rest of the paragraph expands his sense of selves, or roles, into a more varied model for "you," who similarly expands from son into a more generalized audience. What seems to be a picture of self-reliant success is actually a call for imitation. Indeed, what seems to be a self is actually only a book, whose character is as changeable as its style and whose style is as "occasional" as the reasons for writing.

> To which I have besides some other Inducements. Having emerg'd from the Poverty and Obscurity in which I was born and bred, to a State of Affluence and some Degree of Reputation in the World, and having gone so far thro' Life with a considerable Share of Felicity, the conducing Means I made use of, which, with the Blessing of God, so well succeeded, my Posterity may like to know, as they may find some of them suitable to their own Situations, and therefore fit to be imitated. That Felicity, when I reflected on it, has induc'd me some-

times to say, that were it offer'd to my Choice, I should have no Objection to a Repetition of the same Life from its Beginning, only asking the Advantage Authors have in a second Edition to correct some Faults of the first.[19]

The structure of the lengthy sentences repays a closer look. What is the subject of those two long participial phrases? "Having emerg'd . . . and having gone . . ." is centered either in "the conducing Means" or "my Posterity," not in a clearly defined "I." The ambiguity is part of his tactic. It is "Felicity" that "has induc'd me sometimes to say," he continues, in the same vein of detaching motives from himself and attaching them to a more diffuse sense of imitable style. Means and posterity are agents, even goals, for his self-transformation; he is both a man of means and a means of being used by posterity. So at least he pretends. Where Edwards crisply repeats "I, I, I" in simply ordered sentences that conclude with a clear separation from self, Franklin spreads himself into the varied interests of his audience, while paradoxically establishing himself as a fit model. His sentences are a meandering series of subordinations and dependent clauses where the subject never stands still but slips into a subordination to something else the minute we think we see it clearly. Each phrase and sentence artfully qualifies what precedes it, while seeming to elaborate. Nothing can be pinned down. Though "Poverty and Obscurity" have been changed to affluence and reputation, felicity seems to be the true shaping force, with "I made use of"—the real subject—buried in a subordination to a subordination. Thus negative anxieties can be transformed to felicitous success by burying the self in "Means . . . fit to be imitated." The humor of thinking of his life as a book depends on the comfortable distance already established between author as role and author as feeling.

Edwards repeats; Franklin varies. His sentences range from twelve to sixty words in the first paragraph alone, and he styles his vanity with a kind of virtuous shiftiness: past tense to future tense; adjectival clauses and infinitive phrases commingled with a great variety of verbs, usually in the conditional mode and further qualified by succeeding turns of phrase; participial phrases and balanced predicates that establish mutual ironies more than clear judgments. Above all, his self-introduction avoids any introspection that would fix him in a single mold and separate him from an untroubled sense of pleasure or felicity. Accordingly, the conclusion of this very long paragraph (I have omitted two sentences) finally presents him as vain and talkative, but

in ways that make him simply an honest model for everyone's vanity
and talkativeness. For that honesty too, he implies, his audience should
be grateful:

> Hereby, too, I shall indulge the Inclination so natural in old Men, to
> be talking of themselves and their own past Actions, and I shall in-
> dulge it, without being troublesome to others who thro' respect to Age
> might think themselves oblig'd to give me a Hearing, since this may be
> read or not as any one pleases. And lastly, (I may as well confess it,
> since my Denial of it will be believ'd by no body) perhaps I shall a
> good deal gratify my own *Vanity.* Indeed I scarce ever heard or saw
> the introductory Words, *Without Vanity I may say,* &c. but some vain
> thing immediately follow'd. Most People dislike Vanity in others what-
> ever Share they have of it themselves, but I give it fair Quarter
> wherever I meet with it, being persuaded that it is often productive of
> Good to the Possessor and to others that are within his Sphere of
> Action: And therefore in many Cases it would not be quite absurd if a
> Man were to thank God for his Vanity among the other Comforts
> of Life.[20]

In owning it, with sentences more straightforward than before, he dis-
owns it. Vanity becomes an "it," as separate from himself as any other
possession, attributable to everyone else and even—in his most hedged
phrasing—caused by God himself.

The contrast with Edwards is more than thematic. Every sentence is
a seduction rather than a separation. Franklin's humor here depends on
a shared standard of common sense that punctures self-inflation, but it
also implies a denial of feelings that may not be identical with other
people's pleasure. He is repetitively connective: "To which," "That,"
"So," "However," "Hereby," "And," "Indeed," "And therefore" are
words beginning eight of the sixteen sentences. Most of the others
clearly refer back as well as ahead. His style diminishes particular
elements into occasional roles within a broadly flowing sense of pleasure in himself being construed. But "himself" is more a creature of
what he wants others to feel, a device for furthering his own purposes.
Overtly the passage is about why he is writing. Covertly the passage is
about the development of a style that changes personal anxiety about
his son and his beginnings into a general expression of his audience's
pleasure in themselves. There are few better ways of getting quick
approval.

Both Edwards and Franklin present an "I" that is seemingly active
but actually passive. Franklin looks to style for his diffusion of nega-

tives and feelings of separation into connected pleasures, while Edwards brings the self up short with the clarity of contrast. Patriarchal form encourages him to seek God's approval, not the audience's, if indeed he even wrote "Personal Narrative" with an audience in mind. Franklin, whose ideal was the serviceable self rather than the reborn self, depends on a generalized model of public imitation to overcome private worries about alienation from his son, and probably to master more unconscious memories of childhood oppression. The father no longer has the recourse of the greater Father to assuage anxiety. Franklin's multiple strategies of self-presentation, like his benign self-mockery, are also ways of disowning residual resentment against his father for a conflict-free presentation of a paternal voice that anybody could love.[21] There is no tyrant here; merely a man like any other man, though happier and saner in being able to control his destiny.

For Edwards, worldly relations have little to do with inward life. "This I know not how to express otherwise," he says in "Personal Narrative," "than by a calm, sweet abstraction of soul from all the concerns of this world; . . . of being alone in the mountains, or some solitary wilderness, far from all mankind, sweetly conversing with Christ, and wrapt and swallowed up in God." To be sure he was happily married, a devoted and attentive family man, and a minister optimistic to the point of obsessive fantasy about the possibilities for holy community on earth. Throughout the Great Awakening his dreams of apocalyptic social regeneration became more and more public, and at times he ventures the giddy hope that the New Jerusalem is beginning right there in New England. Later, in a lengthy treatise he called for a holy nationwide concert of prayer to bring on the millennium, as they were trying to do in Scotland. During the late 1740s and beyond he eagerly culled newspaper articles about evangelical triumphs or Catholic reversals in the Spanish and French empires to prove the pouring out of the sixth vial.[22] But his unawareness of the world *as world* is the other side of his hypersensitivity to the world as a shadow of God's intentions. Edwards was constantly looking for reasons to be optimistic about preserving God's name, even as Northampton was throwing him out to preserve its own.

Recent scholars have made too much of Edwards's dream of "new heaven, new earth" as a call for shared community. His interpretation of Revelations 21.1 takes care to locate that place "removed at an immense distance from the solar system," though he is more ambiguous about locating New Jerusalem. More important, his concern is with the eternal spiritual community of God, not the "fleeting" physical world of man. Even George Whitefield thought Edwards's faith in the speedy coming of the Lord on earth was an unrealistic fantasy.[23] Edwards's later language of logic, abstraction, and obsessive scripturalism expresses his sense of inward life in God's terms alone, radically disjunct from the world, without the earlier joined polarities of spiritual comprehensiveness and pragmatic good sense that gave Puritan language its human sensitivity and strength.

Conversely, to the degree that Franklin speaks of inward life, he sacrifices his usefulness. Unlike Edwards, he has no qualms about finding worldly masks for his private intensities, because community approval is basic to his self-esteem. However, community for him seems to begin where family leaves off. Not only did he abandon his own family for years, but in some ways his life can be seen as a flight from the Puritan family of his childhood, and from the emotional intensities it induced in him. Born on Milk Street in Boston and baptized by Samuel Willard, he clearly did not have his will broken. Various contemporaries mention his extremes of wrath, and his hatred of tyranny begins, he remarks in the *Autobiography*, with his brother's brutal treatment of him. His family had even expected him to become a minister, since as the tenth son he would be a tithe to the church. His Puritan father laid a heavy hand on his desires to go off to sea, and his uncle Benjamin, after whom he perhaps was named, offered him many shorthand volumes of sermons, as the *Autobiography* recalls.[24] That was a network of interpersonal expectations comprehensive enough to bring anyone to Puritan submission. But Franklin sought a wider world. Where Edwards made similar expectations the essence of true religion, Franklin forsook the role of minister for the role of worldly citizen. He found a language to seal off inward intensities, especially of rage, except as irony, a proclamation of hard work, and a steady mockery of tyrants wherever he found them.[25] The time was ripe for that new language, and we remember him now as an almost unique event: a revolutionary at ease with himself.

The shared fantasy that he offers is the self born of self, though his engaging mask was actually born of managing the preoccupations of his audience:

> *Who is wise?* He that learns from every One.
> *Who is Powerful?* He that governs his Passions.
> *Who is rich?* He that is content.
> *Who is that?* Nobody.

So Poor Richard said in 1755. The sequence moves from instructive envy to the humor of collective self-deprecation. Yet Franklin's equations are characteristic: wisdom comes from listening, power from self-control; riches are found not through ambition but through content-ment. In part these are the complacent formulas of a respectable man disowning his contentious, climbing past. In part they are quite Puritan, if Godless. But they are also the considered statements of one who understands that to be the voice of his community, perhaps even to be the father of his country, he must forswear expressions of personal zeal except in ironic terms.[26] He rechannels anger, not to suppress him-self as Edwards does, but to get his way.

"He makes a Foe who makes a Jest," Poor Richard had said in 1740. Franklin developed a new language, borrowed from English models, for a new community of merchant interests that wished to jest at self on the make, placating foes while highlighting personal success, and overthrowing any rigid authority not hospitable to a world of self-advancement. The genre of cultured commentary on crass bumpkinism would become a staple of nineteenth-century American humor. The price, however, for writers from Franklin to Mark Twain, is that they speak as their audience would wish them to speak.[27] For Franklin the price is not difficult to meet, because he is always aware of what he is doing and what he wants. He brilliantly codifies an American language for role playing, manipulating, and masquerading, all with the most moral intentions. More consciously than most he fit his personality to the mercantile frame. As D. H. Lawrence put it, "He set up the first dummy American."[28] For nineteenth-century writers, much less sure of self and more hostile to community, a desperate or God-mirroring inward-ness seemed the necessary rhetoric for self-definition.

Yet Franklin's language finally reveals a revolutionary, not a phony. One of his finest English hoaxes, "An Edict by the King of Prussia," claiming the king's right to England as the English king was claiming America, ends by appealing to the explicit impossibility that England could "treat its own children in a manner so arbitrary and tyrannical!" In some ways the thought is, and had been, Puritan. In more ways it was his most heartfelt contribution to the energy of a post-Puritan age.

———————— • ————————

As several historians have said, the fantasy of being self-made man-ages feelings of interpersonal anxiety and ambivalence. Michael Kam-men's *People of Paradox* speaks of the "quest for legitimacy" and the "unstable pluralism" that define American life in the eighteenth cen-tury, with Puritan tribalism and "a collective individualism" as basic defenses against anxiety. Gordon Wood has shown the complex emo-tional strains and divisions leading to the Revolution, even as Franklin was giving voice to new mercantile styles of mobility, diffusion, inventiveness, and wit.[29] The tight grip of the patriarchal family in stable agrarian communities was in conflict with a wider culture whose dynamic expansionism rewarded risk, not obedience. The entrepreneurial style balances aggressive wit with cultured models of identity to manage conflict and anxiety, while the pietistic style asserts an older tradition of passionate humility.

"Reason" and "enthusiasm" have been the catchwords for the divisions in style and behavior during the American mid-eighteenth century, though both Franklin and Edwards moved from earlier enthusiasms to a language of reason and order in their later years. It might be more accurate to talk of the entrepreneurial and the pietistic personality. An ethic of freedom and material advancement was proving more attractive than an ethic of belonging. Even the Great Awakening, several have said, gave ordinary people a religiously sanctioned courage to contend with the fathers of society. Yet the fantasy of the greater Father was still intense among the pious, while among the rational an equally pervasive ideal of law became primary.

Franklin embodies the new personality so richly rewarded by his culture. Historians and sociologists have defined the speculative temperament characteristic of modernization as open, independent, ambitious, punctual, assertive over the environment, and oriented toward planing.[30] Jack P. Greene speaks of identity conflict in the eighteenth century as a conflict between the values of hierarchy, subordination, and deference, characteristic of an economy of scarcity, and the expansion, mobility, and prosperity of the market society.[31] Edwards and Franklin mirror these conflicts in values. Yet an antiauthoritarian strain lurks just below the surface of the entrepreneurial faith in law as well as the "new light" faith in awakened religion. Perhaps the finest commentary on the period is Hawthorne's "My Kinsman, Major Molineux," which overtly describes a brash youth's progress from loyalty to laughter in the face of his tarred-and-feathered authority figure, while covertly the story reflects ambivalence and fear in the ghastly divided face of the man leading the mob.

Franklin's style was able to express self-division and ambivalence through irony. He more than Edwards inherits the early Puritan impulse to question earthly authority, though now in the name of right reason rather than the heavenly Father. While he relished mastery, Edwards despised pride. But a language for collective dependence no longer functions in a more expansive, individualistic age, despite Edwards's continuing call for New Jerusalem and apocalypse. The choice is between assertive and submissive styles of being an individual, in this world or the next.

The rest of my chapter will focus on the last real Puritan, the man who tried to keep a language of "affections" tied to the language of faith. In contrast to first-generation writers, Edwards's view of the divine begins with sovereignty over self, not with mothering and community. Community is only a heavenly reward for the faithful. What is missing in Edwards is as important as what is achieved. His Puritanism is a rigorous matter of guilt and patriarchy, without contradiction, yet without double appeal, because he has sacrificed the element of shared human need for a classically obsessive language of guilt and submission to the greater Father. At his best he is the Fra Angelico of logic, luminous and serene—and just as narrowly withdrawn from the world.

His own conversion symbolizes obedience to the father, as Edwards records in his "Personal Narrative," even in his choice of the biblical text that first gave him "a sense of the glory of the Divine Being":

> The first instance that I remember of that sort of inward, sweet delight in God and divine things that I have lived much in since, was on reading those words, 1 Tim. i. 17. *Now unto the King eternal, immortal, invisible, the only wise God, be honor and glory for ever and ever, Amen. . . .* Never any words of scripture seemed to me as these words did. I thought with myself, how excellent a Being that was, and how happy I should be, if I might enjoy that God, and be rapt up to him in heaven, and be as it were swallowed up in him for ever!

The calm abstractions of immortality aim at harmony with universal essence, not particular expressions of character. Edwards apparently began as a sickly, scholarly youth who "had not a strong, loud voice," as Samuel Hopkins wrote; "he was of a tender and delicate constitution," with "but a comparative small stock of animal life."[32] One recalls David Shapiro's connection of the obsessive style to the "feeling of being small." Yet what John Lynen calls the "terrifying *sang-froid*" of Edwards's public voice comes through even on the page. It shows a man "ceasing to be himself by becoming the truth." His "Personal Narrative" is in this sense neither personal nor a narrative, since his major rhetorical technique, the exact repetition of a few key words, lifts the self from a linear life to become one with God's abstract pillar of is. As Lynen says, "Exact repetition . . . suggests that there is a governing vocabulary—a few spare and essential words in which all meanings meet—and that the process of abstraction . . . is the penultimate phase of its journey toward the Word." For that style the text from 1 Timothy was analogue, mirror, and inducement.[33]

Yet there is a more unconscious connection with paternal authority involved. Edwards's father was also named Timothy. He too was a minister, who more successfully than his son held his community to God's standards, though, like his son, not without controversy. In the 1730s he disciplined a young man for marrying without the permission of the wife's father and maintained his position against the vehement wishes of his Connecticut congregation. He refused to hold communion for three years as a consequence.[34] This ministerial strength was uncommon, in an age where the more usual ministerial trend was toward the permissive tactics of Edwards's grandfather, Solomon Stoddard. Though the early childhood details are, as usual, lacking, Philip Greven and Richard Bushman have persuasively argued that Edwards's theology transforms guilt and anger into total submission to the father's sovereignty.[35] The text from 1 Timothy gives his father's stubborn earthly holiness an immortal calm, uncontaminated by a culture where paternal deference was eroding. Calmness was one of Edwards's own most notable characteristics. As the only boy among ten sisters, Edwards may have felt a special need for pure maleness, expressed as scholarly devotion. He found it in rediscovering the language of rebirth so natural to first-generation Puritans. "My heart panted after this, to lie low before God, as in the dust; that I might be nothing, and that God might be ALL, that I might become as a little child."

His image of God is suffused, even in the "Personal Narrative," with vigorous intellectual paradox uniting high and low in oxymoronic splendor: "a sweet conjunction; majesty and meekness joined together; it was a sweet, and gentle, and holy majesty; and also a majestic meekness; an awful sweetness; a high, and great, and holy gentleness." Polarity, as in earlier Puritan writings, rises from divided hearts to God's unity. And like first-generation preachers, his language for the experience of grace is a mixture of vision and taste. " 'Tis as much the nature of one that is spiritually new born, to thirst after growth in holiness," he declares in *Religious Affections*, "as 'tis the nature of a newborn babe, to thirst after the mother's breast; who has the sharpest appetite, when best in health." One of his favorite images for grace is the taste of honey, and "sweet" is his most frequent adjective for holy feelings. Grace "is in its whole nature different from any former kinds of sensation of the mind, as tasting is diverse from any of the other sense . . . as the sweet taste of honey is diverse from the ideas men get of honey by only looking on it, and feeling of it."[36]

But unlike the first generation of Puritans in America, Edwards's vocabulary for faith was predominantly an expression of pure understanding, much more rigorous than in Willard. True religion always begins in the affections, as prompted by right understanding. But intellectual relations reflect the love of pure father for pure son: "The Godhead being thus begotten by Gods loving an Idea of himself & shewing forth in a distinct subsistence or Person in that Idea, there Proceeds a most Pure act, & an Infinitely holy & sacred energy arises between the F. & Son in mutually Loving & delighting in each other, for their love & Joy is mutual, Prov. 8, 30, I was daily his delight Rejoicing alwaies before him. This is the eternal & most Perfect & essential act of the divine nature." The intellectual ecstasy of Edwards's later writings, in particular after his departure from Northampton, depends on ascending from the contaminated body world of desire and resistance to mutual receptivity. Tactile language is for sinners; abstraction is for saints. Even solidity itself is equivalent to sin, for "all that we mean or Can be meant by solidity is Resistance Resistance to touch, the Resistance of some parts of Space." Overcoming resistance, Edwards learned from Shepard, gives the real experience of "Excellency," which Edwards defined as *The Consent of Being to Being, or Being's Consent to Entity.* The more the Consent is, and the more extensive, the greater is the Excellency." And as he says elsewhere in "Notes on the Mind," "nothing belonging to Body, exists out of the mind but Resistance." Divine mind alone can save him from nakedness. "All our good is more apparently from God," he said in his first major sermon, "God Glorified in Man's Dependence," "because we are first naked and wholly without any good, and afterward enriched with all good."[37]

Edwards's early sermons reflect his personal predilection for doctrine and received truth. He offers intimate colloquies and extended metaphors of God as sun and fountain, along with explications of the Bible's doctrinal frame. But he was vividly aware that his audience needed saving. As he comes to talk more specifically to the unregenerate, his frame of reference imperceptibly shifts from oneness with the Divine Mind to an intercourse with human affections. He moves from saints to sinners. At that point the modern reader begins to perk up. Edwards now takes his metaphors and dramatic situations from the world as well as from revealed truth. He spends less time on doctrine, and more on developing a style of "application" to the problem of resistance.

He piles on accretive phrases in longer and longer sentences, developing recurrent negative images with inexorable repetition. John Cotton's repetitive devices seem meandering compared to Edwards's calm force.[38]

"Some talk of it as an unreasonable thing to fright persons to heaven," Edwards once declared, "but I think it is a reasonable thing to endeavour to fright persons away from hell. They stand upon its brink, and are just ready to fall into it, and are senseless of their danger. It is not a reasonable thing to fright a person out of a house on fire?"[39] Later he would conclude, as Shepard had, that even if a sinner did escape the burning house, his selfishness would still bar him from salvation. Fear does not lead to true dependence. But in the heat of the Great Awakening, his mastery of the metaphors of resistance and solidity proved too successful for clear perspective. At times he must have felt that he was dangling his congregations like his famous spiders, over a pit—or that the writhings and agonies in front of him were themselves the pit, while he calmly fixed his eyes on the bell-rope in the back of the church: "What will it signify for a worm, which is about to be pressed under the weight of some great rock, to be let fall with its whole weight upon it, to collect its strength, to set itself to bear up the weight of the rock, and to preserve itself from being crushed by it? Much more in vain will it be for a poor damned soul." Incremental comparisons of physical quantities are his major rhetorical tool for driving home that sense of helpless weight, and the awful melting about to happen. "However before they may seem to harden their hearts, in order to prepare themselves to bear," he says in one sermon, "yet the first moment they feel it, their hearts will become like wax before the furnace."[40] Physical pain, quantified into an eternity of discrete moments, awaits the sinners, expressed in metaphors of weight, motion, animals, and tactility itself. Edwards balances these images with metaphors of light and insubstantiality for the saints, all to the one goal of making sinning affections "sensible."

His most famous sermon of this period, preached at Enfield in July of 1741 and now known as "Sinners in the Hands of an Angry God," gives sinners a consuming weight. The same God that is glorified in man's dependence is eternal wrath to those who resist. Taking his text from Deuteronomy, "Their foot shall slide in due time," he mixes body and temporal images with rhythmic repetition of an incremental inevitability, showing a series of natural objects in the grip of natural forces far beyond personal control. At the beginning his images are conventional, and he shows sinners in their manyness.[41] But as sentences grow in length, the dramatic immediacy of each sinner's situation heightens, until in his application the images focus on the one isolated "you," dangling by a thread over the vast forces of God's flood and fire. Edwards makes no attempt to visualize these forces. Unlike others of his sermons, this one uses no words for color, no words for heat. Instead, the minister concentrates on evoking the eerie suspension of the sinner.[42] And the image of the spider locates all the "affections" in its helplessness: "if God should let you go, . . . all your righteousness, would have no more influence to uphold you and keep you out of hell, than a spider's web would have to stop a fallen rock." Note that the rock is already "fallen."

Soon his most notorious passage reiterates the ugly helplessness and completes the separation between an arbitrarily rescuing Father and the consuming flames: "The God that holds you over the pit of hell, much as one holds a spider, or some loathsome insect over the fire, abhors you, and is dreadfully provoked: his wrath towards you burns like fire; he looks upon you as worthy of nothing else, but to be cast into the fire; he is of purer eyes than to bear to have you in his sight; you are ten thousand times more abhominable in his eyes, than the most hateful venomous serpent is in ours." Edwards has no use here for the slow stages of conversion. As with Cotton, it is all or nothing.[43] By arousing the sinner's own memories of omnipotence when sadistically playing with a bug, and ascribing those feelings to God, Edwards speaks rather freely for the Deity. But the steady, rhythmically parallel beat of those five phrases can even raise a shudder in the modern reader. Simply to describe the feelings evoked as anxious demeans the complexity of Edwards's achievement. We *become* in quick succession the spider, the hand, the "purer eyes," and then the speaker of those words. The parade of semicolons imparts a measured, stately quality to horror and damnation. There are no exceptions made, no limited terms for punishment, no plea bargaining. His voice intimates the absolute distance between the father and his erring children and conveys judgment without mercy. The self stands at the loathsome center of a mutilating experience, and resistances melt away to a gaping passivity.

His follower Thomas Prince once described Edwards as "a preacher of a low and moderate voice, a natural way of delivery; and without any agitation of body, or anything else in the manner to excite attention; except his habitual and great solemnity, looking and speaking as in the presence of God, and with a weighty sense of the matter delivered."[44] Edwards did not need James Davenport's histrionics to bring on a feeling of absolute, merciless judgment, mirroring his own conversion from guilt. The characteristic conversion pattern in the Great Awakening, he reported in *A Faithful Narrative* (1738), begins with sinners being brought by God "to a conviction of their absolute dependence on his sovereign power and grace, and universal necessity of a Mediator, by leading them more and more to a sense of their exceeding wickedness and guiltiness in his sight." As we might expect from his own conviction, he notes that his sermons on God's sovereignty are the ones most responded to.[45] From a helpless awareness of God's wrath and an "abyss" of guilt, the sinner experiences a conversion to joy, expressed with laughter and tears, at the "fullness of Christ." It is a "turning" of the heart, he repeatedly defined, "infusing life into the dead soul," with light either blinding and sudden or slow like the sunrise. Often there is terror, then calm, then light; even more frequently there is great terror, then great light and calm.[46]

His language for conversion is remarkably unmaternal, even unparental. God is judge, not father, at least at this stage. Elsewhere he often defines God's dual excellencies as judge and father: "an infinitely great, pure, holy and heart-searching Judge" and "a gentle and gracious Father and a loving Friend: by the one he is a pure, searching and burning flame; by the other a sweet, refreshing light." At no point, from beginning to end, is God expressed in mothering terms. Though Edwards occasionally uses nursing imagery for human feelings of dependence and loves the word "sweet," his doctrine is God-centered sovereignty and order, with adjectival human feelings of sweetness and light. As a judge, God brings us to "awe and reverence," "to search and humble us." As Father his purpose is "to win and draw and encourage us" through his Son. Guilt, not anxious separation, is the overwhelming feeling of sinners; dependence on the pure Father is the reward of saints. Edwards describes sin as anger and "deformity," as well as filth. Deformity is a physical analogue for the ugly feeling of guilt before the Father's judging perfection of proportion, and a displacement of anger as well.[47]

Similarly, the minister's function is to be the Father's ambassador, not the breast. A minister brings God's light, more pure than milk. As Edwards says, "We had need to be as full of light as a glass is, that is held out in the sun; and with respect to love and zeal, we had need at this day to be like the angels, that are a flame of fire." Ministers are "ambassadors of Jesus Christ"; they are Christ's officers, shepherds, stewards, watchmen, captains, and instruments—but not breasts. Like sinners, they must constantly be aware that Christ is coming any day to judge them, not shelter them, for any lapses in promoting God's work. "The New Jerusalem in this respect has begun to come down from heaven," and anyone not working for it with all his heart and mind will be damned.[48]

Sinners therefore must expect guilt and judgment, not solace and rational comfort. For saints the "joy" is partly a "sweet" dependence, but in intellectual terms; God's love is felt as mind's "consent." Edwards had no difficulty affirming against rationalist criticisms that an "exceeding affectionate" preaching works better "than a moderate, dull, indifferent way of speaking," since for him affections can never be raised except through the understanding, either as "light" or "delusion." The effect of his awakening preaching, however, was to maximize guilt in every way. His major innovation in the Puritan style of making similes is the magnification of high and low to infinite heights and depths of comparative humbling. Not only wrath is brought home, but also an awesome feeling of absolute, helpless smallness in the face of infinite power. As chapter four describes, that feeling is basic to the obsessive style.

Not surprisingly, young children anxiously responded to these expectations, even though they were expressed with such impersonal language. Children may seem innocent to us, Edwards says, acknowledging the changing attitudes to childhood; yet they "are young vipers, and are infinitely more hateful than vipers." He also observes that he has never known "any ill consequence" of frightening children, since truth always does good. Indeed, "there is a strange alteration almost all over New England amongst young people," he asserts in *Some Thoughts*. *A Faithful Narrative* is more precise: "It has heretofore been looked on as a strange thing, when any have seemed to be savingly wrought upon, and remarkably changed in their childhood; but now, I suppose, near thirty were to appearance so wrought upon between ten and fourteen years of age, and two between nine and ten, and one of about four years of age." He tells the case of little Phebe Bartlett in detail because "this last will be most difficultly believed." These are no longer mixed expectations resolved ambivalently at the end of adolescence, but overwhelmingly clear expectations responded to with overwhelming guilt, though Phebe did seem to enjoy crying copiously over her older sisters' sure path to hell.[49]

Edwards's own child-rearing practices reflect his and his wife's judgmental expectations. He was not wrathful but infinitely attentive, spending an hour each evening listening to the day's excitements from his children and slowly turning their minds to the appropriate moral lessons and the Bible. His "careful and thorough . . . government," said one contemporary, subdued "any considerable degree of will and stubbornness" in them, by means of prudent discipline, "exercised with the greatest calmness, and commonly without striking a blow," which "effectually established his parental authority, and produced a cheerful obedience ever after." No child of his could ever stay out after nine, or stay up much later. Philip Greven cites a lengthy passage in the biography of one of Edwards's grandchildren to show how Sarah Edwards was equally calm and thorough in her disciplining, "without loud angry words, much less heavy blows . . . with all calmness and gentleness of mind," compelling obedience by addressing herself "to the reason of her children . . . She had need to speak but once; she was cheerfully obeyed: murmuring and answering again, were not known among them. . . . Her system of discipline, was begun at a very early age, and it was her rule, to resist the first, as well as every subsequent exhibition of temper or disobedience in the child, however young, until its will was brought into submission." One of the Edwards's daughters wrote in 1754 to a friend of whipping their first child Sally, "not quite Ten months old," and records the child's sensitivity to her mother's expectations: "She knows the differance between a Smile and a frown as well as I do. When She has done any thing that She Suspects is wrong, will look with concern to Sce what Mamma Says, and if I only knit my brow, She will cry till I Smile." As early as six and seven, Edwards reports at the height of the Awakening, his own children could reach a conviction of sin and salvation. Writing to Benjamin Colman on March 9, 1741, he says that the past winter was "a time of the most remarkable and visible blessing of heaven upon my family that ever was. . . . I hope that my four eldest children (the youngest of them between six and seven years of age) have been savingly wrought upon."[50]

Tender mothering does not seem to be so tender any more. The moratorium on strict child discipline and expectations, which in earlier Puritan times could extend well past the age of reason, has vanished, at least in the Edwards household. Mother is calm, cool, and zealous at all times, as grave as father was always supposed to be. Mixed expectations are gone; both mother and father are working together at all times to induce a feeling of guilt for any willfulness. Except for his evening hour with the children Edwards seems to have kept austerely distant from family cares, giving himself "wholly to the work of the ministry," as Samuel Hopkins records, with family matters left "almost entirely to Mrs. Edwards."[51] Like the father who maintains an austere distance in the family, Edwards's God is overbearingly patriarchal, without any tender mitigation. In some respects Edwards magnifies Increase Mather's destructive style while also magnifying Willard's style of rational order. Yet while joining the two strands of the obsessive style, his language does not speak to complex ambivalences but only intensifies guilt.

His success was immediate. But his failure was profound, if less immediate. His people felt less guilty than he thought they were, or than he felt himself to be. An older language of Puritanism had articulated ambivalence for over a century. The narrower language of guilt, though searingly pure, did not have the capacity to hold hearts more than momentarily, as an expiation, before people turned back to more material matters. Like the jeremiad but with more brilliance, Edwards's language resolved for his community a more transitional set of feelings than it resolved for himself. While he and his family stayed put, his community's concerns moved on.

The more rigid obsessive styles probably begin in response to cold yet demanding mothering, recent psychoanalytic theory suggests.[52] At least one entry in Edwards's *Images or Shadows of Divine Things*, as Philip Greven notes, explicitly associates the world with a threatening, mutilating mother. "The earth or this earthly world does by men's persons as it does by their bodies: it devours men and eats them up. As we see this our mother that brought us forth and at whose breasts we are nourished is cruel to us, she is hungry for the flesh of her children, and swallows up mankind, one generation after another, in the grave, and is insatiable in her appetite. So she does mystically those that live by the breasts of the earth and depend on worldly things for happiness; the earth undoes and ruins them" (no. 157). Greven observes that Numbers 13.32, which Edwards cites here, says nothing about breasts or mothers, only that a certain land devours its inhabitants, all of whom are "men of great stature." Edwards himself was exceptionally tall. The allegory of this one passage, which after all is a private intellectual exercise based on scriptural language found elsewhere in the Bible, is not the language Edwards chooses for public discourse to frighten his sinners into guilt. Images of devouring, mutilating hell have less importance in his writings than a rhetoric of self-hatred and the body's fatal weight. Yet the fear of being engulfed is as profound in his writings as the joy of being "swallowed up" in God. Though we know nothing about the kind of mothering Edwards received as a child, Philip Greven may well have hit on the truth of the matter in hypothesizing that Edwards, who grew up surrounded by sisters, felt unconscious hostility to women and a fear of being engulfed.[53] Edwards does not often use the earlier Puritan nursing analogies.

Perhaps the real change was in the age at which families chose to break the child's will, and how tender the mothering was until then. The earlier the demand for submission, and the less affectionate the mother except when rewarding good behavior, the more rage is turned against the self as guilt. Imagery of oral devouring also involves some displacement of wrath against the father, by connecting mothering needs with filth and personal hatefulness. Now the father's absolute gravity and security becomes the end point for identity, and vestigial dependence on one's mother is lumped together with hate and oral needs as "deformity." Edwards's language of guilt and fathering is overdetermined by repression of anger at several levels, into an identification with the Father's immortal calm, yet also into imagery bringing back more primal fears. Several psychoanalytic writings on spider phobias, for instance, connect the imagery to infantile anxieties about mothering.[54] As with earlier Puritans, strong fathering was for Edwards at least partly a defense against male anxiety. But the rigidity of his language of sovereignty shows that it was finally his only defense. Need and desire are not allowed any positive expression except in God's name.

Sinful affections, no matter how abased, are still sinful. That was the lesson he learned from the Great Awakening, which had brought out his most passionate, paradoxical hopes for sinning souls. He was much more concerned with forging a holy community than was the English revivalist George Whitefield, whose sermons focus only on personal regeneration. The Puritan hope for redeemed churches, or for Edwards, one church, was rarely so militantly and desperately expressed. But Edwards's later sermons show a marked decrease in applications for sinners, a striking absence of worldly community except in abstract apocalyptic wish fulfillment, and a rigorously logical tone of doctrinal address for saints only. After 1740 his writings concern sanctification, not preparation.[55]

It was as if he had given up on the "spiders marching through the air," the worldly objects that had occupied his youthful empirical energies of observation. Now he would speak only to those admitting complete dependence on God's sovereignty, quite literally, since he tried to make public testimony a requirement for joining the Northampton congregation. His later writings speak primarily to the intellect, not the affections, though with the same expectations of millennial redemption. As early as 1734 he had begun to fight his grandfather's visible sacramental ordinances with an older language of invisible faith.[56] His longer philosophical works show his progression from Bible-centered dependence (*The History of Redemption*), to a concern with religious emotions (*Religious Affections*), to a denial of human agency (*Freedom of the Will*), and finally to an abstract conception of God's bliss (*The Nature of True Virtue*) balanced by a rigidly scriptural exegesis of original sin (*Original Sin*). In retreating from experiential language to a framework of logic and scripture, Edwards not only lost his audience but narrowed himself.

His earlier, private notes had kept attitudes toward the world in an ambivalent suspension of optimism and loathing. *Images or Shadows of Divine Things,* his collection of private typological notes, even welcomes America's mercantile expansion, because "the changing of the course of trade and the supplying of the world with its treasures from America is a type and forerunner of what is approaching in spiritual things, when the world shall be supplied with spiritual treasures from America" (no. 147). Yet he also frequently associates the world with filth, and more fearfully connects volcanoes with orality and wrath.[57] *Religious Affections* (1746) is the high point of his attempt to join earthly language to heavenly realities. Right from the start he strives to bring back a masculine tone for shared feelings of religion: not "weak, dull and lifeless wouldings" but "a fervent, vigorous engagedness of the heart in religion." Rejecting nursing fantasies and images of "babes in Christ" as too weak, he prefers imagery of men fighting and warring with "strength and vigor." His point is to be active, not passive, in the work of rebirth. As with his entry on America's mercantile development in *Images or Shadows*, Edwards likes the phrase "the business of religion." He is a man talking to men,[58] still searching to communicate religious feelings to sinners.

However, his definitions show an absolute gulf between the things of this world and the feelings for God. His polarities are rigorous: love has God for its object, and hatred has sin for its object. Love is the "fountain" of all the affections, because love is the understanding's comprehension of God, just as hatred is the understanding's delusion of self. Most important, truly religious affections are born from above, not from within, as light comes to a glass. Love is an infinite tenderness of heart, just as hate is an infinite hardness or stoniness.[59] It is easy to misread Edwards as calling for human love. But for him human love is a contradiction in terms. Divine love, and only divine love, is the fountain of all religious affections. All other loves are counterfeit forms of pride, from Satan's poisoned fountain. "Love is the spirit of adoption, or the childlike principle." It is a wholly supernatural principle, remaking the self free from wrathful pride. It is "consent," "tenderness," obedience, submission. Tenderness for Edwards begins in Christ-like suffering, not maternal comfort. The "dying Redeemer" is the ultimately affecting thought. Christ's crucifixion shows his virtues "in a manner the most tending to move our affections, of any that can be imagined; . . . to have the greatest, possible tendency to reach our hearts in the most tender part." Similarly, sinners must feel total distress about their physical and spiritual condition, without any hint of self-worth, before the Father is willing to let them depend on him.[60]

Love is from God; only lust is human. The shift to a supernatural frame for right affections is subtle but total. There are no tender mothers available, only hateful or tender hearts before a sovereign judge. Edwards redefines his subject so far as to assert that true religious affections do *not* arise from the heart, but rather "from those influences and operations on the heart, which are *spiritual, supernatural,* and *divine*." Conversely, "the imagination or phantasy . . . is the devil's grand lurking place." Christ lives in those who have become bruised into tender obedience; they "become little images of that Sun which shines upon them," or sap from his root. Edwards contemptuously dismisses the "bribery" of self-love, throwing out the moderate Puritan appeal from Hooker through Willard. Self-love leads only to anger or gratitude, two unholy emotions. A real conversion brings an "entirely new" identity, which earthly language can express only as a sixth sense, like tasting honey for the first time or seeing colors after blindness.[61]

Edwards strives to make the newness comprehensible in worldly terms. He wants sinners to see how fear is only the prelude to extraordinary joy. But the point is lost on anyone who thinks that "Religious Affections" have anything to do with natural affections. For the true saint, love begins with God's pure loveliness, not with God loving them. Appreciation of his holiness may bring God's love as a secondary consideration, but false affections feel just the secondary need. Because sinners see only "the awful greatness of God," not his "moral beauty," they miss his "tender," "lovely," "sweet" excellence. This is not a new doctrine, he says, but a new apprehension of the old miracle that Christ has made available to us in earthly language, as the Word. The invisible, the spiritual, and the "not seen" are the true reality of the Gospel.[62]

True religion therefore begins explicitly in a suppression of self, especially of anger and pride. There is awesome self-hatred in Edwards's theology. "True Christian fortitude consists in strength of mind, through grace, exerted in two things; in ruling and suppressing the evil, and unruly passions and affections of the mind; and in steadfastly and freely exerting, and following good affections." Like Christ, a saint must be "steadfastly maintaining the holy calm, meekness, sweetness, and benevolence of his mind," with no expressions of anger or unquiet, just as the Edwardses at home maintained an atmosphere of sweet obedience, with no contentiousness among their children. In that sense, children are the proper models of faith, since they can be bent to obedient dependence through constant, calm attentiveness. "Little children are not guileful and deceitful, but plain and simple," Edwards writes in *Religious Affections*. "They are yieldable and flexible, and not willful and obstinate; don't trust to their own understanding, but rely on the instructions of parents, and others of superior understanding. Here is therefore a fit and lively emblem of the followers of the Lamb."[63] A true saint is tender, with "a reverential fear," like "the least and tenderest child." He is aware always of God's beauty rather than his own needs. No "boldness" of language or thought; no "bold, familiar and appropriating language" claiming God for our Father; no "over-bearing, high-handed and violent sort of confidence" will do. Edwards sees anger and need as violence; both are eruptive forms of pride. He follows his own maxim by attributing only two— and those the shortest—of his twelve signs of true saving grace to the self's qualities and attributing the rest to God's.[64]

The Father is all, as judge and sovereign. Self must be made nothing. Finally that is true of the world's concerns as well. Earthly language can "shadow forth" God's excellencies, Edwards thought at first. But even by *Religious Affections* his polarities imply that earth and heaven can be joined only on heaven's terms. Language of the damned body is unable to express grace. A growing aloofness from flesh and things, a growing preference for logic and scripture, characterize Edwards's later writings. He would not make the mistake of raising sinning affections again. Ministers should come together to pray, he said, but they should never engage in worldly conversation.[65]

In his "Funeral Sermon" for David Brainerd, the saint who was to have married his daughter, Edwards often returns to the joyful time when man will be "absent from the body" and in the Father's presence. Brainerd, like Edwards, had been deceived by the Great Awakening. "When that false religion, which arises chiefly from impressions on the imaginations, began first to gain a very great prevalence in the land, he was for a little while deceived with it, so as to think highly of it." But "after a little while, he came clearly to see the vanity and perniciousness of such things." As earlier Puritans said of art, nothing that originates in "what is called *an impulse, or a strong impression on his imagination,*" rather than in the Deity, can bring the self to dependence.[66] Now only a language of paradox and abstraction can convey something of the Father. In the realm of philosophic discourse Edwards could make the connections expressing the Father's existence, power, immortality, and excellence.

To choose that language, however, meant that ordinary people would no longer hear him. Edwards's change recapitulates the change from Thomas Hooker to second-generation sermonists, and goes further. Samuel Willard defined the powers of metaphor as "therein dressing up of Heavenly Matter in Earthly Language, and thus accommodating of himself to our capacity: A Metaphor being nothing else but a contracted comparison by which he represents the things of God under the resemblance of things here below."[67] But for Edwards after the early 1740s, common language cannot work God's will. Love, which is the theme of *The Nature of True Virtue,* seems identical with the theme of his sixteen lectures in 1739 on Corinthians, published in 1874 as *Christian Love.*[68] Yet those early 530 pages speak to an audience in colloquial discourse, exhorting and raising the affections, while the later and very brief discourse proceeds by substituting one abstraction for another.

As Edwards had written in his notebooks, he was resolved "to Extricate all Questions from the least confusion or ambiguity of words so that the Ideas shall be left naked." In *Freedom of the Will* (1754) he tries to lift language beyond the sphere of natural resistance to a frame of pure logic. What is "plain and obvious" on the level of common discourse, he declares, can blind us, through false habituation, to the metaphysical level where alone we can glimpse God's truth. Ordinary language can be left to the Franklins, so long as some language of causality can still be found. He knew, without reading Hume, that ordinary language tends, like the age, toward atheistical dispersion. "The doctrine of necessity," he stated, "which supposes a necessary connection of all events, on some antecedent ground and reason of their existence, is the only medium we have to prove the being of God."[69] It seems poetically just, if not a happy ending, that the Puritan effort to purify the Word ended ensnared in theories about the nature of words. To Edwards's horror, the plain style did the devil's work with ease.

While he was preparing his logical masterworks, Edwards had been thrown out of Northampton for his first-generation views. In 1746 he had reasserted the church covenant against "promiscuous admission." At first he was merely denied permission to preach on the theme. In early 1750, since he had persisted, he was dismissed by a vote of 230 to 23 of the (male) members. Master of the Word to the last, Edwards had his subtle revenge in his "Farewell Sermon," preached on July 2, 1750, a bare nine years after his successes at Enfield. Here his style is, as Larzer Ziff has said, like a Jamesian dialogue, secretive, retentive, triumphant in failure, suggesting meanings as much by exclusion as by inclusion.[70] What time and the world condemn, he says, will be exalted by eternity. Rarely had his sentences seemed so calm, controlled, momentous, impassively sure of the outcome to follow this dust and heat. "Yea," he said, grandly appropriating a biblical image, "there is reason to think that often some that are most bold in their confidence of their safe and happy state, and think themselves not only true saints, but the most eminent saints in the congregation, are in a peculiar manner a smoke in God's nose."[71] His own serenity depends wholly on knowing what the Father will do, how he will judge, whom he will pardon.

"Consider of that day," he admonishes in the application, "when you and I shall meet before our Judge, when it shall be examined, whether you have had from me the treatment which is due to spiritual children, and whether you have treated me, as you ought to have treated a spiritual father." His rhetorical strategy could not be more different from Franklin's techniques for ingratiating himself with his son. He secures his language by finding his true audience where Edward Taylor addressed his poems, in an inwardly and eternally present God. His great effort had been to bring the words back into consonance with the Word: "The great thing which I have scrupled in the established method of this church's proceeding, and which I dare no longer go on in, is their publicly assenting to the form of words rehearsed on occasion of their admission to the communion, without pretending thereby to mean any such thing . . . it being, at the same time that the words are used, their known and established principle which they openly profess and proceed upon, that men may and ought to use these words and mean no such thing, but something else of a nature far inferior." Franklin had no trouble developing techniques of irony to say one thing and mean another. He stood before kings and helped carry the Constitution by arguing that no one should put his particular passion before the success of general compromise. Edwards had been kicked out of his little parish for daring to force men toward honesty in their use of words.

It is weak to be "fierce and violent," with "sharp and bitter passions," Edwards had said in *Religious Affections*. That is giving in to pride. Yet his later writings, while purporting to be works of logical speculation, are sometimes given over to a proud contentiousness. "It is one great reason why speculative points are thought to be of so little importance, that modern religion consists so little in respect to the divine Being, and almost wholly in benevolence to men," Edwards once observed.[72] *Freedom of the Will* and *The Nature of True Virtue* are relatively abstract disquisitions. While Franklin inherited Hooker's focus on preparation for right conduct, Edwards moved Shepard's tradition of rigorous law far beyond Willard's God of accommodation to its highest possible plane of rigor. But his last major treatise, *Original Sin*, published posthumously in 1758, shows a more petty, niggling Edwards, not only in its defective logic but more obviously in its inability to stop worrying about refuting John Taylor's book on sin, published nearly twenty years before. As a contemporary reviewer said, "where texts with texts a dreadful war maintain" it might seem tedious to readers, and "useless to the bulk of people."[73] That is exactly the case. The problem goes beyond a bad book, because the reasoning shows a final stage in Edwards's God-centered vision.

Abandoning the usual Puritan argument that we inherit sin from Adam, Edwards declares that we all sin *in* Adam, since he represented man publicly before God. However proud we may be of our individuality, we have to realize that God deals with man as a unity in crucial respects. Perry Miller saw the argument as a grand declaration of man's brotherhood. But Edwards's point is our brotherhood in sin, not grace. This is the fruit of our community with the world.[74] Without God, we are nothing but wrath, because of the heart's depravity. Using almost no imagery, with no examples from experience, Edwards simply asserts that our moral depravity can be shown by "an effectual tendency to destructive vengeance" in everyone. God is not the author of our sin, only the permitter when he withdrew his love from "rebel man," since sin naturally happens in the absence of positive good. The argument lands Edwards in a flat contradiction with the idea of an infinitely sovereign God of order, as his imperative of self-hatred leads him to posit the self's wrath beyond God's control.[75]

Death is not just a fact but a final punishment for anger and pride. Though Edwards repeatedly agonizes over the logical problem of infant deaths, he resolutely asserts the "immense guilt" that every baby has in Adam, even if it never had the chance to sin. His language is entirely concerned with judgment, vengeance, and the logic of punishment. Since our whole duty is love to an infinite God, the least iota of withholding is an infinite sin—again a contradiction, since finite creatures cannot be expected to have infinite feelings. The wish to polarize anger and guilt for anger, like his contempt for Taylor, goes deeper than the logic. "If we should see a wise and just father chastising his child, mixing terrible frowns with severe strokes, we should justly argue, that the father considered his child as having something in him displeasing to him," he says, justifying God's punishment of infants by death. To hope for lesser guilt for babies "relieves nothing but one's *imagination.* . . . it does not at all relieve one's *reason.*"[76]

More important than the argument is the language, which is from scripture rather than experience. His often tortuous explications depend almost completely on biblical texts, though the editor's introduction notes that Edwards confirmed his ideas of original sin through his experience with the Indians. Like Thoreau obsessively measuring natural phenomena around Concord in the last ten years of his life, Edwards subjects his texts to intricate grammatical collation and analysis, while ascribing "unreasonable violence" to Taylor's opposing views.[77] "It signifies nothing, to exclaim against plain fact," Edwards says of Taylor's notion that we are individuals. In one of his rare appeals to natural imagery, he declares that we are diverse, yet one, like the tree and the little sprout from which it began, even though "perhaps not one atom the very same." Thus man is united to Adam in time. Only God has "absolute independent identity." All our oneness is "a merely *dependent* identity" on God, since we are effects, not causes.[78]

That argument vitiates his other argument about man as the author of sin. But the underlying fantasy is clearer than the logic. In language as well as fantasy, Edwards presents a human reality completely dependent on the divine Father for any goodness in the self. God is like "a father, or some great friend and benefactor." He produces everything out of nothing "at each moment." Even when finally humbled in our pride, we are only "by nature, *companions* in a miserable, helpless condition; which, under a revelation of the divine mercy, tends to promote mutual *compassion.*"[79] This is not "new heaven, new earth," by any means. In fact Edwards shows his compassion by immediately declaring that Taylor's doctrine is the one promoting ill will. "Man's nature, as in his native state, is a body of sin, which must be destroyed, must die, be buried, and never rise more." God's community and man's estate have nothing in common. The view of man as a unity is entirely from God's point of view, and God has nothing to do with anyone in that unity except as he is reborn out of it. "If we love not God because he is what he is, but only because he is profitable to us, in truth we love him not at all," Edwards declares, echoing the theme of *Religious Affections*.[80]

The change from the original Puritan double appeal is immense. At its best the language of Puritanism, like the poet's eye described by Theseus in *A Midsummer-Night's Dream*,

> Doth glance from heaven to earth, from earth to heaven;
> . . . and gives to airy nothing
> A local habitation and a name.
>
> (V, i, 13–17)

But with Edwards the world is missing, except as sin or shadows. Taylor is more real to him than Northampton or the Indians. Community attenuates, except as God chooses a few private souls to join his ranks. Collective dependence becomes a personal fantasy, not a shared purpose. Mothering disappears, overwhelmed by the Father's judging sovereignty. Guilt and fear, not need, are the beginnings of saving grace.

Sometimes Edwards would ride his horse into the woods, returning much later with his flowing black cloak nearly covered by random pieces of white paper pinned to it. These were notes that he took in the wilderness, for whatever writing he was doing at the time. Franklin made randomness into an almanac. Edwards turned holy scraps into sermons. Solitary, massive, with God's white words covering a dark body, he was supremely self-controlled, or rather God-controlled, in the world. He spoke to people but did not reach for them—except for those, like his wife and David Brainerd, whom he considered more holy than himself.

In psychological terms, he had destroyed his sense of object relations to keep his sense of fantasy alive. We can see him doing that in the first paragraph of his "Personal Narrative." "The great wrong which Edwards did, which haunts us as an evil dream throughout his writings," concludes his most sensitive biographer, Alexander Allen, "was to assert God at the expense of humanity. Where man should be, there is only a fearful void."[81] When human reality was going Franklin's way, a solitary language of the mind was the last alternative to preserve Puritanism from accommodation to social change. Jonathan Edwards's writings are the grandest, purest statement of the Puritan obsessive style.

Chapter Nine

Freud and the American
Puritan Tradition

> But O, the grievous wrecks of pro-
> fessors. One can see some boards
> and planks at low water, but that
> is all.
>
> Thomas Shepard[1]

"Like all heirs," Stephen Foster writes, "we are less interested in
the careers of our ancestors than in their legacies."[2] The Puritan tradition has had a surprising and continuous impact on subsequent American writers, and its legacy has been frequently examined. My purpose
here is to trace loss, not gain: the loss of a language for establishing
identity within community, securing roles, expressing anxieties, and
joining shared purpose to responsive authority. Puritanism, I have
said, was among many other things an ambivalent response to social
discontents threatening the traditional father's role. The mixed signals
of tender though zealous mothering and grave or anxious fathering
were unified in the Puritan God. The stern fathers who settled New
England may have been as much wish as fact in the early years, and
the collective inward life of the first generation was articulated with
feminine and infantile imagery, the minister serving as their "breast
of God." In slighting feminine and regressive language, later Puritans
left the hollow shell of patriarchal sternness as their stereotypical
testament.

There are broader social reasons for our retrospective perception of
Puritan patriarchy, because Puritanism was one of the first large-scale
responses to a growing division in male and female roles. By Franklin's
time male roles were being defined more in terms of work than family
life, and his model of social usefulness rather than Puritan obedience
proved the more enduring way to success and status. By the nineteenth
century white Protestant America quite blatantly rewards pure ambi-

tion for men, and pure nurturance for women. Such mutually debilitating roles force male feelings of anxiety and dependence to be denied and replaced by aggressive posturing, while the association of women with home, art, and sensitivity is equally constricting. These broad social expectations, though put too simply, are clear enough to readers of any Hawthorne short story. Failing to preserve the Puritan double language for male feelings, the culture moved toward a compensatory ideal of solitary individualism, while making over the Puritan fathers ostensibly as figures to rebel against, actually as men in their own image. Not until Freud do we find a new, nontheological language for male anxiety. The struggle to find some mutuality between social role and personal feeling is obviously still with us, as are the social expectations that divide us from ourselves.[3]

The Freudian and the Puritan are not usually linked by anything more intimate than mutual vindictiveness. But what they share, beyond an intellectual focus on the anxious self, is a vision of social authority and paternal identity quite absent from American expectations. As a mode of therapy, psychoanalysis has gone beyond Freud in many ways, notably in its study of pre-Oedipal dynamics and in its model of mental functioning. Yet "Freudian" can also be taken as an ideology. Freud's impact on two generations of therapists outstrips Calvin's on the American Puritans, and both movements can be analyzed as historical phenomena.[4] To examine the many similarities between Freud's model of the mind and the Puritan faith would require another book; earlier chapters have drawn some parallels between Freud's psychoanalytic concepts and Puritan perspectives.[5] More important to my argument is that Freud's model of Oedipal conflict, like the Puritan model of faith, puts the father's role at stage center.

There are profound, enduring social reasons for American hostility to Freud as well as to the Puritan tradition, even as both continue to have such an astonishing impact. America has been the country that has most completely reconstituted male roles in terms of work rather than family. The American middle-class father is a wistful weekend hope, the "Mom" an omnipresence. The dream of male success in the world of work is given special urgency by massive indifference to failure, without familial and community norms of respect that traditionally validate one's life. Our literature records a sensitivity to male failure as acute as its various "Imperial Self" fantasies of solitary protection. American writing has been notoriously a literature of radically individualized styles asserting "a world elsewhere" than shared community; the forms chosen by our major writers, from Melville and Whitman to Mailer and Ginsberg, seem often provisional, at best attempts to assert the self's organic processes, as in Whitman, and at worst an unintegrated amalgam of the sermon and the almanac, our two most distinctly social genres.[6] The dominant shared fantasy of the American Dream is of the prophetic self in nature watching another self compete in Darwinian worldly combat. That divided self is a residue of a fatherless community: Ishmael and Ahab. A characteristic pattern of failed, anxious, or absent fathers in the lives of classic American authors helps to explain the precariousness of social focus and the exaggerated fantasies of self in American literature.

These are broad strokes on a broader canvas. Nevertheless, they are implicit in the earlier chapters. At the risk of drastically oversimplifying, I would like to draw out their consequences.

Several years ago a brief newspaper article noted the death of one of the first big winners of the Michigan lottery. His wife had found him asphyxiated, sitting at the wheel of his new $20,000 car in their garage, with one foot out of the car door. A suicide, one would think; but not so. "He loved that car," his daughter told reporters. The lottery winner had often sat in it for hours, playing with the stereo, the refrigerator, the bar, the color TV, the tape deck. Apparently he didn't realize that operating those appliances in a closed garage brings in monoxide fumes. The foot out the door shows his belated awareness.

What a Hawthorne short story that would make! A man in a self-wrought womb of material happiness, fiddling and tinkering with his gadgets by the hour, with no thought for wife or daughter, struck dead by the invisible waste from his luxury. The episode lingers in my mind as the quintessential expression of the American Dream. Of course it isn't: the man died, after all, and he had been rewarded without hard work. Most Americans would define the American Dream as a fantasy of family leisure more than as a solitary bath in material things. Yet the image of that man in his luxury car, idle and idling, is a plausible finale to Benjamin Franklin's *Autobiography*. It connotes the worldly satisfactions to which all one's hard work and sociability tend. Franklin too left his wife, for years at a time.

Against material balm most of our literary voices and values have protested. Yet the dominant spiritual articulations of the American Dream, as expressed in Emerson's sense of self-reliance, substitute solitary transcendence for material complacency. Richard Chase's theme has become a truism: that classic American literature lacks a social emphasis, except in prophetic or redemptive terms. In a land where freedom has come to mean elbow room rather than mutuality, our native-grown literature and thought tend away from politics, work, and society. Anarchism still passes for our best philosophy, if we take Robert Nozick's *Anarchy, State and Utopia* as guide. In literature too, Thomas Pynchon's *Gravity's Rainbow* is one of many that exalts redemptive anarchist spontaneity while condemning organized work relations as the tools of bureaucracy and death. The American Dream has never been associated, in any major way, with shared purpose, work, or community. Rather, it stands for a shared fantasy of self, nature, and top of the heap, with overtones of male friendship separate from anxieties about class and women.[7] To the degree that he is separate from his neighbors, a man can respect himself. Uncompromised by bosses, surveying his bigger and bigger lawn, he can dream of being ever more purely alone with an Emersonian wilderness-God.

The Puritans offered a different, more retrogressive fantasy: the strong, tender father who civilizes one's fearful impulses toward interdependent security. Freud's theory of the Oedipus complex recasts the same fantasy in more repressive secular terms. Though Freud discovered that we "internalize the father" by the age of six, the Puritan's mature sense of conscience and the more infantile Oedipal superego are twins. Freud uncovered parricidal feelings, while Puritanism makes submission to the father the end product rather than the beginning of civilized behavior. But inward desire in conflict with external male authority is the conscious world view of both these mental disciplines, at least as the first fathers designed them.

The Puritan and Freudian perspectives on the self both arose from partially submerged, partially conscious ambivalence toward the father's authority in a world that was transforming the father's role. Each system encourages a fantasy of exaggerated patriarchy, to articulate resentment of and wishes for strong male identity on the part of both fathers and sons. Puritanism is as unaware of its resentments as Freudian theory is of its wishes for patriarchy. That inversion has personal and historical dimensions, because these two disciplines mark the beginning and the end of the period in Western history when capitalism took the father away from the bourgeois home. Puritanism differs from Freud in its call for a return to village and family roles, with the father's intimacy on a cosmic scale. Freud stridently called for as much rational autonomy as civilization can bear. Born when the transition from peasant village life to industrial capitalism was well advanced, Freud located identity in one's solitary powers to confront the mind's nonrational sources, while Puritanism gained its sense of manhood from what Freud would call a reaction-formation fantasy. Yet each responded to role dislocation and father-son conflict with ambivalent advocacy of a very traditional male image of dominance and self-control.

Freud himself, that most Protestant of atheistic Jews, wrote *The Future of an Illusion* as a diatribe against the false comfort of religious perspectives. For him, all religion comes from atonement for unconscious parricidal guilt. But his contempt is the public side of a ferocious inward struggle against his wishes for protective authority. Only in 1896, with the death of his own father—a small-time "cloth merchant," like so many Puritans before their emigration—did this forty-year-old medical doctor begin to confess the depth of his own ambivalence toward the modest Jewish tradesman whom he had already replaced with a succession of professionally eminent fathers: Brücke, Breuer, Janet, Charcot, Fliess. One of his most vivid memories was of his father telling him how a Christian had once knocked off Jacob's hat, shouting "Jew, get off the pavement!" Sigmund, wanting a Hannibal-like conclusion to his father's story, was profoundly disappointed to hear that his father had simply picked up the hat.[8] Written in the midst of his climb up Catholic Vienna's strict and awesome ladder of hierarchic apprenticeship, Freud's *Interpretation of Dreams* remains an extraordinary record not only of solitary self-interpretation but of the invention of a patriarch in himself. It is, like those we have seen from Shepard's to Franklin's, a spiritual autobiography, with Freud converting himself to a new order of heroic knowledge. Later, hovering over the Vienna circle that was his chosen elect, Freud too would wish to covenant his spiritual children.

There are many similarities between Freud's restless search for fathers strong enough to initiate him into the mission he craved, and the Puritan quest for a God powerful enough to shelter their social purposes. In one aspect the Puritans were primarily a small, homogeneous group of displaced English weavers and small tradesmen trying to preserve the family's roles on terms they were used to, in a world whose disruption of traditional social authority led to the killing of their king. Like Freud, the Puritan never allowed his feelings to simplify into rebellion. Rather, both looked to Old Testament patriarchs for analogues to express their sense of being "chosen" for loyal opposition, for a pilgrimage to America or into the unconscious that would somehow bring a new consciousness of manly dignity to the old world. Both

Freud and the Puritans also threw their energies into their calling, obsessively so. One of the larger ironies of Freud's life is that the man who supposedly reduced everything to sex devoted himself, even in the midst of great physical pain, to work, work, and more work. He wrote articles right to the end of his life, after twenty-three operations for cancer of the jaw. He even named one of his sons after Oliver Cromwell.[9]

But unlike Freud's, the Puritan sense of patriarchy did not end with the self. The Freudian assumption, which fits equally well with habits of American individualism or with Jonathan Edwards, is that everyone is alone with guilty desires. Freud's life rigidly enacts the nineteenth century's separation of work from home, solitary male ambition from female nurturance in the family. His wife, who is reported to have once said that "psychoanalysis stops at the door of the children's room," laid out his clothes for him, even put the toothpaste on his toothbrush.[10] Earlier Puritans were more flexible than Freud in their vision of social identity, and they found literary and social forms, especially the sermon, to express shared values, shared fears, shared fantasies. Their religion was a comprehensive communal structure that helped to articulate a larger faith in social expression and a more humble sense of what individuals can do without structures of authority and support. It helped to resolve the mixed signals of a society in transition.

Take, for instance, one of the most famous passages in Puritan writing—famous because of its supposedly un-Puritan cast. Samuel Sewall's hymn of praise to Plum Island has often been greeted with a sigh of relief, as if at finding in the midst of arid theologizing one Puritan who sees nature as we do, fresh with intimacy and detail rather than order and abstraction. Yet the assumptions of his language are entirely social, not individual. For him, all natural facts have their place and role in a larger purpose:

> As long as *Plum Island* shall faithfully keep the commanded Post;
> Notwithstanding all the hectoring Words, and hard Blows of the proud
> and boisterous Ocean; As long as any Salmon, or Sturgeon shall swim
> in the streams of *Merrimack*; or any Perch, or Pickeril, in *Crane-Pond*;
> As long as the Sea-Fowl shall know the Time of their coming, and not
> neglect seasonably to visit the Places of their Acquaintance: As long
> as any Cattel shall be fed with the Grass growing in the Medows,
> which do humbly bow down themselves before *Turkie-Hill*; As long as
> any Sheep shall walk upon *Old Town Hills*, and shall from thence
> pleasantly look down upon the River *Parker*, and the fruitfull *Marishes*
> lying beneath; As long as any free and harmless Doves shall find a
> White Oak, or other Tree within the Township, to perch, or feed, or

build a careless Nest upon; and shall voluntarily present themselves to
perform the office of Gleaners after Barley-Harvest; As long as Nature
shall not grow Old and dote; but shall constantly remember to give
the rows of Indian Corn their education, by Pairs; So long shall Christians be born there; and being first made meet, shall from thence be
Translated, to be made partakers of the Inheritance of the Saints in
Light.[11]

The natural objects gain his affection by virtue of how they fulfill their
social duties and relationships. Every particular fact lives through its
connection to larger authority. The island itself must "faithfully keep
the commanded post"; the sea fowl "shall know the Time of their
coming" and seasonably visit; the grass shall "humbly bow down themselves before Turkie-Hill" for cattle to eat; and even the "free and
harmless Doves," who have to find a tree "within the Township" for
their "careless" nests, will "voluntarily present themselves" as gleaners
after the harvest. In a world where roles are voluntary yet obligated, as
Puritan theory says, Christians can be "born" and "made meet" for
biblical language at last (Col. 1.12), "to share in the inheritance of
the saints in light."

Does one failure of faith mean the end, or can the community carry
a lapse? The syntax is deliberately vague; "As long as any" continue,
the vision of the whole is possible, though not secure. Nature herself is
held accountable as teacher "to give the rows of Indian corn their
education, by Pairs." Straying individuals should feel anxious, because
the vision of Christian redemption follows from the harmony of social
functions, not the assertion of individual powers. Group and place are
touchstones for individual identities, which are solidly grounded in
work, and also for the sense of time itself. Here consciousness of the
future is a continuation of the present, where all obligations and
relationships conspire to make men "meet" for the divine translation.

Sewall's language has more to do with roles than patriarchs, though
a traditional deference is clearly implied. In psychoanalytic terms, he
assumes the necessary relation between identity and repression, as well
as between personal identity and group articulation. In our century,
only Faulkner comes close to such social language for natural description, and he too is the tragedian for the downfall of aristocratic fathers,
the Sartorises and Sutpens, who are outfoxed by the grasping, self-reliant
Snopeses. In Norman Mailer's *Why Are We in Vietnam?* or Pynchon's
Gravity's Rainbow, two books whose surfaces are saturated with psychoanalytic and Puritan perspectives, nature is presented as a fantasy of
purity or an agent for apocalypse, but above all as opposed to human

doings. There is none of Sewall's winsome faith that natural work relations reflect human order and righteous purpose. Work alienates, and social authority maims the soul. These books are products of the mainstream shared fantasy in America, which presents the filial self allied with mother nature against the working, failing, fathering world.

———•—•———

What Freud and the first generation of Puritan preachers in America finally share, I believe, is the attempt to articulate a different "structure of feeling," in Raymond Williams's phrase:[12] one that transforms male ambivalence about the father's role into fantasies of authority, community, and dependence. The strain in male identity is the historical context for both theories. The fear is not only of doing battle with a stronger father, but of watching one's father fail in the wider world.

The fear of *group* failure, sheltered by the fantasy of God's nurturing fatherhood, was Puritanism's magnificent motivating solution to the fear of individual failure and conflict. The famous Puritan sense of mission, for which several generations of preachers in America gave funeral orations, carried a sense of fear that later times would amiably transform and forget. Even Sewall's hymn to Plum Island expresses anxiety over failure and a wish to transform individual weakness into group support. There was no "manifest destiny" about those first emigrations. We tend to impart such assurance to John Winthrop's call that "wee shall be as a Citty upon a Hill, the eies of all people are uppon us." But his call continues with a vivid sense of possible failure, not success: "soe that if wee shall deale falsely with our god in this work wee have undertaken and so cause him to withdraw his present help from us, wee shall be made a story and a by-word through the world."[13] Unbelievers can easily miss Winthrop's implication that failure, not success, is what the world is watching for, and what literature would recount. If we prevail, he implies, no one need pay attention but God.

But what sons could measure up to those patriarchal expectations? Second-generation preachers covered their filial sense of inadequacy and competition with a grandiloquent myth of the first generation and a magnified sense of group failure. Their fathers had been sustained by a powerful fantasy of God as a stable, supportive audience as well as parent; theology had given them what Sacvan Bercovitch has called a "comprehensive identity."[14] Their sense of collectivity permitted a covert rebellion against the gentry in the name of higher authority.

Two hundred and fifty years later, Americans would misconstrue Freud by turning his pessimistic account of necessary repression into a problem to be solved on the way to rebelling against the "civilized morality" that they took for the legacy of Puritanism.[15] But even within thirty years, the Puritan confidence that as chosen people they were fulfilling God's purposes was shaken. The original Puritan image of the ever-watchful Father with maternal powers dried up into the petrified, astringent Yankee who could wither his young with a look, or a distance. The father's severity lingered as a symbol of Puritanism, long after the social purpose, the social language, and the infantile fantasies, had gone. That severity, too, was part wish, part reality. Ben Franklin, covertly rebelling against his own father, made the first of his many self-made characters a woman, Silence Dogood, whose "entrance into this troublesome World was attended with the Death of my Father," and whose "indulgent Mother departed this life" within two years, "leaving me as it were by my self, having no Relation on Earth within my Knowledge." This state of affairs, announced in her first epistle in 1722, also inaugurates a new shared fantasy among the sons of Puritanism: to be born of oneself, without the father's help.

In the nineteenth century a more class-stratified and competitive society placed new strains on male roles, without traditional theological props to give meaning to the working world. Women were urged into motherhood and the home, as urban and institutional work began to disrupt the more egalitarian work roles of the agrarian family. The family itself ceased to be a microcosm of the larger society and tended to become a place for child rearing and father's rest and recreation. Men now left the family to work: a simple social reality that had immense consequences for child rearing and social identity. There was a greater pluralism of immigrant groups and American regions and little congruence among the patterns of shared authority from family to government. As the family became more a place for consumption and child rearing, governed by the mother, than a work place governed by the father, the young boy's sense of power and nurturance was inevitably split, or attributed to his mother, until he entered the working world.[16]

Two new fantasy structures evolved to manage these anxieties. One was the idealization of nature as a mixture of escape and self-confrontation, as something apart from what Thoreau called "the mass of men" and their "lives of quiet desperation." The image of nature offered fantasies of solitude, yet with motherly shelter rather than abandonment. It encouraged a transition from aggressive male dominance and sexuality to dependence, and it welcomed the adult into a regressive haven, away from social tensions. It also offered a screen to confront one's hidden "nature."[17] Especially in Hawthorne, but in Cooper too, nature gives birth to the receptive and feminine parts of the self, with woman's secret powers, while exposing all guilty violations of what *The Scarlet Letter* calls "the sanctity of the human heart." The other fantasy, a more strict avoidance of conflict, was individualism.

Both fantasies share a great deal with the Puritan experience. They spring from the tension between failure, guilt for aggressive feelings, the possibilities and risks inherent in mobility of any kind, and the sense that one has incessantly to earn a place in a changing world. They even spring, at least in American literature, from the same New England area and class. In psychoanalytic terms, they are both reaction formations. Identity must be found in the past, or in the woods, or in the idealized female, or in the transcendental mind—not in the conflicts between desire and role, between family background and social expectation. Emerson and Thoreau share a tone of magisterial condescension toward those involved in the dust and heat of the workaday world; to Thoreau all those Irish laborers look alike, and Emerson takes on the more empathetic task of rescuing limp souls from "the downward tendency and proneness of things," though he is equally scornful of laborers at the end of his essay on "Nature." Even Whitman's "Song of Myself," which seems to be celebrating the ordinary world, avoids anxiety and conflict by incorporating everything in an androgynous inner dialogue.[18]

Yet the new fantasy objects of nature and self obviously differ from the Puritan God. These are not fantasies of mutuality and role security on earth and female or infantile submission to the Father in heaven. The controlling abstraction of nature has aspects of the Puritan fantasy of dependence, but the mother is now on the throne. Receptivity to a womb cosmos allows the Imperial Self to stand apart from the social struggle for survival and dominance, even from ego itself. Thoreau dreamed at the end of *A Week on the Concord and Merrimack Rivers*, "Sometimes a mortal feels in himself Nature,—not his Father but his Mother stirs within him, and he becomes immortal with her immortality. From time to time she claims kindredship with us, and some globule from her veins steals up into our own." D. H. Lawrence remarks less cosmically, about Crèvecoeur, "Absolutely the safest thing to get your emotional reactions over is NATURE."[19]

Paradoxically, the double fantasy of self-reliance in a virgin or maternal wilderness was the dream of an upwardly mobile class. It was

a *social* ethic, in which personal failure brought feelings of guilt, not
frustration, solidarity, or anger. The sense of failure that John Winthrop articulated for a group was now brought home to the solitary
self, without the community reinforcement that the Puritan vision encouraged. In Puritan structures of theology and community, men could
share both self-doubt and self-assertion. Now the paradoxical fantasy
of solitary self-assertion and cosmic receptivity, whether expressed as
Natty Bumppo or Emerson's "transparent Eyeball," buried more complex interpersonal issues. Making money, as many foreign visitors observed with astonishment, seemed to be the only male concern, without
any broader articulation of authority or feeling. Privately, as G. J.
Barker-Benfield records, many men simply went crazy. So said Dr.
Edward Jarvis in 1851: In America, where "no son is necessarily con-
fined to the work . . . of his father," every field is open, and all can
"join the strife." Yet these men "are struggling . . . at that which they
cannot reach . . . their mental powers are strained to their utmost
tension. . . . Their minds stagger . . . they are perplexed with the
variety of insurmountable obstacles; and they are exhausted with the
ineffectual labor." What Barker-Benfield calls an "all-male, anti-author-
itarian world" of sons and fathers diffused authority and equated maleness with self-control.[20]

Failure in the new world of capitalism came down most heavily on
the father, who had been supported by the theological language of
patriarchal dominance. The difficulties of second-generation Puritans
show the power of a cultural fantasy that had succeeded too well. The
patriarchal village family in America repressed its aggressive sons,
from Andover to Boston, while the new mercantile culture encouraged
those same sons in their aggressiveness. With the fragmentation of
communal ideology, third-generation Winthrops could grab for land
and advancement.[21] Yet the psychological price for breaking away is
reflected in one of the most stereotypical themes in American literature:
the search for the father, first expressed in the stabilizing and stylized
voice of Benjamin Franklin, but more comprehensively seen in fantasies of flight from civilizing women. Rip Van Winkle's nagging wife
is the given; to be reborn as unencumbered oldster, preferably with
son, is the ideal. The Horatio Alger myth, which along with Franklin's
autobiography was the most influential American version of self-help
and upward mobility, characteristically shows the hero succeeding not
by self-reliance but—just as in Franklin—by seeking fatherly men in
authority who suddenly lift the boy to prominence. "Where is the
foundling's father hidden?" Ahab cries, himself seeking in the whale a

God to overthrow. *The Scarlet Letter* too, at the most obvious level, recounts a search to know the secret of a father's identity. Ike McCaslin seeks "Sam Fathers" for knowledge of the wilderness, and Huck Finn ends his story by proclaiming his flight from "sivilizing" women at home.[22]

The mother was now in charge of child rearing and was expected to be very moralistic about it, while the father took charge of worldly survival. Therefore it was the mother who occasioned strong and contradictory feelings in the middle-class child. The father's image became that of the idealized and vanishing protector—the reverse of the Freudian paradigm. Although Freud said that the Oedipal dilemma was universal, his own mother was authoritarian, his father consciously perceived by his son as weak.[23] In some respects Freud's theory of totemic patriarchy was his own Puritanic wish fulfillment. He too dreamed of Hannibal, Moses, Rome.

So Puritanism remains as a paradox: that at least for the dominant white Protestant tradition, America's first settlers enacted the father's last collective stand in the home. Individualism has been a successor fantasy of traditional male power, but expressed only as self-control: the more inward paradox of feeling dominant without social dominance. From Emerson to James, says Quentin Anderson, "most of the major figures whom we have come to think of as offering a sense of our distinctive qualities were men who had either been let down by their fathers or acted as if they had." His three exceptions, James Fenimore Cooper, Emily Dickinson, and Henry Adams, only prove his rule. These writers, especially the men, have what he calls a "firm, downright—even worldly" dimension. Adams, like Cooper, "was quite sure that our fate was wholly bound up with the fate of the polity."[24]

In fact, almost every major American writer in the nineteenth century *except* Dickinson, Cooper, and Adams had a father who died early, had little authority in the home, or conspicuously failed in business. Melville's father failed twice, once in New York City and once in Albany, where he died quite suddenly when Herman was barely in his teens. Hawthorne's father, a ship captain, died of yellow fever in Dutch Guiana when Nathaniel was four, throwing Hawthorne's mother into a long life of seclusion. Poe's father seems to have run out on the family when Edgar was eighteen months old. He died shortly before his wife died, leaving two-year-old Edgar to be taken from a world of itinerant actors and raised by a solid, conservative, repressive stepfather. Emerson's father, a minister and respected civic leader, took ill with a lung hemorrhage when his son was five, to die when Waldo was eight.

Emerson's family history is riddled with other deaths and sicknesses. Thoreau, Whitman, and James were very much "mama's boys," whose fathers either did not merit or did not gain their sons' respect.

My point is not to show how neurotic American literature is as a result of this pattern of trauma, but rather to suggest that the pattern of paternal failure, weakness, or absence has more than biographical significance. It provided an unconscious motive for fashioning a literature that could express personal conflicts in public language. After the Civil War, when writers from the Mid-West began to refashion American literature in more realistic ways, nuclear family anxieties take more overtly social forms, with less primacy given to the Imperial Self. Nevertheless, despite their many differences, the Twains, Hemingways, Fitzgeralds, and Faulkners have similar family tales to tell. The failed father, despite Puritanism's legacy, has been one of America's most consistent products, at least in families from which great writers, our psychic barometers, have come.

The father in industrial times has traditionally mediated between the family and the larger world of work. The lack of such mediating influences was what Tocqueville noted in American democracy. In America, he said, "each citizen is habitually engaged in the contemplation of a very puny object: namely, himself. If he ever looks higher, he perceives only the immense form of society at large or the still more imposing aspect of mankind. . . . What lies between is a void."[25] Tocqueville saw America's self-preoccupation simply as an unfortunate natural outgrowth of democratic principles, though the authoritarian Puritans had in fact begun the practice. But whether social or psychological, the American father's desire for individual success and family recuperation—what we now know as the American Dream—lacks the language of social purpose that animated early American patriarchy. It also lacks the shared vocabulary of emotion that Puritanism developed to express and alleviate male fears.

There are more emotions than pride, as Freud and the Puritans knew, and there are more roles for men than patriarch, as they often forgot. Yet the Puritan vision of God and Freud's model of the unconscious, like other immigrant faiths, tried to invent a structure of feeling that united needs and feelings with work and parenting. The limits of reactionary patriarchal beliefs should be amply evident, as our society struggles toward equality of men and women, whose feelings this study has deliberately underplayed. Yet the strength of the Puritan tradition remains fresh. More significant even than their tenacity of mind, which most historians still take for Puritanism's primary legacy, is their will toward a language of shared feelings and secured social roles. To dismiss the Puritan tradition as irrelevant patriarchy is to dismiss the complex ways that Puritan theology and social structure redirected resentment, ambivalence, anxiety, and desire into mutual support. In their social emphasis, even in their patriarchal fantasies, Freud and the Puritans provide a way of seeing the absence at the heart of the American Dream.

Notes

Introduction

1. Thomas Shepard, *Parable of the Ten Virgins* (London, 1660), p. 6.
2. Increase Mather, *David Serving His Generation* (n.p., 1697), p. 31, Cotton Mather, *A Father Departing* . . . (Boston, 1723), pp. 22–23.
3. Samuel Willard, *A Compleat Body of Divinity* . . . (Boston, 1726), p. 32. Shepard's simile comparing sin to a menstruous cloth is also from the Bible.
4. John Cotton, *A Brief Exposition of the whole Book of Canticles* . . . (London, 1642), pp. 240–241; cf. 1 Peter 2.2 and 1 Corinthians 3.2. See John Robotham, *An Exposition On the whole booke of Solomons Song* . . . (London, 1651), pp. 209–216 (ministers as breasts), 467–468 (beauty of church), 681 ("Equalitie in Womens Breasts, make, much for the beautie of them"), 697, 720–721, for various allegorical interpretations of breasts in the Song of Solomon.
5. Thomas Hooker, *The Soules Vocation* (London, 1638), p. 306; Willard, *Compleat Body*, p. 131. Cotton's *Spiritual Milk* was published in Cambridge, Mass., in 1656.
6. See Peter Laslett, *The World We Have Lost* (New York, 1965), a demographic study showing that the nuclear family antedates industrialization. Melville's linked analogies are in *Moby-Dick*, ch. 70.
7. Joan Webber, *The Eloquent "I": Style and Self in 17th Century Prose* (Madison, 1968), p. 137; also Owen C. Watkins, *The Puritan Experience* (London, 1972), p. 228.
8. Thomas Hooker, *A survey of the summe of Church Discipline* . . . (London, 1648), part 1, pp. 188, 186.
9. Sigmund Freud, "Family Romances" (1908), Standard Edition, vol. 9, pp. 237–241, and his letter to Fliess of May 20, 1898.
10. Thomas Playfere, *The whole Sermons* . . . (London, 1623), p. 230, from "A Sermon Preached at *Whitehall* before the King on Tuesday after Lo Sunday. 1604," on 2 Corinthians, 3.18. Cf. Horton Davies,

Worship and Theology in England From Cranmer to Hooker 1534–1603 (Princeton, 1970), pp. 236–237.

11. John Norton, *The Heart of N- England rent at the* BLASPHEMIES *of the Present Generation* . . . (Cambridge, New England, 1659), p. 22.

12. See Webber, *The Eloquent "I"*, and Watkins, *Puritan Experience*, p. 25. For comparisons between Anglican and Puritan theology, see John F. New, *Anglican and Puritan: The Basis of Their Opposition, 1558–1640* (London, 1964), and Davies, *Worship and Theology*, pp. 40–75; also pp. 227–254 on Anglican preaching and pp. 255–324 on Puritan worship and preaching.

13. On Puritan intensities, see Davies, *Worship and Theology*, pp. 41, 428; M. M. Knappen, *Tudor Puritanism: A Chapter in the History of Idealism* (Chicago, 1939), p. 341; and Patrick Collinson, *The Elizabethan Puritan Movement* (Berkeley, 1967), pp. 26–27.

14. On Anglican patriarchal rhetoric, see Michael Walzer, *The Revolution of the Saints: A Study in the Origins of Radical Politics* (Cambridge, Mass., 1965), pp. 149, 184–198. On the increase in patriarchal rhetoric during early seventeenth-century England, see Gordon J. Schochet, *Patriarchalism in Political Thought: The Authoritarian Family and Political Speculation and Attitudes Especially in Seventeenth-Century England* (New York, 1975), especially chs. 4–6; also Lawrence Stone, *The Family, Sex and Marriage In England 1500–1800* (London, 1977), especially pp. 151–218, "The Reinforcement of Patriarchy." Both Schochet and Stone tend to take rhetoric for reality.

15. Hooker, *Survey*, part 1, pp. 3, 107, 206. Also see part 2, pp. 72–74, on the necessity for voluntary feelings in subjection.

16. For three uses of the phrase "nursing fathers," see Henry Bullinger, *The Decades*, reprinted in *Puritan Political Ideas, 1558–1794*, ed. Edmund Morgan (n.p., 1965), pp. 26–27; Edward Hopkins and William Goodwin, 1647 preface to Hooker's *Survey*, p. 9; and Thomas Cobbett, *A Fruitfull and Usefull Discourse Touching the Honour due from Children to Parents, and the duty of Parents towards their Children* . . . (London, 1656, 1st pub. New England 1654), p. 235. Willard's *Compleat Body* never mentions the phrase in a year's worth of lectures on the Fifth Commandment (pp. 597–655).

17. Hooker, *Survey*, part 1, p. 107; Willard, *Compleat Body*, pp. 98–99.

18. On the Puritan definition of "church" and "meeting house," see Davies, *Worship and Theology*, p. 429.

19. John Dod and Robert Cle[a]ver, *A Godlye Form of Household Government* (London, 1621, 1st ed. 1614), epistle dedicatory by Cleaver. Robert Cushman's *The Sin and Danger of Self-Love* is cited as the first published American sermon by John Seelye, *Prophetic Waters: The River in Early American Life and Literature* (New York, 1977), p. 126. Cushman was a layman.

20. For a helpful essay reviewing the history and meanings of ambivalence,

see Alex Holder, "Theoretical and Clinical Aspects of Ambivalence," *The Psychoanalytic Study of the Child*, 30 (1975), pp. 197–220.

21. Hopkins and Goodwin, preface to Hooker's *Survey*. Hopkins and Goodwin give "mixed fellowships, and other pollutions" as a major reason for emigrating. For more on Ramist polarities, see Perry Miller, *The New England Mind: The Seventeenth Century* (New York, 1939); Walter J. Ong, *Ramus, Method, and the Decay of Dialogue, from the Art of Discourse to the Art of Reason* (Cambridge, Mass., 1958); David L. Parker, "Petrus Ramus and the Puritans—The 'Logic' of Preparationist Conversion Doctrine," *Early American Literature*, 8 (1974), pp. 140–162; Keith L. Sprunger, "Ames, Ramus, and the Method of Puritan Theology," *Harvard Theological Review*, 59 (April 1966), pp. 133–151; and Charles Feidelson, Jr., *Symbolism and American Literature* (Chicago, 1953), pp. 77–118.

22. On "breaking the will," see John Demos, *A Little Commonwealth: Family Life in Plymouth Colony* (New York and London, 1970), and Philip Greven, *The Protestant Temperament: Patterns of Child-Rearing, Religious Experience, and the Self in Early America* (New York, 1977). Demos's book is technically about a separatist colony, but his Eriksonian observations apply more broadly.

23. Recent studies suggest that Freud may have reduced fathering complexities to parricidal feelings because he was blocked here, as he was in his feelings toward women and aesthetics, by his own defenses. A provocative though too patriarchal view is Arthur Efron's "Freud's Self-Analysis and the Nature of Psychoanalytic Criticism," *The International Review of Psycho-Analysis*, 4 (1977), pp. 253–280. For more pre-Oedipal studies, see Jim Swan, "*Mater* and Nannie: Freud's Two Mothers and the Discovery of the Oedipus Complex," *American Imago*, 31 (Spring 1974), pp. 1–64; Paul Roazen, *Freud And His Followers* (New York, 1975), pp. 44–45, 397–398; and especially Jack J. Spector, *The Aesthetics of Freud: A Study in Psychoanalysis and Art* (New York, 1972).

24. Richard Bushman, *From Puritan to Yankee: Character and the Social Order in Connecticut, 1690–1765* (Cambridge, Mass., 1967); Philip Greven, *Four Generations: Population, Land, and Family in Colonial Andover, Massachusetts* (Ithaca, 1970); and Emory Elliott, *Power in the Pulpit in Puritan New England* (Princeton, 1975). Timothy Breen's *The Character of the Good Ruler: A Study of Puritan Political Ideas in New England, 1630–1730* (New Haven, 1970) studies conscious ideas of Puritan authority.

25. For the class background and social homogeneity of Puritanism, see Christopher Hill's *Society and Puritanism in Pre-Revolutionary England* (New York, 1964); Herman Israel, "Some Religious Factors in the Emergence of Industrial Society in England," *American Sociological Review*, 31 (October 1966), pp. 589–599; Carl Bridenbaugh, *Vexed*

and Troubled Englishmen 1590–1642 (New York, 1968); Wallace Notestein, *The English People on the Eve of Colonization 1603–1620* (New York, 1954), among many others. Walzer's *Revolution of the Saints* tries to counter Hill's focus on "the industrious sort" with a picture of Puritanism as "the political religion of intellectuals (ministers) and gentlemen" (p. 328). On this point, as on several others, I disagree with Walzer's emphasis, although his argument may hold better for later English Puritanism. As Knappen says in *Tudor Puritanism,* still one of the liveliest and most balanced studies of the early Puritans, they were controversialists but not intellectuals (p. 367). Darrett B. Rutman, *American Puritanism: Faith and Practice* (Philadelphia, New York, and Toronto, 1970) argues for New England's continuity with England's peasant traditions and associates the emigrants' religious ardor with identity crises. T. H. Breen's "Persistent Localism: English Social Change and the Shaping of New England Institutions," *William and Mary Quarterly,* 32 (January 1975), pp. 3–28, has persuaded me that New England vigorously perpetuated the English village tradition in all its contrariety; see the various recent studies of Puritan villages, especially Greven's work on Andover and Kenneth A. Lockridge, *A New England Town: The First Hundred Years* (New York, 1970), on Dedham. Puritanism must also be seen in the broader sense of crisis established by Lawrence Stone in *The Crisis of the Aristocracy: 1558–1660* (London, 1971). For more general arguments connecting religion to a shared sense of powerlessness, see Keith Thomas, *Religion and the Decline of Magic* (New York, 1971); Peter Berger, *The Sacred Canopy: Elements of a Sociological Theory of Religion* (New York, 1967), especially p. 38, suggesting that religion "legitimates" the father's authority in times of stress; and W. Carey McWilliams, *The Idea of Fraternity in America* (Berkeley, 1973), p. 105.

26. On Puritanism as a "reaction formation," see Zevedei Barbu, *Problems of Historical Psychology* (New York, 1960), pp. 183–187. Greven is wrong to say in *The Protestant Temperament,* p. 347, that "the evangelical experience was not conservative in any sense but truly radical." In that respect he is in agreement with Alan Heimert's *Religion and the American Mind from the Great Awakening to the Revolution* (Cambridge, Mass., 1966).

27. Puritanism as a dream of order allaying conflict is Walzer's view in *Revolution of the Saints;* see also Michael McGiffert's introduction to *God's Plot: The Paradoxes of Puritan Piety, Being the Autobiography & Journal of Thomas Shepard* ([Amherst], 1972). Michael Kammen's *People of Paradox: An Inquiry concerning the Origins of American Civilization* (New York, 1972) speaks of a legacy of Puritan "tribalism" as a defense against "unstable pluralism" in American life.

28. See Phyllis Greenacre, "The Family Romance of the Artist" (1968), reprinted in her collected essays, *Emotional Growth,* vol. 2 (New York,

1971), pp. 503–528. The classic texts connecting anality to cultural experience are Erik Erikson, *Young Man Luther: A Study in Psychoanalysis and History* (New York, 1958), and Norman O. Brown, *Life Against Death: The Psychoanalytic Meaning of History* (Middletown, Conn., 1959). A useful critique of Brown is in chapter two of Frederick Crews, *Out of My System: Psychoanalysis, Ideology, and Critical Method* (New York, 1975); the last chapter is a critique of psychoanalytic reductionism. Michael Paul Rogin, *Fathers & Children: Andrew Jackson and the Subjugation of the American Indian* (New York, 1975), applies theories about anality and pre-Oedipal dynamics to social behavior in Jacksonian America, and Norman N. Holland's *The Dynamics of Literary Response* (New York, 1968), pp. 31–48, usefully though reductively summarizes the stages of growth and gives literary applications.

29. Demos, *A Little Commonwealth;* R. V. Schnucker, "The English Puritans and Pregnancy, Delivery and Breast Feeding," *History of Childhood Quarterly,* 1 (Spring 1974), pp. 637–658.

30. Cotton Mather, *Magnalia Christi Americana* (Hartford, 1855, 1st ed. 1702), vol. 1, p. 522. Most descriptions of Puritan child rearing have stressed discipline and depravity. See Sanford Fleming, *Children & Puritanism* (New Haven, 1933), and Bernard Wishy's more balanced *The Child and the Republic: The Dawn of Modern American Child Nurture* (Philadelphia, 1968). Joseph E. Illick, "Child-Rearing in Seventeenth-Century America," in *The History of Childhood,* ed. Lloyd deMause (New York, 1974), pp. 303–350, asserts that Puritan child-rearing practices express parental goals of self-control, projected onto children as willfulness. Greven's *Protestant Temperament,* while stressing issues of discipline and control, usefully emphasizes Puritan ambivalence to childhood rather than Puritan theories of depravity. See also Bogna W. Lorence, "Parents and Children in Eighteenth-Century Europe," *History of Childhood Quarterly,* 2 (Summer 1974), pp. 1–30, which characterizes upper-class parents as "indifferent" and middle-class parents as "intrusive," even terrorizing; Steven R. Smith, "Religion and the Conception of Youth in Seventeenth-Century England," *History of Childhood Quarterly* 2 (Spring 1975), pp. 493–516; Ross W. Beales, Jr., "In Search of the Historical Child: Miniature Adulthood and Youth in Colonial New England," *American Quarterly,* 27 (October 1975), pp. 379–398); and John Demos, "Developmental Perspectives on the History of Childhood," *The Family in History: Interdisciplinary Essays,* ed. Theodore K. Rabb and Robert I. Rotberg (New York, 1973, 1st pub. 1971), pp. 127–140.

31. Robinson, *Works* (1851), quoted by John Demos in "Demography and Psychology in the Historical Study of Family Life: A Personal Report," in *Household and Family in Past Time,* ed. Peter Laslett (Cambridge, 1972), p. 566.

32. Cotton Mather, *A Family Well-Ordered* (Boston, 1699), pp. 35–36, 20.

33. See Beales, "In Search of the Historical Child," and especially Edmund Morgan, *The Puritan Family: Religion & Domestic Relations in Seventeenth-Century New England*, rev. ed. (New York, 1966, 1st ed. 1944). On farming out children to other families, see also Stone, *Family, Sex and Marriage*, pp. 108–109. Greven, *Protestant Temperament*, pp. 45–46, makes too much of little boys wearing female clothing.

34. Elliott, *Power in the Pulpit*, p. 74, quotes the Italian observer more fully; cf. Ivy Pinchbeck and Margaret Hewitt, *Children in English Society*, vol. 1 (n. p., 1969), pp. 25–26.

35. There are almost no accounts of Puritan lives from female or children's points of view, and very few of anyone's childhood. Puritan biographies and autobiographies focus primarily on the "conversion experience" that lifted individuals from sin to significance. See Cecelia Tichi, "Spiritual Biography and the 'Lords Remembrancers,'" *William and Mary Quarterly*, 28 (January 1971), pp. 64–85, reprinted in *The American Puritan Imagination: Essays in Revaluation*, ed. Sacvan Bercovitch (London, 1974), pp. 56–73.

36. See Holland, *Dynamics of Literary Response*, and his more recent *Poems in Persons* (New York, 1973) and *Five Readers Reading* (New Haven, 1975); also Bleich, "Pedagogical Directions in Subjective Criticism," *College English*, 37 (January 1976), pp. 454–467, and *Subjective Criticism* (Baltimore and London, 1978).

37. The basic history of New England ministers and sermons is David Hall's *The Faithful Shepherd: A History of the New England Ministry in the Seventeenth Century* (Chapel Hill, 1972).

38. Thomas, *Religion and the Decline of Magic*, pp. 163–164.

39. Quoted by Elliott, *Power in the Pulpit*, p. 55.

40. See Spector, *Aesthetics of Freud*, and Erikson's classic study of Freud's dream of Irma's injection, "The Dream Specimen of Psychoanalysis," *Journal of the American Psychoanalytic Association*, 2 (1954), pp. 5–56. I am avoiding Jung here. Although Jung was overtly more sensitive to literature and form than Freud was, his theories ultimately lead to diffused and static archetypal grandiosities, his own Family Romance, rather than to a sense of specific contexts and conflicts.

41. Chilton Latham Powell, *English Domestic Relations 1487–1653* (New York, 1917), p. 128.

42. See Darrett Rutman, *Winthrop's Boston* (Chapel Hill, 1965), and Stephen Foster, *Their Solitary Way: The Puritan Social Ethic in the First Century of Settlement in New England* (New Haven, 1971), for accounts of Puritan contradictions. A recent history of disunity in Connecticut is Paul R. Lucas, *Valley of Discord: Church and Society along the Connecticut River, 1636–1725* (Hanover, N.H., 1976). The most notable advocate of intellectual consensus, after Perry Miller, is Sacvan Bercovitch in *The Puritan Origins of the American Self* (New Haven and London, 1975).

43. Ludwig Lewisohn, in *Expression in America* (New York, 1932), used Freud as a club to belabor Puritanism's influence. He and H. L. Mencken helped set the equation of Puritanism with repressiveness in popular thinking.

44. Recent studies arguing that Puritans internalized authority are Walzer, *Revolution of the Saints* and Larzer Ziff, *Puritanism in America: New Culture in a New World* (New York, 1973). The literature on the Protestant ethic is enormous. The Weber-Tawney thesis has been much criticized for slighting Puritan continuities with Anglican and even medieval practices; see George H. and Katherine George, *The Protestant Mind of the English Reformation 1570–1640* (Princeton, 1961). For an acerbic sociological critique of the Georges, see David Little's *Religion, Order, and Law: A Study in Pre-Revolutionary England* (New York, 1969), which offers a sophisticated defense of Weber. Little overemphasizes the urban and democratic aspects of Puritanism, but he is right to stress the difference between voluntary and involuntary obedience and the consequent ambivalences required of the Puritan. See also Edmund Morgan, "The Puritan Ethic and the American Revolution," *William and Mary Quarterly*, 24 (January 1967), pp. 3–43, which focuses on the idea of the calling, and Robert S. Michaelsen, "Changes in the Puritan Concept of Calling or Vocation," *New England Quarterly*, 26 (September 1953), pp. 315–336. See Hill's *Society and Puritanism* for a discussion of Puritan views on idleness. Stephen Foster's *Their Solitary Way* is a lively study of Puritanism as a reactionary social ideology which subverted itself in every way toward guiltless capitalism. Knappen's *Tudor Puritanism* finds an "exceedingly indirect" relationship with capitalism, at best a "negative" destruction of old traditions (p. 422).

45. On conflicts with neighbors as a partial explanation of witchcraft accusations, see Thomas, *Religion and the Decline of Magic*, and Paul Boyer and Stephen Nissenbaum, *Salem Possessed: The Social Origins of Witchcraft* (Cambridge, Mass., 1974), who place the witchcraft episode in the context of a transition from a peasant economy to mercantile capitalism. A complementary analysis of witchcraft in England is A. D. J. Macfarlane, *Witchcraft in Tudor and Stuart England: A Regional and Comparative Study* (London, 1970), especially pp. 205–206, on the tensions between individual upward mobility and the decline of informal neighborly institutions. Norman Cohn sees that "peasant" level of conflict coexisting with demonological fears among the European intelligentsia, in *Europe's Inner Demons: An Enquiry Inspired by the Great Witch-Hunt* (London, 1975). A more psychoanalytic study is John Demos, "Underlying Themes in the Witchcraft of Seventeenth-Century New England," *American Historical Review*, 75 (June 1970), pp. 1,311–1,326. Frederick C. Drake counteracts the usual focus on Salem by citing several earlier instances in his "Witchcraft in the American

Colonies, 1647–1662," *American Quarterly*, 20 (Winter 1968), pp. 694–725.

46. See Leo F. Solt's critique of Christopher Hill in "Puritanism, Capitalism, Democracy, and the New Science," *American Historical Review*, 78 (October 1967), pp. 18–29, and Kai Erikson, *Wayward Puritans: A Study in the Sociology of Deviance* (New York, 1966), p. 50.

47. For William Carlos Williams's apt phrase, see his chapter on "Voyage of the Mayflower," *In the American Grain* (New York, 1925).

48. See Holland, *Dynamics of Literary Response*, and Simon O. Lesser, *Fiction and the Unconscious* (New York, 1957). Holland is no longer working with this model but rather with "identity themes," a concept derived from Heinz Lichtenstein that allows him to discuss individual styles without referring to repression. See his "UNITY IDENTITY TEXT SELF," *PMLA*, 90 (1975), pp. 813–822. Edward W. Said, in *Beginnings: Intention and Method* (New York, 1975), sympathetically criticizes the structuralist tendency to avoid repressive aspects of language and civilization in favor of a search for order and category in language alone (pp. 282–346).

49. Michael McGiffert, "American Puritan Studies in the 1960's," *William and Mary Quarterly*, 27 (January 1970), pp. 36–67, called for a "new paradigm" focusing on emotions in the same way that previous Puritan historians had focused on intellectual aspects.

50. See Robert G. Pope, "New England versus the New England Mind: The Myth of Declension," *Journal of Social History*, 3 (Winter 1969), pp. 95–108.

51. Quoted by Morgan, *Puritan Family*, p. 164, from *A Brief Exposition with Practical Observations upon the Whole Book of Canticles* (London, 1655), p. 209. Elsewhere Cotton cautions against taking such comparisons too literally, e.g., *Christ the Fountaine of Life* (London, 1651), pp. 137–138, where he cautions against thinking we can eat Christ "goblet by goblet."

52. I take the idea of literature as mirror from Donald W. Winnicott, "The Mother as Mirror," in *The Predicament of the Family*, ed. P. Lomas (London, 1968); also Winnicott's *The Maturational Processes and the Facilitating Environment* (London, 1965), or *The Family and Individual Development* (New York, 1965). In *Playing and Reality* (London, 1971), which reprints "Mirror-role" (pp. 111–118), Winnicott also develops a theory of "transitional objects," with playing as an intermediate area between psychic reality and shared reality. Art and religion, he says (p. 13), provide that intermediate area for adults.

Chapter One

1. M. M. Knappen, *Tudor Puritanism: A Chapter in the History of Idealism* (Chicago, 1939), p. 440. See E. K. Chambers, *The Elizabethan Stage*,

4 vols. (Oxford, 1923), vol. 1, p. 255; M. C. Bradbrook, *The Rise of the Common Player: A Study of Actor and Society in Shakespeare's England* (Cambridge, Mass., 1962); Louis B. Wright, *Middle-Class Culture in Elizabethan England* (Ithaca, 1958, 1st pub. 1935), pp. 603–654; and especially Elbert N. S. Thompson, *The Controversy between the Puritans and the Stage* (New York, 1903).

2. Horton Davies, *Worship and Theology in England From Cranmer to Hooker 1534–1603* (Princeton, 1970), p. 318. In *The War Against Poetry* (Princeton, 1970), Russell Fraser criticizes those who say Puritan attacks against the stage were only social. Lawrence A. Sasek, in *The Literary Temper of the English Puritans* (Baton Rouge, 1961), also emphasizes the Puritans' moral critique of drama and dramatic conventions.

3. See Fraser, *War Against Poetry*, and Christopher Hill, *Society and Puritanism in Pre-Revolutionary England* (New York, 1964). See Winton U. Solberg, *Redeem the Time: The Puritan Sabbath in Early America* (Cambridge, Mass. and London, 1977), pp. 46–56, for an explanation of Puritan hostility to ritual, especially drama: "Traditional customs appealed to man's physical nature and touched the irrational and unconscious side of his being" (p. 48).

4. Cited by Hugh Martin in *Puritanism and Richard Baxter* (London, 1954), p. 95.

5. Excerpted in H. C. Porter, *Puritanism in Tudor England* (London, 1970), p. 124. Patrick Collinson gives an account of Field's central role for Elizabethan Puritanism in *The Elizabethan Puritan Movement* (Berkeley, 1967). Porter notes as an irony of Field's life (p. 120) that one of his seven children was later kidnapped and became a boy player in the Burbage company, where he grew up to be a playwright.

6. William Perkins, posthumously published in 1613; reprinted by Everett Emerson in *English Puritanism from John Hooper to John Milton* (Durham, 1968), pp. 157–161.

7. Martin, *Puritanism and Richard Baxter*, p. 92.

8. Cited by Fraser, *War Against Poetry*, p. 9.

9. Dod and Cle[a]ver, *A Godlye Form of Household Government* (London, 1621, 1st ed. 1614), section E 4. For Fenner, see Fraser, *War Against Poetry*, pp. 18, 10. See also William Rankins, *The Mirrour of Monsters: wherein is described the vices caused by sight of playes* (London, 1587).

10. Cited by Hill, *Society and Puritanism*, pp. 508–509. Collier led the Puritans to victory over the stage in Parliament.

11. Stephen Gosson, *The School of Abuse* . . . (1579), ed. Edward Arber (London, 1869), p. 24. Gosson's first version finds some plays tolerable, including "a pig of mine owne Sowe," and cites classical authorities rather than the Bible. His much harsher 1582 version cites biblical reasons, and by the late 1590s he was a parson. Fraser, *War Against Poetry*, pp. 72–74, suggests he was bought by city authorities. Cf. Thompson, *Controversy*, pp. 76–79. The quotation from Richard Rogers

is in his *Practice of Christianitie* (1618), p. 404; from Edmund Rudierde, in his *The Thunderbolt of Gods Wrath* (1618). Both are cited in Fraser, *War Against Poetry*, pp. 116, 23–24.

12. Cited by Owen C. Watkins, *The Puritan Experience* (London, 1972), p. 1.

13. Saint Augustine, *The City of God*, trans. John Healey (1610, rev. 1620), ed. R. V. G. Tasker, (London, 1945), vol. 1; book 1, ch. 31 ("delicate vanity"); book 2, ch. 28 ("holy doctrine of God's word"); book 2, ch. 14 ("figments of their own lusts"). Rome was sacked by the Goths in 410 A.D., and *The City of God*, written by St. Augustine in Carthage, appeared in 426 as a response to the question of God's intention (see book 1, ch. 31).

14. Philip Stubbes, *Anatomie of Abuses* (1583), edited by F. J. Furnivall (London, 1879). See especially pp. 140–146.

15. Ibid., pp. 169 ("Devils brest"), 144 ("marke the flocking").

16. Furnivall's introduction to Stubbes's *Anatomie* reprints Nashe's response, "Almond for a Parrat" (1589), p. 36.

17. Ibid., pp. 38–39.

18. John Rainolds, *The Overthrow of Stage-Playes* (Oxford, 1629, 1st ed. 1599), printer's preface.

19. Ibid., pp. 4, 10–11, 14–15 ("apparell"), 104, 108ff.

20. Thompson, *Controversy*, p. 162. Prynne's biographer is William M. Lamont, *Marginal Prynne 1600–1669* (London and Toronto, 1963), quotation p. 1; also William Haller, *The Rise of Puritanism* (New York, 1938), p. 219 ("pathological"), and pp. 218–225; Martin, *Puritanism and Baxter*, p. 91 ("extremist"); George H. and Katherine George, *The Protestant Mind of the English Reformation 1570–1640* (Princeton, 1961), p. 141 ("paranoid"). See also Fraser, *War Against Poetry*, p. 168.

21. Lamont, *Marginal Prynne*, pp. 13, 32, quotation p. 228.

22. Prynne, *Histrio-mastix* . . . (London, 1633), p. 171. The text also italicizes "we . . . affords?"

23. This list is "m" and "n" of a much longer list.

24. *Histrio-mastix*, dedication and pp. 190, 193, 201, 210–211.

25. Ibid., pp. 546–547. (The pagination is confused in the middle; pp. 514–567 is Folio, with every other page numbered. Regular pagination begins again at p. 545.)

26. Ibid., p. 7. On pomp and vanity, see p. 47.

27. Ibid., pp. 374–375.

28. See Natalie Zemon Davis, *Society and Culture in Early Modern France* (London, 1975), especially ch. 5. She sees sexual inversion as a form of cultural play, encouraging social protest as well as symbolizing social disorder.

29. See Christopher Haigh, *Reformation and Resistance in Tudor Lancashire* (Cambridge, 1975); R. C. Richardson, *Puritanism in North-west England: A Regional Study of the Diocese of Chester to 1642* (Manchester,

1972); Roger B. Manning, *Religion and Society in Elizabethan Sussex: A Study of the Enforcement of the Religious Settlement 1558–1603* (Leicester, 1969).

30. See Keith Thomas's *Religion and the Decline of Magic* (New York, 1971), and Alan Macfarlane's *Witchcraft in Tudor and Stuart England: A Regional and Comparative Study* (London, 1970); also C. L. Barber's *Shakespeare's Festive Comedy: A Study of Dramatic Form and Its Relation to Social Custom* (Princeton, 1959), which speaks of the opposition between older village traditions and the "anxious" centers of change. Jonas Barish, in his essay "Exhibitionism and the Anti-Theatrical Prejudice," *English Literary History*, 36 (1969), pp. 1–29, and especially in his *Ben Jonson and the Language of Prose Comedy* (Cambridge, Mass., 1967), pp. 197–204, observes that Puritan preachers united with city officials to impose on the stage a new, constricted language with morality as its theme and repetition as its style. L. C. Knight's *Drama and Society in the Age of Jonson* (London, 1937), is an impassioned, romantic analysis of Elizabethan and Jacobean drama as village folk language being threatened by anomic, impersonal new forces.

31. See Collinson, *Elizabethan Puritan Movement*, and Perry Miller's *Orthodoxy in Massachusetts 1630–1650: A Genetic Study* (Cambridge, Mass., 1933).

32. Collinson describes several flagrant attacks on the queen by members of Parliament in the 1570s. Though Fraser in *War Against Poetry* interprets the Puritan attacks on the stage as a covert attack by the city against the throne, most of his evidence comes from tracts hostile to Puritanism. It was not authority as such that Puritans questioned, but *impure* authority. Prynne, for example, was clearly a snob, and both Rainolds and Stubbes took care to distinguish "honorable" people from "the ruder sort." See Sasek, *Literary Temper*, p. 121.

33. Collinson, *Elizabethan Puritan Movement;* Robert G. Pope, *The Half-Way Covenant: Church Membership in Puritan New England* (Princeton, 1969).

34. John Milton, "On the new forcers of conscience under the Long Parliament," 1647. The poem is, among other things, an attack on William Prynne. In psychoanalytic terms, polarization is one of the most accessible defenses against incompatible feelings about the same object.

35. Samuel Willard, *A Compleat Body of Divinity* . . . (Boston, 1726), p. 37.

36. Cited by George H. and Katherine George, *Protestant Mind*, pp. 338–339.

37. Haller, *Rise of Puritanism*, pp. 142, 223.

38. Kenneth Burke, *Attitudes toward History*, 2nd ed. (Boston, 1959), p. 24; Hill, *Society and Puritanism*, pp. 463–465. Cf. Paul Delany's excellent Marxist analysis of Shakespeare's ambivalent sympathy for aristocratic values at bay, *"King Lear* and the Decline of Feudalism," *PMLA*, 92 (May 1977), pp. 429–440.

39. See Michael Goldman, *Shakespeare and the Energies of Drama* (Princeton, 1972). Goldman stresses the self-consciousness of the play, the nagging pulse of irritation sounding throughout, and the theme of strangeness. Several other critics have commented on the ambiguity of "won-d'red father" (IV,i). It may be a final irony that stage plays were prohibited in Stratford itself, a center of Puritanism since Cartwright had preached there, in 1602. Emerson, *English Puritanism*, p. 260.

Chapter Two

1. See Russell Fraser, *The War against Poetry* (Princeton, 1970), p. 91, citing Peter Ramsey's *Tudor Economic Problems* (London, 1963); on Elizabethan conflicts and changes, see Patrick McGrath, *Papists and Puritans Under Elizabeth I* (London, 1967), and William P. Haugaard, *Elizabeth and the English Reformation: The Struggle for a Stable Settlement of Religion* (Cambridge, 1968), which analyzes the 1563 Convocation in detail. McGrath sees Puritans basically as controversialists, fearing the modern and disliking the status quo. Unlike most scholars, he finds Puritan influence relatively weak among townsmen and the urban classes, at least in the mid-sixteenth century (p. 384).

2. Carl Bridenbaugh, *Vexed and Troubled Englishmen 1590–1642* (New York, 1968), p. 396. See Emery Battis, *Saints and Sectaries: Anne Hutchinson and the Antinomian Controversy in the Massachusetts Bay Colony* (Chapel Hill, 1962), for a detailed analysis of the migration, and especially T. H. Breen and Stephen Foster, "Moving to the New World: The Character of Early Massachusetts Immigration," *William and Mary Quarterly*, 30 (April 1973), pp. 189–222. Breen and Foster note the equal balance of men and women, the preponderance of "relatively small nuclear families," the absence of the poor, and the probability of some congruence between disgruntled urban tradesmen and disgruntled Puritans, at least for the emigration in 1637.

3. Richard Baxter, *Reliquiae Baxterianae* (London, 1696), p. 30; written in 1683. See Mildred Campbell, "Social Origins of Some Early Americans," in *Seventeenth Century America*, ed. James M. Smith (Chapel Hill, 1959), pp. 63–89; also George Homans, "The Puritans and the Clothing Industry," *New England Quarterly*, 13 (1940), pp. 519–529.

4. See Christopher Haigh, *Reformation and Resistance in Tudor Lancashire* (Cambridge, 1975), and R. C. Richardson, *Puritanism in Northwest England: A Regional Study of the Diocese of Chester to 1642* (Manchester, 1972).

5. A fascinating study of instability and crisis in the cloth trade is B. E. Supple's *Commercial Crisis and Change in England 1600–1642: A Study in the Instability of a Mercantile Economy* (Cambridge, 1959). Supple is especially acute on governmental shortsightedness and the drastic

effects of foreign currency manipulations, though no one connected depressions to foreign currency or to governmental intervention against industrialization and diversification.

6. Francis J. Bremer, *The Puritan Experiment: New England Society from Bradford to Edwards* (New York, 1976), pp. 18–19; his source is the Short-Title Catalogue.

7. M. M. Knappen, *Tudor Puritanism; A Chapter in the History of Idealism* (Chicago, 1939), p. 353; cf. Battis, *Saints and Sectaries*, pp. 255 ff., and Breen and Foster, "Moving to the New World."

8. David Hall, *The Faithful Shepherd: A History of the New England Ministry in the Seventeenth Century* (Chapel Hill, 1972), p. 68. Cf. H. C. Porter, *Puritanism in Tudor England* (London, 1970), which focuses on the more antiauthoritarian and separatist writers.

9. Breen and Foster, "Moving to the New World," p. 214.

10. Dod and Cle[a]ver, *A Godlye Form of Household Government* (London, 1621, 1st ed. 1614), section F 4.

11. William Bradshaw, *English Puritanisme Containing The maine opinions of the rigidest sort of those that are called Puritanes In the Realme of England* (London, 1605), p. 10.

12. See Natalie Zemon Davis, *Society and Culture in Early Modern France* (London, 1975), ch. 1, for the high incidence of aggressive Protestantism among skilled young craftsmen in untraditional trades in Lyon. Mildred Campbell's *The English Yeoman under Elizabeth and the Early Stuarts* (London, 1967, 1st ed. 1942), also emphasizes the Elizabethan yeomen's tendency to be Puritan (p. 292) and to be ambitious, aggressive capitalists rather than peasants (pp. 103–104). On the other hand, see Daniel Walker Howe, "The Decline of Calvinism: An Approach to its Study," *Comparative Studies in Society and History*, 14 (June 1972), pp. 306–327, for connections between Calvinism and anxiety.

13. Paul S. Seaver, *The Puritan Lectureships: The Politics of Religious Dissent 1590–1662* (Stanford, 1970); also Patrick Collinson, *The Elizabethan Puritan Movement* (Berkeley, 1967), especially on the Society of Feofees.

14. T. Jackson, *A Treatise containing the Originall of Unbeliefe* (1625), quoted by Keith Thomas, *Religion and the Decline of Magic* (New York, 1971), p. 664.

15. Quoted by Collinson, *Elizabethan Puritan Movement*, p. 79.

16. On aristocratic ambition, see Anthony Esler, *The Aspiring Mind of the Elizabethan Younger Generation* (Durham, 1966).

17. Quoted by George H. and Katherine George, *The Protestant Mind of the English Reformation 1570–1640* (Princeton, 1961), p. 292.

18. Roger B. Manning, *Religion and Society in Sussex: A Study of the Enforcement of the Religious Settlement 1558–1603* (Leicester, 1969), p. xi.

19. Everett Emerson, *English Puritanism from John Hooper to John Milton* (Durham, 1968), pp. 56, 63.

20. Field, 1570s, quoted by Collinson, *Elizabethan Puritan Movement*, p. 107. Wentworth is cited by Porter, *Puritanism in Tudor England*, p. 153. After thirty-one days Wentworth returned to Parliament. In 1573 a Puritan tried to kill Sir Christopher Hatton for being a covert Catholic, but wounded Sir John Hawkins instead (Emerson, *English Puritanism*, p. 20). The queen's speech is cited by Collinson, p. 20.

21. Porter, *Puritanism in Tudor England*, pp. 85–88. (The dialogue, held in June 1567, was printed in 1593.)

22. Collinson, *Elizabethan Puritan Movement*, p. 196.

23. Ward, *The Simple Cobbler of Aggawam in America* (1647), excerpted in *The Puritans: a Sourcebook of Their Writings*, ed. Perry Miller and Thomas H. Johnson, rev. ed. (New York, 1963), vol. 1, p. 229. Shepard, *The Sincere Convert* (London, 1664), p. 7.

24. Cited by Manning, *Religion and Society in Sussex*, p. 166.

25. Collinson, *Elizabethan Puritan Movement*, pp. 94–97. Knappen is wrong to say that "when laymen definitely secured the upper hand, Puritanism soon ceased to be Puritanism" (*Tudor Puritanism*, p. 353). That process consistently renewed the Puritan impulse for 200 years.

26. Winthrop's Journal (1639), quoted by Perry Miller, *Orthodoxy in Massachusetts 1630–1650: A Genetic Study* (Cambridge, Mass., 1933), pp. 217–218; Willard, *A Compleat Body of Divinity . . .* (Boston, 1726), p. 181.

27. On connections between radical Puritans and Quakers, see Geoffrey F. Nuttall, *The Holy Spirit in Puritan Faith and Experience* (Oxford, 1947), who says Quakers made the Spirit, not the Word, primary authority (p. 20); cf. Jackson I. Cope, "Seventeenth-Century Quaker Style," *PMLA*, 71 (September 1956), pp. 725–754, for a detailed analysis of Quaker stylistics, which are intensely personal without a sense of order or group. Larzer Ziff, *The Career of John Cotton: Puritanism and the American Experience* (Princeton, 1962), especially pp. 140, 164, describes Cotton's intellectual struggle against his antinomian tendencies.

28. *Diaries of Oliver Heywood*, ed. J. H. Turner (Brighouse, England, 1883), vol. 1, p. 23.

29. See Esler, *Aspiring Mind*; Joan Thirsk, "Younger Sons in the Seventeenth Century," *History*, 54 (October 1969), pp. 358–377; also Robert Brenner, "The Social Basis of England's Commercial Expansion, 1550–1650," *Journal of Economic History*, 32 (March 1972), pp. 361–384.

30. Quoted by the Rev. A. F. Scott Pearson, *Thomas Cartwright and Elizabethan Puritanism 1535–1603* (Cambridge, 1925), p. 3.

31. See Gordon J. Schochet, *Patriarchalism in Political Thought: The Authoritarian Family and Political Speculation and Attitudes Especially in Seventeenth-Century England* (New York, 1975), who argues that patriarchal theories of the state, notably Robert Filmer's, brought long-standing assumptions to consciousness in response to threats from new

contractualist theories, though the patriarchal response assumed a unity of state and society in a society that was rapidly splitting into separate spheres (pp. 55–57). Cf. Schochet's earlier essay, "Patriarchalism, Politics and Mass Attitudes in Stuart England," *The Historical Journal,* 12 (1969), pp. 413–441; also Lawrence Stone, *The Family, Sex and Marriage in England 1500–1800* (London, 1977), pp. 151–218. Various writers on psychoanalysis, notably David Bakan in *The Duality of Human Existence* (Chicago, 1966), pp. 205–230, have suggested revising Freudian theory to include the father's ambivalent attitudes toward the son.

32. Norton, *Abel Being Dead yet speaketh* (London, 1658), pp. 10–11; Ziff, *Career of John Cotton,* pp. 22–23. Cotton Mather's *Magnalia Christi Americana* (Hartford, 1855, 1st ed. 1702), vol. 1, p. 253, says Cotton's father Roland was a reconciler, "preferring the *consolations* of a *peacemaker,* before all the *fees* that he might have got by blowing up of *differences.*" Mather also mentions that Roland Cotton examined himself every night to discern any bad deeds committed during the day. Of Cotton's mother, Mather says only that she was "pious." Mather also says (p. 254) that some found in John Cotton's early "eminency" the reason why his father's clients were "more than a little multiplied."

33. Neal, *The History of New-England* . . . (London, 1720), vol. 1, p. 288; Ziff, *Career of John Cotton,* pp. 63–64, 75, 78–79. Cotton's letter to the bishop is reprinted in Alexander Young's *Chronicles of The First Planters of The Colony of Massachusetts Bay, from 1623 to 1636* (Boston, 1846), pp. 434–437. See also Hall, *Faithful Shepherd.*

34. See Ziff, *Career of John Cotton.* Jesper Rosenmeier, "The Teacher and the Witness: John Cotton and Roger Williams," *William and Mary Quarterly,* 25 (July 1968), pp. 408–431, says that the real issue was Williams's sense of redemption beyond this world as opposed to Cotton's unwillingness to separate spirit from flesh in interpreting Christ's incarnation. Sacvan Bercovitch places these differences in the context of allegorical typology (Williams) versus historically continuous typology (Cotton) in "Typology in Puritan New England: The Williams-Cotton Controversy Reassessed," *American Quarterly,* 19 (Summer 1967), pp. 166–191.

35. Shepard's autobiography is reprinted in *God's Plot; The Paradoxes of Puritan Piety, Being the Autobiography & Journal of Thomas Shepard,* ed. Michael McGiffert ([Amherst], 1972) pp. 33–71, with marginalia pp. 72–74, quotations p. 37.

36. McGiffert, *God's Plot,* introduction, pp. 3–4, quotations pp. 38–39.

37. A note in Shepard's manuscript of the autobiography; *God's Plot,* p. 72.

38. Ibid., pp. 144, 158. Cf. McGiffert's introduction, pp. 26, 7. For discussion of Cotton's and Shepard's sermon styles, see chapter 6.

39. Winthrop is cited by McGiffert, *God's Plot,* p. 8; Shepard by Hall, *Faithful Shepherd,* p. 164 (from *The Sound Believer*).

40. *God's Plot,* p. 52; McGiffert's introduction, pp. 18–19.
41. Ibid., pp. 98, 135–136, 137.
42. Ibid., pp. 70–71.
43. Ibid., pp. 33–36, 57–63.
44. Ibid., McGiffert's introduction, p. 5.
45. Alan Macfarlane, *The Family Life of Ralph Josselin, a Seventeenth-Century Clergyman: An Essay in Historical Anthropology* (Cambridge, 1970), pp. 7–16, quotation p. 16.
46. Ibid., p. 126.
47. Ibid., pp. 110–111 (Macfarlane), 116, 95 (daughter), 119–120 (Thomas), 118 (Macfarlane), 120–122 (John), 125 (dead child), 125 (Macfarlane). Cf. Lawrence Stone, *Family, Sex and Marriage,* pp. 178–193, on the decrease in parental control over children's marriages in the seventeenth century, especially in the lower classes.
48. Macfarlane, *Josselin,* pp. 169, 176, 170.
49. The laments of Cotton Mather and Samuel Danforth are excerpted by Robert H. Bremner in *Children and Youth in America: A Documentary History,* ed. Bremner, vol. 1:1600–1865 (Cambridge, Mass., 1970), pp. 46–49. Danforth is cited here from Mather's *Magnalia,* vol. 2, p. 65.
50. Bremner, *Children and Youth,* p. 48; the diary entry is Nov. 22, 1713.
51. Ibid., p. 111.
52. *Diaries of Oliver Heywood,* ed. Turner, vol. 1, pp. 157–159, 19–20. The next quotations are taken from vol. 1, pp. 20–32.
53. Ibid., pp. 30–31, also pp. 84–87, 295, 319–324. The Event Book is repeated in vol. 3, pp. 150–152.
54. Ibid., vol. 1, pp. 32, 81–82.
55. Ibid., pp. 316–318.
56. Ibid., pp. 341–342.
57. Ibid., pp. 319–325, 340.
58. Ibid., pp. 169–170, 295–298, 57; see also pp. 232, 237 on "my father Angier."
59. Ibid., vol. 3, pp. 297, 300–301, 224.
60. Robert C. Black III, *The Younger John Winthrop* (New York and London, 1966), pp. 3–18.
61. See Louise Thorn Golding, *An Elizabethan Puritan: Arthur Golding the Translator of Ovid's Metamorphoses and also of John Calvin's Sermons* (New York, 1937).
62. See Frank Shuffelton, *Thomas Hooker 1586–1647* (Princeton, 1977), p. 6; Martin, *Puritanism and Richard Baxter* (London, 1954), p. 12. Baxter converted at fifteen because of his father's example (p. 36).
63. On Preston, see Emerson, *English Puritanism,* p. 223; on Ames, see Keith L. Sprunger, *The Learned Doctor William Ames: Dutch Backgrounds of English and American Puritanism* (Urbana, 1972), p. 8. On Whitefield, see Philip Greven, *The Protestant Temperament: Patterns of*

Child-Rearing, Religious Experience, and the Self in Early America (New York, 1977), p. 24.

64. Cited by Emerson, *English Puritanism*, p. 102.

65. Raymond P. Stearns, *The Strenuous Puritan: Hugh Peter, 1598–1660* (Urbana, 1954), pp. 3, 9, 16, 438, viii, 128–129.

66. J. H. Adamson and H. F. Folland, *Sir Harry Vane: His Life and Times (1613–1662)* (n.p., 1974), pp. 147, 32, 50–52, 143, 333.

67. Battis, *Saints and Sectaries*, p. 9.

68. Cited in Ola Elizabeth Winslow, *Master Roger Williams: A Biography* (New York, 1957), p. 28. Williams's father was a minor London tailor, and Williams's life shows several Family Romance aspects, notably in his adolescent apprenticeship to Sir Edward Coke, who "was often pleased to call me son" (p. 49).

69. See Robert L. Moore, "Justification without Joy: Psychohistorical Reflections on John Wesley's Childhood and Conversion," *History of Childhood Quarterly*, 2 (Summer 1974), pp. 31–52. See Philip Greven, *The Protestant Temperament*, pp. 36–38 on Susanna Wesley's controlled, methodical bringing up of the founder of Methodism; p. 132 for Wesley's ambivalence toward his mother, and pp. 90–92 for Wesley's religious language of conversion; also Stone, *Family, Sex and Marriage*, pp. 467–468.

70. Baxter, cited by Joan Webber, *The Eloquent "I": Style and Self in 17th Century Prose* (Madison, 1968), p. 125. Baxter was, strictly speaking, not a Puritan but a nonconformist.

Chapter Three

1. On children as little adults, see Philippe Ariès, *Centuries of Childhood: A Social History of Family Life* (New York, 1962); for a critique of Ariès, showing the existence of youth as a separate stage before the eighteenth century, see Natalie Zemon Davis, *Society and Culture in Early Modern France* (London, 1975), e.g., p. 108. A helpful overview is John R. Gillis, *Youth and History: Tradition and Change in European Age Relations 1770-Present* (New York, 1974). Cleaver, *A Briefe Explanation of . . . the Proverbs of Salomon* (London, 1615), p. 92.

2. Ivy Pinchbeck and Margaret Hewitt, *Children in English Society*, vol. 1, (n.p., 1969), p. 267. See also Lawrence Stone, *The Family, Sex and Marriage in England 1500–1800* (London, 1977). Stone finds the Puritans more attentive in their patriarchy than the earlier mode, but more repressive (pp. 155, 158, 177, 217), a view I challenge. Stone's bias toward what he calls the autonomous individualism of the eighteenth-century aristocratic family leads him to denigrate almost any sense of group or intimate mutual expectations as constricting or

malicious; e.g., "The Elizabethan village was a place filled with malice and hatred, its only unifying bond being the occasional episode of mass hysteria" (p. 98), also pp. 99, 102. That Puritans wrote most of the child-rearing handbooks, despite the "enormous preponderance" of Anglicans, only proves that "Puritans were abnormally concerned about children and their upbringing" (p. 176). He sums up the Puritan family dynamic as "psychological coolness and physical severity" (p. 177), with "psychic numbing" at every stage (p. 101). For other references, see the introduction, note 30; for American child rearing, the bibliography in Philip Greven's *The Protestant Temperament: Patterns of Child-Rearing, Religious Experience, and the Self in Early America* (New York, 1977).

3. Stone, *Family, Sex and Marriage*, p. 27. Arthur W. Calhoun, *A Social History of the American Family* (Cleveland, 1917), vol. 1, p. 72, notes that New England deliberately used the family for welfare and correction.

4. Richard Greenham, "Of the good education of children," cited by Everett Emerson, *English Puritanism from John Hooper to John Milton* (Durham, 1968), pp. 152–153.

5. John Dod and Robert Cle[a]ver, *A Godlye Form of Household Government* (London, 1621, 1st ed. 1614), section S 4; William Gouge, *Of Domesticall Duties . . .* (London, 1622), reprinted in *The Works of William Gouge . . .* (London, 1626), vol. 1, p. 313. Chilton Latham Powell, in *English Domestic Relations 1487–1653* (New York, 1917), notes that these works of Gouge and Cleaver—who was the primary author of *Godlye Form*—went through many editions. *Godlye Form* was the longest family manual to date, with whole passages lifted from other works (pp. 132–133). Gouge went through twelve editions, ten after 1626.

6. Gouge, *Domesticall Duties*, pp. 90–91; Dod and Cleaver, *Godlye Form*, sections B 1 and D 1 – D 2. Many Puritan writers used the phrase "a little commonwealth"; *Godlye Form* begins, "An Houshold is as it were a little Commonwealth, by the good government whereof, Gods glorie may be advanced, and the commonwealth which standeth of severall families benefited." In part the Puritan emphasis on the importance of each little commonwealth was intended to diminish the greater commonwealth to its proper place.

7. Michael Walzer, *The Revolution of the Saints: A Study in the Origins of Radical Politics* (Cambridge, Mass., 1965); Stone, *Family, Sex and Marriage*; Greven, *Protestant Temperament*. Walzer oddly concludes that "fondness and maternal solicitude" were "aspects of repression" (p. 192). Stone makes nothing of the evidence for good mothering in the early years, even while citing it (pp. 160–168). Greven, while agreeing that the father was "more usually associated with authority and the mother with love" (p. 22), sees maternal love in the evangelical family

primarily as strict religious zeal. Roger Thompson, in *Women in Stuart England and America: A Comparative Study* (London, 1974), implies the reverse of my thesis by claiming that New England had more tender mothering and Old England had more repressive patriarchy, because in New England women were freer to follow their softer and softening nature (p. 157). Francis J. Bremer, in *The Puritan Experiment: New England Society from Bradford to Edwards* (New York, 1976), p. 179, at least notes that the Puritan family was first loving, then authoritarian. Edward Shorter, in *The Making of the Modern Family* (New York, 1975), dismisses premodern mothering entirely, as does Lloyd deMause in his lengthy introduction to *The History of Childhood*, ed. deMause (New York, 1974).

8. Gouge, *Domesticall Duties*, p. 296. Cf. Stone, *Family, Sex and Marriage*, pp. 426–432, on relaxed mothering in the first eighteen months; also R. V. Schnucker, "The English Puritans and Pregnancy, Delivery and Breast Feeding," *History of Childhood Quarterly*, 1 (Spring 1974), pp. 637–658.

9. Gouge, *Domesticall Duties*, pp. 286–289. Robert Pricke, in *The Doctrine of Superiority, and of Subjection, Contained in the Fift Commandement* . . . (London, 1609), waxes more eloquent on the function of nipples (section K): "To what end doeth the providence of God yeeld unto the woman two Pappes, as it were fountaines, and that in the most comely and fit place of her bodie? & besides that, filled them with most sweet and pretious liquor" if not to nourish her infant "& so set forth the glorie of God"?

10. Dod and Cleaver, *Godlye Form*, section P 3 – P 4; Gouge, *Domesticall Duties*, p. 290; Pricke, *Doctrine of Superiority*, section H 3. Stone mistakenly locates the Puritan emphasis on breast-feeding in his third stage of eighteenth-century affective Individualism (*Family, Sex and Marriage*, pp. 426–432, 730). See Samuel Willard, *A Compleat Body of Divinity* . . . (Boston, 1726), p. 602, for later New England advice urging tender mothering in the early years.

11. Gouge, *Domesticall Duties*, pp. 229, 291–292.

12. Stone, *Family, Sex and Marriage*, says that the infant's passage through the oral and anal stages was "probably relatively easy, with milk on demand, late weaning and late toilet training" (p. 160). However, he also stresses the negative effects of swaddling (which reduces the heartbeat and induces sleep by immobilizing the baby) and wet-nursing, which deprives the baby of the mother. Advice on toilet training does not appear until the very end of the seventeenth century; the culture as a whole was without hygiene (p. 160). See John Demos, *A Little Commonwealth: Family Life in Plymouth Colony* (New York and London, 1970), for a more positive view of mothering and swaddling.

13. Robert Cleaver, *A Briefe Explanation of the Whole Booke of the Proverbs of Salomon* (London, 1615), pp. 352–353 ("St. Paul"); Pricke, *Doc-*

trine of Superiority, section K ("wives head"); Gouge, *Domesticall Duties,* p. 302 (King, Priest, and Prophet); Dod and Cleaver, *Godlye Form,* section L 4 (long quotation); Robert Bolton, *The Works* (London, 1631–41), vol. 2, *Some General Directions for a Comfortable Walking with God . . .* (1st pub. London, 1638), p. 244 (heads); Pricke, *Doctrine of Superiority,* section I 3.

14. Dod and Cleaver, *Godlye Form,* section F 3 ("outward affaires"), section M 3 ("molestation" and "medling"); also sections D 4 to F 2 on husband's worldly duties and sections F 3 to F 4 on wife's household duties; Gouge, *Domesticall Duties,* pp. 168–169, on woman governing religious observances if man is "blockish."

15. Bolton, *Works,* vol. 2, p. 249 ("Priest and Pastour"); Dod and Cleaver, section D 4, both quotations.

16. Gouge, *Domesticall Duties,* p. 304 ("spirituall food" by "nurses and mothers"); Smith, *A Preparative to Mariage . . .* (London, 1591), p. 74; Pricke, *Doctrine of Superiority,* section H 2, on correction. Pricke's instructions add that we should not deal with the ignorant as with the knowing, nor with the "weake, and sickely" as with the strong, "nor with timerous and mild natures, as with those that are bold and stubborne."

17. Dod and Cleaver, *Godlye Form,* section T 4 ("apish"); Gouge, *Domesticall Duties,* p. 306.

18. *The Child-Bearers Cabinet* (London, 1652) cited by Joseph E. Illick, "Child-Rearing in Seventeenth-Century America," in *The History of Childhood,* ed. deMause, p. 311; Anne Bradstreet cited in Elizabeth Wade White, *Anne Bradstreet "The Tenth Muse"* (New York, 1971), p. 43; for modernized spelling, see Bradstreet's *Works,* ed. Jeannine Hensley (Cambridge, Mass., 1967), pp. 240–241; Gouge, *Domesticall Duties,* p. 297.

19. Lord Chesterfield's letter is excerpted in Pinchbeck and Hewitt, *Children in English Society,* vol. 1, p. 298. Aubrey is cited by Illick, "Child-Rearing," p. 312.

20. Gouge, *Domesticall Duties,* p. 313; Cleaver, *Briefe Explanation,* p. 153; Dod and Cleaver, *Godlye Form,* sections T 1 and D 4. Gouge, p. 313, finds excessive severity "the more unnaturall."

21. Gouge, *Domesticall Duties,* p. 307 ("mothers peculiar care," "governour," "home experience confirmeth"); Cleaver, *Briefe Explanation,* p. 68; Dod and Cleaver, *Godlye Form,* section K 4.

22. William Whately, cited by Emerson, *English Puritanism,* p. 274. Cf. David Stannard, "Death and the Puritan Child," *American Quarterly,* 26 (December 1974), pp. 456–476; also his "Death and Dying in Puritan New England," *American Historical Review,* 78 (December 1973), pp. 1,305–1,330, and Stannard's recent book, *The Puritan Way of Death: A Study in Religion, Culture, and Social Change* (New York, 1977). Though Stannard notes the relatively low infant mortality rates in New

England and the "genuine love" parents felt for children (*Puritan Way of Death*, pp. 51–56), he finds that discipline, "restraint and even aloofness" characterize the Puritan family in large part because of parental expectations that at least two children would die before the age of ten. He argues more from the logic of his assumptions than from child-rearing evidence. See Bremer, *Puritan Experiment*, p. 180, for relevant statistics.

23. Alice Judson Ryerson, "Medical Advice on Child Rearing, 1550–1900," *Harvard Educational Review*, 31 (Summer 1961), pp. 302–323, suggests a clear growth in repressivenesss in advice books after 1750. I am indebted for this reference to Nancy Goldberger.

24. Dod and Cleaver, *Godlye Form*, section S 4.

25. Bunyan's poem is cited in Stone, *Family, Sex and Marriage*, plate 13. It is from *Divine Emblems* (1686). Greven's *Protestant Temperament* also notes the change from obedient children to rebellious teen-agers (pp. 55–61), though he draws different conclusions.

26. See Natalie Zemon Davis, *Society and Culture in Early Modern France* (London, 1975), especially chs. 4 and 6.

27. On "good enough" mothering, see Winnicott, *Playing and Reality* (London, 1971), pp. 10, 13; also his radio talks to parents, collected as *The Child, the Family, and the Outside World* (New York, 1964), e.g., p. 25 on "mothers who are ordinarily good."

28. Cleaver, *Briefe Explanation*, p. 68; Pricke, *Doctrine of Superiority*, section B 3.

29. Pricke, *Doctrine of Superiority*, section K.

30. Cleaver, *Briefe Explanation*, pp. 205, 207–208; Cleaver italicizes "He that loveth . . . to him." On the other hand, Cleaver also says (pp. 360–361) that it is good to use the rod because a child's reason is "weake."

31. Gouge, *Domesticall Duties*, p. 298, also table of contents IV; Pricke, *Doctrine of Superiority*, section B.

32. Robinson cited by George H. and Katherine George, *The Protestant Mind of the English Reformation 1570–1640* (Princeton, 1961), p. 277; Dod and Cleaver, *Godlye Form*, sections F 4 to O 3; Gouge, *Domesticall Duties*, p. 74; Dod and Cleaver, *Godlye Form*, section L 4.

33. Dod and Cleaver, *Godlye Form*, section L 4; Gouge, *Domesticall Duties*, table of contents.

34. Dod and Cleaver, *Godlye Form*, section L 3; Smith, *Preparative to Mariage*, pp. 59, 58 (margin).

35. *John Cotton on the Churches of New England*, ed. Larzer Ziff (Cambridge, Mass., 1968), p. 330; published in 1648—long after Anne Hutchinson—as "The Way of Congregational Churches Cleared"; Hooker, *A survey of the summe of Church Discipline* . . . (London, 1648), part 3, p. 6.

36. On unrestrained women and restraint of Puritan women, see R. C.

Richardson, *Puritanism in North-west England: A Regional Study of the Diocese of Chester to 1642* (Manchester, 1972), pp. 105–110. Emerson's *English Puritanism* reprints Thomas Gataker's "A good wife Gods Gift," pub. 1624 (pp. 203 ff.); Gataker rails against contentious and disloyal wives. See also Davis, *Society and Culture in Early Modern France*, responding to Keith Thomas, "Women and the Civil War Sects," *Past and Present*, 13 (1958), reprinted in *Crisis in Europe 1560–1660: Essays from "Past and Present,"* ed. Trevor Aston (London, 1974), pp. 317–340; Davis finds (p. 82) that Protestant commitment "complemented in a new sphere the scope and independence that the women's lives had already had."

37. Bolton, *Works*, vol. 2, p. 254; Dod and Cleaver, *Godlye Form*, section L 3 – L 4.
38. Pricke, *Doctrine of Superiority*, section K; Bolton, *Works*, vol. 2, p. 245. By silently deleting Bolton's citation of Ambrose, Walzer misinterprets the thought as sexist when in fact Bolton is wrenching Ambrose into an argument for equality of men and women; see *Revolution of the Saints*, p. 193.
39. Bolton, *Works*, vol. 2, p. 246; Dod and Cleaver, *Godlye Form*, section I 4.
40. Gouge, *Domesticall Duties*, pp. 223–224, 224–226; Paul Baynes cited in Bremer, *Puritan Experiment*, p. 24; Gouge, pp. 43–44.
41. Richard Sibbes, *The Riches of Mercie* (1638), quoted in the Georges' *Protestant Mind*, p. 283.
42. Dod and Cleaver, *Godlye Form*, section K 4; Cotton Mather, *A Family Well-Ordered* (Boston, 1699), p. 41; Cleaver, *Briefe Explanation*, p. 153.
43. Cleaver, *Briefe Explanation*, p. 239; Dod and Cleaver, *Godlye Form*, section P 4; Gouge, *Domesticall Duties*, pp. 180–181.
44. Gouge, *Domesticall Duties*, Epistle Dedicatory to his "patrons," his parishioners. Gouge's life, which was compulsively ordered even by Puritan standards, is trenchantly sketched in the *Dictionary of National Biography*.
45. On mothers wielding the rod, see Cleaver, *Briefe Explanation*, p. 382. Cleaver elsewhere (*Godlye Form*, section D 4) makes the father the proper disciplinarian.
46. Cf. Philip Greven's *Protestant Temperament*, especially pp. 124–140 on "Brides of Christ: Femininity, Masculinity, and Sexuality." Greven takes the feminine imagery used by evangelical men simply as a denial of their sexuality, while I suggest other and more positive connections to good mothering.
47. Daniel Rogers, *Matrimoniall Honour: or, The mutuall Crowne and comfort of godly, loyall, and chaste Marriage* . . . (London, 1642), pp. 13, 47, 279 ("breasts"), 154, 279–280.
48. Ibid., pp. 89, 91–93.

49. Ibid., p. 299. Stone, *Family, Sex and Marriage*, pp. 167–178, mistakenly says this passage is plagiarized; cf. Levin L. Schüking, *The Puritan Family, a Social Study from the Literary Sources*, trans. Brian Battershaw, 2nd ed. (London, 1969, 1st pub. 1929), p. 75. Schüking elsewhere states that Rogers "displays the most penetrating understanding of the essential character of women" (p. 46), with unprecedented "respect" for women in *Matrimoniall Honour;* see pp. 19, 25–27, 35–36, 43–44, 53, and also 89 on the "negligible role of motherliness" and consequent superficiality in the Puritan family.

50. Rogers, *Matrimoniall Honour*, pp. 265, 304 ("good drudge," "good wife"), 278.

51. Ibid., pp. 266, 211–212, 221, 135 ("drudgery"), 162, 81.

52. The *Dictionary of National Biography* notes that Giles Firmin's *Real Christian* was written to counter Rogers's despondency. Rogers was the eldest son of the Elizabethan Puritan Richard Rogers.

53. Dod and Cleaver, *Godlye Form*, section M 2; Bolton, *Works*, vol. 1, p. 48; Rogers, *Matrimoniall Honour*, p. 178.

54. Rogers, *Matrimoniall Honour*, pp. 81, 251, 238, 242. On "cross," see pp. 81, 214–217, 274. Cf. Dod and Cleaver, *Godlye Form*, section L 4: "As the provision of household dependeth onely on the husband; even so the honour of all dependeth onely of the woman."

55. Rogers, *Matrimoniall Honour*, pp. 188–189.

56. Willard, *Compleat Body*, pp. 184–187 (April 19, 1692); also pp. 597–655 on the Fifth Commandment. Willard says "parents," not "father" or "mother," for duties at every stage, even the first (p. 602), where mothering is implicit. He rarely differentiates fathers from mothers and says of husband and wife (p. 609) that "of all the Orders which are unequals, these do come nearest to an Equality, and in several respects they stand upon even ground."

57. Rogers, *Matrimoniall Honour*, pp. 254–256, 281.

58. Thomas Cobbett, *A Fruitfull and Usefull Discourse* . . . (London, 1656), esp. pp. 96, 65, 225. Arthur Calhoun, in *A Social History of the American Family*, vol. 1, writes of the New England tendency toward "patriarchal clans" (p. 80), with fathers governing households of up to thirty people. As Cobbett said, "Children are to rise up and stand bare" in the presence of their parents; they must bow, speak reverently, subject themselves to "seasonable corrections, *Heb.* 12.9," etc. (pp. 89–91). Calhoun observes that proper New England children had to address their parents as "esteemed parent" or "honored sir and madam" (p. 111).

59. Bishop William Fleetwood, *Relative Duties* . . . (London, 1705), pp. 5, 7, 59–62, 86, 175, 292. Stone, in *Family, Sex and Marriage* (pp. 240–241), says Fleetwood "sets out the new doctrine" of reciprocal duties, though the Puritans had been advocating it for a hundred years.

60. On Becon's *Boke of Matrimony*, see Pinchbeck and Hewitt, *Children in English Society*, vol. 1, pp. 13–15. On continuities between the Puritan

domestic ideal and Catholic or medieval attitudes, see Knappen, *Tudor Puritanism,* pp. 451–455.

61. *Diaries of Oliver Heywood,* ed. J. H. Turner, (Brighouse, England, 1883), vol. 1, pp. 50–54. Cf. Roger Thompson, *Women in Stuart England and America,* p. 89.
62. Heywood, *Diaries,* vol. 1, pp. 46–50, 66.
63. Ibid., pp. 41–44, 160.
64. Ibid., pp. 58–61.
65. Ibid., pp. 209, 62–64.
66. Ibid., pp. 65–69, 176–177.
67. Ibid., pp. 65, 239. Cf. Jackson I. Cope, "Seventeenth-Century Quaker Style" PMLA, 71 (September 1956), pp. 725–754, who shows that the Quakers have no sense of physical location in their moments of strong emotion.
68. Cotton Mather, *Parentator . . .* (Boston, 1724), p. 3.
69. See B. R. Burg, *Richard Mather of Dorchester* (n.p., 1976), pp. x, 6–7, 18–19, 30–37, 64, 87, 112 on Richard's various failures and disappointments.
70. See Kenneth Murdock, *Increase Mather: The Foremost American Puritan* (Cambridge, Mass., 1926), pp. 39, 51; Cotton Mather, *Parentator,* pp. 3–11.
71. Robert Middlekauff, *The Mathers: Three Generations of Puritan Intellectuals, 1596–1728* (New York, 1971), pp. 93, 86; Murdock, *Increase Mather,* p. 96. Middlekauff states that Increase reverted to his father's opinion the year before Richard died, but Robert G. Pope, in *The Half-Way Covenant: Church Membership in Puritan New England* (Princeton, 1969), p. 51, says it was the year after, in 1670. Pope finds that Increase's opposition may have been a declaration of independence.
72. Middlekauff, *Mathers,* concludes too simply that Increase turned to his father in his conversion out of love.
73. Stone argues (*Family, Sex and Marriage,* pp. 15, 75–80, 159–161, 194) that the absence of oral trauma and anal training may make psychoanalytic insights irrelevant to the study of premodern child rearing, though on pp. 194–195 he asserts that other kinds of Puritan repression combined to produce "adults who were cold, suspicious, distrustful and cruel."
74. On the "double bind" theory, see G. Bateson, D. D. Jackson, J. Haley, and J. H. Weakland, "Toward a Theory of Schizophrenia," *Behavioural Science,* 1 (1956), pp. 251–264. On the "schizophrenogenic" mother, see Frieda Fromm-Reichmann, "Notes on the Development of Treatment of Schizophrenics by Psychoanalytic Psychotherapy," *Psychiatry,* 11 (1948), pp. 263–273.
75. For a close reading of *Hamlet* along these lines, see my essay, "The Woman in Hamlet: An Interpersonal View," in *Signs,* 4 (Winter 1978), pp. 291–308. A remarkable study of collusion and mixed signals in

eleven families is R. D. Laing and Aaron Esterson, *Sanity, Madness and the Family* (London, 1964). Esterson expanded one chapter into *The Leaves of Spring: A Study in the Dialectics of Madness* (London, 1970).

Chapter Four

1. For the concept of "false self" as accommodation to expectation, see R. D. Laing, *The Divided Self: An Existential Study in Sanity and Madness* (London, 1960).
2. Although Freud changed his views and in *The Problem of Anxiety* (New York, 1936, 1st ed. 1925) said that anxiety is prior to and produces the need for defenses, I do not believe the change is helpful.
3. Thomas Hooker, *A survey of the summe of Church Discipline . . .* (London 1648), part 1, p. 10.
4. Edmund Morgan, *Visible Saints: The History of a Puritan Idea* (New York, 1963), p. 70.
5. Cf. Owen C. Watkins, *The Puritan Experience* (London, 1972), pp. 227–228.
6. Keith Thomas, *Religion and the Decline of Magic* (New York, 1971), p. 14.
7. See Henri F. Ellenberger, *The Discovery of the Unconscious: The History and Evolution of Dynamic Psychiatry* (New York, 1970), p. 486, for Freud's adoption of the term "defense" from Meynert.
8. On "anal character" see Freud, "The Predisposition to Obsessional Neurosis" (1913), which first connected anal erotism and obsession; Karl Abraham, "Contributions to the Theory of the Anal Character" (1921), in *On Character and Libido Development, Six Essays by Karl Abraham,* ed. Bertram D. Lewin (New York, 1966), pp. 165–187; and Erik Erikson's section on the Yurok fishermen in his *Childhood and Society,* 2nd ed. (New York, 1963), pp. 166–186. For relations between impulses toward purity and concerns with boundaries see Mary Douglas, *Purity and Danger: An Analysis of Concepts of Pollution and Taboo* (London, 1966), and Natalie Zemon Davis, *Society and Culture in Early Modern France* (London, 1975), ch. 6, esp. pp. 178–179.
9. H. R. Beech, ed., *Obsessional States,* (London, 1974), p. 5; Henry V. Dicks, *Clinical Studies in Psychopathology. A Contribution to the Aetiology of Neurotic Illness* (London, 1939), pp. 55–76. The classic summation of orthodox psychoanalytic views on obsession is in Otto Fenichel's *The Psychoanalytic Theory of Neurosis* (New York, 1945), ch. 14.
10. See Jack H. Kahn, *Job's Illness: Loss, Grief and Integration* (Oxford, 1975).
11. Robert Cawley, "Psychotherapy and Obsessional Disorders," in *Obsessional States,* ed. Beech, pp. 271, 273.

12. See Harry Trosman, "After *The Waste Land:* Psychological Factors in the Religious Conversion of T. S. Eliot," *International Review of Psycho-Analysis,* 4 (1977), pp. 295–304. Freud was the first to call compulsion neurosis a private religion, saying obsessions reverse the drives from active aggression to passive submission; Freud, "Notes upon a Case of Obsessional Neurosis" (1909), in *Collected Papers,* vol. 3, trans. Alix and James Strachey (London, 1953), pp. 296–383; the patient is commonly known as the Rat Man.

13. Freud, "Notes upon a Case of Obsessional Neurosis," pp. 368 (chief objects of doubt), 379 (masturbation).

14. The Dr. Schreber case is in Freud's "Psycho-Analytic Notes upon an Autobiographical Account of a Case of Paranoia (Dementia Paranoides)" (1911), in *Collected Papers,* vol. 3, pp. 387–470. On the discovery of the father's book, see Morton Schatzman, "Paranoia or Persecution: The Case of Schreber," *History of Childhood Quarterly,* 1 (Summer 1973), pp. 62–88; also Schatzman's "The Schreber Case," *History of Childhood Quarterly,* 2 (Winter 1975), pp. 453–456, and his *Soul Murder: Persecution in the Family* (New York, 1973).

15. Oscar Pfister, *Christianity and Fear: A Study in History and in the Psychology and Hygiene of Religion,* trans. W. H. Johnston (London, 1948), pp. 390–455; Heije Faber, *Psychology of Religion,* trans. Margaret Kohl (London, 1976); W. Lloyd Warner, *The Living and the Dead. A Study of the Symbolic Life of Americans* (New Haven, 1959). A somewhat more subtle version of Warner's equation of Protestantism with masculinity, Catholicism with the mother, is Walter J. Ong's "The Lady and the Issue," chapter 11 of his *In the Human Grain: Further Explorations of Contemporary Culture* (New York and London, 1967).

16. Melanie Klein, "The Early Development of Conscience in the Child" (1933), in *Contributions to Psycho-Analysis 1921–1945* (London, 1952), pp. 267–277; also *The Psycho-Analysis of Children,* 3rd ed. (London, 1954, 1st pub. 1932), esp. ch. 9, "The Relations between Obsessional Neurosis and the Early Stages of the Super-Ego," pp. 210–244; also pp. 11–12 and ch. 3, "An Obsessional Neurosis in a Six-Year-Old Girl," pp. 65–93.

17. Harry Stack Sullivan, *Conceptions of Modern Psychiatry* (London, 1955), pp. 112–119, 122; *The Interpersonal Theory of Psychiatry,* ed. Helen Swick Perry and Mary Ladd Cawel (London, 1955, 1st pub. 1953), pp. 318–319.

18. David Shapiro, *Neurotic Styles* (New York and London, 1965), pp. 23–53.

19. Shapiro, "Speech Characteristics of Some Rigid Characters," a talk given April 16, 1977, at the City College of New York's graduate center, and private conversation thereafter.

20. Erik Erikson, *Young Man Luther: A Study in Psychoanalysis and History* (London, 1959), p. 64, also pp. 58–74, 87–93, 118 (anal stage). On

comparing Luther and Freud, see pp. 146–148, 151, 245–247. Erikson stresses that Luther's mother is totally "eclipsed" (p. 62, also pp. 68–69). In *The Dynamics of Literary Response* (New York, 1968), Norman N. Holland discusses "anal writings" in detail, e.g., p. 40. A helpful and sympathetic critique of Erikson's book, finding that Erikson overstates the villainy of Luther's father, is *Psychohistory and Religion: The Case of "Young Man Luther,"* ed. Roger A. Johnson (Philadelphia, 1977).

21. Cf. Robert Waelder, "The Psychoanalytic Theory of Play," *Psycho-analytic Quarterly,* 2 (1933), pp. 208–224. Waelder says play helps children to master "indigestible" experience through repetition.

22. Erikson, *Young Man Luther,* p. 72.

23. See Alan Black, "The Natural History of Obsessional Neurosis," in *Obsessional States,* ed. Beech, pp. 19–54, esp. pp. 22, 30, 37.

24. Reinhard Bendix and Guenther Roth, *Scholarship and Partisanship: Essays on Max Weber* (Berkeley, 1971), p. 206, also pp. 188–206, "Japan and the Protestant Ethic."

25. See Freud, "Family Romances" (1908), Standard Edition, vol. 9, pp. 237–241, and his letter to Fliess of May 20, 1898; Phyllis Greenacre, "The Family Romance of the Artist" (1968), reprinted in her collected essays, *Emotional Growth,* vol. 2 (New York, 1971), pp. 503–528. Linda Joan Kaplen surveys the literature in "The Concept of the Family Romance," *Psychoanalytic Review,* 61 (Summer 1974), pp. 169–202. The first application of the concept to literary and mythological themes was by Otto Rank in *The Myth of the Birth of the Hero,* 1st pub. 1914; see also Ernst Kris, *Psychoanalytic Explorations in Art* (New York, 1952), pp. 69–72.

26. Samuel Willard, *A Compleat Body of Divinity* . . . (Boston, 1726), p. 903; John Norton, *The Orthodox Evangelist* . . . (London, 1654), p. 133; Thomas Hooker, *The Christians Two Chiefe Lessons, viz. Self-Denial, and Selfe-Tryall* (London, 1640), p. 288; Hooker, *The Soules Humiliation* (London, 1637), pp. 214–215.

27. Freud, *Moses and Monotheism,* trans. Katherine Jones (New York, 1939), p. 71.

28. See Emil Oberholzer, Jr., "The Church in New England Society," in *Seventeenth Century America,* ed. James M. Smith (Chapel Hill, 1959), pp. 143–165; on family disputes, see p. 150.

29. The epigraph from James 1.18 is as cited by Willard, *Compleat Body,* p. 819.

30. Willard, *Evangelical Perfection* (Boston, 1700, 1694 lecture), p. 182. Richard Sibbes, *Works,* ed. A. B. Grosart (Edinburgh, 1862–64), vol. 5, p. 25; Thomas Shepard, *Parable of the Ten Virgins,* in *Works* (New York, 1967, reprinting 1853 Boston ed.), vol. 2, p. 172; *John Cotton and the Churches of New England,* ed. Larzer Ziff (Cambridge, Mass., 1968), p. 81 ("Keys of the Kingdom," 1644).

31. Willard, *Compleat Body*, p. 12; Peter Bulkeley, *The Gospel-Covenant: Or, the Covenant of Grace Opened*, 2nd ed. (London, 1651, 1st pub. 1646), p. 193; Hooker, *Survey*, part 1, p. 3.

32. Norton, *Orthodox Evangelist*, p. 72; Richard Mather, Preface to *The Summe of Certain Sermons upon Genes. 15, 6* (Cambridge, N.E., 1652). Cf. Norton, *Orthodox Evangelist*, pp. 332, 343, and Bulkeley, *Gospel-Covenant*, p. 173.

33. Richard Mather, *A Farewell Exhortation to the church and people of Dorchester in New England* (Cambridge, New England, 1653), p. 18; Willard, *Compleat Body*, pp. 134, 42. The next few pages are filled with imagery of sunlight and ocean for God, though Willard adds an unintended irony, at least to English ears, when he says "There is in him an Infinite Redundancy" (p. 48).

34. Hooker, *The Saints Guide* (London, 1645), p. 30; *The Soules Vocation* (London, 1638), p. 658.

35. Shepard, *Parable*, in *Works*, vol. 2, p. 322; Norton, *Orthodox Evangelist*, pp. 94–95; Willard, *Compleat Body*, p. 892.

36. Shepard, *Parable*, in *Works*, vol. 2, pp. 429, 309. Second-rank Puritan ministers, e.g., John Norton, tended to use more distanced similes of order and authority, without fusing authority with intimacy.

37. Cotton, *A Practical Commentary . . . [on] John*, 1st epistle (London, 1656), pp. 40–41; Bulkeley, *Gospel-Covenant*, p. 250; Shepard, *Parable*, in *Works*, vol. 2, p. 583.

38. Cotton's poem is printed in John Norton's eulogy, *Abel being Dead yet speaketh . . .* (London, 1658), p. 28.

39. Winthrop's *Model of Christian Charity* is reprinted in *Puritan Political Ideas, 1558–1794*, ed. Edmund Morgan (n.p., 1965), quotations pp. 87–92.

40. Hooker, *Survey*, preface; Shepard, *Parable*, in *Works*, vol 2, p. 473 ("earthly minds"); Shepard, *The Sincere Convert* (London, 1664, delivered 1641), p. 13. Hooker's simile about the difficulties of giving birth to truth was written, or rewritten, after Hooker's huge manuscript had been lost at sea on its way to England. Hooker had to write it again and died just before it was finished—a testament, if not to a sense of mission, at least to self-discipline.

41. Bulkeley, *Gospel-Covenant*, p. 80; Shepard, *God's Plot: The Paradoxes of Puritan Piety, Being the Autobiography & Journal of Thomas Shepard*, ed. Michael McGiffert ([Amherst], 1972), p. 209. M. M. Knappen is wrong to note "the surprising lack of christological thought" in Puritanism (*Tudor Puritanism, A Chapter in the History of Idealism* [Chicago, 1939], p. 376), though Christ in Tudor Puritanism did not have the overwhelming emphasis he had in New England, especially for second-generation ministers. Cf. Sacvan Bercovitch, *The Puritan Origins of the American Self* (New Haven and London, 1975), p. 19 on self-confrontation through Christ, and pp. 23–25 on the spiritual

biography as a model of Christic identity, though that too may have been a post-Elizabethan development.

42. Bolton, *Works* (London, 1631–41), vol. 1, p. 87 ("The Second Asise Sermon," London, 1635); John Robotham, *An Exposition On the whole booke of Solomons Song . . .* (London, 1651), p. 29. For brief applications of various images for Christ, see Norton, *Orthodox Evangelist*, pp. 284–285, and Bulkeley, *Gospel-Covenant*, p. 50.

43. Willard, *Fountain Opened* (Boston, 1700), p. 37; *Brief Discourse* Boston, 1686), p. 134; Cotton, *Commentary on John*, p. 12; Shepard, *God's Plot*, p. 121.

44. Bulkeley, *Gospel-Covenant*, p. 188; Willard, *The Child's Portion* (Boston, 1684), p. 70; Hooker, *Soules Humiliation*, p. 75.

45. Ernest Jones, *Essays in Applied Psycho-analysis*, vol. 2 (London, 1951), p. 423.

46. Shepard, *Parable*, in *Works*, vol. 2, pp. 48, 69, 40; *Sincere Convert*, pp. 103–104.

47. Cotton, *Commentary on John*, p. 218; *A Brief Exposition Of the whole Book of Canticles . . .* (London, 1642), pp. 15–16; Shepard, *The Sound Believer . . .* (London, 1659), p. 311; John Dod and Robert Cle[a]ver, *A Godlye Form of Household Government* (London, 1621, 1st ed. 1614), section K 4.

48. Emory Elliott, *Power in the Pulpit in Puritan New England* (Princeton, 1975), pp. 13–14.

49. Hooker, *The Unbeleevers Preparing for Christ* (London, 1638), p. 38; Shepard, *Parable*, in *Works*, vol. 2, pp. 592, 174 ("swaddling-clouts").

50. Alan Simpson, *Puritanism in Old and New England* (Chicago, 1955), p. 2. Willard, *Compleat Body*, pp. 489–491; Bulkeley, *Gospel-Covenant*, p. 255, also pp. 241–273 on sanctification. Cf. Philip Greven, *The Protestant Temperament: Patterns of Child-Rearing, Religious Experience, and the Self in Early America* (New York, 1977), pp. 62–99.

51. Winthrop, quoted by Edmund Morgan in *Visible Saints*, p. 72; Shepard, *Sound Believer*, p. 155. Cotton, *Commentary on John*, p. 258, declares that man is "but a shrimp in grace."

52. R. Mather, *Farewell Exhortation*, p. 3; Cotton, *The Way of Life* (London, 1641), p. 28; Shepard, *Parable*, in *Works*, vol. 2, p. 62; Cotton, *Way of Life*, p. 97.

53. Hooker, *The Christians Two chiefe Lessons* (London, 1640), p. 20.

54. See Freud, *Totem and Taboo: Resemblances between the Psychic Lives of Savages and Neurotics* (1913), Standard Edition, vol. 13, pp. 1–161. In *The Pursuit of the Millennium* (London, 1957), Norman Cohn discusses psychodynamics in medieval millennial sects that were similar, though expressed with more overt aggression. Cleo McNelly's "Natives, Women and Claude Lévi-Strauss: A Reading of *Tristes Tropiques* as Myth," *Massachusetts Review*, 16 (Winter 1975), pp. 7–29, shows unconscious fears of otherness, linked with natives and women, in Lévi-

Strauss and Conrad's *Heart of Darkness;* her analysis of how "the act of knowing" becomes an act of "dominance" has application to Freud as well as to her critique of structuralism.

55. Norton, *Orthodox Evangelist,* pp. 251–282, quotations pp. 282, 338.

56. Ibid., p. 347; Shepard, *Parable,* in *Works,* vol. 2, p. 215; Willard, *Compleat Body,* p. 514.

57. Shepard, *Parable,* in *Works,* vol. 2, pp. 104 ("hewings and hammerings"), 227 ("riches"), p. 80 ("heart"), and 533 ("sucking out the sweet"); Willard, *Compleat Body,* p. 533. By contrast, Owen C. Watkins observes in *The Puritan Experience* (London, 1972), God is seldom mentioned in Quaker narratives, which emphasize "human sensibility and intuition" (pp. 230–231).

58. Hugh Peter, *A Dying Fathers Last Legacy to an Only Child* (London, 1660), p. 101. The phrase "Flying to the American Strand," heading this section, is taken from the Vergilian first sentence of Cotton Mather's *Magnalia Christi Americana* (Hartford, 1855, 1st ed. 1702), p. 25.

59. See John C. Miller, *This New Man, The American: The Beginnings of the American People* (New York, 1974), pp. 4–10, 98 ff.

60. Foster, *Their Solitary Way: The Puritan Social Ethic in the First Century of Settlement in New England* (New Haven, 1971), p. 155. On Indians, Alden T. Vaughan's *New England Frontier: Puritans and Indians 1620–1675* (Boston, 1965) is too benign, while Larzer Ziff is too harsh in *Puritanism in America: New Culture in a New World* (New York, 1973), pp. 143–145. See also Kai Erikson, *Wayward Puritans: A Study in the Sociology of Deviance* (New York, 1966), pp. 188 ff.

61. Foster, *Their Solitary Way,* p. 157.

62. Hooker, *Survey,* part 1, pp. 16, 69; Cotton Mather's 1690 Nehemiah sermon is excerpted in *Puritan Political Tradition,* ed. Morgan, p. 243.

63. Bolton, Works, vol. 1, p. 149 (*Foure Last Things*).

64. For continuities and similarities with non-Puritan beliefs, see Timothy Hall Breen, "The Non-Existent Controversy: Puritan and Anglican Attitudes on Work and Wealth, 1600–1640," *Church History,* 35 (1966), pp. 273–287. Calvin is cited (from the *Institutes*) by Joseph E. Illick, "Child-Rearing in Seventeenth-Century England and America," reprinted in *The History of Childhood,* ed. Lloyd deMause (New York, 1974), p. 330.

65. Cotton, *The Pouring Out of the Seven Vials,* 3rd sermon on the sixth vial (London, 1642), p. 14.

66. Hill, *Society and Puritanism in Pre-Revolutionary England* (New York, 1964), p. 141.

67. See Cecelia Tichi, "Spiritual Biography and the 'Lords Remembrancers,'" *William and Mary Quarterly,* 28 (January 1971), reprinted in *The American Puritan Imagination: Essays in Revaluation,* ed. Sacvan Bercovitch (London, 1974), pp. 56–73; also Daniel Shea, *Spiritual Autobiography in Early America* (Princeton, 1968).

68. Lockridge, *A New England Town: The First Hundred Years* (New York, 1970), p. 19, and T. H. Breen, "Persistent Localism: English Social Change and the Shaping of New England Institutions," *William and Mary Quarterly*, 32 (January 1975), pp. 3–28.

Chapter Five

1. Shepard, *The Parable of the Ten Virgins*, in *Works*, vol. 2 (New York, 1957, reprinting 1853 Boston ed.), p. 402. *Parable* was first published in 1660. Shepard is ostensibly quoting the Bible (Judg. 9. 54).

2. See, among many others, Richard Bushman, *From Puritan to Yankee: Character and the Social Order in Connecticut, 1690–1765* (Cambridge, Mass., 1967), p. 18. Two recent histories of unconscious dynamics in American history see patriarchal sternness as the essence of Puritanism. Michael Paul Rogin's *Fathers & Children: Andrew Jackson and the Subjugation of the American Indian* (New York, 1975) takes a neo-Freudian and Kleinian perspective to damn Puritan rigidity, while Richard Slotkin's *Regeneration Through Violence: The Mythology of the American Frontier, 1600–1860* (Middletown, Conn., 1973) takes a neo-Jungian perspective to damn Puritan rigidity. Slotkin in particular, though interesting on the failure of the "father myth," often misstates specific aspects of the Puritan experience. Annette Kolodny's *The Lay of the Land* (Chapel Hill, 1975) is more complex and sympathetic, while also stressing a rapist masculine mentality.

3. For fears of the "mutilating mother," see Joseph C. Rheingold, *The Mother, Anxiety, and Death: The Catastrophic Death Complex* (Boston, 1967). For the fantasy of good mother and bad mother as a resolution of primary ambivalence, see Harry Stack Sullivan, *The Interpersonal Theory of Psychiatry*, ed. Helen Swick Perry and Mary Ladd Gawel (New York, 1953), pp. 85–91, 111–124; also various works by Melanie Klein, e.g., "Some Theoretical Conclusions Regarding the Emotional Life of the Infant" (1952), reprinted in her *Envy and Gratitude & Other Works 1946–1963* (n. p., 1975), pp. 61–76 especially, and "The Oedipus Complex in the Light of Early Anxieties" (1945), reprinted in *Contributions to Psycho-Analysis 1921–1945* (London, 1968), especially pp. 346–348.

4. Shepard, *Parable*, in *Works*, vol. 2, p. 50. The original version, from *Parable of the Ten Virgins* (London, 1660), p. 27, is even more truculent, lacking the first question mark, the exclamation mark, and other punctuation marks.

5. Miller, *The New England Mind: The Seventeenth Century* (New York, 1939), p. 298.

6. Hooker, *The Preparing of the Heart for to Receive Christ* (1640), reprinted by Larzer Ziff in his anthology, *The Literature of America:*

Colonial Period (New York, 1970), p. 158. Ziff notes that the sermon was preached before Hooker came to America in 1633. I am unable to find the sermon listed in the bibliography establishing the Hooker canon, done by Sargent Bush, Jr., in *Thomas Hooker: Writings in England and Holland, 1626–1633*, ed. George H. Williams, Norman Pettit, Winfried Herget, and Sargent Bush, Jr. (Cambridge, Mass., 1975). Other ministers gave the Word and grace the more active role, especially Cotton; see Norman Pettit, *The Heart Prepared: Grace and Conversion in Puritan Spiritual Life* (New Haven, 1966). See also Babette May Levy, *Preaching in the First Half Century of New England History* (Hartford, 1945); W. Fraser Mitchell, *English Pulpit Oratory from Andrewes to Tillotson . . .* (London, 1932), and Horton Davies, *Worship and Theology in England From Cranmer to Hooker 1534–1603* (Princeton, 1970). David Hall's *The Faithful Shepherd: A History of the New England Ministry in the Seventeenth Century* (Chapel Hill, 1972) is a comprehensive survey of New England Puritan preaching in theory and practice.

7. Norton, *The Orthodox Evangelist . . .* (London, 1654), Epistle Dedicatory.

8. Richard Baxter, *Reliquiae Baxterianae* (1696), part 1, p. 32, quoted by Perez Zagorin, *The Court and the Country: The Beginning of the English Revolution* (New York, 1970), p. 182; Hooker, *Writings in England and Holland*, p. 244. The sermon is "The Danger of Desertion" (April 1631).

9. Francis J. Bremer, *The Puritan Experiment: New England Society from Bradford to Edwards* (New York, 1976), p. 26, also p. 28; see also Darrett Rutman, *American Puritanism: Faith and Practice* (Philadelphia, New York, and Toronto, 1970).

10. The English preacher is Edward Dering, cited by Everett Emerson, *English Puritanism from John Hooper to John Milton* (Durham, 1968), p. 59.

11. On the plain style as "party badge," see Miller, *The New England Mind: The Seventeenth Century*, pp. 331–361; also Miller, *Nature's Nation* (Cambridge, Mass., 1967), pp. 208–240, on "An American Language."

12. Willard, *A Compleat Body of Divinity . . .* (Boston, 1726), p. 31, also p. 32; Norton, *Orthodox Evangelist*, p. 196.

13. As Hawthorne said in his English Notebooks, "The Puritans showed their strength of mind and heart by preferring a sermon an hour and a half long, into which the preacher put his whole soul, and lopping away all these externals, into which religious life had first leafed and flowered, and then petrified." Quoted by Barriss Mills in "Hawthorne and Puritanism," *New England Quarterly*, 21 (March 1948), p. 88.

14. On the Puritan use of conscience rather than the rod to internalize rules and expectations, see Philip Greven, *The Protestant Temperament: Patterns of Child-Rearing, Religious Experience, and the Self in Early America* (New York, 1977), pp. 49–55. The John Norton quotation is from *The Heart of N– England rent at the BLASPHEMIES of the*

Present Generation . . . (Cambridge, New England, 1659), p. 51. Norton continues: It is "the judgement of a mans self, answering unto the judgment of God concerning him."

15. Chauncy is quoted by Cotton Mather in his *Magnalia Christi Americana* (Hartford, 1855, 1st. ed. 1702), vol. 1, p. 471.

16. Cotton Mather reports Stone's opinion in *Magnalia,* vol. 1, p. 437; Pricke, *Doctrine of Superiority* (London, 1609), section F 2. This is one of four duties necessary for ministers to be spiritual fathers. Hooker, "Spiritual Munition," reprinted in *Writings in England and Holland,* p. 42.

17. Shepard, *Parable,* in *Works,* vol. 2, pp. 494, 484.

18. Ibid., p. 497. This edition says "flit milk"; the 1660 edition, part two, p. 97, says "slit-milk."

19. Ibid., pp. 41, 27; Cleaver, *A Briefe Explanation of the Whole Booke of the Proverbs of Salomon* (London, 1615), p. 91. Breast similes were even used occasionally for reverse argumentation, as when William Gouge cites 1 Peter 2.2 on the milk of the Word to prove why infants desire the breast; see *Of Domesticall Duties* . . . (London, 1622), p. 286.

20. *John Cotton on the Churches of New England,* ed. Larzer Ziff (Cambridge, Mass., 1968), p. 341 ("The Way of Congregational Churches Cleared," 1648). Thomas Hooker has a lengthy simile on the minister's various roles as nurse, steward, and archer in *The Soules Preparation for Christ* . . . (London, 1638, 1st pub. 1632), pp. 62–63. See also Frank Shuffelton, *Thomas Hooker 1586–1647* (Princeton, 1977), pp. 178–179, on the offices of pastor and teacher, and Norton, *Heart of New England rent,* pp. 13–18.

21. Epigraph to Hall's *Faithful Shepherd;* Hooker, *The Soules Exaltation* (London, 1638), p. 36.

22. Norton, *Orthodox Evangelist,* p. 25; Shepard, *Parable,* in *Works,* vol. 2, p. 131; Hooker, *The Soules Vocation* (London, 1638), p. 469. Hooker also defines God's promise as "the immortal seed of God's word whereby the Spirit breeds this faith in the hearts of all that are his" (*Writings in England and Holland,* p. 182, "The Poor Doubting Christian Drawn Unto Christ," 1629). Sometimes he also compares the delivery of God's Word "to an arrow." The English Puritan Robert Bolton defines Puritans as those who "walke precisely" (Eph. 5.15) in God's Word and thus purge themselves of "their owne bloud, wallowing in the dunge (so the word signifies in the Text) of their owne naturall corruption" (*Works* [London, 1631–41], vol. 4, pp. 254–255).

23. Willard, *Compleat Body,* pp. 821, 826, also p. 821: "The Word is compared to Seed in Conversion, so to Food and Nourishment in regard of Edification . . . Milk for new-born Christians, and strong Meat" for older ones, 1 Peter 2.2.

24. In *The Puritan Origins of the American Self* (New Haven and London,

1975), Sacvan Bercovitch wrongly attributes the obliteration of the distinction between metaphoric and literal to Puritan plain style, which for him is "a conventionalized rhetoric that blurs the difference between metaphor and experience" (pp. 29–30). The blurring may be somewhat more characteristic of second-generation rhetoric, his real subject. But it is far more typical of the Quakers.

25. Shepard, *The Sound Believer* . . . (London, 1659), p. 155; Cotton, *A Practical Commentary* . . . *[on] John* (London, 1656), p. 338.

26. Shepard, *Parable*, in *Works*, vol. 2, p. 59; Mather, *Sermon Occasioned by the Execution of a Man found Guilty of Murder* (Boston, 1686), p. 13.

27. Hooker, *Danger of Desertion* (London, 1641, probably preached just before Hooker left England for Holland in 1631; see bibliographical note in *Writings in England and Holland*, p. 410), p. 6.

28. Cotton, *The Bloudy Tenent, Washed* . . . (London, 1647), p. 129; Bulkeley, *The Gospel-Covenant* . . . (London, 1651, 1st pub. 1646), p. 14. See William J. Scheick, "The Widower Narrator in Nathaniel Ward's *The Simple Cobbler of Aggawam in America*," *New England Quarterly*, 47 (March 1974), pp. 87–96, for Ward's more comic equation of toleration with whoredom and pure marriage with truth; King Charles himself, Ward says, has a whorish heart.

29. Cynthia Griffin Wolff, "Literary Reflections of the Puritan Character," *Journal of the History of Ideas*, 29 (January–March 1968), p. 15, on heavenly community as opposed to "intolerable loneliness" on earth; also Edmund Morgan, *The Puritan Dilemma: The Story of John Winthrop* (Boston, 1958), p. 12: "The Puritan loved his God with all the sensual abandon he denied himself in dealing with the world." Greven's *Protestant Temperament*, pp. 62–64, finds less regressive transformation and more return to early childhood obedience and discipline in Puritan conversion dynamics.

30. Willard, *Brief Discourse*, (Boston, 1686), pp. 84–85; Shepard, *God's Plot: The Paradoxes of Puritan Piety, Being the Autobiography and Journal of Thomas Shepard*, ed. Michael McGiffert ([Amherst], 1972), p. 101; Shepard, quoted in *American Thought and Writing, The Colonial Period*, ed. Norman Grabo and Russell B. Nye (Boston, 1965), p. 99, from *The Sincere Convert*.

31. John Bowlby, *Attachment and Loss*, vol. 2 (New York, 1973), especially pp. 27–32, 375–398.

32. Willard, *Compleat Body*, p. 212.

33. Hooker, *The Application of Redemption* (London, 1659, 2nd ed., first pub. 1656). Quotation in *The Puritans*, ed. Perry Miller and Thomas H. Johnson, rev. ed. (New York, 1963), p. 296. Hooker, *Poor Doubting Christian* (London, 1629), p. 37. Hooker, *Application*, quoted in *The Puritans*, ed. Miller and Johnson, p. 299. Shepard, *Parable*, in *Works*, vol. 2, p. 166.

34. Shepard, *Parable,* in *Works,* vol. 2, pp. 392–394, 22; Cotton, "A Sermon Delivered at Salem," in *John Cotton on Churches of New England,* p. 60.
35. Shepard, *Parable,* in *Works,* vol. 2, pp. 154, 163, 32. In *Compleat Body,* Willard usually describes sin in anal terms of filth, disorder, or anger, e.g., pp. 203, 273.
36. Shepard, *Parable,* in *Works,* vol. 2, p. 122; Cotton, "Sermon Delivered at Salem," p. 58; Shepard, *Parable,* in *Works,* vol. 2, pp. 55, 134, 133, 54.
37. See Lyle Koehler, "The Case of the American Jezebels: Anne Hutchinson and Female Agitation during the Years of Antinomian Turmoil, 1636–1640," *William and Mary Quarterly,* 31 (January 1974), pp. 55–78, which argues too simply that antinomianism was "an ideology through which the resentments [women] intuitively felt could be focused and actively expressed" (p. 78), and Koehler's spirited rejoinder to a lengthy critique a year later (January 1975, pp. 164–178). Ben Barker-Benfield, "Anne Hutchinson and the Puritan Attitude toward Women," *Feminist Studies,* 1 (Fall 1972), asserts that the Puritan metaphor of mystical marriage encouraged men to dominate women so as to identify with their dominant God, a dubious conclusion disputed by Margaret W. Masson in "The Typology of the Female as a Model for the Regenerate: Puritan Preaching 1690–1730," *Signs,* 2 (Winter 1976), pp. 304–315. Also relevant is Doris Grieser Marquit, "The Feminine in Puritan Spiritual Autobiography," paper delivered at the December 1976 meeting of the Modern Language Association.
38. Shepard, *Parable,* in *Works,* vol. 2, pp. 377, 402.
39. Bulkeley, *Gospel-Covenant,* pp. 326–327; Hugh Peter is cited in *Antinomianism in the Colony of Massachusetts Bay, 1636–38,* ed. C. F. Adams (Boston, 1894), p. 329. In *Puritan Origins of the American Self* Sacvan Bercovitch too simply makes Anne Hutchinson's antinomianism a case of individuality versus social duties (p. 93) rather than assurance versus doubt within a context of sex-role expectations, pp. 93–94. Winton Solberg cites Winthrop in *Redeem the Time: The Puritan Sabbath in Early America* (Cambridge, Mass. and London, 1977), p. 144.
40. Roger Thompson, *Women in Stuart England and America: A Comparative Study* (London, 1974). Emory Elliott's *Power in the Pulpit in Puritan New England* (Princeton, 1975) is a more judicious examination of the growing role of women in second-generation churches.
41. On Sarah Hutchinson, Anne Yale Hopkins, and other women, see Thompson, *Women in Stuart England and America;* also Elizabeth Wade White, *Anne Bradstreet "The Tenth Muse"* (New York, 1971), pp. 172–177.
42. Shepard, *Parable,* in *Works,* vol. 2, pp. 520, 514, 519, 267, 284. Shepard is very clear on the role women are expected to play; see *Parable,* p. 382, also p. 517.

43. *The Works of Anne Bradstreet,* ed. Jeannine Hensley (Cambridge, Mass., 1967), pp. 16–17. Poem cited in the next paragraph is "The Author to her Book" (p. 221).
44. Cotton, *John Cotton on Churches of New England,* p. 67 ("Sermon Delivered at Salem"); Cotton also cites Numbers xix, 13,14, and Leviticus xix, 17. Shepard, *Parable,* in *Works,* vol. 2, pp. 33, 150.
45. Cotton, *Way of Life,* p. 379; Shepard, *Sincere Convert,* p. 37; Hooker, *Soules Vocation,* p. 371; idem, *The Saints Dignitie and Dutie* (London, 1651), pp. 59–60; *Edward Taylor's Treatise Concerning the Lord's Supper,* ed. Norman S. Grabo (Michigan, 1966), p. 157.
46. Shepard, *Sound Believer,* pp. 84, 130.
47. Shepard, *Parable,* in *Works,* vol. 2, pp. 392–393. Cf. Elliott on masturbation in *Power in the Pulpit,* p. 34; he correlates second-generation fears (e.g., Wigglesworth's diary) with patriarchal repression. See also the anonymous *The Pure Nazarite* (1723), p. 6. For a history of the increasingly severe taboo on masturbation in western Europe at this time, see Robert H. MacDonald, "The Frightful Consequences of Onanism; Notes on the History of a Delusion," *Journal of the History of Ideas,* 28 (July-September 1967), pp. 423–431. Cf. also Philip Greven, *Protestant Temperament,* pp. 55–56.
48. Hooker, *Unbelievers,* pp. 105–106. Haller is cited by Owen C. Watkins, *The Puritan Experience* (London, 1972), p. 20.
49. Hooker, *The Christians Two chiefe Lessons* (London, 1640), p. 250. The two lessons are "Self-Deniall, And Selfe Tryall." Cotton, *Commentary on John,* p. 40.
50. Bradstreet, "Of the Four Ages of Man," in *Works,* p. 54. For the conventional image of "breeding teeth," see Joseph E. Illick, "Child-Rearing in Seventeenth-Century America," in *The History of Childhood,* ed. Lloyd deMause (New York, 1974), p. 313. For Bradstreet's attitude toward infancy as one aspect of Puritan ambivalence, see Greven, *Protestant Temperament,* pp. 28–31.
51. Bulkeley, *Gospel-Covenant,* pp. 162–163; Pricke, *The Doctrine of Superiority* (London, 1609), section G 4.
52. Cf. Illick, "Child-Rearing," and Greven, *Protestant Temperament,* pp. 28–31. Lloyd deMause has said, in the introduction to *The History of Childhood,* p. 10, that "the use of the child as a 'toilet' for adult projections is behind the whole notion of original sin." Peter N. Carroll, in *Puritanism and the Wilderness: The Intellectual Significance of the New England Frontier 1629–1700* (New York, 1969), p. 124, observes that early Puritan attitudes toward the Indians were like their attitudes toward children; they viewed Indians not as agents of the devil but as soil, albeit rocky and barren soil, for planting.
53. *John Cotton on Churches of New England,* ed. Ziff, pp. 191–192 ("Way of Congregational Churches Cleared"); Bradford, *Of Plymouth Plantation, 1620–1647,* ed. S. E. Morison (New York, 1975), p. 24.

54. See Arthur W. Calhoun, *A Social History of the American Family from Colonial Times to the Present*, vol. 1 (Cleveland, 1917), on New England's patriarchy and group orientation, esp. ch. 4, pp. 67–82. Mather's testament cited in Kenneth Murdock, *Increase Mather: The Foremost American Puritan* (Cambridge, Mass., 1926), pp. 72–73. Philip Greven's thesis, in *Protestant Temperament*, that the evangelical pattern of child rearing develops in self-contained households without grandparents (who tend to be indulgent) and without any group supports to alleviate parental repression, is in many respects opposed to mine. He argues, wrongly I think, that migration augmented that pattern by isolating the family (pp. 25–28). John Cotton's government of his family resembles Increase Mather's; see Cotton Mather's *Magnalia*, vol. 1, pp. 277–278, for his deliberate distance except at morning and evening prayer.
55. On swaddling, see Illick, "Child-Rearing," esp. pp. 325–327.
56. Ibid., pp. 325–326; also John F. Walzer, "A Period of Ambivalence: Eighteenth-Century American Childhood," in *History of Childhood*, ed. deMause, pp. 351–382, especially 365–366.
57. Sewall and Shepard both cited in Illick, "Child-Rearing," pp. 325–326; Bradstreet, meditation 38, in *Works*, p. 279.
58. On Locke and toilet training, see Illick, "Child-Rearing," pp. 331, 318–321; John Barnard cited by John F. Walzer, "Period of Ambivalence," p. 365, from *A Call to Parents and Children* (Boston, 1737), p. 22; Hooker and Bradstreet cited by Illick, "Child-Rearing," p. 350, Eliot cited p. 328.
59. Barnard cited by John F. Walzer, "Period of Ambivalence," p. 373, from *Call to Parents and Children*, p. 28. On the other hand, as Walzer says, Josiah Smith and Samuel Moody said play was fine as long as children were thinking of Christ. All three were eighteenth-century writers, however. On the control of play in Jonathan Edwards's household, see Greven, *Protestant Temperament*, p. 47.
60. Cobbett cited by Illick, "Child-Rearing," p. 316; see also Ivy Pinchbeck and Margaret Hewitt, *Children in English Society*, vol. 1 (n.p., 1969), pp. 18–20; John Davenport, *The Saints Anchor-Hold, in all Storms and Tempests* . . . (London, 1661), pp. 4–5. Cotton Mather cited in Calhoun, *Social History of the American Family*, vol. 1, p. 113, from *A Family Well-Ordered*; see also Greven, *Protestant Temperament*, p. 52.

Chapter Six

1. A good summary and critique of Miller's life and work is Robert Middlekauff's "Perry Miller" in *Pastmasters: Some Essays on American Historians*, ed. Marcus Cunliffe and Robin W. Winks (New York, Evanston, and London, 1975), pp. 167–190.

2. Peter Bulkeley, *The Gospel-Covenant* . . . (London, 1651, 1st pub. 1646), p. 413.

3. Owen C. Watkins, *The Puritan Experience* (London, 1972), p. 1. Watkins more properly points to a major limitation in *our* experience of the literature, since the written works are only a small part of a larger community of dialogue; see p. 31.

4. For such studies see Robert Middlekauff, *The Mathers: Three Generations of Puritan Intellectuals, 1596–1728* (New York, 1971); Sacvan Bercovitch, *The Puritan Origins of the American Self* (New Haven and London, 1975); also his "Horologicals to Chronometricals: The Rhetoric of the Jeremiad," in *Literary Monographs,* vol. 3, ed. Eric Rothstein (Madison and London, 1970), pp. 1–124; and Emory Elliot, *Power in the Pulpit in Puritan New England* (Princeton, 1975). David L. Minter, in *The Interpreted Design as a Structural Principle in American Prose* (New Haven and London, 1969), sees the first generation setting up a grand design whose failure the second generation must redeem through interpretation, a cycle he finds recurring throughout American literature (chs. 2 and 3). John Seelye, in *Prophetic Waters: The River in Early American Life and Literature* (New York, 1977), sees the second generation overthrowing the first generation's centripetal design for imperialist expansion.

5. Everett Emerson, in *English Puritanism from John Hooper to John Milton* (Durham, 1968), p. 45, counsels us to "avoid generalizations about *the* Puritan style," since a common style did not emerge in England until the 1620s and 1630s. Horton Davies, in *Worship and Theology in England from Cranmer to Hooker 1534–1603* (Princeton, 1970), notes several varieties of plain style (pp. 308–316).

6. See Joan Webber, *The Eloquent "I": Style and Self in 17th Century Prose* (Madison, 1968), especially her chapter on "Donne and Bunyan: The Styles of Two Faiths." William Haller, in *The Rise of Puritanism* (New York, 1938), mentions Puritanism's characteristic "diffuseness and tautology" (New York, 1957, p. 143). Larzer Ziff's "Literary Consequences of Puritanism," *English Literary History,* 30 (September 1963), pp. 293–305, reprinted in Sacvan Bercovitch's *The American Puritan Imagination: Essays in Revaluation* (London, 1974), pp. 34–44, speaks of Puritanism's "characteristic combination of plainness, passion, and allegory"; see also Kathrine Koller's "The Puritan Preacher's Contribution to Fiction," *Huntington Library Quarterly,* 4 (August 1948), pp. 321–340. George Williamson, *The Senecan Amble: A Study in Prose Form from Bacon to Collier* (London, 1951), discusses the transition from playing with sounds (Euphuism) to making pointed sense (Senecan), pp. 262–273.

7. Jonas Barish, *Ben Jonson and the Language of Prose Comedy* (Cambridge, Mass., 1967), pp. 198–199.

8. In "Piety and Intellect in Puritanism," *William and Mary Quarterly,* 22

(July 1965), Robert Middlekauff speaks of how the Puritan penchant for allegory "routinized their emotions" and supported "the pre-eminence of the intellect in Puritan mind and character" (pp. 469–470).

9. Christopher Bollas suggests that style may be an unconscious interpretation of self, a speech to inward needs by "re-collecting" repressed attributes. See his "Character: The Language of Self," *International Journal of Psychoanalytic Psychotherapy*, 3 (1974), pp. 397–418.

10. Hooker, *The Application of Redemption* (London, 1659, 1st ed. 1656), p. 5.

11. Hooker, *The Unbeleevers Preparing for Christ* (London, 1638), pp. 27–28.

12. Bercovitch, *Puritan Origins of the American Self*, p. 31.

13. See Frank Shuffelton, *Thomas Hooker 1586–1647* (Princeton, 1977), pp. 3–9.

14. Hooker, *Application of Redemption*, pp. 85, 17–18. See E. F. Bradford, "Conscious Art in Bradford's *History of Plymouth Plantation*," *New England Quarterly*, 1 (April 1928), pp. 133–157, for a study of Lyly's influence on another semi-Puritan stylist.

15. Detailed studies of Hooker's art and thought are, most notably, Norman Pettit, *The Heart Prepared: Grace and Conversion in Puritan Spiritual Life* (New Haven, 1966), and Pettit's essay, "Hooker's Doctrine of Assurance: A Critical Phase in New England Spiritual Thought," *New England Quarterly*, 47 (December 1974), pp. 518–534; John T. Frederick, "Literary Art in Thomas Hooker's *The Poor Doubting Christian*," *American Literature*, 40 (March 1968), pp. 1–8; the four essays by George H. Williams, Norman Pettit, Winfried Herget, and Sargent Bush, Jr., in their edition of *Thomas Hooker: Writings in England and Holland 1626–1633* (Cambridge, Mass., 1975); Perry Miller's essay, "Thomas Hooker and the Democracy of Connecticut," reprinted in *Errand into the Wilderness* (Cambridge, Mass., 1956), which includes a critique of Vernon Louis Parrington; Everett Emerson's introduction to *Redemption: Three Sermons* (Gainesville, Fla., 1956); and Alfred Habegger, "Preparing the Soul for Christ: The Contrasting Sermon Forms of John Cotton and Thomas Hooker," *American Literature*, 41 (1970), pp. 342–354; also Shuffelton's *Thomas Hooker*, which emphasizes Hooker's primary role as preacher.

16. Hooker, *The Saints Dignitie and Dutie* (London, 1651), pp. 4–5; Cotton Mather, *Magnalia Christi Americana* (Hartford, 1855, 1st ed. 1702), vol. 1, p. 335; cf. David Hall in *The Faithful Shepherd: A History of the New England Ministry in the Seventeenth Century* (Chapel Hill, 1972), p. 77; Hooker, *Foure Learned and Godly Treatises* (London, 1638), p. 209; Hooker, *The Saints Guide* (London, 1645), p. 29.

17. See George Williams's biographical sketch, in *Thomas Hooker: Writings in England and Holland*, pp. 1–35; also Pettit's essay, "Hooker's Doctrine of Assurance," Shuffelton also describes the Joanna Drake episode in

detail, *Thomas Hooker,* pp. 29–68, and connects it to the stages of conversion Hooker develops in *The Poore Doubting Christian.* Hooker's
ability to deal with cases of conscience, for which he set aside one day
each week, was legendary.

18. *Writings in England and Holland,* p. 200 ("The Faithful Covenanter,"
ca. 1629), p. 195; *The Christian's Two chiefe Lessons* (London, 1640),
pp. 238–239; *The Soules Vocation* (London, 1638), p. 600.

19. Hooker, *Foure Learned and Godly Treatises,* p. 7; *The Soules Exaltation* (London, 1638), pp. 71–72; *The Soules Preparation for Christ*
(London, 1638), p. 10.

20. *The Soules Ingraffing into Christ,* pub. in *The Soules Implantation . . .*
(London, 1637), p. 133; *Saints Dignitie,* p. 97; *Writings in England
and Holland,* p. 78 ("The Church's Deliverances," 1638, 1st delivered
1626). Shuffelton notes that Hooker especially favored engrafting and
implanting similes for his Essex farmers (*Thomas Hooker,* p. 93).

21. Morgan, *The Puritan Family: Religion & Domestic Relations in Seventeenth-Century New England,* rev. ed. (New York, 1966, 1st ed. 1944),
p. 175. Morgan portrays Hooker as "a man who retained the original
impulse of the Reformation, a man who spoke his words to sinners
rather than saints."

22. Hooker, *Saints Dignitie,* p. 240; *Danger of Desertion* (London, 1641,
probably preached just before Hooker left England for Holland in 1631,
see bibliographical note in *Writings in England and Holland,* p. 410),
p. 14.

23. Cf. Pettit, *The Heart Prepared.*

24. Hooker, *Christians Two chiefe Lessons,* pp. 32–33, 38, 58; *The Poore
Doubting Christian* (London, 1629, in *Writings in England and Holland,* p. 180), p. 363; *Saints Guide,* p. 155. Stressing Hooker's "logical
intricacy," and his use of dialogue and "'tough acute disputations'" to
preach to the understanding, Shuffelton (*Thomas Hooker,* pp. 107, 67),
slights the force of Hooker's dramatic voice and similes yoking nature to
understanding. Shuffelton also overemphasizes Hooker's wish to take
his flock out of the world, e.g., p. 292. Hooker's aim was more to
connect than to separate.

25. Hooker, *Unbeleevers,* p. 200; *Christians two chiefe Lessons,* pp. 210–
211. Cf. Shuffelton's analysis of Hooker's rhythms and "almost cinematic"
sense of drama (pp. 112–115).

26. Hooker, *Application of Redemption,* p. 48; cf. Miller, *The New England
Mind: The Seventeenth Century* (New York, 1939), pp. 240–241.
Hooker, *Soules Vocation,* p. 287.

27. Hooker, *Souls Humiliation,* p. 74; contemporary quoted by Cotton
Mather, *Magnalia,* vol. 1, p. 345.

28. Shuffelton, *Thomas Hooker,* pp. 166–183 on community, especially his
persuasive explanation that Hooker moved to Connecticut (pp. 197–
210) in part because he found his role as peacemaker being transformed

into that of disputant. At Hartford only one person was admonished and one excommunicated in Hooker's fourteen years (p. 228), though internal dissension left the church "hopelessly fragmented" within a dozen years of his death (pp. 228, 281). The Cotton poem in praise of Hooker is in the preface to Hooker's *A survey of the summe of Church Discipline* . . . (London, 1648).

29. Neal, *The History of New-England* (London, 1720), vol. 1, p. 271; Mather's story is cited in Shuffelton, *Thomas Hooker*, pp. 220–224, quotations p. 220. Shuffelton also notes that Hooker's sermons more frequently urge parents to attend to their children than vice versa (p. 221).

30. Hooker, *Saints Guide*, p. 69; *Foure Learned Treatises*, pp. 79–80, 275–276, 207; *Soules Preparation*, p. 74.

31. Hooker, *Soules Vocation*, p. 174; *Soules Exaltation*, p. 102; *Soules Implantation*, p. 132. Cf. *Soules Implantation*, p. 87.

32. Shuffelton, *Thomas Hooker*, pp. 281–288.

33. Cf. Peter Bulkeley, *The Gospel-Covenant* . . . (London, 1651, 1st pub. 1646), in which father-son analogies are even more frequent than imagery of the sun. John Davenport, in *The Saints Anchor-Hold* . . . (London, 1661), stresses God's various roles (pp. 103–104, 128–130); all his images are of the father's stern power, not the helping hand of Hooker's imagery.

34. The "Son of Thunder, Shower of Rain" phrase is a conventional way of polarizing the minister's semiparental virtues. See Watkins, *Puritan Experience*, pp. 8–9. For John Norton's legalism, see his *The Heart of N- England rent at the* BLASPHEMIES *of the Present Generation* . . . (Cambridge, New England, 1659), e.g., pp. 30–31, where civil order is equivalent to the Trinity.

35. Larzer Ziff, *The Career of John Cotton: Puritanism and the American Experience* (Princeton, 1962), p. 252.

36. Shepard, *God's Plot: The Paradoxes of Puritan Piety, Being the Autobiography & Journal of Thomas Shepard*, ed. Michael McGiffert ([Amherst], 1972), p. 74; Shuffelton, *Thomas Hooker*, p. 252. This judgment is unfair to Cotton; cf. Ziff's analysis in *Career of John Cotton* and his introduction to *John Cotton on the Churches of New England*, ed. Larzer Ziff (Cambridge, Mass., 1968); also Shuffelton's analysis of Cotton's preparational differences with Hooker (*Thomas Hooker*, pp. 239–242, 246–258, 262–263). The crucial difference is that Hooker saw ingrafting as a lifelong psychological process, while Cotton imagined conversion as an abstract instantaneous perfection, with preparation coming after union with Christ.

37. Everett H. Emerson, *John Cotton* (New York, 1965), p. 97, speaks of Cotton's virulent anti-Catholicism.

38. Cotton, *A Practical Commentary* . . . *[on] John* (London, 1656), p. 331; Norman S. Grabo, "John Cotton's Aesthetic: A Sketch," *Early*

American Literature, 1 (Spring 1968), pp. 4–10, quotation, p. 7. For Cotton as consolidator, see Ziff, *Career of John Cotton,* p. 105.

39. Cotton, *Christ the Fountaine of Life* . . . (London, 1651), pp. 10 (vision of happiness), 13 (dream of obedience; I have substituted "scares" for "deares").

40. Cotton, *God's Promise to his Plantations* . . . (Boston, 1686, 1st pub. London, 1634), p. 8; Pettit, *Heart Prepared.*

41. Cotton, *God's Mercie mixed with his Justice* . . . (1641), reprinted with introduction by Everett H. Emerson (Gainesville, Fla., 1958), p. 38; Cotton Mather, *Magnalia,* vol. 1, p. 274; Cotton, *The Way of Life* . . . (London, 1641), p. 10.

42. Cotton, *Christ the Fountaine,* pp. 15–16.

43. Cotton, *Commentary on John,* pp. 325, 407; William Hubbard quoted by Perry Miller, *Orthodoxy in Massachusetts 1630–1650* (Boston, 1933), p. 248; Cotton, *Way of Life,* pp. 40–41; *The Puritans,* ed. Perry Miller and Thomas H. Johnson, rev. ed. (New York, 1963), vol. 1, p. 318.

44. Cotton, *Christ the Fountaine,* pp. 14, 131. Cf. John Davenport's use of spider imagery in *The Saints Anchor-Hold, in all Storms and Tempests* . . . (London, 1661): he says the hope of sinners "shall be *as a spiders web,* finely spun, but not firm, its but an hope of their own making, as the spiders web is wrought out of its own bowels; and, as the spider thinks it self, when it is lodged in its web, so they think themselves safe in their false hope; but as the spiders web is easily and suddenly swept away, so shall their hope be . . . *Isa.* 14.23" (p. 89). For Davenport the simile overwhelms the thought; in Cotton's hands it is a subtle illustration of his theme, showing "exactitude" even as it "wheels about."

45. Cotton, *Commentary on John,* p. 338; Grabo, "John Cotton's Aesthetic," p. 6.

46. Cotton, *A Brief Exposition of the whole Book of Canticles* . . . (London, 1642), pp. 191–192; *Commentary on John,* p. 107.

47. Cotton, *Christ the Fountaine,* p. 213. For Williams's side of the controversy, see Perry Miller's critical anthology, *Roger Williams: His Contribution to the American Tradition* (New York, 1953), pp. 101–205.

48. *Christ the Fountaine,* pp. 71–72; *Gods Mercie,* pp. 40–41; *Way of Life,* p. 475.

49. Cotton, *Spiritual Milk* . . . (Cambridge, N.E., 1656), p. 2; Ziff, *Career,* p. 154; Cotton, *Commentary on John,* p. 230. See Hall, *Faithful Shepherd,* pp. 25–120, 159–166, on Cotton's role.

50. Cotton, *Commentary on John,* pp. 40–41.

51. Cotton, *Way of Life,* pp. 98–99.

52. Ziff, *Career,* p. 165; Cotton, *Gods Promise,* p. 6.

53. *Johnson's Wonder-Working Providence 1628–1651,* ed. J. Franklin Jameson (New York, 1959), pp. 136, 94; Jonathan Mitchell, preface to Shepard's *Parable,* in *Works,* vol. 2 (New York, 1967, reprinting 1853 Boston ed.); Neal, *History of New-England,* vol. 1, p. 278. Mitchell's

preface states that almost all of Shepard's work was published from notes; "only about a sheet himself wrote out in his lifetime," he says parenthetically.

54. See Pettit, *Heart Prepared*, p. 107, comparing Shepard and Hooker; also Shuffelton, *Thomas Hooker*, p. 292, and Hall, *Faithful Shepherd*, p. 167, on Shepard's legalism.

55. McGiffert, introduction to *God's Plot*. On Calvin, Shepard writes to a friend, in *Certain Select Cases Resolved . . .* (London, 1648), pp. 138–139: "Again you ask me, whether *Calvin* doth not express fully my thoughts about our spiritual union, in his *lib. 4, cap. 17.* I answer, I have forgot what he hath writ, and my self have read long since out of him, and for the present I have no books about me where I am, and therefore cannot satisfie you in this, neither know I when I shall seeke to finde out the book and place." One suspects a bit of disingenuousness here.

56. Shepard, *Parable*, in *Works*, vol. 2, p. 134.

57. Shepard, *Certain Select Cases*, pp. 4–5; *Sincere Convert*, p. 35.

58. Shepard, *Parable*, in *Works*, vol. 2, p. 449; *Sincere Convert* (London, 1664), pp. 47, 48.

59. On Shepard's disavowal of *Sincere Convert*, see Mather, *Magnalia*, vol. 1, p. 389; *Sincere Convert*, p. 29; *The Sound Believer* (London, 1659), p. 100.

60. Shepard, *Parable*, in *Works*, vol. 2, p. 28.

61. Ibid., pp. 26, 194, 248.

62. Ibid., p. 471; *Certain Select Cases*, p. 216.

63. Shepard, *Sincere Convert*, pp. 190, 19, 27.

64. Shepard, *Parable*, in *Works*, vol. 2, pp. 113–117; *God's Plot*, p. 60.

65. *Sound Believer*, p. 305; *Parable*, in *Works*, vol. 2, p. 46.

66. *Parable*, in *Works*, vol. 2, pp. 43–44, 613, 255–256. The original edition (London, 1660), part one, p. 164, reads "run for a spurt," not "run for a while."

67. Ibid., p. 73; *Sound Believer*, pp. 116–117.

68. *Sound Believer*, p. 230; *Certain Select Cases*, pp. 104–105.

69. *Sincere Convert*, p. 184.

70. See *God's Plot*, p. 71; *Sincere Convert*, p. 32.

Chapter Seven

1. On frontier pulpits versus Boston drawing rooms, see James W. Jones, *The Shattered Synthesis: New England Puritanism before the Great Awakening* (New Haven and London, 1973), e.g., p. ix.

2. Pettit, *The Heart Prepared: Grace and Conversion in Puritan Spiritual Life* (New Haven, 1966), p. 206.

3. Cotton Mather, *Magnalia Christi Americana* (Hartford, 1855, 1st ed.

1702), vol. 1, p. 66; Jonathan Mitchell's marginalia quoted by Miller in *The New England Mind: The Seventeenth Century* (New York, 1939), p. 473. Ezekiel Rogers is also cited in Mather's *Magnalia*, reprinted in *Children and Youth in America: A Documentary History*, ed. Robert H. Bremner, vol. 1 (Cambridge, Mass., 1970), p. 36.

4. Cotton Mather said women outnumbered men in the faithful by three to one: "There are three Maries to one John." Cited by Roger Thompson, *Women in Stuart England and America: A Comparative Study* (London, 1974), p. 11; see also pp. 94–95. Cf. Emory Elliott, *Power in the Pulpit in Puritan New England* (Princeton, 1975), who argues that a growing orientation of New England Puritanism toward comfort parallels the increased female role in the church and in the home, since "the mother had replaced the father as the spiritual leader of the household" (p. 57), a view I question.

5. Robert G. Pope, *The Half-Way Covenant: Church Membership in Puritan New England* (Princeton, 1969), suspects that the term "half-way covenant" originated in the 1760s to deride Edwards's followers (p. 8). On the striking decline in conversions from the first to the second generation, see Kenneth Lockridge, *A New England Town: The First Hundred Years* (New York, 1970), pp. 33–34, also 79, 85 on feelings of "failure."

6. Pope, *Half-Way Covenant*, p. 151.

7. Robert Middlekauff, *The Mathers: Three Generations of Puritan Intellectuals, 1596–1728* (New York, 1971), p. 114, notes the fragmentation of the community implicit in the jeremiad, which seems to have been so named by Perry Miller in *The New England Mind: From Colony to Province* (Cambridge, Mass., 1953), pp. 19–39. In *The Interpreted Design as a Structural Principle in American Prose* (New Haven, 1969), David Minter argues that the jeremiads were pleasing because their ritual humiliation told the fathers' story while avoiding the fathers' inherited task. Stephen Foster, *Their Solitary Way: The Puritan Social Ethic in the First Century of Settlement in New England* (New Haven and London, 1971), has a similar sense that the jeremiads avoided real issues. Frank Shuffelton's *Thomas Hooker 1586–1647* (Princeton, 1977) points out the absence of terror, the focus on "external peccadilloes and lapses" and natural disasters, and suggests that preachers used the jeremiad form "to guard the entrance to the church rather than as a stimulant for conversion" (p. 293).

8. Foster, *Their Solitary Way*, e.g., p. 126. Sacvan Bercovitch, in "Horologicals to Chronometricals: The Rhetoric of the Jeremiad," *Literary Monographs*, vol. 3, ed. Eric Rothstein (Madison and London, 1970), pp. 1–124, sees the jeremiad as the seedbed for all of American literature. He overemphasizes the "unshakable optimism" that finally becomes reset in the theme of the prophetic self.

9. Shepard, *Parable of the Ten Virgins*, in *Works*, vol. 2 (New York, 1967, reprinting 1853 Boston ed.), p. 65.

10. David Stannard in *The Puritan Way of Death: A Study in Religion, Culture, and Social Change* (New York, 1977) shows connections between the jeremiad, growing extravagance in escapist funeral rituals, and a loss of felt community after the first generation.

11. Hoar, *The Sting of Death and Death Unstung* (Boston, 1680), p. 7.

12. Ibid., pp. 11, 24.

13. Norton, "A Funeral Elogy Upon . . . Anne Bradstreet," at the end of her *Several Poems* (Boston, 1678), quoted by Elizabeth Wade White, *Anne Bradstreet "The Tenth Muse"* (New York, 1971), p. 366.

14. Webber, *The Eloquent "I": Style and Self in 17th Century Prose* (Madison, 1968), p. 136. Cf. E. Brooks Holifield, *The Covenant Sealed: The Development of Puritan Sacramental Theology in Old and New England, 1570–1720* (New Haven, 1974), who finds that the original Puritan distrust of visible symbols yielded to a "sacramental renaissance," in part to magnify the minister's status. This development parallels the growing physicality in second-generation discourse.

15. Willard, *A Compleat Body of Divinity* . . . (Boston, 1726), pp. 234–242.

16. Allan I. Ludwig, *Graven Images: New England Stonecarving and Its Symbols, 1650–1815* (Middletown, Conn., 1966). Ludwig's assertion that visual iconography of death had always been natural to American Puritans is questionable, since the earliest illustrations date from the second generation.

17. Hall, *The Faithful Shepherd: A History of the New England Ministry in the Seventeenth Century* (Chapel Hill, 1972), p. 195.

18. Robert Middlekauff, *Mathers*, p. 94, notes Mather's self-concern.

19. Colman, *The Prophet's Death Lamented and Improved* . . . (Boston, 1723), p. 36.

20. Hall, *Faithful Shepherd*, p. 268, notes that Increase "fell into the habit of announcing that each sermon was his final message to an erring people."

21. Mather, *Heavens Alarm to the World* (Boston, 1682), pp. 30, 37; idem, *The Day of Trouble is Near* . . . (Cambridge, Mass., 1674), p. 23. Many Puritans spoke of the evils of long hair; among the "Provoking Evils" listed by the 1675 General Court in explanation for the Indian attacks is the fact that "long haire, like weomens haire, is worne by some men." *Puritan Political Ideas, 1558–1794*, ed. Edmund Morgan (n.p., 1965), pp. 227–228.

22. Mather, *The Day of Trouble is Near* . . . (Cambridge, New England, 1674), pp. 9 (loins), 13 (sheep), 23 (diamonds); *David Serving His Generation* (preached December 1697), pp. 25–26 (service), 16, 25. Cotton Mather, *A Father Departing* (Boston, 1723), p. 27.

23. Mather, *Day of Trouble*, p. 26; Middlekauff, *Mathers*, p. 105.

24. Mather, *Heavens Alarm to the World*, pp. 27–28; Middlekauff, *Mathers*, p. 328.

25. Mather, *A Call from Heaven, To the Present And Succeeding Genera-tions* . . . (Boston, 1685), p. 29; *Two Sermons Testifying against the Sin of Drunkenness* . . . (Cambridge, Mass., 1673), p. 26; *A Sermon . . . Preached on a Publick Fast* . . . (Boston, 1682), pp. 19–20.

26. Mather, *The Divine Right of Infant-Baptisme* (Boston, 1680), p. 9. The sword was one of his favorite images for God's power.

27. Colman, *The Prophet's Death Lamented and Improved* . . . (Boston, 1723), p. 36. Sacvan Bercovitch notes Cotton Mather's "strange identi-fication with Jesus" as part of Cotton's strategy of transforming defeat into victory through the imagination; see "Cotton Mather," in *Major Writers of Early American Literature*, ed. Everett Emerson (Madison, 1972), pp. 7, 93–149.

28. Samuel Willard is also very physical in imagining Christ's sufferings on the cross; see *Compleat Body*, pp. 402–405. There were no vital organs pierced; thus Christ died a lingering death, which was especially cruel because the whole weight of Christ's body was on the nails in the palms and the soles, "having the greatest concourse of the nerves" (p. 402). "Look upon this bloody Saviour . . . and then say, what Love is com-parable to his? . . . look yourselves into Raptures: Meditate, till you find your selves transported, and your Affections all on a Blaze" (p. 405).

29. Mather, *Two Sermons Testifying against the Sin of Drunkenness* . . . (Cambridge, New England, 1673), p. 23; introduction to *A Course of Sermons on Early Piety* . . ., by eight Boston ministers (Boston, 1721), pp. iii–v.

30. Willard, *Impenitent Sinners Warned* . . . (Boston, 1698), p. 40. Cf. Elliott, *Power in the Pulpit*, p. 163. Elliott sees Willard as more comfort-ing and assuring than I do (pp. 14, 160–177); also Jones, *Shattered Synthesis* (pp. 54–75) presents Willard as orthodox but liberalizing in his concern with happiness. Seymour Van Dyken, in *Samuel Willard, 1640–1707: Preacher of Orthodoxy in an Era of Change* (Grand Rapids, Mich., 1972), notes the absence of chiliastic fantasy in Willard's orthodoxy, as contrasted with Increase Mather (p. 190). This biography also records that Willard was the son of a relatively distinguished Puri-tan and that Willard's mother died soon after he was born (pp. 11–14). Ernest Benson Lowrie, *The Shape of the Puritan Mind: The Thought of Samuel Willard* (New Haven, 1974), also emphasizes Willard's theology of happiness; for him Willard's central theme is God's accommodation to man's capacities.

31. Willard, *A Brief Discourse of Justification* (Boston, 1686), p. 16. His God is often a rather mechanical one; as he says in *The Fiery Tryal no strange thing* (Boston, 1682), p. 18, "There is a higher hand moving all these lesser wheels."

32. Willard, *The Truly Blessed Man* . . . (Boston, 1700), p. 47.

33. Willard, *Impenitent Sinners Warned*, p. 48; Jones, *Shattered Synthesis*,

p. 55. *A Compleat Body of Divinity* . . . comprises 220 lectures delivered once a month, on Tuesday afternoons, from 1687–88 to 1707 with surprisingly few omissions, until Willard's health failed. It was published in Boston in 1726 by several printers' hands, as 914 double-columned pages in a huge volume. The pagination skips from p. 159 to p. 176; later, on p. 666, there is a printer's apology because another printer had started subsequent pages at p. 581. So there are two sets of pp. 581–666. The full title is *A Compleat Body of Divinity in Two Hundred and Fifty Expository Lectures on the Assembly's Shorter Catechism.* It is actually 220 lectures, with 26 others prepared. Willard skipped September, December, and February of 1692–93, the time of the witch trials. As Lowrie says, in *Shape of the Puritan Mind,* pp. 3–4, the book is surprisingly quotable for being half again as long as Calvin's *Institutes,* but that is not to say it holds the attention without effort.

34. Willard, *Compleat Body,* pp. 1–2, 7, 8. Other citations to *Compleat Body* are incorporated in the text.

35. Willard, *Compleat Body,* e.g., pp. 42–44, 99, and 121 on means and ends. When describing what to him are the two most "mysterious" Gospel doctrines, the three-in-one Trinity and Christ as both God and man, he says, "These things confound carnal reason, and surprize the humane understanding; it would lose it self in the speculation, did not faith come in and support it" (p. 293). Earthly language is inadequate because it is part of time, while God is eternal (pp. 59–63). But God adapts himself to our minds, and his language therefore addresses our understanding, will, and affections (p. 63). In doing so, God's style is "for the most part plain," but "with powerful majesty" (p. 19).

36. Willard's argument against the *"Enthusiasts"* is that they listen to "a secret, and oftentimes a violent impulse, and back them with carnal Reasonings" (p. 28).

37. For Willard hierarchy sets value, and wrath brings disorder. Once hierarchy and rank are accepted, self-love becomes permissible if one loves oneself as part of the whole. See Lowrie, *Shape of the Puritan Mind,* pp. 106–107.

38. On the problem of how sin is physically transmitted, Willard says, "And all the arguings I have met with on this subject, seem obscure and unintelligible. And I believe it is one of the Judgments of God which are unsearchable. It is then a point of Faith" (p. 198). Avoiding any imputation of sin to Eve or to the mother's body, or to bodies in general, he emphasizes rational understanding, not blame. When Willard speaks later of original sin, he refuses to discuss how it is communicated because "we took notice of that under a former Question, so far as we might with sobriety" (p. 209).

39. Election will remain forever a secret, Willard says in his six sermons on the issue. You must wait upon God's love (pp. 246–271). As Willard

concludes. "When we have run things up to the divine will, we have gone as high as we can" (p. 260).

40. On speaking "synecdochically," see p. 600; also pp. 123, 472.

41. *Brief Discourse,* pp. 122–123; *The Child's Portion Or the unseen Glory of God, Affected, and Proved* . . . (Boston, 1684), p. 144.

42. Willard, *The High Esteem Which God hath of the Death of his Saints* (Boston, 1683), p. 12.

43. Willard, *The Child's Portion,* pp. 17, 66; *Checkered State* (Boston, 1701), one of the italicized uses.

44. Willard, *Child's Portion,* pp. 53–54; Pemberton, *A Funeral Sermon on the Death of that Learned and Excellent Divine, the Reverend Mr. Samuel Willard* (Boston, 1707), p. 63. However, Pemberton's extracts in the preface to *Compleat Body* also call Willard "my Translated Father . . . a Pastor, Father and Friend." Cf. Elliott, *Power in the Pulpit,* p. 16; Lowrie, *Shape of the Puritan Mind,* p. 9.

45. Cotton Mather cited by Thompson, *Women in Stuart England and America,* p. 147; see pp. 147–151 for evidence of lenient parents in second-generation New England. Cobbett, *A Fruitful and Usefull Discourse* . . . (London, 1656, 1st pub. New England 1654), p. 188; see pp. 186–213 on the "arising generation."

46. Cobbett, *Fruitfull and Usefull Discourse,* pp. 198, 227–230, 187. Cobbett also observes, p. 187, that men's hair cannot be "so long as womens, who are naturally of a moyster temper," for which he is thankful.

47. On James Janeway's *A Token for Children* (Boston, 1781, 1st ed. 1671) and parental expectations, see Joseph E. Illick, "Child-Rearing in Seventeenth-Century England and America," reprinted in *The History of Childhood,* ed. Lloyd deMause (New York, 1974), pp. 317–318, and John F. Walzer, "A Period of Ambivalence: Eighteenth-Century American Childhood," in the same book, p. 361. On parental innocence and patriarchal inability to adapt to change, see Thompson, *Women in Stuart England and America,* p. 152. In *Power in the Pulpit,* pp. 79–80, Emory Elliott suggests that early childhood conversions were an "artificial form of self-trust" that "collapsed" in adolescence for lack of relation between childhood piety and adult roles. Some converted children, like some of the witches, were male. John F. Walzer connects these conversions to projected parental guilt.

48. Middlekauff, *Mathers,* pp. 201, 365; Christopher Bollas, private conversation.

49. On Timothy Root, see Thomas H. Johnson, "Jonathan Edwards and the 'Young Folks' Bible,'" *New England Quarterly,* 5 (January 1932), pp. 37–54. A less pungent version is in Herbert Wallace Schneider, *The Puritan Mind* (Ann Arbor, 1961, 1st pub. 1930), pp. 131–132.

50. Loren Baritz, *City on a Hill: A History of Ideas and Myths in America* (New York, 1964), p. 57.

Chapter Eight

1. Wigglesworth is quoted (from his diary) by Stephen Foster, *Their Solitary Way: The Puritan Social Ethic in the First Century of Settlement in New England* (New Haven, 1971), p. 121. Franklin's first version of Poor Richard's statement about hope (1736) is more earthy than Father Abraham's recasting (1758) of it as "He that lives upon Hope dies fasting," though the first may have been a misprint. See James A. Sappenfield, *A Sweet Instruction: Franklin's Journalism as a Literary Apprenticeship* (Carbondale and Edwardsville, Ill., 1973), p. 152.

2. Brooks, *America's Coming-of-Age* (New York, 1915). A recent restatement of Brooks's thesis is Quentin Anderson, "Practical and Visionary Americans," *American Scholar*, 45 (Summer 1976), pp. 405–418. Some studies that have connected Edwards and Franklin are John Lynen, *The Design of the Present: Essays on Time and Form in American Literature* (New Haven, 1969); Michael Kammen, *People of Paradox: An Inquiry Concerning the Origins of American Civilization* (New York, 1972), pp. 195–197; Robert F. Sayre, *The Examined Self: Benjamin Franklin, Henry Adams, Henry James* (Princeton, 1964), pp. 34–37; and Herbert Wallace Schneider, *The Puritan Mind* (Ann Arbor, 1958, 1st pub. 1930), pp. 102–155 on Edwards and pp. 237–256 on Franklin as practical Puritan.

3. See Paul Conner, *Poor Richard's Politicks: Benjamin Franklin and his New American Order* (New York, 1965), pp. xi, 212–217. Cf. David L. Parker, "From Sound Believer to Practical Preparationist: Some Puritan Harmonics in Franklin's Autobiography," in *The Oldest Revolutionary: Essays on Benjamin Franklin*, ed. J. A. Leo Lemay ([Philadelphia], 1976), pp. 67–75.

4. Sappenfield, *A Sweet Instruction*, and Daniel B. Shea, Jr., *Spiritual Autobiography in Early America* (Princeton, 1968), connect Franklin to the tradition of spiritual narrative.

5. See Sappenfield, *Sweet Instruction*, and Conner, *Poor Richard's Politicks*. Hume's letter (1774) is cited by Conner, p. 151. John Lynen, in *Design of the Present*, analyzes the *Autobiography* as a "double perspective" of the mature Franklin on the early Franklin, with each incident as a successive approximation of the mature self; cf. P. M. Zall, "A Portrait of the Autobiographer as an Old Artificer," in *The Oldest Revolutionary*, ed. Lemay, pp. 53–65. On the Godfrey incident, see J. A. Leo Lemay, "Benjamin Franklin," in *Major Writers of Early*

American Literature, ed. Everett Emerson (Madison, 1972), pp. 211–212.

6. A fine essay on Franklin's mask making is John Griffith's "Franklin's Sanity and the Man behind the Masks," in *The Oldest Revolutionary,* ed. Lemay, pp. 123–138. For Griffith "it is the story of learning to be approved of" (p. 129), through the winning "fabrication" of a tone of calmness, sanity, and control.

7. Franklin's letter to his mother cited by Schneider, *Puritan Mind,* p. 249. See Claude-Anne Lopez and Eugenia W. Herbert, *The Private Franklin: The Man and His Family* (New York, 1975), on Franklin's no-saying father. The *Autobiography* tends to idealize the father, Lopez and Herbert observe, while "unfairly" casting his brother James, who actually liberated Benjamin, as the villain (p. 9). On Philadelphia as "the most unfettered middle-class community of the Western world," see Carl and Jessica Bridenbaugh, *Rebels and Gentleman: Philadelphia in the Age of Franklin* (New York, 1942), especially pp. 361–364.

8. See Lynen, *Design of the Present,* p. 136, on Franklin's role playing. Conner's *Poor Richard's Politicks* suggests that Franklin's models of personal and political order are opposite to his real sense of himself. Bruce Ingham Granger's *Benjamin Franklin: An American Man of Letters* (Ithaca, 1964) studies the growth of his style in relation to "a genteel, coffeehouse audience of merchants and professional men" (p. 21). Granger shows Franklin consistently revising, even in the *Autobiography,* to replace colloquial with reputable expressions (e.g., pp. 229–235).

9. The quotations are from the *Autobiography,* part 1. I use the term "false self" more loosely here than R. D. Laing does in *The Divided Self: An Existential Study in Sanity and Madness* (London, 1960). Franklin develops his false self quite consciously, whereas Laing's definition has to do with more unconscious accommodation. On Franklin's wife see Lopez and Herbert, *The Private Franklin,* p. 91.

10. Franklin's lack of inwardness is what so exercised D. H. Lawrence and Melville, among many others. In this respect the contrast between Franklin and Edwards seems to show the opposite of the " 'low gradient' affect" Lawrence Stone associates with the Puritans, and the "'steep gradient' affect" he associates with the eighteenth-century upper bourgeoisie and squirarchy (see *The Family, Sex and Marriage in England 1500–1800* [London, 1977], p. 268), unless high affect means superficial sociability. Richard Hofstadter's *America at 1750: A Social Portrait* (New York, 1971), p. 62, points out that Franklin was one of only two descendants of indentured servants who attained the heights that Franklin implies everyone can reach with hard work.

11. David Minter argues that Franklin's project of arriving at moral perfection arises during his journey back to Philadelphia, the most anxious time in his life. Having failed in his grand plans and having been

victimized by friends and authorities, he now tries to remold himself toward social service as he reenters a strange new world. See *The Interpreted Design as a Structural Principle in American Prose* (New Haven and London, 1969), pp. 80–84.

12. Edwards continued to dream of holy community on earth; see *An Humble Attempt To promote Explicit Agreement and Visible Union of God's People in Extraordinary Prayer* . . . (Boston, 1748), in *The Works of Jonathan Edwards,* vol. 5, ed. Stephen J. Stein (New Haven and London, 1977), pp. 307–436.

13. Franklin, *Autobiography,* reprinted in *Anthology of American Literature,* ed. George McMichael (New York, 1974), p. 350. The text is from the 1964 edition established by L. W. Labaree and others. Edwards, "Personal Narrative," in *Jonathan Edwards: Representative Selections,* ed. Clarence H. Faust and Thomas H. Johnson, rev. ed. (New York, 1962), pp. 70–71.

14. The word "autobiography" was coined in 1797 and popularized by Robert Southey in 1809. (See the *O.E.D.* and 1972 supplement. I am indebted for this reference to Barrie Daniels.) Franklin usually referred to his unfinished manuscript as "memoirs." Puritan spiritual autobiographies bore a wide variety of titles; see Owen C. Watkins, *The Puritan Experience* (London, 1972), especially his bibliography of primary sources. The word "autobiography" retrospectively imposes a more conscious self-coherence on the provisional sense of self that Franklin was aiming for, or the God-centered self striven for in Puritan narratives.

15. David Minter, in *Interpreted Design,* pp. 72–73, suggests a possible element of wish in Edwards's experience of the orthodox conversion pattern.

16. Shea, *Spiritual Autobiography,* pp. 163–164.

17. Edwards, "Personal Narrative," in *Representative Selections,* ed. Faust and Johnson, all quotations, p. 57. As Minter notes, *Interpreted Design,* pp. 74–76, Edwards's beginning is "treated gently" compared to the terror and stern order of his second awakening, when the self's needs yield to the pattern and "pure lyricism" of God's design.

18. Franklin, *Autobiography,* in *Anthology,* ed. McMichael, pp. 286–287. See Lopez and Herbert, *Private Franklin;* also Thomas Fleming, *The Man Who Dared the Lightning: A New Look at Benjamin Franklin* (New York, 1971), which popularizes the drama of Franklin's relationship with his son (bridge of words, p. 206).

19. Franklin, *Autobiography,* p. 287.

20. Ibid.

21. See Betty Kushen, "Benjamin Franklin, Oedipus, and the Price of Submission," *Literature & Psychology,* 25 (1975), pp. 147–157, which stresses Franklin's paternal role and "oral inhibition"; G. J. Barker-Benfield, *The Horrors of the Half-Known Life: Male Attitudes toward*

Women and Sexuality in Nineteenth-Century America (New York, 1976), p. 29; and Richard L. Bushman, "On the Uses of Psychology: Conflict and Conciliation in Benjamin Franklin," *History and Theory,* 5 (1966), pp. 225–240.

22. According to his opponents, Edwards even said the apocalypse was starting in Northampton, a charge he vehemently denied. See *Apocalyptic Writings, Works,* vol. 5, ed. Stein, intro. pp. 28–29. On Edwards's newspaper cullings, see pp. 253–284 for negative events from 1747 to 1757, mostly 1747–48, and pp. 285–297 for hopeful evangelical events. The *Humble Attempt* is scriptural not experiential in its language, though in his eagerness to bring on the millennium through a concert of prayer he waffles on the major objection that it would set up a human ritual (pp. 368–370). On Edwards's call for the New Jerusalem in New England, see *Works,* vol. 4, ed. C. C. Goen (New Haven, 1972), *The Great Awakening,* especially *Some Thoughts Concerning the Present Revival of Religion in New-England* (1743), pp. 353–358, 384–385. Again his argument is entirely from the Bible, except to say that Christ as sun will rise in the West, since that is "contrary to the course of this world" (p. 357). He also argues that the New Jerusalem will happen in New England since the colony is the last and weakest. In his introduction to volume 5 of the *Works,* Stephen J. Stein calls Edwards's reasoning in these pages "strange" and "tortured" (p. 28).

23. On "new heaven, new earth," see *Apocalyptic Writings, Works,* vol. 5, ed. Stein, pp. 140–142. Edwards says the New Jerusalem will not be in the solar system (pp. 149–158, 166–167). But he also says the New Jerusalem will be the church in this world (pp. 197–198, 415–416). In either case, he means spiritual, not physical realities (p. 167). "New Jerusalem" is from Isaiah 65.17–19, also Ezekiel 40–48. Edwards says it means the church before the end of the world in the Old Testament; after the end of the world, in the New (pp. 197–198). It seems to me that "new heaven, new earth" represents his private fantasy more than any sensitivity to real community. For Whitefield's sense that Edwards's hopes were "premature," see Stein's introduction, pp. 86–87. Edwards's theology was always God centered rather than world centered. In the list of his sixty-six sermons on Revelations at the end of *Works,* vol. 5, there is not one on Rev. 21.1. For a different view, see Alan Heimert, *Religion and the American Mind from the Great Awakening to the Revolution* (Cambridge, Mass., 1966), which sees a radical pietistic thrust for holy community leading to the American Revolution. A succinct critique of Heimert's view is in Edmund Morgan's review, *William and Mary Quarterly,* 24 (July 1967), pp. 454–459. James West Davidson, *The Logic of Millennial Thought: Eighteenth-Century New England* (New Haven and London, 1977), makes a complex and persuasive case for locating the roots of millennial thought in exemplary conversion, not social action; see especially pp. 215–230, 258–260, de-

fining millennial thought as fundamentally apolitical. A more sympathetic use of Heimert, similarly flawed I think, is in Philip Greven's
*The Protestant Temperament: Patterns of Child-Rearing, Religious Ex-
perience, and the Self in Early America* (New York, 1977), e.g., pp.
10–11 and the epilogue. See also Cushing Strout, *The New Heavens
and New Earth: Political Religion in America* (New York, 1974), pp.
1–76.

24. See Lopez and Herbert, *Private Franklin,* p. 68; also Arthur Bernon
Tourtellot, *Benjamin Franklin: The Shaping of Genius—The Boston
Years* (Garden City, N.Y., 1977), pp. 3–4. Franklin's father Josiah was
a covenanted Puritan who converted shortly after he arrived from England in 1683.

25. See John Griffith, "The Rhetoric of Franklin's 'Autobiography,'"
Criticism, 13 (Winter 1971), pp. 77–94. On the New England style
of suppressing anger, see Michael Zuckerman, *Peaceable Kingdoms:
New England Towns in the Eighteenth Century* (New York, 1970), pp.
61–84, especially p. 64, and Greven's *Protestant Temperament.*

26. Poor Richard quoted in Sappenfield, *Sweet Instruction,* p. 165. On
Franklin's wish to be father of his country, see Conner, *Poor Richard's
Politicks,* pp. x, 136–148.

27. Poor Richard's 1740 saying is cited in Frances M. Barbour, *A Concor-
dance to the Sayings in Franklin's "Poor Richard"* (Detroit , 1974), p. 71.
In "Franklin's Sanity" John Griffith provocatively suggests that negative
responses to the *Autobiography* have to do with the reader's uneasiness
about role playing. However, for Griffith to deny any unconscious conflicts in Franklin (p. 136) diminishes his subject's complexity.

28. See Lawrence's chapter on Franklin in *Studies in Classic American
Literature* (New York, 1955, 1st pub. 1923). In *Puritan Mind,* p. 250,
Schneider criticizes Lawrence for mistaking Franklin's instrumental
values as ideal values.

29. Kammen, *People of Paradox,* pp. 75–81. See Ernest Lee Tuveson,
Redeemer Nation: The Idea of America's Millennial Role (Chicago and
London, 1968). Wood, *The Creation of the American Republic, 1776–
1787* (Chapel Hill, 1969), pp. 113–114 (on resentment and ideology)
and passim; also Wood's "Rhetoric and Reality in the American Revolution," *William and Mary Quarterly,* 23 (January 1966), pp. 3–32, especially p. 26.

30. See Richard Brown, "Modernization and Modern Personality in Early
America, 1600–1865—A Sketch of a Synthesis," *Journal of Interdisciplinary History,* 2 (Winter 1972), pp. 201–228; he derives his frame
from Alex Inkeles, p. 216. See also Thomas C. Cochran, "The Business
Revolution," *American Historical Review,* 79 (December 1974), pp.
1,449–1,466, which argues that growth of an entrepreneurial group
with freedom to manipulate was prior to and necessary for a tech-
nological revolution. A major study of personality and modernization is

Alex Inkeles and David H. Smith, *Becoming Modern: Individual Change in Six Developing Countries* (London, 1974), which suggests more adaptibility in the personality than is granted by Freudian theory, though the authors neglect to mention what happens to those who don't adapt.

31. Greene, "Search for Identity: An Interpretation of the Meaning of Selected Patterns of Social Response in Eighteenth Century America," *Journal of Social History*, 3 (Spring 1970), pp. 189–220. See also Kenneth Lockridge, "Social Change and the Meaning of the American Revolution," *Journal of Social History*, 6 (Summer 1973), pp. 403–439, who argues that the revolution offered a "crusading ideology" for rural groups to defend a premodern way of life (p. 428). In *Puritanism and the Wilderness: The Intellectual Significance of the New England Frontier 1629–1700* (New York and London, 1969), Peter Carroll suggests that the Puritan "inability to select alternatives" shows their bankruptcy in an expanding society; they were unable to resolve conflict except through organic ideals of cohesion (p. 128). See also John Seelye's analysis of Puritan maps for their concentric rather than expansionist perspectives, in *Prophetic Waters: The River in Early American Life and Literature* (New York, 1977), p. 138.

32. Edwards, "Personal Narrative," in *Representative Selections*, ed. Faust and Johnson, p. 59; Samuel Hopkins, *The Life and Character of the Late Reverend Mr. Jonathan Edwards* (Boston, 1765), reprinted in *Jonathan Edwards: A Profile*, ed. David Levin (New York, 1969), pp. 1–86, quotations pp. 47, 40, 42.

33. Lynen, *Design of the Present*, pp. 111–114.

34. On Timothy Edwards, see Hopkins, *Life and Character;* also Richard L. Bushman, *From Puritan to Yankee: Character and the Social Order in Connecticut, 1690–1765* (Cambridge, Mass., 1967), pp. 153–154; Greven, *Protestant Temperament*, pp. 52–53; and Strout, *New Heavens and New Earth*, p. 31.

35. Greven, *Protestant Temperament*, pp. 109–113, and Richard Bushman, "Jonathan Edwards as Great Man: Identity, Conversion, and Leadership in the Great Awakening," *Soundings*, 52 (1969), pp. 15–46, have placed Edwards's Oedipal conflicts in a social perspective of widespread guilt for drives toward wealth and power. Greven suggests an unconscious hostility to women (pp. 132–133) as well as the suppression of an enormous amount of anger (pp. 109–113). Cf. Strout, *New Heavens and New Earth*, pp. 32–33. Robert D. Rossel, "The Great Awakening: An Historical Analysis," *American Journal of Sociology*, 75 (May 1970), pp. 907–925, suggests a variety of fragmentations and separations leading to anxiety.

36. Edwards, *Religious Affections*, ed. John E. Smith, *Works*, vol. 2 (New Haven, 1959), pp. 377, 205–206.

37. Edwards, "An Essay on the Trinity," *Representative Selections*, ed.

Faust and Johnson, p. 377; "Of Being," *Representative Selections,* p. 22; "Notes on the Mind," *Representative Selections,* p. 35; "Essay on the Trinity," *Representative Selections,* p. 95. Perry Miller's *Jonathan Edwards* (New York, 1959; 1st pub. 1949), an extraordinarily exciting intellectual extravaganza, sets Edwards in the wrong direction by allying him more with Locke and Newton than with Shepard; cf. Wallace E. Anderson, "Immaterialism in Jonathan Edwards' Early Philosophical Notes," *Journal of the History of Ideas,* 25 (April-June 1964), pp. 181–200.

38. For another analysis of Edwards's style and imagery, see Annette Kolodny, "Imagery in the Sermons of Jonathan Edwards," *Early American Literature,* 7 (Fall 1972), pp. 172–182.

39. Quoted by John H. Gerstner in *Steps to Salvation: The Evangelistic Message of Jonathan Edwards* (Philadelphia, 1960), p. 30.

40. Edwards, "The Future Punishment of the Wicked," *Representative Selections,* ed. Faust and Johnson, pp. 144, 145.

41. Edwin H. Cady, in "The Artistry of Jonathan Edwards," *New England Quarterly,* 22 (March 1949), pp. 61–72, rather nicely calls the early imagery "footless" (p. 64).

42. Ibid., p. 69.

43. On stages of conversion, see Norman Pettit, "Hooker's Doctrine of Assurance: A Critical Phase in New England Spiritual Thought," *New England Quarterly,* 47 (December 1974), pp. 518–534.

44. Thomas Prince is cited by C. C. Goen, introduction to Edwards's *Works,* vol. 4, p. 72.

45. Edwards, *A Faithful Narrative . . .,* written 1736 (London, 1737; Boston, 1738), in *Works,* vol. 4, ed. Goen, p. 163, also p. 168.

46. Ibid., pp. 174–179. On "conversion" as a turning of the heart, see also Edwards, *Original Sin,* in *Works,* vol. 3, ed. Clyde Holbrook (New Haven and London, 1970), pp. 363–366.

47. Edwards, *Some Thoughts Concerning the present Revival* (1743), in *Works,* vol. 4, ed. Goen, p. 463. On sin as deformity, see *Some Thoughts,* pp. 461–463; also *Religious Affections,* which contrasts religion's "entireness and symmetry of parts" with "maimed and monstrous" false religion (p. 147, also p. 326). For images of sin as the more conventional filth, dung, and world's dirt, see *Images or Shadows of Divine Things,* ed. Perry Miller (New Haven, 1948), numbers 109, 115, 116 (pp. 91–94), also numbers 122, 195 (pp. 96, 128).

48. Edwards, *Some Thoughts,* pp. 507 (cf. Psalm 104.4), 511 ("ambassadors"); see pp. 374–379, on duties of ministers as representatives of Christ on earth and "the captains of the host in this war" (p. 374), and p. 346 on successful conversions, even among Indians and Negroes, as intimating that the New Jerusalem "has begun to come down from heaven."

49. Edwards, *Some Thoughts,* pp. 394, 326; *A Faithful Narrative,* p. 158. Phebe Bartlett's case is described pp. 199–205.

50. Edwards's letter to Benjamin Colman cited by Goen, introduction to *Works*, vol. 4, p. 73. See Hopkins, *Life and Character*, also Greven, *Protestant Temperament*, pp. 32–33; on Edwards's daughter, pp. 35–36.

51. Hopkins, *Life and Character*, p. 49.

52. Christopher Bollas has suggested the relationship between obsessive rigidity and cold yet demanding mothering, in conversation. See Melanie Klein, "An Obsessional Neurosis in a Six-Year-Old Girl," chapter 3 of *The Psycho-analysis of Children*, 3rd ed. (London, 1954), pp. 65–93, for an instance of a girl who had trained herself in cleanliness by the age of one year, without any severity on the part of her mother, because she was so anxious to please as a result of several earlier privations. Klein finds more unconscious fantasies of envy and destruction at work as well. See also Leanne Domash, "The Development of Tenderness in a Six-Year-Old Boy," *International Review of Psycho-Analysis*, 5 (1978), pp. 65–70, suggesting that obsessionals are "self-parenting" to avoid the mother's failure to be organizer and shield for the self.

53. Greven, *Protestant Temperament*, pp. 132–133, also pp. 79–80 on Edwards's unusually tall stature and his imagery equating height with danger.

54. On spider phobias and unconscious anxieties about mothering, see Ralph B. Little, "Oral Aggression in Spider Legends," *American Imago*, 23 (Summer 1966), p. 176; Richard Sterba, "On Spiders, Hanging and Oral Sadism," *American Imago*, 7 (March 1950), pp. 21–28; Melitta Sperling, "Spider Phobias and Spider Fantasies," *Journal of the American Psychoanalytic Association*, 19 (1971), pp. 472–498; she states (p. 491) that the spider symbolizes "the split-off pregenital and potentially psychotic core," representing both patient and mother; also Howard F. Gloyne, "Tarantism," *American Imago*, 7 (March, 1950), pp. 29–42. Joseph C. Rheingold has described the consequences of a primal fear of "the mutilating mother" in *The Mother, Anxiety, and Death: The Catastrophic Death Complex* (Boston, 1967), which also illuminates some psychodynamics of apocalyptic fantasies. For a broader psychoanalytic study of mothering and religious feelings, see Irving B. Harrison, "On the Maternal Origins of Awe," *Psychoanalytic Study of the Child*, 30 (1975), pp. 181–196. Of course the evidence for all these psychoanalytic connections comes from an age when mothers are more exclusively in charge of children.

55. On the change from preparation to sanctification in Edwards's writings after 1740, see Alan Heimert, review of Gerstner's *Steps to Salvation* in *American Literature*, 32 (January 1961), pp. 470–473.

56. On visible sacraments, see E. Brooks Holifield, *The Covenant Sealed: The Development of Puritan Sacramental Theology in Old and New England, 1570–1720* (New Haven and London, 1974), pp. 192 ff., on Edwards's opposition to the sacraments, pp. 228–229.

57. Edwards, *Images or Shadows,* numbers 147 (p. 102), 157 (p. 109), also 84 (p. 83).
58. Edwards, *Religious Affections,* pp. 99–100.
59. Ibid., pp. 104, 108, 149, 114.
60. Ibid., pp. 150–151, 124, 179. On Edwards's focus on Christ, see Stein, introduction to *Works,* vol. 5, p. 52. On Christ as "dying Redeemer" "manifested in his dying agonies, his bloody sweat, his loud and bitter cries, and bleeding heart, and all this for enemies," see *Religious Affections,* p. 123; on the necessity for total distress, see p. 152.
61. *Religious Affections,* pp. 197, 288 (imagination), 200–201. On "bribery," see pp. 240–241; on anger and gratitude from self-love, p. 243; on conversion, blindness, and tasting, pp. 204–208.
62. Ibid., pp. 246–248 (God's loveliness), 263–265 (what sinners see), 278–284 (new apprehension), 271 (Christ), 291–292 ("not seen").
63. Ibid., pp. 350, 349.
64. Ibid., pp. 364 (fear, child), 170–171 (bold language and confidence), The two shortest signs are the eighth and the ninth.
65. See *Some Thoughts,* in *Works,* vol. 4, p. 507.
66. Edwards, *Representative Selections,* ed. Faust and Johnson, p. 177.
67. Willard quoted by Elliott, *Power in the Pulpit,* pp. 171–172.
68. *Christian Love,* ed. Rev. Tryon Edwards (Philadelphia, 1874, 1st ed. London, 1851).
69. Notebook entry quoted in Arthur Cushman McGiffert, *Creative Lives: Jonathan Edwards* (New York, 1932), p. 10; Edwards, *Freedom of the Will,* in *Works,* vol. 1, ed. Paul Ramsey (New Haven and London, 1957), p. 420. See Paul R. Baumgartner's essay, "Jonathan Edwards: The Theory behind His Use of Figurative Language," *PMLA,* 78 (September 1963), pp. 321–325, for a summary of how Edwards would have liked language to integrate images and shadows into a seamless whole.
70. Ziff's observation was made in a 1966 Berkeley graduate seminar. On the 230–23 vote for dismissal, see Goen, introduction to *Works,* vol. 4, pp. 87–88. Edwards left for Stockbridge in 1751.
71. Edwards, "Farewell Sermon" (July 2, 1750), reprinted in *Selected Sermons of Jonathan Edwards,* ed. H. Norman Gardiner (New York, 1904); quotation p. 126. The sermon is dated here as June 22, 1750; Goen dates it July 2 in his introduction to *Works,* vol. 4, p. 87.
72. Edwards, *Religious Affections,* pp. 351–352; the remark on speculation and benevolence cited by Perry Miller, introduction to *Images or Shadows,* p. 17; "Farewell Sermon," p. 125.
73. The 1767 reviewer (for the *Monthly Review*) is cited in Holbrook's introduction to *Original Sin,* p. 98. As Holbrook notes, Edwards seems to have had no sense of the nature of the controversy after Taylor's book was published in either 1738 or 1740. Holbrook's analysis of Edwards's argument (pp. 27–67) shows Edwards often foundering.

74. *Original Sin,* intro., p. 101. For Edwards's argument on sinful brotherhood, see pp. 253–260, and especially pp. 389–412.
75. On destructive vengeance, see ibid., p. 110; "rebel man," pp. 383, 381, also 390–393.
76. On death as punishment and therefore proof of sin, see ibid., pp. 206–219; on infant deaths, pp. 215–219, 265–268, 342–343, 407–412; on guilt, p. 132; quotation on father-child punishment, p. 215; imagination vs. reason, p. 410. Holbrook's introduction brings out the contradictions.
77. On Taylor, see ibid., pp. 326, 379. Edwards flares up at Taylor more frequently as the text wears on. Particularly tortuous is his attempt to say children are wicked since they come from the womb (Psalm 58.3), while saying Isaiah 49.1 (prophets in the womb) must mean from "the beginning of existence," not birth, since otherwise it would connote infant purity (pp. 265–268). See also Edwards's attempt to wriggle out of the Apostle's discussion of " 'those that had not sinned after the similitude of Adam's transgression' " (pp. 341–342) and his analysis of the names Adam gave to Eve (p. 256).
78. Ibid., pp. 394, 397.
79. Ibid., pp. 402, 146 (God as father), 424. The last quotation is the basis for Perry Miller's optimistic claim about Edwards's brotherhood. It is, in any case, one brief paragraph in a list of secondary objections answered.
80. Ibid., pp. 371, 144.
81. Alexander Allen, *American Religious Leaders: Jonathan Edwards* (Boston, 1889), p. 388. As Hopkins says, *Life and Character,* p. 49, "He was less acquainted with most of his temporal affairs than many of his neighbors; and seldom knew when and by whom his forage for winter was gathered in, or how many milk kine he had; whence his table was furnished, etc." James Carse argues for "a radical this-worldliness" to Edwards in *Jonathan Edwards & The Visibility of God* (New York, 1967), p. 162, though he admits Edwards "was never fully engaged" in the world (p. 181).

Chapter Nine

1. Thomas Shepard, *Parable of the Ten Virgins,* in *Works,* vol. 2 (New York, 1967, reprinting 1853 Boston ed.), p. 177.
2. Stephen Foster, *Their Solitary Way: The Puritan Social Ethic in the First Century of Settlement in New England* (New Haven, 1971), p. 155. Ursula Brumm, in *American Thought and Religious Typology,* trans. John Hooglund (New Brunswick, 1970), traces Puritan continuities.
3. On male and female divisions in the nineteenth century, see especially Ann Douglass, *The Feminization of American Culture* (New York, 1977), and G. J. Barker-Benfield, *The Horrors of the Half-Known Life: Male Attitudes Toward Women and Sexuality in Nineteenth-Century America* (New York, 1976); also Annette Kolodny, *The Lay of the Land*

(Chapel Hill, 1975), Michael Paul Rogin, *Fathers & Children: Andrew Jackson and the Subjugation of the American Indian* (New York, 1975), and Richard Slotkin, *Regeneration Through Violence: The Mythology of the American Frontier, 1600–1860* (Middletown, Conn., 1973). For a useful corrective to male preaching, showing the reality of female sexual feelings, see Carl N. Degler, "What Ought To Be and What Was: Women's Sexuality in the Nineteenth Century," *American Historical Review*, 79 (December 1974), pp. 1,467–1,490. George Santayana graphically described the fantasized self-images of male-female polarity at the end of the nineteenth century as masculine skyscraper will against a female maiden-aunt atmosphere; see Kevin Starr's analysis of Santayana and the genteel tradition in *Americans and the California Dream 1850–1915* (New York, 1973), pp. 419–421.

4. See Henri F. Ellenberger, *The Discovery of the Unconscious: The History and Evolution of Dynamic Psychiatry* (New York, 1970); Nathan G. Hale, Jr., *Freud and the Americans: The Beginnings of Psychoanalysis in the United States, 1876–1917* (New York, 1971); Philip Rieff, *The Triumph of the Therapeutic: Uses of Faith After Freud* (New York, 1966); Paul Roazen, *Freud And His Followers* (New York, 1975), and Juliet Mitchell, *Psychoanalysis and Feminism* (New York, 1974), among other recent studies of the Freudian movement. One scholar who has connected Freud and Puritanism is Cushing Strout in *The New Heavens and New Earth: Political Religion in America* (New York, 1974), esp. pp. 27, 32–33, 38.

5. See Howard Feinstein, "The Prepared Heart: A Comparative Study of Puritan Theology and Psychoanalysis," *American Quarterly*, 22 (Summer 1970), pp. 166–176; also David Bakan, *Sigmund Freud and the Jewish Mystical Tradition* (Princeton, 1958). Ellenberger, in *Discovery of the Unconscious*, p. 544, criticizes Bakan for making too much of Freud's fears of anti-Semitism.

6. See Richard Poirier, *A World Elsewhere: The Place of Style in American Literature* (New York, 1966).

7. Richard Chase and Lionel Trilling are commonly credited with the idea that American classic novels differ from European counterparts in their more asocial concern with self; see Chase's *The American Novel and Its Tradition* (Garden City, N.Y., 1957), though F. O. Mattheisson aptly contrasts the Protestant inwardness of American literature with English traditions of character in *American Renaissance: Art and Expression in the Age of Emerson and Whitman* (London, Toronto, and New York, 1941), pp. 72, 234–236, 270–271, and elsewhere. For criticism of the thesis, see Cushing Strout, "From Trilling to Anderson," *American Quarterly*, 24 (Winter 1972), pp. 601–606; Maurice Gonnaud, "Emerson and the Imperial Self," *1975 English Institute Essays*, pp. 107–128; and especially Nicolaus Mills, *American and English Fiction in the 19th Century: An Antigenre Critique and Comparison* (Bloomington, 1973),

which argues that the differences between American and English classic fiction have far more to do with transcendent versus social style than with "romance" versus "novel." Marius Bewley, in *The Eccentric Design: Form in the Classic American Novel* (New York, 1959), offers an earlier comparative study. Richard Brodhead takes Mills's thesis a further step, in *Hawthorne, Melville, and the Novel* (Chicago and London, 1976), by describing the ways Hawthorne and Melville use conventions of "portentous romance" and "comic realism" to undermine both forms. Leslie Fiedler, in *Love and Death in the American Novel* (New York, 1960), first described the pervasive American theme of male friendship in the wilderness, though Fiedler sees the fantasy simply as regression from adult fears of heterosexual love.

8. Freud, *The Interpretation of Dreams*, trans. James Strachey (New York, 1965, 1st ed. 1900), pp. 239–240.

9. A striking reinterpretation of Freud's *Interpretation of Dreams* as a political rather than a sexual or Oedipal wish fulfillment, along some of the lines I am suggesting for Puritanism, is Carl Schorske's "Politics and Patricide in Freud's *Interpretation of Dreams*," *American Historical Review* (April 1973), pp. 328–347.

10. See Ellenberger, *Discovery of the Unconscious* p. 458; also Roazen, *Freud and His Followers*. A Freud disciple said, "If I had had such a wife, I too could have written all those books" (Roazen, *Freud and His Followers*, p. 57).

11. The Sewall passage is reprinted at the end of the first volume of the anthology edited by Perry Miller and Thomas H. Johnson, *The Puritans*, rev. ed. (New York, 1963), p. 377.

12. See Raymond Williams, *The Country and the City* (New York, 1973).

13. Winthrop, "A Model of Christian Charity" (1630), reprinted in *Puritan Political Ideas*, ed. Edmund Morgan (n.p., 1965), pp. 92–93. The "city on a hill" image comes from Matthew 5.14. The passage is preceded by Winthrop's impassioned appeal for "our Community as members of the same body." Other Puritans used the phrase from Matthew to exhort their communities toward a special self-consciousness.

14. *The American Puritan Imagination: Essays in Revaluation*, ed. Sacvan Bercovitch (London, 1974), p. 8.

15. Freud, "Civilized Sexual Morality and Modern Nervousness" (1908), reprinted in Freud's *Sexuality and the Psychology of Love*, ed. Philip Rieff (New York, 1963), pp. 20–40. On the American reception of Freud's theories, see Hale, *Freud and the Americans*, pp. 462–480.

16. This is obviously oversimplified. In *Homicide in American Fiction 1798–1860* (Ithaca, 1957), David Brion Davis discusses the father's absence as a loss of superego in the culture; his perspective is more conventionally Freudian. For the shift toward mother-dominated homes, see Richard Sennett, *Families against the City: Middle Class Homes of Industrial Chicago, 1872–1890* (Cambridge, Mass., 1970); Barker–Benfield,

Horrors of the Half-Known Life; and Douglas, *Feminization of American Culture.* Douglas's book has been attacked by David Schuyler, "Inventing a Feminine Past," *New England Quarterly,* 51 (September 1978), pp. 291–308, for various errors, overstatements, and projections of contemporary feminism, but her central argument about male and female polarization is unchallenged. Alexis de Tocqueville noted the decline of the father's authority in preindustrial American families; see *Democracy in America,* vol. 2, ed. Phillips Bradley (New York, 1945, 1st pub. 1840), pp. 202–207. Two essays by Ruth H. Bloch pinpoint the change in sex roles and give an incisive overview: "American Feminine Ideals in Transition: The Rise of the Moral Mother, 1785–1815," *Feminist Studies,* 4 (June 1978), pp. 101–126, and "Untangling the Roots of Modern Sex Roles: A Survey of Four Centuries of Change," *Signs,* 4 (Winter 1978), pp. 237–252. Laurel Thatcher Ulrich sets the change from Puritan prescriptions for female godliness, strength, and mutuality with men to genteel prescriptions for motherly tenderness even earlier in the eighteenth century; see "Vertuous Women Found: New England Ministerial Literature, 1668–1735," *American Quarterly,* 28 (Spring 1976), pp. 20–40. Also see Alexander Mitscherlich, *Society Without the Father: A Contribution to Social Psychology,* trans. Eric Mosbacher (New York, 1969, 1st pub. 1963).

17. See Joel Porte, *The Romance in America: Studies in Cooper, Poe, Hawthorne, Melville, and James* (Middletown, Conn., 1969).

18. On Whitman's androgynous resolution of conflict, see Albert Gelpi, *The Tenth Muse: The Psyche of the American Poet* (Cambridge, Mass., and London, 1975), pp. 153–216. Stephen A. Black's *Whitman's Journeys into Chaos: A Psychoanalytic Study of the Poetic Process* (Princeton, 1975) is a perceptive and sensitive account of Whitman's efforts and ultimate failure (after 1865) to transform his unconscious conflicts into poetry; Stephen E. Whicher's *Freedom and Fate: An Inner Life of Ralph Waldo Emerson* (Philadelphia, 1953) is still the best study of the anxieties underneath Emerson's compensatory prose. For the development of the term "individualism" in France in the 1820s by conservatives and its transformation by Americans who took Tocqueville's condemnation for positive description, see Steven Lukes, "The Meanings of 'Individualism,'" *Journal of the History of Ideas,* 32 (January-March 1971), pp. 45–66.

19. Thoreau, *A Week on the Concord and Merrimack Rivers* (Cambridge, Mass., 1961, 1st pub. 1849), p. 404; Lawrence, *Studies in Classic American Literature* (New York, 1955, 1st pub. 1923), p. 33.

20. Barker-Benfield, *Horrors of the Half-Known Life,* pp. 29 (Jarvis), 30. Among the studies of anxiety in nineteenth-century American life are Marvin Meyers, *The Jacksonian Persuasion: Politics and Belief* (Stanford, 1957) and Lawrence J. Friedman, *Inventors of the Promised Land* (New York, 1975), which connects male anxieties to the pressure on

"True American Womanhood" to embody a stable mothering and soft feminine role (pp. 133–178). See also Page Smith, "Anxiety and Despair in American History," *William and Mary Quarterly*, 26 (July 1969), pp. 416–424.

21. See Richard S. Dunn, *Puritans and Yankees: The Winthrop Dynasty of New England 1630–1717* (Princeton, 1962). The transformation of the European Jewish family, whose patriarchal family structure compensated for social oppression, especially of Jewish men, into the matriarchal American middle-class family has many similarities with the process I am describing here.

22. Thomas Wolfe puts the father theme at the center of his work, in *The Story of a Novel* (1936, cited by Erik Erikson, *Young Man Luther: A Study in Psychoanalysis and History* [New York, 1958], p. 119): "From the beginning . . . the idea, the central legend that I wished my book to express—had not changed. And this central idea was this: the deepest search in life, it seemed to me, the thing that in one way or another was central to all living was man's search to find a father, not merely the father of his flesh, not merely the lost father of his youth, but the image of a strength and wisdom external to his need and superior to his hunger, to which the belief and power of his own life could be united."

23. As Henri Ellenberger says of Freud's mother (*Discovery of the Unconscious*, p. 426), "Testimonies about her concord on three points: her beauty, her authoritarian personality, and her boundless admiration for her firstborn Sigmund." She was Jacob Freud's third wife, half his age. Jacob is described as easygoing and poor.

24. Quentin Anderson, *The Imperial Self: An Essay in American Literary and Cultural History* (New York, 1971), p. 16. Cf. Davis's *Homicide in American Fiction*, which concludes that the violence in early American literature was generated both by materialistic expansion and by the accompanying emasculation of paternal sources of authority. For these reasons, feminist critiques of patriarchy, especially Juliet Mitchell's otherwise excellent *Psychoanalysis and Feminism*, are wrong to assume that the father's dominance in the home parallels male dominance in business.

25. Alexis de Tocqueville, *Democracy in America*, ed. Bradley, vol. 2, ch. 18, p. 82. In *The American Novel and Its Tradition*, pp. 1–28, Richard Chase finds this "void" at the heart of the American romance. Cf. Philip Slater, *The Pursuit of Loneliness: American Culture at the Breaking Point* (Boston, 1970), a sensitive analysis of American denials of engagement, community, and dependence, which suffers from a rather Puritan sense of imminent apocalypse.

Index

A

Act of Uniformity, 62
Adams, Henry, 269
adolescence, 15, 78–79
aggression, 112, 124
alcoholism, 42
Alger, Horatio, 268
Allen, Alexander, 257
ambition, Puritanism and, 46, 49
ambivalence: authority and, 3, 37, 45, 49, 239; child rearing and, 56, 98, 101, 102; defenses from, 40, 107, 116; Family Romance, 118; Godly submission, 106–107; in language 19; obsessive style, 111; Puritanism and, 10, 12, 69, 101; self and, 98, 105, 135–136; society and, 136; stage plays, 24; in Word, 108
Ambrose, St., 83
American Revolution, 233
Ames, William, 67, 83
anal fantasy, sources of, 14
anal imagery: Puritan language, 14, 110, 111; sin, 156–157; social context of, 120–121; virtue and, 111; Willard, 212, 217
anal sadism, 111–112
Anatomie of Abuses, The (Stubbes), 26, 28
Anderson, Quentin, 269

Andros, Sir Edmund, 134
anger: conversion experience, 112; Cotton, 52; repression of, 13, 15, 41; as sin, 4; Willard, 213
Angier, Elizabeth, 94–95
Anglicans and Anglicanism, 3, 155; authority and, 46, 49; Catholicism and, 147; child-rearing literature, 70, 77, 80; nursing imagery, 5, 8; political theories, 51; preaching among, 122; Puritans contrasted, 5–6, 7, 9, 108, 128, 142, 146, 212; ritual, 44; self-interest, 90, 91; stage plays and, 23; state authority, 110
antiauthoritarian, 46–48, 239, 268
antinomian controversy: Cotton, 52, 175; father/son, 68; Shepard and Hutchinson, 55, 151–152; sin, 151
Antony and Cleopatra (Shakespeare), 35
anxiety: ambivalence and, 105, 107; Puritanism, 36, 45; sex role, 12, 86–87; social structure, 42, 120; transformation of, 4, 126; as virtue, 9, 108–109
apprenticeship, 15, 43, 60
aristocracy, child rearing, 50–51, 76
Aristotle, 31, 76
Arminians, 9, 226
art, 115; *see also* stage plays
assassination, 41, 47